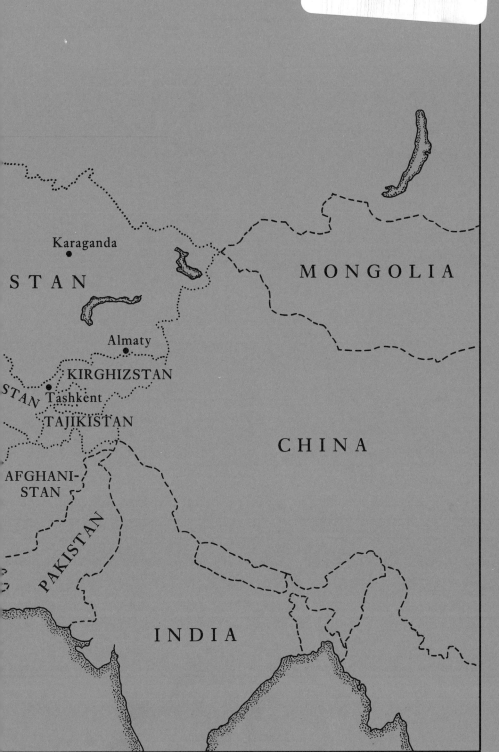

Karaganda

STAN

MONGOLIA

Almaty

KIRGHIZSTAN

STAN Tashkent

TAJIKISTAN

CHINA

AFGHANI-
STAN

PAKISTAN

INDIA

*The Lost
Heart of Asia*

By the same author

The Lost
Heart of Asia

COLIN THUBRON

HEINEMANN : LONDON

First published in Great Britain 1994
by William Heinemann Ltd
an imprint of Reed Consumer Books Ltd
Michelin House, 81 Fulham Road, London sw3 6rb
and Auckland, Melbourne, Singapore and Toronto

Reprinted 1994 (twice)

A CIP catalogue record for this book
is available at the British Library
Hardback isbn 0 434 77976 8
Paperback isbn 0 434 00139 2

Typeset by Falcon Graphic Art Ltd., Wallington, Surrey
Printed and bound in Great Britain by
Mackays of Chatham plc, Chatham, Kent

For my Mother

Author's Note

This journey was undertaken during the first spring
and summer of Central Asia's independence from
Moscow. A brief visit the year before yielded some
valued friends; but in the shadow of political
uncertainty the identity of several people recorded
here has been disguised.

Years earlier I had travelled in the nearer Moslem
world, then the European Soviet Union (for which I
learnt a halting Russian) and eventually China. Central
Asia supplied the final, most elusive piece of this
personal jigsaw.

Contents

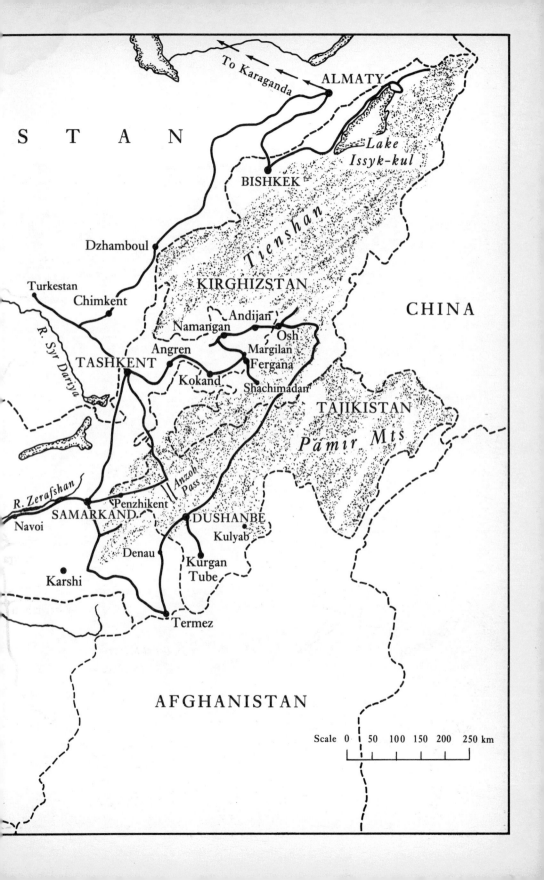

1

Turkmenistan

The sea had fallen behind us, and we were flying above a desert of dream-like immensity. Its sands melted into the sky, corroding every horizon in a colourless light. Nothing suggested that we were anywhere, or even moving at all. The last solid objects in the universe were the wing-tips of the plane. Yet when I stared at the faces dozing or brooding around me, I felt that only mine did not belong in this sun-stricken wilderness. They were wide-boned faces, burnished and still. They slept.

We had turned along the forties latitude now, midway between Gibraltar and Beijing, into the world's heart. It was a childish concept, I suppose – that the world had a heart – but it had proved oddly durable. As a boy I had soon lost the notion that one day I might slither down the North Pole or run my finger-tips along a red-hot Equator. But unconsciously I had gone on feeling that somewhere in the core of the greatest land-mass on earth, beyond more familiar nations, there pulsed another country, half forgotten, to which the rest were all peripheral.

Yet even on the map it was ill-defined, and in history only vaguely named: 'Turkestan', 'Central Asia', 'The Land beyond the River'. Somewhere north of Iran and Afghanistan, west of the Chinese deserts, east of the Caspian Sea (which lay far behind us now), this enormous, secret country had turned in on itself. Its glacier-fed rivers – the Oxus and Jaxartes of the ancients, the Chu and the Zerafshan – never reached the ocean, but vanished in landlocked seas or died across the desert. The Himalaya cut off its mountains from any life-giving monsoon where the

1

Pamirs rose in a naked glitter of plateaux, so high, wrote Marco Polo, that no bird flew there and fire burnt with a pale flame in which you could rest your hand.

Yet this region stretched from the Kazakh steppes to the Hindu Kush. It was larger than Western Europe and split by atrocious geographic extremes. While the Pamirs lay under permafrost, the Karakum desert beneath us could simmer for weeks at a time in 105°F in the shade, and its flatlands harden to a surface like levelled stone.

'There's nothing to see down there,' said the Uzbek seated beside me. 'It's the Turcomans' country' – and his voice darkened in despisal. 'They're shepherds.' Then, alerted by my clumsy Russian, he asked: 'Are you from the Baltic?'

'No, England.'

'England.' He contemplated the word as if waiting for something – anything – to flutter into his mind. 'That is next door to America ....'

I stared down. The plane's fuselage was gliding above a wasteland where faint tracks wandered. Here and there, as in some anatomical chart, canals and arteries converged over the blank tissue of the sand, or spread into dark fields. Occasionally, too, the soil whitened to saline flats, where all shrubs had withered away, or never been. But against the desert's enormity these features looked as slight as craters on the moon. For mile upon mile the only colour was a terrible, famine-breathing platinum, less like pure sand than the pulverised clay of the empires which had petered out in its dust: Persia, Seleucia, Parthia, Macedon .... It was awesome and somehow expected: that the heart of the world was not a throbbing organ but a shifting question-mark.

People had filled it with their inner demons. In ancient times it was the domain of Cimmerian hordes who lived in perpetual mist, and of the dread Scythians with their horses and gold. It became a corridor awash with nomad nations. For centuries it would remain silent and the movements of its peoples unknown, then it would unleash its wild cavalry west and east –

Scythians, Huns, Turks, Mongols – to unwrap the softened empires round them. It was the hinterland of God's vengeance.

Its strangled rivers also nurtured empires of its own, muffled to Western ears by the vastness surrounding them. They left themselves behind in cities and tombs broken over the encroaching wilderness or in the river valleys. Only after the fifteenth century, when the Mongol empire fractured and the Silk Road died, did this fearful heartland sink out of history, splintered into obscure khanates and tribal pastures. Four centuries later the Russian empire easily devoured it, and its noise was heard only dimly, through Moscow, as if it were a ventriloquist's dummy.

'You will go to Samarkand and Tashkent,' the man beside me said. It sounded more a command than a question. 'But you won't go to Tajikistan, there is fighting there. They are fighting everywhere now. Nobody knows what the future is ....'

But my journey unravelled in my mind through six thousand miles of mountain and desert. The Soviet system of tourism had broken up, and I had secured my visa by pre-booking rooms in a chain of grim hotels, which I would often ignore. The old order – all Soviet Central Asia – was cracking apart, and its five republics, artificially created by Stalin, had declared their sovereignty a few months earlier. Uzbekistan, Tajikistan, Kazakhstan, Turkmenistan, Kirghizstan – suddenly the Soviet tide had ebbed from these shadowy Moslem nations and had left them naked in their independence. What would they become? Would they hurl themselves into the Islamic furnace, I wondered, or reconvene in a Communist mass? I could conceive their future only in the light of powers which I already knew: Islam, Moscow, Turkey, the West.

To the south, for more than an hour now, the snow-peaks of the Kopet Dagh, the 'Dry Mountains', had guided us eastward. Adrift in a sea of haze, they drew the ancestral battle-line between the Turkic and Persian worlds. For more than two hundred miles they followed us like the first waves of an ocean poised to come crashing out of the Iranian plateaux barely thirty miles to the south.

Then we started to descend over a wide oasis. Beneath us the snake of the Karakum Canal was taking silt and water to the Caspian Sea. The collective farms looked as neat as Roman camps, bisected by pale streets where nothing moved. A voice over the Tannoy announced that in ten minutes we would be landing in Ashkhabad.

Ashkhabad: the capital of Turkmenistan evoked no feelings at all. Turkmenistan was one of the poorest and wildest of the old republics of the USSR, a desert region huger than Germany, peopled by less than four million souls. Over a century ago its inhabitants had been oasis farmers or stockbreeding nomads, whose raids had filled the markets of Bukhara and Khiva with thousands of Persian slaves. Now Turkmenistan had discovered oil, gas and minerals, and – it seemed – the habits of dictatorship. With the collapse of the Soviets, little had changed in its government except the formal abolition of Communism.

Watching the passengers as we came in to land, I realised that the broad Mongol visage belonged to Kazakhs and Uzbeks, who were travelling on east. But the Turcoman faces were fiercely individual and anarchic. Sometimes they showed brown hair with long jowls and slender noses. A few might have been German or English. Two seats from mine an oval-faced woman with blue eyes was breast-feeding a blue-eyed baby. In front of her lolled a turbaned mullah whose beard bifurcated down his chest from concave cheeks. As they all hunted for their luggage under the seats of the groaning Tupolev, I saw that they had scarcely a suitcase between them, but heaved out packages trussed with frayed string, bedrolls and splitting bags. They seemed like nomads still: predators and opportunists, whom history had caught in mid-migration.

Their capital, when I reached it, did not seem theirs at all, but a Russian city, almost featureless. I wandered its streets in bewilderment: streets funnelled through avenues of firs and plane trees, a placeless greenery. A century before, only a few hovels had clustered here, but the military station which replaced them

4

had bequeathed wide roads laid out for army wagons and artillery. In 1948 Ashkhabad was pulverised by earthquake, killing 110,000 people. Now all was modest, low, temporary-looking. The city had a passive strangeness. It seemed half empty. Ministries, colleges and institutes deployed in pastel colours and bland classical orders. Here and there some mock-oriental tiles or plasterwork made a concession to local culture, but the hammer-and-sickle and Red star still stamped every gate and pediment. Nobody had chiselled them away, or seemed even to notice them. They remained behind with a recessional foreboding.

The streets were still full of Russians: lumbering young men in jeans, and heavy-hipped women with hennaed hair and worn faces. In the parks the gossiping war veterans were still ribboned in their medals, and robust female gardeners bent among rose-beds. I longed to talk to someone. The youths loitering under the chestnut trees, and the young mothers walking their children, teased me with the mysteriousness of a people still unknown. What did they do when they were not here? What were they thinking? Momentarily they inhabited a milieu of maddening remoteness.

Along a track between trees, two small girls were riding a children's railway. They perched at little wheels, and thought they were steering the train, while their mother sat and watched. We joked a little as her girls steered themselves importantly, but our laughter sounded fragile and empty. Perhaps the illusion of control was too adult a sorrow. She was half Russian, it turned out, and half Armenian, and until the year before had been married to a Turcoman. The small girls, with their primrose skin and black eyes, were the fruit of this union. But she wanted to go to Russia now. 'We all do. My Russian friends talk of nothing else. Some have already gone. My grandparents arrived as farmers at the time of the czars – there was land hunger in Russia then – so I haven't known any country but this.'

'You belong here?'

She hesitated. 'In a way.' Perhaps she belonged nowhere

5

now. She had one of those Slavic faces which ignite into a sentimental sadness that is paradoxically touching. 'It'll be hard to go back. It's not even "back" really.' She trembled a little as she spoke. 'But they're making it hard for us. If you want a job you have to apply in Turcoman. The first question they ask you is: Do you speak Turcoman?' But I've never learnt this language....' She said this with a wondering regret, as if she suddenly saw that there was a culture here, not a dying irrelevance. All her life it had been these half-noticed Turkic peoples who had been compelled to learn Russian. Now, overnight, she was a foreigner in her own birthplace.

I asked: 'But where will you go?'

'I don't know. I have relatives in Moscow, but it's impossible to find work there. Two-room apartments cost a million and a half roubles .... It's too hard a place.' She added sadly: 'Harder than here.' The toy railway-train had squeaked to a halt, and her girls were clambering out. She exploded, suddenly bitter: 'But these people will regret it when we go! The Russians run everything here! We're the only people who make things work. When we're gone, what will their future be?'

The future was moving through the city round us, of course, but it remained opaque. The Turcomans inhabited these streets and flats like strangers. They walked in shabby jackets and dusty shoes. Their women put on flowered dresses and the same melancholy jackets; but their heads flashed with silk scarves over the fall of glossy pigtails. Occasionally an old man in a towering sheepskin hat or blue turban seemed to have hobbled out of another time, or a young bride shimmered past in ankle-length velvet.

Yet they moved in a Soviet city. Suddenly they had inherited all the structures and institutions of another civilisation. For decades Moscow had tried to assimilate them to a nationless stereotype – a *Homo Sovieticus* – and in this their own culture had been buried. Even the street names – Gagarin Prospect, Lenin Avenue – remained, for the moment, unaltered. Only Karl Marx Square had become Turkmenistan Square, and the cynically

6

named Freedom Prospect had been renamed after Makhtumkuli, the eighteenth-century founder of vernacular Turkic literature, whose portrait now stared from the walls of offices and institutes as if he were president.

Scanned from any height, the city looked impermanent, almost pastoral: a shanty-town whose tin and asbestos roofs drowned in trees against the vaporous Kopet Dagh. Sometimes I had the fancy that it was an enormous cantonment, built to accompany some truly Turcoman town which had vanished. But this other town was unimaginable.

As I roamed the sanitised squares and boulevards, the depth of this people's change was impossible to know. They seemed cauterised. Even the Russians did not appear to own this metropolis, but carried with them a look of rural displacement. They trudged the pavements like farmers. It was as if the city itself belonged to nobody. With its grid-iron streets and screening trees and aseptic monuments, it was the perfect laboratory for the Communist experiment, where disparate peoples would be blended, and the world made simple.

*

It was early April, and a warm rain pattered out of the sky. It polished the avenues to brilliant green, stirred stagnant ponds in the wells of numberless flat-blocks and hatched a swarm of pink umbrellas above the women. Whenever a wind blew, it seeped through the frames of my hotel window.

But little else entered the hotel. It was a parody of the self-defeated Soviet world which had built it. It reeled across the sky in a cliff of balconies and porticoes. But inside, everything fell to bits. Stone-flagged floors spread a mausolean gloom through reception and dining-rooms, overcast by fretted ceilings. In the bedrooms nothing worked, but everything – fridge, television, telephone – was represented. My bath might have been designed for a cripple, and the plasterboard furniture, varnished malignant black, was breaking up. Electric wires wandered nomadically about the walls, and a tiny rusted fridge doubled as

7

a bedside table, and sighed disconsolately all night. The coming months would blind me to such trivia, I knew; but for the moment I observed them in disordered fascination. Even in this near-rainless land, damp had mounded up loose plaster behind the splitting wallpaper, and etched it with a sepia tidemark.

Outside, the corridors were dark. That spring the instability of Central Asia had warned foreigners away. Only in the dining-room a little orchestra of tambour, drum and accordion played Turkic pop songs to a delegation from Ankara.

I found a telephone that worked, and rang a number given me in England. It belonged to a Turcoman writer. He had been a secret dissident, a friend had told me, and had only been published after *perestroika*. And that was all I knew.

In fact his whole people were elusive to me. They had emerged into known history only in the fourteenth century – a Caucasoid race tinged with Mongol blood – and their country, along with all Central Asia, had been almost impenetrable until 150 years ago. Then, for a brief half-century before the Bolshevik turmoil, European travellers had brought back contradictory tales of them. The Turcomans were wild and depraved, they said: a proud, ignorant and inhospitable people, robed outlandishly in scarlet gowns and topped off by monstrous sheepswool hats. They could ride for eighty miles a day and survive on nothing but bruised wheat and sour milk. They were at once gluttonous, austere, affable, thieving, immodest, anarchic and frank. For a pittance they would slip a knife into you.

So when Oraz appeared in my hotel, a cloud of mirages trembled and evaporated. He had a regular, handsome face with high, furrowed cheeks and a trim physique. He looked smart, dapper even, yet not quite comfortable, as if this status – or whatever it was – had been awkwardly won. He was nearing fifty, but there was something boyish in him. It was an odd mixture, a little disconcerting.

'You don't know our city? Then we'll walk it together!'

Little by little, beneath his acquired suavity, I watched a raw Turcoman emerging. The rumoured coarseness and danger had gone, but he walked for hours with a hardy lightness, and talked in fluent, stressless Russian, with an innocent pride in his borrowed city. For twelve years he had worked as a civil servant in the prime minister's office, he said – and pointed out a nondescript building. 'I wrote my first novel there.'

'Actually *in* the prime minister's ...?'

'Yes, I began it when Brezhnev was still alive. It took me six years. It was about corruption in government, and it was obvious where my material came from. I made a study of it.'

It had been a precarious, near-foolhardy undertaking. Perhaps it explained the animal alertness in him. I said: 'But what did you expect of the future?'

'I didn't imagine the book would ever see the light of day.' He smiled. Those years seemed far away now. 'I remember thinking the manuscript would be passed round among my friends. But no, I wasn't really frightened, not for myself. Just for my children.'

Yet he had gone on with that secret, apparently futureless labour, year after year, and I could not tell whether he had done so out of disgust with his surroundings – in self-cleansing – or from a writer's fascination with his material. 'But even in the middle of the Brezhnev years and all the hypocrisy,' he said, 'I didn't believe people could go on for ever living lies. Not for ever. It had to end.'

For a man born in the Stalin era, it was a high hope. But his was an instinctive and obscurely irrepressible faith, grown out of the surety that indoctrination must falter in the end, because every generation was born innocent. 'At the moment everything's in chaos, and everyone's bitter,' he said. 'Our lives have become too expensive, ever since *perestroika*. But it had to happen. It may be hard now, but it will get better ....' *Perestroika*, after all, had transformed his life. He had to believe in it, in the freer future. He was, in a sense, its symbol and harbinger.

He was walking in a nervous, high-strung stride. He seemed at once buoyant and vulnerable. His novel had sold an astonishing sixty thousand copies in Turkmenistan. 'It was the first thing

9

of its kind allowed here,' he said, 'a scandal.'

But I questioned aloud how his nation would extract itself from the Soviet shadow. Of all the people in the old Union, these were the least prepared for independence. For seventy years Communist models and propaganda, collectives and institutes, had overlain all Central Asian. Then, overnight, as in some schoolchild's fantasy, the teachers had gone away, leaving behind the message that the lesson was wrong.

'But we were never close to the Russians,' Oraz said. 'We Turcomans have an utterly different character. Have you heard of Turcoman *chilik*? It's something like our essence. It means independence, even idleness, and hospitality and courage. It's a kind of pride. The Russians chose to flout it. If a woman touches a man in public, for instance, that is against *chilik*. Modesty between the sexes goes deep with us. Even in marriage, we never kiss in front of our children. All that is private.' *Chilik* seemed to express a sober, Turkic dignity. It eschewed passions, or any violent self-seeking. 'But of course since the Russians came, all that has been diluted. Even the idea of dictatorship is alien to us. We were always free....'

A moment later we passed the newly opened Iranian embassy – a drab tenement riddled with nesting pigeons – and he looked at it with distaste. 'Our temper is different from the Iranians' too. That fundamentalism won't come here. We're a sane people.'

He was describing an old north–south watershed: the divide between an effervescent Persia and the more slow-tempered Turk. He spoke as if there was something unmanly in extremism. Besides, the Iranians were Shia, and barely a century ago the Sunni Turcomans had enslaved them as worse than unbelievers.

'Our people aren't interested in dogma. We don't persecute anyone for his beliefs. Some of the Russians may be leaving – those not born here – but most will stay. They're welcome to stay – but not as rulers. This is our land, and it will be a good place.' He laughed a blithe, confident laugh.

His patriotism was guileless, often naïve. He believed in his

10

people's inherent righteousness, as the Russians had once believed in theirs. The Turcomans were naturally peaceable, he said. It was a myth of Soviet historians that they had ever warred among themselves. We passed a statue of Stalin's henchman Kalinin, which would soon be replaced by a monument to Turmenistan's first prime minister, shot for his patriotism in 1941. 'Nobody knows where he's buried, but he'll have a memorial here.' As we tramped across a cenotaph to the Second World War dead, Oraz said: 'This, at least, we share with the Russians. The victory over Fascism!'

It was one of those overblown yet harrowing monuments that cover the old Soviet Union: a statue of motherhood towering opposite an eternal flame shut in by blood-red marble pillars. The dead were still remembered in mounds of chrysanthemums and gladioli. But the eternal flame had gone out. Its broken gas-vent hissed faintly. I did not have the heart to tell Oraz that many thousands of Central Asia's soldiers, embittered by Stalin, had deserted to the Germans.

Yet he seemed, for the moment, immune to disillusion. He was bright with an imagined future. I feared for him. I wondered if anyone of his generation had believed in Communism at all.

'Maybe one per cent.' He laughed harshly.

'The very poor?'

'No! The others. The officials.' We had entered a park where a statue of Lenin survived. It hovered angrily above us. 'And now they don't know what to believe.'

Lenin stood on a ziggurat brilliant with Turcoman tilework, and lifted a declamatory arm towards Iran. Beneath, an inscription promised liberation to the peoples of the East.

'There are fifty-six Lenin monuments in the city,' Oraz said. 'This one will stay and the rest will go.' He was striding round the dried fountains which circled the monument, suave in his suit and tie, while above him the baggy-trousered Lenin crumpled his cloth cap in his hand. 'Maybe in time this one will go too. But not now.'

I felt perversely glad that it would remain: a gesture of

11

moderation, and a fragile acknowledgement of the past. A group of visiting farmers was posing beneath it for a snapshot. The photographer – a dour youth in a T-shirt blazoned 'USA: Nice Club' – arranged them in a crescent of interlaced arms and cheerless faces. I thought: so people still come to be photographed here, out of habit, or some tenuous loyalty.

But as the youth adjusted his tripod, I peered through the lens and saw that his clients were framed against the plinth of oriental ceramic, which rose to the top of the photograph and amputated Lenin somewhere in the sky. 'We don't include him any more,' the youth said. 'He's out of fashion.'

But what, I wondered, could replace him? As Oraz and I trudged around the state exhibition hall that evening, I felt the Turcoman culture slipping irretrievably away. The modern paintings regaling the walls celebrated it only in synthetic images – tribespeople plucking lutes or riding through misted mountains in a swirl of antiquated robes. The artists were tourists in their own past. At the end of the hall a sixty-foot-long Turcoman rug, rumoured the largest in the world, hung in a crimson waterfall of patterned symbols.

'I wish I could read these for you,' Oraz said, pointing out emblematic horses and birds' eyes. 'They would tell you half our history.' He shook his head. 'But I can't.' Even the classic art of poetry, he said, was dying.

'Does nobody write it any longer?'

'Oh yes. Everybody *writes* it. But nobody reads it.'

That night, wandering the emptied streets alone, I came upon the marble podium where the Turcoman president and his ministers had once saluted May Day parades. Until a few months before, it had been the city's political heart. Now it glimmered derelict beyond the street-lamps. As I climbed on to its rostrum, the marble and limestone carapace of its walls was cracking under my hands. The crowning statue of Lenin had gone – as if an enormous bird had flown from its roost – but the pedestal, torn in its removal, had been boarded round by wood painted to resemble stone, as if the wreckage of those stupendous foot-prints was still too painful to expose.

I stared down on the avenue beneath, thickened to seven lanes for the passage of parades. A wind stirred dead leaves over the steps. I remembered what Oraz had said about the people's disbelief in Communism. Yet that night I fancied that it still pervaded the sleeping city – in the slogans which nobody had dared wipe from the walls, in the jargon on people's lips, even in Lenin's statue lingering in the park nearby, warning that his ghost be not provoked.

*

Korvus was an old man now. Beneath a burst of white hair his face shone heavy and crumpled, and his eyes watered behind their spectacles. Thirty years ago he had been Turkmenistan's minister of culture, and a celebrated poet; and he was a war-hero in his country. Authority still tinged his stout figure as he greeted me. He wore an expensive Finnish suit and a gold ring set with a carnelian. Yet a Turcoman earthiness undermined this prestige a little, and a loitering humour.

He seemed to live in schizophrenia. His public life had been spent in Soviet government, but his house nested in a Turcoman suburb sewn with family courtyards, vine-shadowed, where the hot water ran in fat pipes on struts above the lanes, and people shed their shoes before entering the homes, in the Islamic way.

He ushered me indoors. He looked gentle, preoccupied. He lived with the family of his eldest son – the hallway was scattered with toys and shoes – and as I entered the sitting-room I stopped in astonishment. I had stepped into an engulfing jungle of Turcoman artefacts. It was as if I had dropped through the floor of the bland Soviet world into an ancient substratum of his people's consciousness. Phylacteries in beaten silver set with semi-precious stones, horsewhips and quivers and camel-bells, the tasselled door-frame of a yurt tent still darkly brilliant in vegetable dyes – they covered the walls with a barbarian intricacy.

'My son and his wife collect them,' the old man said. He

13

looked vaguely unhappy.

'They're magnificent.'

He sat beside me on a divan. I could not tell what he was thinking. His whole life had been directed towards a Soviet future, in which national differences would disappear. Yet for years, piece by piece, his son had been harvesting his people's past and pouring it over the walls in a lavish, speechless celebration. It hung before the old man now like an indictment. It was the history he had abandoned.

But after a while he said sombrely: 'I think it is right that this has happened, and that we have our freedom. It is right that the old Union is split up.' He spoke as if he had fought against each sentence before it had conquered him. He did not look at me. 'Although the war seemed to unite us.'

The war: he had returned from it with a chestful of medals – 'like Brezhnev,' he laughed. He had survived the ferocious tank-battle of Kursk, and fought through the terrible winter of 1942–3, when the thrust of the whole war changed and the world was lost to Hitler. His face ignited as he spoke of it. He relaxed into its simplicity. Things had been easier then. Somewhere in the fields of south Ukraine, he said, he had attacked a German tank single-handed and been hit by shell splinters. 'I regained con-sciousness in the snow, covered in blood.' Humorously he patted his chest and back, wriggling his short arms around his body. 'I didn't know if I was alive. How were my legs? They were still there. My head? That was on. But my back and side were ripped, and my hand a mass of ligaments. So I packed snow round my wounds, and the German fire missed me and I crawled away. Later one of our officers – a hooligan type with a motorcycle – charged up and filled me with vodka and drove me off. I was operated on in a field hospital under gas, and woke like this.' He held up his hand. I saw that two fingers were gone, their stubs welded in a wrinkled trunk. He grinned at it.

In the bleak, triumphant years after the war, he had gone to Moscow to study. Perhaps he had believed in the Soviet unity

14

then. He had married a Russian orphan, and returned to Ashkhabad a hero. He chuckled and drew his maimed hand across his chest to conjure ranks of medals. Later he had written poems about the war, and love lyrics. He had become head of the Turkmenia Writers' Union, then its Minister of Culture in the sixties.

But how much had he invested in his authority, I wondered? Had he believed in Marxism-Leninism or in literature or, arcanely, in both? It was hard to ask. He looked so old now, and somehow depleted, yet comfortable. He had taken off his jacket and put on a lumpy cardigan. His damaged hand rested on his knees. But his wife lived in Moscow – she did not care for Ashkhabad, he said – and he came and went between them, not exactly separated. His life seemed now to have resolved into these divided loyalties. They were perhaps his truth.

I wondered how easily this family cohabited: the failing war-hero and his film-director son Bairam – who was working on a study of Red Army atrocities – and a garrulous, ten-year-old grandson. A depthless chasm of experience seemed to gape between them all.

Bairam came in later, pale and ebullient, without the look of closed unsureness which I often saw about me in the streets. He grew excited by my interest in Turcoman things, and presented his collection piece by piece, unrolling hundred-year-old kelims at my feet in a patter of discriminatory pride. These were not the soulless products, dull with aniline dyes, which 200 underpaid girls (he told me) turned out in the local Soviet-built factory. They were works of love and patience, whose skills had been inherited from mother to daughter. He brought in jewellery too: necklaces which had flooded the breast with lapis lazuli and silver bells; enamelled and filigreed frontlets that clipped on to the woman's ears before cascading about her in a tumult of chains. They trickled like water through my fingers.

Meanwhile the old man switched on the television which stood among the nomad regalia, and drank brandy mixed with Pepsi Cola. 'I used to drink too much,' he said to no one in particular. 'But I hardly drink now.' On his chosen channel the Ashkhabad Orchestra, dressed in white tie and tails, was playing Moussorgsky.

Bairam was full of projects. He was working on a film which would have been unthinkable two years before, he said. It was a documentary on his people's flight from the Red Army during the forced collectivisation in the 1930s, when a million Turcomans and others had fled into Iran and Afghanistan.

He spoke like his father, in sudden bursts of feeling, while still holding up jewellery for me to admire. 'We're even showing a sequence on the Red Army machine-gunners mowing down the refugees in the mountain passes. Yes, this happened.' He held up an amethyst frontlet, as if it might have belonged to the dead. 'The film is being bought by Moscow television! They asked us to cut out what the Red Army did, but we said no. So they're transmitting it whole!' He let out an airy laugh. It was an astonishing reversal of power.

His father went on listening to Moussorgsky, but after a while ambled out into his courtyard. It must have been simpler to survive the war and all the Stalin years, I thought, than to meet this shock of independence. But Bairam waved the notion away. 'No, not for my father. He was already independent. He never believed in the Party. He left it twenty-four years ago.'

I asked in astonishment: 'Why?' Leaving the Party was tantamount to suicide.

'There was a sort of scandal ... when he was Minister of Culture. They said he travelled too much – in Turkey and India. The KGB got after him.'

I thought: so in Moscow's eyes his ideas had become contaminated. 'What did he do after that?'

'There was nothing he could do. After you'd left the Party, that was the end of you. There was no chance of a job. So he sat at home and wrote poetry ....' He smiled weakly. 'That's how I remember him, all my childhood.'

So whatever had happened, I had not understood; and the old man's look of hurt and reconciliation sprang from something older than his country's independence. A little later I asked him about Oraz – who had written his subversive novel from the heart of government – and Korvus only said: 'I know who you mean by this man.'

The note of censure was unmistakable. A residual loyalty to the system, perhaps, had been disturbed by that betrayal. He himself had simply resigned, and become a poet.

*

On Sundays, when the central market opened, the farmers spilt into the city. Behind their hillocks of tangerines, pomegranates, beetroot, peppers and dried apricots, they waited from early morning with dogged unconcern: a people whose faces expressed all the fierce gamut of Turcoman change. There were Mongoloid faces whose cheeks had stayed creaseless into old age, and long Caucasoid ones with startling pale eyes, and Bedouin visages where the beetling noses erupted beneath tapered brows. A few of the older women, in the remembered modesty of youth, still touched their concealing scarves to faces no longer beautiful, and squatted all day before a cupful of onions or carrots from their private plots.

The shoppers trudged disconsolately among them. Sudden inflation had sent the fragmented Soviet Union into shock. Everybody was complaining. Everybody had a dirge of comparative prices on his lips. 'One kilo of meat costs a hundred roubles now … last year it was just ten! Everything was better under Brezhnev ….' And the Russians who moved among them looked as poor as the rest.

It was here that I met the artist Momack. He was drifting about, like me: a slight, middle-aged man in baggy jeans and trainers. In this rough ambience he looked faintly theatrical. He had the sensitised melancholy of a king in a Persian miniature. A satiny beard swarmed blackly up to his cheekbones and liquid eyes. He felt close to these farmers, he said. They seemed nearer to his people's roots. But I could not imagine them feeling close to him.

17

He drove me to his studio in a twenty-year-old Zhiguli saloon. Years ago, he said, he had daydreamed of selling all his paintings and buying a Mercedes Benz. 'I love those cars.' He tapped his splintered windscreen. 'But instead I've got this.' The Zhiguli might have been assembled from scrap metal. It moved in spasms, and swung about like an artist's mobile.

We clattered down Gogol and Pushkin streets – 'I hope they keep those names,' he said. 'They were real people, writers not politicians ….' He hated politics. Even Islam was not a belief to him, but a habit. It had always rested lightly on the pastoral Turcomans. He had counted three new mosques being built in the city, he said, but they signalled a mild cultural resurgence rather than a doctrinaire revolution. 'We Turcomans never so deeply believed. We never had many mosques. It was enough just for five or six people gathered in a house to pray….I remember that as a child.'

His studio stood in a suburb still scattered with the dwellings of 1948 earthquake victims. The building had lain derelict for years, until he and some friends had restored it. Now it had become a nest of gaunt ateliers where nobody seemed to be working. A debris of sculpture lumbered its courtyard – two decapitated leftovers of Socialist Realism carved in silver-painted polystyrene, and a discarded portrait-bust.

We went down an echoing corridor, where outsize stoves loomed like pillars. In the studio was a primitive press for Momack's etchings. He sat down awkwardly. His life's work lay stacked around us, unsold. The canvases banked up in shelves or were heaped against the walls. As a student he had become infatuated by Picasso and Chagall, and over the years his paintings had grown dangerously unrepresentational. They had sold only to friends. After *perestroika*, he said, he had enjoyed some acclaim in Moscow and even Eastern Europe. But life was hard now, he was so isolated. He supported two daughters by his first wife, and by his second a little son, who had yesterday been circumcised and cried all night.

Hesitantly he showed me some pictures. His early oils were

romanticised scenes of Turcoman village life, and faltering essays in Picasso. But his etchings and watercolours were besetting and strange. Obsessively he had painted weddings and mirages. Above all, mirages. It was as if his people's past shimmered just out of reach, maddening and ungraspable to him. His figures were like ghosts. They walked or rode in abstract deserts and mountain-valleys, and they reeked of melancholy. They were people in moonlight, in flight. Their shadows on the sand or rock were as important as they were, and were often doing something different.

'These are only attempts,' he said. 'You can never achieve what you want, can you?'

The grief in him, the hunt for some rootedness in the past of his violated people, perhaps arose from an orphan's distress. His father and two small sisters had been killed in the 1948 earthquake, leaving his mother pregnant with him; and when he was only thirteen, she too had died.

'Perhaps that's why I'm already going white ....' He touched a plume of ashen hair spurting back from his temples. He was still only forty-three. No wonder all his pictures seemed to weep for a lost motherland. He had chosen to inhabit the fringes of his city, among the victims, and his friends came from the minority peoples who float between the Russian and Turkic populace in all the capitals of Central Asia: Armenians, Tartars, Jews, Koreans, Poles.

Had he conceived of his painting, I wondered, as a way back to his past?

'No, no, nothing like that now.' His expression dissolved into a kind of tragic softness. 'It's only line and colour. That's all. Line and colour. No, I haven't rediscovered my culture, just extended my technique.'

Some of his pictures descended into a peculiar literalness. In one the words of an illuminated Turkish manuscript hung like a curtain behind a bearded artist. But the composition dwindled away in four parts, the words faded and the figure was pared to a shadow. 'This tells that without knowledge of his past a man is

19

nothing,' Momack said pedantically. 'He can't understand him-self. He disappears.'

Now he was fingering a watercolour labelled *Marriage: a Study of Old and New*. A village bridal dress – the vivid crimson of fertility – lay in a museum vitrine, brilliant but inaccessible; while beside it, in virginal white, posed a Western mannequin bride. Under her veil, she was naked.

*

I longed to find some geographical heart to this diffused nation, but there was none. It owned no Vatican, no Acropolis. Its peo-ple had perhaps drifted westwards into the Karakum desert in the tenth century, but even this is unsure. Late in the nineteenth century the advancing Russians found them scattered beneath the Kopet Dagh foothills in fortress villages and nomad camps. Of all the Central Asian peoples the Turcomans had the firmest sense of their own nation, and the strongest will to fight. Yet even amongst them this statehood was a cloudy concept. They thought of themselves first by tribe – Tekke or Yomut or Salor – and their frontiers were in constant flux.

Only the little town of Geok-Tepe, I thought – some twenty miles north of the Iranian foothills – might have covertly been remembered as a national shrine. In 1879 the Turcomans had thrown back a czarist army from its walls in a rare reverse for the imperial arms in Central Asia, but two years later the Russians returned under their sanguinary general, Skobelev – 'Old Bloody Eyes', as the Turcomans came to call him – and laid siege to Geok-Tepe again.

Inside its three miles of mud-built ramparts the most savage and powerful of the tribes, the Tekke, had assembled ten thou-sand mounted warriors for a last stand. Artillery failed to dismantle this redoubt, so the Russians sent in sappers to mine the soft earth beneath its walls. After twenty days of siege, a two-ton explosion and a rain of artillery blew a breach almost fifty yards wide, killing hundreds of defenders; then the Russian infantry charged forward with their bands playing, and streamed through the breach. Hand-to-hand fighting broke the dazed Turcomans. They fled out of the fortress with their women and children, and were massacred indiscriminately in their thousands. For years afterwards the plains were scattered with human bones, and the tribespeople only had to hear a Russian military band playing for their women to start wailing hysterically and their men to fall on their faces in terror.

Yet Geok-Tepe became a legend of heroic failure, and when I mentioned it to Korvus's son Bairam, he grew excited and insisted on driving me there. It was only fifty kilometres away, he said. He knew a local historian who would join us. We would go to the burial-place of the Turcoman war-leader Kurban Murat. 'We'll have a party!'

By the time we left next morning, the party had mushroomed uncontrollably. We clattered out of the city in a Volga saloon stuffed with his friends from the state television company. There was a mocking film-director, already drunk, a mouse-like scriptwriter, and a cloudless colossus of a historian with a pock-marked face. Scenting festivity, they had abandoned their desks *en masse* and were stirring up a carnival euphoria.

Even before we left the outskirts, they had waylaid a friend in his butcher's shop. Through a swinging jungle of fly-blown cow and sheep, we thrust our way into a mud-floored storeroom and squatted down in this sordid secrecy for a random picnic. Roundels of bread and saucers of cucumber appeared, and soon the tiny room resounded to the splash and gurgle of vodka. An infectious jubilation brewed up. We toasted one another's countries, families, businesses, futures and pasts. Turcoman and Russian oratory blundered together in helpless pastiche. Occasionally the butcher came in to snatch up a knife or a bloodstained apron. But we were soon past caring. Shoulders and necks were clasped in inebriate brotherhood, and bawdy jokes recycled as the film-director implacably refilled every-body's glass.

Even in my vodka-soaked trance, I recognised the director's strangeness. He was the group's self-appointed jester, but he had the face of a ravaged clown. With his every movement a shock of greying hair floundered above two goitrous eyes. Much of his humour was lost to me, but the rest was subtly self-degrading. The others laughed sycophantically. The role of joker had become his distinction, his passport. He appeared close to breakdown. 'English culture! Turcoman culture!' He lifted a shaking glass. 'These are high cultures! Not like the Russians ....' Our glasses clashed. 'I love England .... Most of all I love Princess Anne! That is a beautiful woman!' His eyes came bulging close against mine. He was slopping vodka into my glass. 'Vodka's the cure for everything!'

Only the historian did not drink. 'He is a very serious man,' the clown gabbled. 'He wants to talk history with you. But he says drink fucks his brains.'

The historian's face cracked into a smile, which survived there senselessly a long time later, as if he had forgotten it. All his moods traversed these slow gradients, and remained stranded in his expression after all feeling must have gone.

By now the damp from the earth floor was seeping up through our socks and trousers. But we settled drunkenly into the last crusts and dregs. With dimmed amazement I remembered that the men squatting in this butcher's store were the sophisticates of Ashkhabad. But their formal shirts and ties now looked like pantomime, and our party seemed to unleash in them some deep, earthen craving, older than Islam.

An hour later we were meandering over a potholed road towards Geok-Tepe. For miles Ashkhabad seemed to extend itself over the scrubland in scattered villages of pale-bricked cottages and dishevelled gardens. The country had a vacant, incomplete look, as if it were earmarked for a suburb, and was waiting. Pylons and telegraph poles criss-crossed the plains in a dirty spider-web. Heaps of piping and rubble littered the roadsides. Every building appeared to be unfinished or falling down, with no moment between consummation and decay.

We passed cement and asbestos works, and wine distilleries. Then cotton fields and vineyards appeared, and collective farms named 'Sun' or 'Glory', adorned by faded slogans celebrating strength and labour. Once we crossed the Karakum Canal flowing westwards seven hundred miles from the Amu Dariya, the classical Oxus, to fertilise all these oases beneath the Kopet Dagh. It ran in a brown tumult between concrete banks and encroaching reeds.

Soon afterwards, driving through pastureland, we came upon an enormous graveyard. Many dead from the Geok-Tepe massacre had been interred here, and a year afterwards the Turcoman leader Kurban Murat was buried amongst them. He was not only a warrior but a Naqshbandi Sufi, a holy man, and his tomb became a lodestar for pilgrims, and a token of resistance. Far into the Soviet era it was secretly venerated. 'It had just decayed to a mound,' the historian said, 'but people remembered it.'

We scrambled through a gap in the concrete wall. The saint's tomb had been clumsily rebuilt: a brick cube under a clay dome. We had all sobered a little, and now went swaying in silence through the grass towards it. All around us heaved an ocean of nameless mounds misted with white poppies. The historian said: 'Two of my great-grandparents were killed in that battle. They're buried here too.' He knew the place, but did not go there. He eased open the door to the tomb of Kurban Murat. Only the director remained outside, suddenly ashamed or indifferent, running his hands over his face in the Moslem self-blessing.

We peered into a wan light shed by the perforated dome. We were alone. The grave-mound swelled huge and constricted in its walls. It was covered in green silk. At its head, pilgrims had left variegated stones, and several hundred roubles lay there untouched. Three times we circled the grave anti-clockwise in the Moslem way, squeezing along the walls. Nobody spoke. Then suddenly, violently, at the grave's head, my companions prostrated themselves and struck their foreheads against its mound. I gazed at them in mute surprise. All at once the place reverberated with the ancient, tribal prestige of the dead, and of all the unutterable past. Their foreheads were covered with dust when they rose.

Next moment we were outside, among the graves again. A few swallows were twittering in the grass. 'Many people come here on the anniversary of the battle' – the historian snaked out his arm to conjure queues – 'especially the descendants of the dead.' But the dead were mostly anonymous. Here and there a Turcoman samovar, discoloured and rusting, betrayed the presence of a grave, or an inscribed headstone showed. But most were marked only by the raw earth breaking through a weft of shrubs and poppies.

'Do the Naqshbandi come?' I had read that they still pervaded Central Asia.

But he said: 'No. They're not important. Our religion is older than theirs, older than Islam. We have our own faith. That's why we can't accept fundamentalism, or Iran, or any of that.' His face confronted mine like a blank moon. He wanted me to understand. 'The people who come to our shrines, they're not exactly Moslems, you see, although they are called that. Their belief is earlier...different.'

Lingering beside this clannish mausoleum – the lair of a sainted warrior – I believed him. It reeked of ancestor-worship. The formal practice of the mosque, all the structures and theologies of urban Islam, seemed far away. This was a secret place of tribal memories, and anger. 'The Russians killed fifteen thousand of us on that day, many of them women and children, and lost three thousand of their own.' The historian stared across the rough, earthen sea. 'They were barbarians.'

Yet he had invented the number of enemy dead. Against the piteous Turcoman casualties, the Russians (perhaps minimising) put their own at fewer than 300. But the historian's history was glamorous and simple. He was rebuilding his country's past as dangerously free of truth as the Russians had once created theirs. Wandering the graves, he claimed a 7000-year ancestry for the Turcomans in this land, as if they were the pure descendants of Neolithic men. He had reconstructed them not as idolatrous slavers who had veneered themselves with a more sophisticated

24

faith, but as an ancient, homogeneous people steeped in early wisdom.

Now the director was stumbling along the path beside us. 'It's not our tragedy!' His shirt gaped open above a straggling tie. 'It's *their* tragedy, the Russians' tragedy! It's the Russians who had to leave this country, not us. Like the British from India or the French from Algeria!' His clownish eyes strayed over me. 'Like all colonialism – it's the tragedy of the colonisers!'

I mumbled uncertainly. Colonialism seemed to resolve into no such easy patterns. He was drinking himself to death like any Russian.

'It's *their* disaster, *their* mistake!' His arm trembled towards the graves: 'These others were not mistaken ....'

An hour later, as we motored towards Geok-Tepe, the odd, reckless fervour overtook him again, and he insisted on stopping. Nobody dared refuse him and soon we were all lolling in the grass with two more bottles of vodka and a bag of half-liquefied cheese. Beside us glinted a stagnant pool, where a concrete sluice was channelling away water from the Karakum Canal. It gurgled miserably. By now my head had floated clear of my body, and my feet were unfamiliar to me. I recognised them dimly at the far end of my legs. The self-made clown had turned us all into children. We laughed in a gale of idiot mirth whenever he opened his mouth. A few dusty shrubs concealed our scandal from the road. 'This is a beautiful Turcoman place,' he cried, and everybody laughed.

I was aware only of the historian secretly condescending, touching my arm from time to time, and his eyes said: I'm sorry. And sometimes Bairam pushed bread and cheese at me and whispered: 'Eat, eat, don't just drink. Save yourself ....'

I longed to tip away my glass unseen, but the director watched me with fevered eyes every time he refilled it, and demanded toast after toast. Then – half in jest at first, half in absolution – he would slither his hands over his face in the Moslem blessing, until they were squirming down his cheeks in cynical desperation. But he muttered: 'I'm grey. Only good men go grey .... Look at these others ....' He got up and staggered in the grass. 'This is a beautiful place .... Will you give my love to Princess Anne?... Our is a high culture ....'

We never reached Geok-Tepe, but somehow circled back to Ashkhabad in a nimbus of alcohol. At the hotel, where my floor-lady usually sat at her post in bored watchfulness, the desk was vacant and I fumbled in its drawer for my room-key. Then I stopped. A piece of paper had caught my eye. With a shock I found myself reading a report on my own movements. Scrupulously it noted the times I had left and entered my room, and the identity of those who had visited me. I felt slightly sick. An old tension took hold of me, familiar from twelve years before, when the KGB had dogged me through the western Ukraine. The paper reminded me of what I already knew, but which in the pleasure of the day I had forgotten: that this was not a free country.

But to whom, I wondered, did the local KGB report? Were they being cleansed of their Russian element and turning purely Turcoman, or had the links with Moscow been preserved? Above all, what was their point? But most likely, I thought, they would change only with the slowness of those Jurassic sauropods which possessed two brains, one in the head, one in the base of the tail: an organism of unwieldy, vegetable instinct. For a while they would simply continue doing what they had been programmed to do, however senseless, because that is what they had always done.

The next moment my floor-lady appeared, agitated. An obese Russian *babushka* with hennaed curls and pencilled eyebrows, she too seemed to belong to a fading species. She greeted me with a wriggling wave of her fingers, then groped for my key in her pocket, shooting me smiles. 'How stupid of me ....'

*

Next day I revived my plans to reach Geok-Tepe. A driver named Safar offered to take me seventy miles for barely two dollars (the devaluation of the rouble had turned the dollar to gold) and we set off past the same factories, cotton-fields and jaded pasturelands. The country grew poorer as we went. The cottages spawned shacks of corrugated tin: animal pens, dwellings, lavatories. Weather-blackened men idled in the door-ways with dark, Bedouinish women in black dresses and flaring headscarves. Over the grasslands roamed flocks of karakul sheep and lambs – the source of astrakhan wool – and small, one-humped camels. But the fields were fringed with salinated marsh which shone like dirty snow.

By now the Kopet Dagh mountains were teeming across the southern horizon, and dropping their foothills in our path. A storm raged beyond them, discolouring the sky. Suddenly a mili-tary airfield appeared. Outside their camouflaged bunkers, the jet fighters were all pointed at Iran thirty miles away over the mountains. I was unsure if foreigners were permitted on this road, but the old rules had broken down, and the airfield was circled only by broken barbed-wire and derelict watch-towers where nobody watched. The next moment we were past.

I wondered what people thought of this arsenal in their midst – the forces of the Commonwealth of Independent States – but Safar only shrugged. He had done his military service in a chem-ical warfare unit near Bukhara, he admitted, and he didn't mind the Russians. 'We can get on with them. They're all right. The Russians won't go away.'

But they were already going away, I knew.

I wondered about Safar. A dust of white hair flew back from his brows, and his long face was deeply lined. Yet all the lines had gone the right way, and his nose craned over a loose, laughing mouth.

But his life unfolded in tragedy, as I was now expecting here. In the earthquake, when he was only a boy, he had lost his three-year-old sister buried under the debris, and his father had disappeared long before during the Stalin years.

'I never knew him. He was a trader in salt over the border in Iran.' He gestured at the mountains. 'He married my mother over there – Turcomans spread all over the border – but he was

27

arrested as a *kulak* in 1936 and taken away to Siberia. My mother is ninety now, but still remembers. He returned to her for a month, then was rearrested, and years later she got a letter from a fellow-exile, saying he had died out there, near Novosibirsk. That was how we knew.'

For a while, beneath the mountain walls, a paler line of ramparts had been rising, and now loured on its hill to our south. It was a Parthian palace-city, over two thousand years old. And that was the sorcery of this land. For miles it lay empty of anything but modern villages or state farms, and then – as if the intervening centuries had concertinaed – the dry air or shifting sand would have preserved an ancient era in dreamlike isolation, like this city of Nisa.

Barely eighty years after Alexander the Great marched through this region to India, the half-nomadic Parthians rebelled against his successors and were establishing their own empire. Nisa must have marked the northern limit of their domination, and it looked formidable still. Nothing stirred there. But near its gates a shy greeting sounded and we glimpsed in the spectral light a red-headed boy with pale eyes. He vanished into the ruins. He might have belonged anywhere: to Persia or Macedon or even (my imagination vaulted) to those broken Roman legionaries whom the Parthians marched eastward after the battle of Carrhae.

Ahead of us the city seemed as ghostly as he. Built of baked earth, it shared its colour with the dust around it. Wind, rain and the pulverising sun had eliminated all its detail and left behind a tawny labyrinth of walls and towers. I tramped its corridors in fading anticipation. So substantial were its halls that I expected any moment to encounter something intimate or particular. But the sixty-foot ramparts and the bastions knuckling out of them were smoothed to precipices, and the passageways ran beneath like natural gulleys. Even the circular throne-room, once statued with the half-deified princes who ruled here, showed only a shell. The earth was absorbing the whole city back into itself. It was falling out of focus.

Mentally I tried to furnish it with artefacts I had seen in the Ashkhabad museum. They had betrayed a city infected by a mongrel Hellenism. I remembered statuettes in translucent marble, and stupendous ivory drinking-horns. Only from these horns could I dimly sense the city. Their bases flowered into carved dragons with ebullient tusks and firebird wings, but the decorative tiers swarming up their stems were ringed by half-Greek figures, who made war or sacrifice in postures of faded grace, or clashed their cymbals at some forgotten rite.

Yet the city itself had died. My feet fell disembodied in its dust. Here and there courses of hefty baked brick still showed clear in the walls, only to be engulfed again. I was wandering a monochrome maze. An east wind beat in my ears, but seemed to touch nothing else. Once only, on a distant battlement, I glimpsed the uncanny, red-haired boy, watching.

We approached Geok-Tepe at dusk. Safar was neither bitter nor reverent at reaching his people's Calvary, but chattered on with a hardy brightness. Southward, the mountains lifted to grassy plateaux rolling with thunder-clouds. We crossed a lonely railway-line.

'That was why we went to war with the Russians,' Safar said. 'They wanted to bring the railway here, but we Turcomans hated it.' Unconsciously he was peddling a Soviet version of the conflict, I suspected: an interpretation of czarist imperialism which made the Turcomans look backward. As for the Russians, a confusion of motives – the greed for trade and raw materials, a hunt for secure borders, outrage at the slave-traffic in Slavs – drove the czarist empire piecemeal to the walls of Geok-Tepe. In the end the void and weakness of all this land – a simple power-vacuum – sucked the Russians in.

At first we glimpsed nothing but a small town scattered in the distance, and the quiet railway. Then we were driving beside the concrete enclosure of a collective farm, which masked other, older walls. Intentionally, perhaps, it had been sited here to lay the past to sleep. It was called 'Peace'. But after a while

29

its vineyards petered out, and there moved over the pastureland a low switchback of earth ramparts, like the spine of a serpent buried in the scrub.

We scrambled up it. Beside us a crenellated outwork had disintegrated to a stump, bristling with artemisia. A drift of barbed wire crowned the summit. As I reached it, I stopped in amazement. Below me, as far as I could see in the dusk, there fell open an immense quadrangle of ramparts almost three miles in circumference. It glimmered over the plain and was utterly deserted. Here 35,000 Tekke tribespeople, with 10,000 mounted warriors, had assembled in a teeming tent-city. Some of the battlements stood only twelve feet high now – after the siege their upper courses had been stripped away to cover the slain – but for hundreds of yards they rose eerily intact. Their double parapet ran in a worn corridor where the loopholes and rifle-pits had eroded to cracks or wholesale breaches. In those embrasures, after the battle, many men were found still sitting where they had been shot, some of them dead for days, their heads slumped between their knees.

We came to where a new tomb was being built. Its foundations enclosed a stone marker with the name of the dead leader and the fatal date, 1881. Safar dropped to the earth, whispering prayers, then we circled the grave together. I asked if it had been accurately remembered. 'Yes,' he said. 'Local people remember these things. And they paid for the tomb.'

For a while, in the thickening twilight, we stumbled along those haunted ramparts. They ran before us in hillocks of connected earth, slashed by floodwaters and artillery. Beyond the mound where the Turcomans had set up a battery and observation-post, the southern walls had melted into twilight and the fatal breach was subsumed beneath the collective farm. Somewhere nearby the Russians' redoubt had pushed to within seventy yards of the fortifications as they mined beneath them, so that their soldiers could hear the Turcoman sentinels chatting together, wondering why the infidels were drilling their snouts into the ground like pigs. After the mines exploded and the breaches were stormed, panic had swept through the Turcoman camp. Most of the fighting men took to their horses and streamed out through rents in the walls where we now walked, and hordes of terrified civilians followed them. For more than ten miles the Russians pursued them over the plains, scything them down in their thousands: old men, women and children.

Now, as we strayed inside the enceinte, I realised that all around us the earth was rumpled into mounds. They lapped to our feet in a pitiful ocean. It was impossible not to tread on them, they were so many, spiked with camel-thorn and all unmarked. The morning after the battle, 6500 corpses had been counted inside the fort, with 8000 more who had been massacred in flight.

'Nobody knows who lies there,' Safar said. 'It was the Russians who buried them.'

I gazed numbly. They had simply been covered with earth where they fell.

By the time Safar and I returned to the car it was dark, and we had both gone silent. Our headlights wavered bleakly over the road. Opposite the main breach, I had read, the Russians raised a memorial to their fallen. 'I saw it three months ago,' Safar said. 'It's nothing much.'

But guiltily I asked to visit it. The tolerance which had left it standing touched me with bemused warmth.

Yet as we circled along the railway Safar grew bewildered. 'I thought it was here,' he said, 'I'm sure it was.' Three or four times we traversed the same road, but he recognised nothing. Around us the town had become a warren of underpowered lights in blank windows.

Suddenly he lifted his hands in perplexity. 'There it is!'

I craned forward. 'Where?'

'There!'

Wanly, as if throwing a tenuous halo round an object of dubious sanctity, our headlamps had alighted on a hillock of dust and rubble. Safar wrenched the car away from it. 'They made a job of that!'

31

We asked a passer-by what had happened.

'I don't know,' the man answered. 'It just disappeared.'

'How?'

The man's face puckered into a laugh, then he said with grave matter-of-factness: 'They say God did it in the night!'

2

The Desert of Merv

Eastward from Ashkhabad my train lumbered across a region of oases where rivers dropped out of Iran to die in the Turcoman desert. In one window the Kopet Dagh mountains lurched darkly out of haze, and repeated themselves in thinning colours far into the sky. Beyond the other rolled a grey-green savannah, gashed with poppies. Over this immensity the sky curved like a frescoed ceiling, where flotillas of white and grey clouds floated on separate winds.

Once or twice under the foothills I glimpsed the mound of a *kurgan*, broken open like the lips of a volcano – the burial-place of a tribal chief, perhaps, or the milestone of some lost nomad advance. Along this narrow littoral, a century ago, the Tekke Turcomans had grazed their camels and tough Argamak horses, and tilled the soil around forty-three earthen fortresses. Now the Karakum Canal ran down from the Oxus through villages with old, despairing names such as 'Dead-End' and 'Cursed-by-God', and fed collective farms of wheat and cotton.

The train was like a town on the move. In its cubicles the close-tiered bunks were stacked with Russian factory workers and gangs of gossiping Turcomans. Grimy windows soured the world outside with their own fog, and a stench of urine rose from the washrooms. But a boisterous freedom was in the air. Everyone was in passage, lightly uprooted. They gobbled salads and tore at scraggy chicken, played cards raucously together and pampered each other's children, until the afternoon lunch-break lulled them into sleep. Then the stained railway mattresses were

33

deployed over the bunks, and the corridor became a tangle of arms and projecting feet in frayed socks. From a tundra of sheets poked the beards of Turcoman farmers, and the weathered heads of soldiers resting on their caps. Matriarchs on their way to visit relatives in the next oasis lay mounded under blankets or quilted coats, and young women curled up with their children in their arms and their scarves swept over their faces.

Two hundred miles east of Ashkhabad, where the soil shelved into ridges of scrub-speckled sand, a harsh wind sprang up. It whined against our windows and liquefied the plain and sky to a single, yellowed light. Suddenly ploughed tracts and irrigation channels appeared, and the glisten of flooded rice-fields; and soon afterwards a withered forest of telegraph-poles, pylons and cranes preceded the suburbs of Mari. I had time for a spy's glimpse into back yards – a view of cherished private plots and straggling geese – before we jolted to a halt.

Mari was a scrawl over the oasis, built piecemeal in a pallid, dead brick. Between flat-blocks and bungalows I tramped towards a heart which was not there. I found a bleak hotel. Towards evening, sitting in its hall before a black-and-white television, I heard that Najibullah had been deposed in Afghanistan. But there was nobody in the lobby with whom to share this; and the news went on. With a dim dissociation, as if I were receiving reports from a distant planet, I heard that the Danes had rejected the European Exchange Rate Mechanism and that there was to be a memorial concert for Freddie Mercury at Wembley.

But nothing from the outlandish present seemed real that night. It was the past which impinged. Somewhere on the fringe of this unlovely town lay the ruined caravan-city of Merv, lodestar of the Silk Road for two thousand years, and capital of the gifted and tragic Seljuk Turks: a rich city, sometimes cultivated and benignly powerful, which had nurtured its heterogeneous citizens in a common passion for trade.

I wandered out into the warm night of Mari. The few street-lamps shed down squalor. The only open restaurant served coarse vegetable soups, with lumps of mutton and goat in sticky

34

rice. I padded down unlit alleys towards a thread of music, and emerged beneath flat-blocks to see a floodlit wedding feast. The guests were sitting at long trestle tables under a ceiling of vines, or dancing in a clearing of beaten earth. I watched them from the darkness. They seemed to be celebrating with an isolated fragility. They danced all together with their arms dangled above their heads. They might have been actors on a faraway stage. Nothing seemed solid. Distance muted the gorging and tippling at the tables to an elfin conviviality. The speeches and the clash of toasts dwindled to murmuring and tinkling. The women shimmered in claret-coloured velvets and harlequin headscarves, and the young men flaunted black bomber-jackets and flared jeans.

Adding to the strangeness, there were Russians among them: big, blond men who danced, and affectionate young women kissing their Turcoman friends. They swayed and sang faintly to the plangent music – Turc and Slav together – in a tableau of fairytale unity.

I wanted to believe in this unity. The material divide between conqueror and conquered had always been slim here, so that the poorer people, I thought, might painlessly integrate. But the Russians' conviction of their cultural superiority, and the Turcomans' deep conservatism, played havoc with this hope. Safar had told me that it was almost unknown for a Turcoman family to yield its daughter to a Russian man. So, as I watched, the feasting and dancing assumed the make-believe of an advertisement, and I was not surprised when the Russian guests departed early, their presence a fleeting token, while the Turcomans danced on into the night.

*

The taxi-driver had scrutinous eyes in a harsh face. For twenty miles we travelled towards Merv through a thin dawn light and a flotsam of houses and factories. Two centuries ago the oasis had been laid waste by the emir of Bukhara who destroyed its irrigation systems and resettled its inhabitants. It seemed never to have recovered. After the Russian conquest it became a place of

35

exile for disgraced army officers, and its native inhabitants gained a reputation for perfidy. 'If you meet a viper and a Mervi,' said other Turcomans, 'kill the Mervi first and the viper afterwards.'

The driver kept patting his hair and moustache in the cracked mirror. He conformed disturbingly to the Mervi cliché, and nothing softened the narrow distrust in his face. What was I doing here, he demanded? Why did I want to see this old place? 'In England, the cities are all beautiful.'

'No ....'

'In England the roads are all good.' We were crashing over potholes. 'How is the food situation in England? Do you have camels and deserts?'

'No.'

'So it's mountains.' He looked at me with the sharp, frustrated violence of his incomprehension. He spoke Russian only in a rasped assembly of fragmented words. 'Will you exchange your watch for mine?... How much does a car like this cost in England?' It was a clapped-out Lada, in which a jungle of wires poured beneath the dashboard. Every few minutes he stopped to take on or drop off other passengers. They looked as poor and hard as he. I asked about a nearby mosque, but nobody knew where it was. There was a mosque in the centre of town somewhere, they said, but no, they didn't know its name. They scarcely spoke Russian.

Soon afterwards the driver stopped on the edge of a wilderness ruffled into heaps and ridges, and said with mystified contempt: 'This is it.'

I got out and started to walk. The land looked violently unnatural, almost featureless. For a long time only the curious quality of the earth – a terrible, powdery deadness – betrayed that I was treading through the entrails of a city. It might have been sieved through the bodies of insects, so fine was it: the two-thousand-year detritus of pulverised brick, cloth, bone. It spirted beneath every footstep with a tiny, breathy explosion. Everywhere it was heaped into obscure shapes which might once have been walls, pathways, rooms, or nothing. They were bearded with grey goosefoot and camel-thorn, and seamed with a rubbled earth which had disintegrated beyond meaning, but was not virgin.

For hours I stumbled in ignorance across the wasteland. I had expected to meet a few other travellers, but there was none – I had seen no Westerner since entering Turkmenistan. Once, in the lee of buried ramparts, I came upon a herd of auburn-coated camels grazing on nothing: prehistoric-looking beasts with undernourished humps. And once a pair of fishing-eagles rose in silence from a reed-choked canal.

This hint of biblical nemesis, and the hugeness of the city's dereliction, started to take on a cruel glamour. No ruined city I had ever seen – not Balkh nor Nineveh nor Ctesiphon – had delivered quite such a shock of desolation as this. It measured fifteen miles from end to end. Even in April the sun flailed down (and the temperature can reach 160°F, the hottest in the old Soviet Union). A line of battlements rose and glimmered across the wilderness for mile after broken mile. Here and there, out of their wind-smoothed walls, a ghostly tower erupted; but more often they broke into separated chunks and seemed only to emphasise, by their vast and futile compass, the void inside them. Once or twice a fortified hill stood up naked and sudden, as if a great levelling tempest had burst across the oasis and inexplicably missed it.

Everything seemed of equal age, or none. But in fact Merv was many cities. It may have been founded by the dynasty of Alexander the Great, but in 250 BC it passed to Parthia, and here the 10,000 Roman legionaries captured in the defeat of Crassus were brought exhausted into slavery. An apocryphal story sites *The Thousand and One Nights* in Merv, and in the late eighth century Muqanna, the Veiled Prophet of Khorasan, kindled schism here against the occupying Arabs.

In the heart of its lush oasis, where the Silk Road between China and the Mediterranean gathered and disgorged its luxuries and ideas, it became, after Baghdad, the second city of the Islamic world. Home to Hindu traders and Persian artisans, it

37

swelled to a mighty cosmopolis of races and interests, with rich libraries and a celebrated observatory, and was the seat of a Christian bishopric as early as the fifth century.

But it reached its zenith under the Seljuk Turks, who filtered southwards from the Aral Sea late in the tenth century, established their capital here in 1043, and pushed their empire deep across western Asia. Under the prodigious sultan Alp Arslan their dominion stretched from Afghanistan to Egypt, and in 1071 they advanced into Asia Minor, crushed a vast and motley Byzantine army at the battle of Manzikert, and captured the emperor. Alp Arslan, 'the valiant lion', became a paradigm for his people. High-minded, generous and austere, he redeemed himself from sainthood by some bursts of intemperance and exorbitant quirks of dress. He accentuated his enormous height with a towering hat, and his moustaches were so long that he knotted them behind his head before hunting. On his return to the capital, at the head of a 200,000-strong army, he was about to pass judgement on a captive commander at his feet, when the man plunged a knife into his heart. 'You who have witnessed the glory of Alp Arslan exalted to the heavens,' ran his epitaph, 'come to Merv, and you will see it buried in the dust.'

But the tomb, and the inscription, have gone. In 1221 the Mongols of Genghiz Khan overswept the whole country. The terror they inspired quakes in the descriptions of Moslem writers still. The barbarians were as many as grasshoppers, they wrote: squat, foul-smelling men whose skin was tough as shoe-leather and pitted with lice. Their arrows turned the sky to a sea of reeds, and their horses' neighing shut the ears of heaven.

The sack of Merv was one of the most atrocious in history. Toloi, the Khan's youngest son, granted its inhabitants their lives if they surrendered, so they opened their gates, and were driven out on to the plain. Then each Mongol soldier, it is fantastically recorded, was ordered to decapitate between 300 and 400 citizens, and within a few hours they had slaughtered over half a million. Systematically they wrecked and fired the city: irrigation works, mosques, tombs. Then they vanished with the same phantom speed as they had come. It was a frequent Mongol ruse. They did not go far. Timidly the runaway survivors crept back into their ruins, and must have wandered them in stunned hopelessness. Then, suddenly, the Mongols returned, and completed their massacre.

More than a century later, the city still lay in ruins, and the sands were flowing over it. Now the remains of the later town destroyed by the Bukhariots had flopped into dust alongside. Tramping across the debris between them, I came upon the graves of half-remembered holy men. Cemeteries covered the dunes all around in a chaotic counterpane of humped earth spiked with poles and rotting flags. The whine of flies and the slap of stiffened cloth in the wind seemed to accentuate the silence. Far from any town, people had returned here in their thousands to be buried, drawn by some atavistic memory. Many tombs had been newly restored, ringed with walls or railings, freshly confident in their faith.

I reached a mound where a building survived in twin arches, half restored. It abutted a pair of graves under little cupolas, and the signs of worship were all about. The tombs, the perimeter fence, even the bushes around it, had been knotted with thousands of rags torn from pilgrims' clothes in token of prayer. It was as if a great gale of rubbish had blown through, and left its wreckage dripping from every barb.

As I loitered in the arches' shade, a crocodile of eight young women came winding up a track from nowhere. I watched them with the apprehension of a hunter, in case they might dart away. But instead they dropped their shoes and bags at the shrine's vanished entrance – as if shedding their modernity – and crowded into a narrow, vaulted chamber, where I could hear them praying. Then, barefoot, in a shimmer of magenta and ultramarine dresses, they circled the graves three times in silence, stopping to touch their temples to its stone. They smoothed their palms over its grille then over their faces, kissing the iron. They seemed at once stately and humble, lost in a contrite love-making. As they finished, they gathered up pebbles

39

and dust close to the graves, and the eldest – a dark, angry-looking Amazon – tied a white scarf to the fence. Five minutes later, scenting another grave to petition, they had trailed away over the wilderness in a brilliant caterpillar, and I heard their laughter chirruping over the dunes.

Gingerly I approached the room where they had prayed. I had imagined it empty. But I eased open the door on a cave cluttered with fantastical bric-à-brac. From its walls dangled out-size wooden pots and ladles, with curling posters of Mecca and the holy places of Bukhara, and the shelves were crammed with candle-stubs and a litter of cloudy bottles. A wooden platform, smothered with soiled quilts, almost filled the floorspace, and on this, under the dim light shed by a dome, an old woman was sitting. She looked huge and sorcerous in the gloom. Her body was swathed in stained and ragged crimson, and a massive silver frontlet, littered with perforated coins and semi-precious stones, cascaded over her breast. On a ledge behind her, his mouth level with her ear, perched a shaven-headed boy. As I entered, the woman's creased hands lifted automatically in prayer, but in her face everything – all vitality, insight, emotion – had vanished long ago, and the eyes which wandered over mine were mute and undreaming.

I asked about the two graves. But the boy only glared back at me beneath fierce brows, and the woman went on rasping her inscrutable prayer. I crouched down on my haunches in involuntary deference. The boy watched me unblinking, like a black Ariel. Hesitantly I pushed some money over the quilt, imagining that the woman was praying for me. But after she had stopped she did not take it, or even notice me. Drenched in jewellery like an ancient bride, she seemed to be waiting for something, and I could not rid myself of the impression that this vaulted chamber was her chosen tomb, where her posthumous sanctity would grow unimpeded, until it too became a place of pilgrimage.

I got up and crossed into sunlight, where swallows were dipping between the arches of the ruined mosque. Broken scaffolding clung to them, and a winch had congealed beneath to a mass of rust and snapped wires. After a while a faint, rhythmic pinging sounded from a ruined-looking dwelling. I had assumed it too squalid for habitation, but when I peered inside I saw an old man touching an elfin hammer to a little anvil. In front of him lay a miniature lathe and a box of gouging and chipping tools – all as intricate and fragile-looking as he – and with these he was creating miniature jewellery and the unearthly, silvery music whenever his hammer struck.

He lived here, I discovered, with the old woman among a muddle of chipped dishes and indecipherable effects, and he carved Islamic crescent moons out of wood or ivory, which he sold to pilgrims. As I came in, he asked me to sit by him. Tentatively I enquired after the saints buried here, and wondered if he was their guardian.

His voice came thin and musical: 'They were soldiers, martyrs. When? I don't know, but in the century of the great sultans. Their history is written in Arabic and Persian. You can't find it in Russian.' He added in faint reproof: 'People should learn the holy languages. You can learn one in a few months if your will is strong enough, and if your heart is right.' He massaged his heart with a tiny fist. 'Look.' He rummaged among his tools and from a carefully beribboned cloth picked out a Koran in Arabic. 'People should read this!'

Yet his own eyes twinkled over it unseeing; he could no more read it than I could. It was a talisman only. In the Stalin years a whole generation of educated Turcomans, the Arabic speakers, had been despatched into oblivion.

I took it from him and turned the sacred pages. 'Where did you get it?'

'From Iran. Sometimes they come here, those people, and from Afghanistan.'

'You favour that system, that ...' – the word whispered like a secret – 'fundamentalism?'

For a moment he went on chipping at the ivory in his hands. Suddenly I realised how I hung on his reply. Here, if anywhere,

41

among the poor and pious, must be the breeding-ground for an Islamic resurgence.

But he answered simply, finally: 'No. We don't need that here.' He jerked his chin to the south. 'That's for people over there.'

It was strange, I thought. Superficially the soil for fundamentalism was perfect here: the deepening poverty and sense of historical wrong, the damaged pride. But in fact the old man's response was typical of his people. The idea of religion as a doctrinaire moulder of society seemed shallow-rooted among them, and their faith to thrive somewhere different, somewhere more sensory and pagan.

'All those laws and customs ....' The old man resettled his grimy skull-cap. 'They don't matter. What matters is underneath this!' – he plucked at his jacket – 'What matters is the heart!'

He laid down his gouge and tried to activate a blackened gas-ring. The old woman came in and circled round him, while he gestured her on little errands just beyond his reach – to collect a teacup here, remove a slipper there. She had lost her strangeness now. She moved about him with a slow, desanctified tread. 'She's deaf,' he said. But his voice was too weak to shout at her. It fluted. His thin legs stuck out unnaturally in front of him.

'Our country's had enough of other people's interference,' he said. 'Our whole world is committing suicide.' He sliced his hand across his throat in ghostly sacrifice. 'All these trains, aeroplanes and cars, when what we need is food! Our soil can give us three crops a year, but what do we usually get? One! All we plant is cotton, but you can't *eat* cotton. You just sell it for roubles. That's what our country's done. And you can't eat money either.' He picked up a rouble note and munched it in phantom frustration. 'Nobody works now. People have to work. Then, God willing, everything will bear fruit ....'

His talk was a goulash of Islamic custom and Marxist work ethic. But his own work was almost done, he said. Two years ago he had been restoring the nearby mosque arches, when he fell and severed his spinal cord. From his hips down, he was

42

paralysed. Yet he mentioned this with the same goblin brightness as he described everything else, illustrating his fall with the
crash of his little fist on to the quilt. I remembered the scaffolding outside from which he must have toppled, and realised now
why his legs were so thin, thrust in front of him. He moved
them about with his hands. 'Nothing!' He touched the base of
his spine. 'Nothing!' Then he pointed to the door. 'I go about on
that now. I made it myself.' My gaze followed his finger, and
alighted on one of those heartrending trolleys which cripples
ride in India and Iran – wheeled boards, which they propel over
the tarmac with their hands.

He must have seen my expression. 'It doesn't matter,' he said.
'My life is over now. My children are all grown up. They don't
need my help any more.' He retrieved the Koran from my lap. 'I
can die now.'

His manner refused all pity, but I took up one of his crescent
moons before I left, and handed him a fifty-rouble note.

He looked at it without interest. 'Do you have kopeks in
England?'

'We have coins.'

'Next time you come, bring me some of those. I work them
into ornaments. Afghan pilgrims give me coins.' I remembered
the perforated coppers which flowed over the old woman's
breast, stamped with Afghan lions. I realised too now why he
kept asking her to do simple things around him, just out of his
reach. 'Metal and ivory are all right. Paper is useless.'

Living among graves, and surrounded by the wreckage of
centuries, the huge woman and her pigmy consort touched me
with irrational sadness. But there was nothing real I could give
them.

*

Towards dusk I reached a seventh-century citadel crumbling on
its mound. Its battlements resembled a rectangle of vast clay logs
upended side by side, and I wondered why this petrified stockade had not been manned against the Mongols. But perhaps the

43

human heart, in the old man's words, had not been right, and now the crenellations had worn away and the entrance-ramp was blurred into the sand.

I waded across stagnant ditches, and skirted a seasonal pond where a flock of black-winged stilts was tiptoeing through the shallows. Ahead of me, a giant mausoleum reared out of nothing above the littered plain. For forty feet into the air its cube of walls loomed blank. It had been heavily restored, and only a pair of high doors broke its austerity. But near its summit it opened on an ornamental portico, and above its drum, from which all decoration had gone, a great dome hovered.

This was the tomb of the much-loved Seljuk sultan Sanjar, grandson of Alp Arslan, whose rule vacillated for fifty years across the eastern provinces of the disintegrating empire. At first his triumphs over Turkic enemies shored up his delicate realm, but in middle age disasters made his name a byword for humiliation. In 1156, at the age of seventy, he died in a half-ruined city and was entombed in the mausoleum which he had built himself, and called 'The Abode of Eternity'.

He was succeeded by chaos, in which his memory glittered. The form of his tomb – its walls closed against the earth but open to heaven – signalled to his people that he was perhaps alive, and might return to resurrect his empire. But inside I found an echoing emptiness. The whitewashed walls lifted to an octagon from whose pendentives floated a cavernous inner dome. It moaned with the beat of pigeon wings. Decorative strapwork, still painted blue, radiated over its surface and meshed at its apex in an eight-pointed star. But vertically beneath it, in the centre of the floor, a plain grave, protected by a sheet against pigeon droppings, subverted the glory of the ruler with the platitude of death.

*

'You watch out in those ruins,' said Murad the lorry-driver. 'They're haunted.'

'Who by?'

44

'I don't know. People have been heard crying there.' He was trying to dissuade me from returning. He was jaunty and impetuous, and wanted me to join him on a picnic in the desert. 'And that castle you saw,' he went on, 'there's gold buried all round, but nobody can find any. Its sultan kept a harem of forty women there and a tunnel leads from it underground to the other end of the city. It's dangerous.'

These fables of gold and tunnels attend ruins all across the Islamic world, so I agreed to the picnic instead, and the next moment we were crashing through the side-alleys of Mari recruiting his friends. He blasted his horn and bawled his invitation beneath half a dozen tenement-blocks, until a flock of grizzled heads sprouted from rotting oriels and balconies, to bellow down their assent or refusal. Then he would march inside to harry them, yelling for me to follow. We bounded up stair-wells fetid and awash with recent rain, where bottles and cigarette stubs and sometimes broken condoms floated. We were joined by a big, hirsute man with violent eyebrows and a lax, cruel mouth. Then came a wizened old Mongoloid clutching a lute in a velvet case. And soon we were careering across the desert in a gust of anticipation, while over the hummocks around us the goosefoot and artemisia thinned, and all signs of habitation vanished.

After an hour Murad's face – a quivering profile of high bones – quickened into expectation. 'We're here!'

He veered over virgin sand and we settled in a dip between the dunes. A weft of yellow and mauve vetch shone all over the savannah, and poppies turned the ridges scarlet. He had forgotten nothing. A felt carpet, such as once covered Turcoman yurts, was unravelled over the sands. Bags of spiced mutton appeared, with two charred samovars, an outsize stewing-pot, a basket of raw vegetables, sheafs of kebab-skewers and some fire-blackened bricks. As we scavenged for dead saxaul – the wind-blown plant whose pallid stems litter the whole country – a familiar euphoria broke out. Their voices were light and bantering. Their bodies seemed balanced only precariously on their bow-legs, as if they longed to leap on horseback. Soon we had a triple blaze of fires going. The samovars were cremated in a nest of flaming branches, the shashlik oozed and spat over charcoal heaps, and the stewing-pot – into which Murad had tossed a calf's head – simmered balefully on a brick hob. The men's faces lit up in sybaritic grins. The bitterness left the big man's mouth and the Mongoloid's face dimpled into glee.

'Isn't this better than home?' he cried, as we settled ceremoniously on the carpet. 'Nothing compares with this!'

Soon the shashlik was being thrust triumphantly from hand to hand. Dribbling blood and fat, it was tough as rope. But the three men swallowed each morsel wholesale, or clamped it between their teeth like mastiffs and worried it to and fro, until it separated with a noise like tearing sheets. They celebrated every mouthful with a carnivorous burp, and dipped gluttonously into mountains of radishes and olives. The brief respites between skewers resounded with an anticipatory grinding of gold and ivory molars and the smack of oily lips. They looked artless and timeless. At any moment, I thought, they might break into shamanistic chant or propose a raid. The time was not long past when their ancestors had cantered eighty miles a day to harvest Persian slaves – the Mongoloid's father might just have known it – and the desert still seemed subtly to nourish them. Their earthquake-stricken country gave no confidence in building, or perhaps in any permanence at all. Better the open sky!

Assiduously they plied me with the tenderest chunks of shashlik, but my teeth recoiled even from these. I smuggled them out of my mouth and secreted them wherever I could: in the bush behind me, under the sand between my knees, in my shirt pockets. Murad kept thrusting more at me, the point of his skewer threatening my chest. But he was grinning with hospitality. They all were. The big man detached the most succulent nuggets to press on me, with the crispest onions. But soon my pockets sagged with the telltale meat, and a betraying stain of fat was spreading across my shirt-front.

As I masticated despairingly on another hunk, I bit on some-

46

thing hard, and assumed it was mutton-bone. Then I realised that it was one of my own bones I was chewing. I had lost a tooth. Neurotically I ran my tongue back and forth over the gap. Nobody else noticed. I longed to inspect it in a mirror, but I could picture it well enough: the double rank of ivory now breached by a slovenly void, as obvious as a fainted guardsman. Viewed from the right, I might pass muster. But seen from the left, I thought, I must show a Dracula-like unreliability. Would I be refused permits, visas, even hotel bedrooms, I wondered, on account of this lost incisor? Would conversations dry up the moment I grinned?

These broodings were halted by the arrival of soup. Murad elevated the cauldron above his head as if at a pagan Eucharist, while the calf's head bobbed obscenely to the surface. The big man skimmed off the fat and threw it on the sand. Then we drank, and it was delicious. Fumbling in my rucksack, I found a packet of English cheese biscuits and passed them round complacently. They nibbled them without comment. Later I noticed Murad dropping his into the sand.

Little by little the party's spirit mellowed. The men's quick, guttural language was mysterious to me, but they translated their jokes into a babbling Russian, and finally Murad conjured up three bottles of vodka. 'This is the whole point!' He slopped it into shallow glasses, and we flung them back in one gulp, Russian fashion, at every toast. Only the old Mongol refused to drink at first. It suborned his stomach, he said. 'He's an *ishan*, a holy one!' roared the big man, mocking.

'They drink most of all!' retorted the Mongol, and they were rolling in the flowers with laughter.

Some charred pots of green tea created a moment's hiatus. Then the vodka-drinking went on. Sometimes, secretly, I spilled mine into the sand, but Murad replenished my glass at every toast, and fatally I lost count of them. Meanwhile they absolved themselves with blessings, and peppered their talk with 'If God wills!' or 'Thanks be to God!', while pouring out the forbidden spirit. Then they expatiated on remedies for hangover, and confided the medicinal properties of saxaul root or green tea (sovereign against headaches if you inhaled the aroma between cupped hands).

'Try it! Try it!' But it was too late. The vodka had already detached me, and I was seeing them all from far away. Sitting cross-legged on their carpet among the flowers, they seemed to have regressed into a Persian miniature. Yet squatting amongst them was this outlandish foreigner, with a black stain advancing over his shirt . . . .

The big man turned to me with inebriate slowness and asked: '*Where* are you from then?' All countries, I think, lay in mist to him beyond the oasis of his own. 'London? That's in America!'

'No, no!' yelled Murad. 'Great Britain!'

The giant looked bewildered, but said: 'Aah.'

'Margaret Thatcher!' mused the Mongol. 'She is very beautiful. I did not think that such an old woman could be so beautiful. So slender!' He shook his own hands in congratulation. 'Who is president of Great Britain now then? Does she have a son?'

By now the shadows of the shrubs were wavering long over the dunes, and the sand grew more deeply golden, the sun descending. The men picked their teeth and let out soft whistles of contentment. For a while the Mongoloid had been plucking the poppies round him, and munching them. But now he took out his *dutah* – the frail-looking Turcoman lute shaped like a long teardrop – and started to play. From this coarse instrument he conjured tiny, plangent sounds on two wire strings, to which he sometimes sang, or half-spoke – but the words, he said, were untranslatable – about love, longing, and the passing of every-thing. His voice was a husky shadow. His shaven head, furred over by a grey and white chiaroscuro, bent close over the strings, as if striving to hear. He had never been taught to play, he said, but had learnt by listening to the old bards in his youth. Yet his gnarled fingers fluttered along the wires, and long after his right hand had plucked one, his left darted up and down the lute's stem, while the notes faded.

Far away on the horizon, billowing black into the sky, an

enormous column of smoke was ascending, where some oil installation had gone up in flames.

The sun dropped into the dunes. The last of the shashlik, ignored, had charred to a line of basalt pebbles, and a post-prandial weariness descended. The last song left the old man's lips, and he eased the *dutah* back into its velvet sheath. Our picnic had shrunk to husks and rinds. Flies were glued to every abandoned scrap. We groped to our feet and began to clear up. The old man was slapping his head against the flies. He cleaned the skewers by stabbing them into the sand, as the Romans had cleaned their armour. Nobody seemed to notice the long trail of dung-beetles on a gastronomic pilgrimage to the bush behind me.

The vodka had vanished too, and all the way back to Mari my head was separating from my body. I glimpsed it swaying in the lorry's mirror. Whenever I opened my mouth my missing tooth struck me with a seedy shock. It had not so much dropped out as disintegrated, and had left a stunted fang dangling above the gap like a yellow stalactite. But by the time we reached Murad's house in a village on Mari's outskirts, I had ceased to care. My legs dropped from the lorry independently, and embarked on a wavering half-life of their own.

I remember his home only as a series of vodka-sickened lantern-slides which light up in my memory even now with a tinge of shame. Two women in native dresses are standing near the doorway. They are Murad's wife and eldest sister. His wife comforts her small son over something as he sobs against her breast. I greet them feebly. The half-light from the door, or an overhanging vine, seems to turn them biblical. I imagine I am back in Syria. The starlight shows a private vegetable patch, and two cows standing under a byre. A puppy wags a disfigured rump. To save it from being mauled by other dogs, its ears and tail have been sliced off with a razor.

My legs carried me weightlessly into the bare interior. In its reception room a dresser shone with cheap ornaments, and a television stood mute. Murad was drunk too, strutting and shouting.

49

The women looked at us with the indulgence accorded to hopeless children.

The drink-haze lifted a little on a mild-faced schoolmaster who was invited in to speak English with me. He did so in a doggerel monologue of Dickensian sentences, once or twice beginning 'It is painful to reflect ....' or 'As is my wont ....' Meanwhile I propped myself on a cushion like an indolent sultan, and tried not to sink into catalepsy. A young musician, too, was summoned from the village to amuse me. In the middle of his improvised concert, I watched through dulled eyes as he slapped two batteries into his *dutah* – 'It makes a bigger noise like this!' – before launching into new arpeggios.

The music tinkled far away. A great tide of blackness was lapping up behind my eyes. I remember hoping, as they thudded shut, that this would be construed as ecstasy at the *dutah* music rather than a bursting headache. Whatever happens, I thought, I mustn't sleep.

Then I slept.

3

Bukhara

For 800 miles the Karakum desert ripples towards Afghanistan in pale yellow waves. Bordered to the south by the Kopet Dagh and the Hindu Kush, and to the north by the long hypotenuse of the Oxus river, this shifting, fine-grained wilderness throws up no landmark, no distinctive feature at all, but is fringed by choked wells and salinated fields. A Roman historian remarked in astonishment that its people could travel only by the stars, like sailors.

From my train window it guttered through a triple haze. Misted by my hangover and by the smeared glass, the whole wasteland was dimly in motion. Almost unnoticeably, a light wind was lifting the feathery grains off the dunes, until every surface fell faintly out of focus. For mile after stricken mile the sallow crescents rolled to the skyline – not in sculptured contours, but in shuffling ridges and rotted-looking mounds.

Across these wastes, in 329 BC, Alexander the Great had marched his 60,000-strong army to the Oxus under a scourging sun, and here, when a soldier brought him water in his helmet, he refused to drink while his army was dying of thirst, and poured the water into the sands.

Later expeditions were drastically depleted, or vanished altogether. General Skobelev, moving against Merv in 1881, started out with a pack train of 12,000 camels, and ended with only 600 living; and the formidable General Kaufmann salvaged barely one twelfth of 20,000 camels and horses from his desert march on Khiva in 1873.

51

The failing of water glares over the whole region. Tributaries of the great rivers peter out in sand-cluttered gullies, and whole lakes shrivel to beds of salt. Irrigation has both extended and thinned its resources. Even the inland seas – the Aral, the Caspian, the mountain-ringed Issyk-kul – are gradually emptying.

The family seated beside me looked out of the window with loathing. As the void deepened, they let out a rasping 'Eah!' or 'Fffft!', and cuffed away the view with their hands. 'It's hopeless,' the woman said. 'You can't do anything with it.'

They were stout and old, with thick bodies and coarse necks: a Russian couple with their small granddaughter. They wore an identical look of clouded defence. In their shared face a tundra of cheeks and jowls overpowered all else, isolating their vision and squeezing their mouth to a fleshy bud. The small girl's plaits were gathered up under frothy muslin ribbons and a Mickey Mouse hairclip, but already she reproduced her grandparents' stolid stare.

The old man had worked in the oil-wells at Nebit Dagh near the Caspian for forty-five years, and a Soviet work-medal drooped from his lapel. Every spring, before the heat came – 'A wind brings the sand out of Afghanistan like a sauna,' he said – they escaped northward to a dacha near Samara in the Russian heartland. There they lived on fruit and vegetables which the woman had grown and bottled the year before, and would return south only when the snows came.

In the cubicles around us the Turcomans lay asleep on the railway's flowery pillows. Their padded coats dangled decorously from every hook, but the faces coddled below were those of Hunnish destroyers. Their beards forked angrily over the clean sheets. Their young women, descendants of those Amazons who had followed their men into battle, lay fully dressed in a glitter of gold-threaded headscarves and ear-pendants.

A hundred years ago the building of this Trans-Caspian railway had set the seal on their nation's defeat. Its earthworks and cuttings were hacked out by 20,000 native and Persian labourers, while two battalions of soldiers spiked down the rails behind them. Along this thin line the trains dithered at less than fifteen miles per hour, but by 1895 it had linked Russian dominions from the Caspian to Tashkent, and hung a Damoclean sword over Persia.

Now the train pushed through a howling wilderness towards the Uzbekistan frontier. A tempest dimmed the sky with sand and tumbled the torn-up saxaul from dune to dune. Local Turcomans say that the sand-grains in each dune cling together like tribespeople and never intermingle, but towards evening our view had liquefied into a tawny mist. Once or twice we passed impoverished villages, with camels wandering in the dust-blown streets, and the desert heaped at their walls. The sun dangled above like a tarnished coin.

'How frightful!' chorused the family. They were dreaming of the green north, the cool winds and marshy fields round Samara.

An hour afterwards we clanked through the sprawl of industrial Chardzhou and minutes later, as the last suburbs disappeared, we were crossing the Oxus. It moved in a huge question-mark over the barren earth: less like a natural river than an act of fate. Both its source and its end were far away. In the past, before irrigation depleted it, it flooded to a diameter of five miles, and even now, confined to its banks, it measured over half a mile across. It flowed with a soft, muscular ease. Silt-mounds glistened on its surface like the backs of drowned whales, or were smoothed into temporary islands, so that it appeared to be entering its estuary four hundred miles too soon.

For a precious minute the train crossed its bridge. I stared at it with boyish excitement – few Westerners had ever seen it – and with a faint sickness of nostalgia which I could not identify. This was the immemorial divide between the Persian and Turkic worlds, and in its 1500-mile flow from the Pamirs to the lifeless Aral Sea, I fancied that it scarcely belonged to the present at all. Turkic peoples call it Amu Dariya, 'the River-sea', so vast does it seem, and Arab geographers long considered it the earth's mightiest river. In Persian legend (and the epic of Matthew Arnold) Rustam had killed his son Sohrab on its banks. Alexander's army steered itself across in five days on inflated tent-skins stuffed with brushwood, and seventeen centuries later the Mongol emperor Tamerlane crossed it the other way to conquer the world.

I had time to glimpse two or three antiquated ferries churning between the mud-flats, and the span of a new lorry bridge. Then the desert circled us again, and we were riding into the night across the unmarked frontier of Uzbekistan towards Bukhara.

As if emboldened, an Uzbek youth perched on our bunk and started to ask questions. His skull-cap was faded green, and his shoes scuffed. The Russians watched him with furious suspicion. The old man answered him only by thin smiles, and the woman was violently silent. But the youth affected not to notice. When he offered the woman a drink from his bottle of lemon juice, she almost screamed her refusal, and glowered in disbelief when he passed it to their granddaughter. 'No, no, no!' And the little girl, infected by the nervousness all around her, echoed: 'No, I don't want it, no ....'

The youth turned to me. 'Where are you from?'

'He's Ukrainian!' the woman barged in. 'He's a teacher! He's just going to a hotel in Bukhara.'

The Uzbek's eyes glided over me. He looked delicate, amused, harmless. It was impossible to tell what he wanted. He murmured: 'Ukrainian ....' and moved away.

The woman said: 'You be careful. It's dollars they want. They'll kill you for them.' She pointed her fingers to her head and pulled an imaginary trigger. 'They're shooting foreigners for their dollars now. Pff! ... Pff! ... Pff!'

'It's worse in Russia,' the man said. 'There it's got terrible.'

'But it's coming here too,' the woman said. 'There won't be travellers here much longer.'

I sank into an uneasy quiet. Outside, the train's headlamps wobbled myopically over the same mutilated-looking desert. Nothing betrayed that we were entering the most ancient and populous country of Central Asia, its settled heart, or that the nomad wastes would soon give way to the watered valleys of Transoxiana, 'the Land beyond the River'.

Across this region, for some two thousand years, the Silk Road had nourished caravan-towns – Samarkand, Bukhara, Margilan – whose populace had spoken an Iranian tongue. The Uzbeks were latecomers, migrating south at the end of the fifteenth century. They took their name from a khan of the Golden Horde, for their origins were Turkic, but already their blood was mixed with Iranians', and they added only the last layer to a palimpsest of peoples identifying themselves less by nation than by clan. On my map Uzbekistan made a multi-coloured confusion. It was shaped like a dog barking at China. A country of twenty million – more than seventy per cent of them Uzbeks – it butted against the Tienshan and the Pamir mountains in green-tinted lowlands and a sudden spaghetti of roads. But it remained an enigma: a land whose Communist rulers had persisted in power under another name, offering only lipservice to Islam, and loosening the economy without promise of democracy.

As we pulled in to Kagan, the station of Bukhara, the woman hissed in my ear: 'Mix only with Russians! Say you're an Estonian! *Never* talk to Uzbeks!'

I got out into the warm night. My rucksack felt suddenly heavy. I had contracted her fear, a little. I kept glancing behind me; but the families tramping along the platform looked docile and self-absorbed. A lonely goods train stood under the stars.

A century ago, when the railway first neared the city, the people had never set eyes on such a thing. It was beneath the dignity of the emir of Bukhara – a vassal of the Russians since 1868 – to travel on a train, and its pernicious track had to skirt the holy city by ten miles. People dubbed it 'the Devil's Wagon'. Yet the moment it arrived at Kagan, they crammed into the open wagons in their hundreds and would wait ecstatically for hours to witness it puffing its inexplicable smoke and to feel the exquisite terror of its movement.

Now I trudged out of a silent station and into the lamp-lit

55

night. A perverse excitement was stirring me. Bukhara! For centuries it had glimmered remote in the Western consciousness: the most secretive and fanatical of the great caravan-cities, shored up in its desert fastness against time and change. To either side of it the Silk Road had withered away, so that by the nineteenth century the town had folded its battlements around its people in self-immolated barbarism, and receded into fable.

I started up the road towards scattered lights and a dark hotel.

*

The sun rose on a chalk-pale city. Its heart was a mud-floored labyrinth where cars petered out. The lanes meandered in ravines of brick and stucco, so that I found myself tunnelling for miles between blank walls where whitewashed clay and weathered door-frames propped each other up, old and new together, in a patchwork of splintering plaster. Ranks of timbers poked out of walls like the cannon from some rotting man-o'-war, or lifted whole storeys clear across the alleys. In these blind wanderings the lightly carved doors, bossed and ringed with brass, stood habitually shut. Sunlight never reached them. The streets curved ahead of me like an ambulatory full of closed chapels. Only occasionally, where some mangy Cerberus nested in an open doorway, I would glimpse beyond a deep passage a courtyard where roses bloomed or a bicycle rusted or a stairway wriggled down from a balcony.

Meanwhile, a motley of citizens sauntered by. A few still went in the long, multi-coloured coats of tradition; and blue or green skull-caps perched on every other head. But an unravellable mix of Turk and Iranian subsumed every face. Aquiline features and vivid, open eyes betrayed a people chiefly Tajik – the early Persian inhabitants – but other faces smoothed to steppeland masks in which the eyes became passing details and the eyebrows refined to feathery arcs.

Once I was overtaken by a groom on the way to his bride: a sheepish-looking youth, outlandishly sashed and turbaned. He went among cheering friends who hoisted four-foot horns into the air and made a rude, unearthly braying. Behind them skipped a street-gang of girls whose members were half-recognisable: the tomboy leader flashing her adult teeth, the rebel, the joker, the beauty, and the sissy tagging along behind.

After they had gone, one of them returned, slopping in slippers too big for her. She had the wide-set eyes and fair complexion of the Russians, and blonde curls trickled under her headscarf. She looked like a miniature charlady. She asked: 'Have you got a dog? So have we, but it's old. I hoped you might get another one from America ....'

I asked her, in the boring way of adults, what she wanted to do after she finished school.

But she walked away. 'I'll be a young woman, then a mother, then an old woman ....' Her walk slowed to a dark saunter, and she looked back suddenly over her shoulder. '.... Then a corpse.'

The alleys twisted into clearings, where I came upon a holy man's grave, restored forty years after its destruction under Stalin. A fig tree marked the mound, which was strewn with candle-stubs, and a horse-tail banner had been raised above it again. At such moments the Communist era shrank to a thin wave in a timeless sea. So too, in the tea-houses of the Lyab-i-Khauz, where the lanes opened on a pool ringed with medresehs – religious schools – an immemorial conclave of old men lolled on wooden divans as if nothing had ever changed. Their heads were knotted in pale blue turbans or piled with sheepskin hats. Beards dribbled from their chins like fine wire. They sat at ease cross-legged, or dangled a hedonistic limb over the divan's edge, while the proprietors shuffled amiably between them, pouring out green tea from cracked pots. A gentle euphoria was in the air. Nothing sounded but the clink of china and a genial murmur of conspiracy. A breeze blew ripples over the water. Around them the religious schools looped in high gate-ways and blind arcades, in whose spandrels flew faience phoenixes. Here and there a façade cast a band of Koranic script into the sky, and under nearby plane trees a statue of Khodja

Nasreddin, the wise fool of Sufi legend, rode his mad-faced mule.

'What would he make of us now? Everything's gone mad!' I had sat down mistakenly beside a man who was angry-drunk. 'Look at our Uzbekistan! We've got cotton, gold, skins, oil, uranium, marble, but we all live like rats!' His raucous voice split paradise apart. The seraphic faces of the old men turned sleepily towards us. 'Our families should be ten times richer than the French! Our potential is greater than Saudi Arabia's! We could buy America!'

The man was fired by some frenetic inner violence, yet his face was soft and idle, and his mouth self-mocking.

I began: 'Then things will get better ....'

But his voice dropped into conspiracy. 'No, we were sold off years ago, under Brezhnev, under Rashidov. Moscow said "Give!" and we gave. And it's still going on. The Uzbek and Russian leaders kiss on TV, like tarts. Our president's spunkless, he's frightened somebody'll shoot him. He's *their* man.' A treacherous knowledge curled his lips. 'Oh yes. I know things. Big Brother is still Big Brother!'

In the coming months I would hear this litany often: a distrust of all political leadership, and a lament for riches which the Russians had spirited away.

I said: 'You're free to trade outside Russia now. You can do your own deals.'

He waved a chubby finger. 'I tell you the Russians won't let us go. A hundred years ago those pederasts in the Kremlin looked about and saw that Britain and America were taking colonies... so why not Russia? They'll go on bleeding us ....' He seemed to be acting two people: one rabid and hyperbolic; the other detached, wryly amused, and perhaps despairing. He had pared history into a play for shadow-puppets.

'Now all we need is to be left alone with our land,' he said. 'Just to live quietly with the earth. The earth was given to everyone. It can feed and clothe us all.'

This mystique of the land, too, would grow familiar. In the

absence of human heroes, it had become the repository of patriotism, of the purity in the people's soul. The Russians had exploited and polluted the earth, but it belonged to those who loved it, and would requite them in the end.

The smile of self-parody had left the man's face. He began: 'Before Alexander of Macedon died, he said: *Only make sculptures of my hands to stand above my grave! Just my hands and the earth! These are my tools!*'

'Did he say that?'

'He said we achieve through labour ....'

It was a grotesque fusion of legend and Communist work ethic. The man started to ramble. He nibbled crusts left over on the table. Oral epics of Alexander have pervaded this country since antiquity. In remote valleys, far into this century, clan chieftains claimed descent from him.

'You remember!' The man stood up. 'I'm not a fool. My grandfather was a prophet in his village. He had the gift of second sight. I have it too ....' He teetered above me. 'And I tell you everything will get worse. Everyone is a tyrant, a thief or a slave!' He drifted morosely away among the divans. 'There's nothing in between ....'

I got up and started towards the city's heart. The lanes had loosened into squares and boulevards impenetrable to cars, where starved canals ran deep in their stone gullies. Suddenly I entered a dust-filled wasteland fringed by a pale host of mosques and medresehs. The din and pall of restoration shook the air. The earth dazzled. The buildings glared in a blank, shadowless uniformity. Dressed in cement-coloured brick, they had not the rich plentitude of the tiled mosques of Iran, but were patterned only sparsely with a glaze of indigo or green. For the rest, they were the colour of the earth beneath them: a dead platinum. It was as if the dust had hardened into walls and turrets and latticed windows. Everything – even the clay-coloured sky – shone with the same bleached stare.

But above, in radiant atonement, hovered a tumult of turquoise domes. Beyond the high gateways and *iwans* – the great vaulted porches – they swam up from their drums like unearthly fruit, and flooded the sky with the heaven-sent blue of Persia. From a distance they seemed to shine in unified aquamarine, but in fact the tiles which coated them were subtly different from one another, so that they spread a vibrant, changing patina over every cupola: eggshell, kingfisher, deep sapphire.

These mosques and medresehs were mostly raised by the successors of Tamerlane or by the sixteenth-century Sheibanids, the first and most glorious Uzbek dynasty that succeeded them. Little that is older survives. In 1220 Genghiz Khan had laid waste a city already more than a thousand years old, and only the stupendous Kalan minaret, muscling 148 feet into the sky, was intentionally spared. Once the minaret served as a beacon for caravans over the night desert and in the degraded years of the last emirs condemned criminals were pushed from its summit. It is a mammoth, unlovely thing. Its colours have all but gone – the surging Arabic script in tilework fallen away – but its raised brick-patterns survive near-perfect, and mount to a rich gallery upheld on scalloped corbels.

I lingered beneath, touched by vertigo at the criminal's body hurtling towards me, and the ground where I stood rushing up to meet him. But only the call to prayer was sounding, plangent and weak from the summit, and two women were sweeping the dust beneath.

I moved away. The blanched aridity all around oppressed me inexplicably, as though the city were dying instead of being restored. Even the dust seemed to have been leached by some ghostly peroxide. But in fact Bukhara was being resurrected indiscriminately: walls rebuilt shoddily *en masse*, tilework reproduced wholesale. Work had started in the Soviet period, but events had overtaken it, and the mosques which had been reconstituted cold in the service of art or tourism were stirring again with a half-life of their own.

Even as I looked, white-turbaned students filed out of the Mir-i-Arab medreseh and into the Ulug Beg medreseh beyond. I had seen them before, hurrying through the markets where they bought nothing, and they stung me with curiosity. I followed them in idle frustration. A look of enclosed earnestness marked them off. I had the illusion that through them I might unravel the country's identity, as if it owned some unified and comprehensible heart. But I did not know if they were the future or the past.

I followed them to the Ulug Beg medreseh, built by the grandson of Tamerlane, and peered in. A few men and boys were walking under the arcades. The double tiers of cells looked empty. But as I hesitated, a diffused hum of Koranic chant rose from the depths of the building, as if it were a vast hive to which the bees were returning.

Then a surly guardian ordered me back. He was filled with suppressed anger. I remembered the same anger in the holy places of Iran and Iraq. 'This isn't open any more. This is for Moslems.' He could not bear to look at me.

I sensed anger in myself too, welling up to meet his. I did not understand it. I found myself challenging him to accept me, asking ingenuous questions. 'How many pupils do you have here?'

He said pugnaciously: 'Four hundred, with the Mir-i-Arab.' The numbers had doubled in two years.

'And how long do they study?'

'Five years.' But his eyes would not meet mine, as if mine might contaminate his, or perhaps soften them. He fixed his stare over my head.

I noticed the inscription carved in Kufic above the gate. It belonged to the time of the liberal sultan Ulug Beg, who had promoted the study of astronomy and the sciences. 'What does it say?'

The man parroted angrily: '"It is the sacred duty of every Moslem man and woman to pursue knowledge."'

I said bloodlessly: 'That's nice.' He glared. 'I've heard there's fine tilework inside.'

'You can read it in books.' He turned his back on me. 'This place is for Moslems.'

Silently, I promised to return.

The heresy incipient in Ulug Beg (who was murdered by puritan reactionaries in 1449) ran riot in the seventeenth-century medreseh opposite, the towering and dilapidated Abdul Aziz Khan. Here, in the dying sunlight, I found a portal tiled with chrysanthemums and cherry blossom; but amongst them, flouting the Islamic ban on portraying animate things, serpents writhed from the ground, masquerading as vase-handles, and blue-headed parakeets flew in pairs towards the sun. Inside, a robust caretaker indicated the outline of a man painted in the *mihrab* – the niche facing Mecca – a terrible heresy, which delighted her. 'Look! Can't you see him? There's his beard...his eyes....' But I could make out nothing.

An undertow of apostasy has pervaded Central Asia always. The Uzbeks carried traces of shamanism into the Sunni orthodoxy of their settled lives, and a countervailing underworld of Persian demons had been throbbing for centuries beneath the surface of the great caravan-cities. Twenty feet beneath the floor of the Attari mosque I saw the stones of a Zoroastrian fire-temple; and fire, I was told, is still carried like an ancestral memory at the head of some Moslem wedding processions here. With a twinge of suspicion now, I remembered meeting years ago in Jerusalem the last of a sect of Bukhariot Sufis, who contemplated God by staring into flames.

Water too: the holiness of springs proved ineradicable. The pagan veneration of a deep well under the city walls was long ago sanctified by an enfolding mosque. It became the Spring of Job (a prophet adopted by the Moslems) who was said to have struck water from the ground to succour the parched inhabitants. The Russians turned the shrine into a museum, and I found it lined with vitrines illustrating the triumphs of Soviet irrigation. But nobody was looking at them. Instead, a party of peasant women was heaving up ice-cold water from the well among the showcases, splashing it over their wrists and heads with little mewling cries, and carrying it away in phials.

It was the failure of water, as well as conservative ferocity, which hurried on the isolation of Bukhara. The Zerafshan river, flowing five hundred miles out of the Pamirs, expends its last breath on the oasis, and is withering away. To north and west the sands have buried a multitude of towns and villages which the exhausted irrigation could not save.

Even in the nineteenth century, the accounts of travellers were filled with ambiguity. To Moslems Bukhara was 'the Noble, the Sublime'. It was wrapped round by eight miles of walls and fortified gates, and its mosques and medresehs were beyond counting. The Bukhariots, it was said, were the most polished and civilised inhabitants of Central Asia, and their manners and dress became a yardstick of oriental fashion. The men minced on high heels – a pompous, trotting gait was much admired – and turbans clouded their heads in as many as forty folds of dazzling muslin. Some dignitaries drove in carriages; others, sporting thigh-length boots with dandily pointed toes, rode thoroughbreds harnessed in turquoise and gold. Beneath their horsehair veils the women walked in the most caressing silks in Asia; they joined their eyebrows in a double arc of black antimony, and anointed their fingernails with balsam. Even in decline, the bazaars were rumoured magnificent, and teemed with Hindus, Persians, Jews and Tartars.

Yet this splendour barely concealed an inner wretchedness. Men who walked abroad like kings returned at night to hovels. The city gates and walls were a gimcrack theatre-set, and the famed medresehs in decay. The emir's spies terrorised the whole populace, and cannabis was so endemic that it reduced half the government to apathy. From time to time a plague of cholera swept through a populace already riddled with dysentery and typhoid. Those who bathed or drank at the public pools contracted the repulsive guinea-worm, which could be eased out of their flesh only by a skilled barber lancing their skin and coiling the worm – sometimes four feet of it – on to a stick.

As for women, only beggars took to the streets barefaced (in the hope of being chosen for a harem) and even amongst the veiled it was *bon ton* to affect decrepitude. No man was seen with a woman. Their incarceration turned men to pederasty, and at night homosexual gangs haunted the streets. Ordinary people seemed inured to cruelty and subterfuge. Scarcely a Westerner dared enter before the 1870s.

Yet religious obscurantism was tainted with hypocrisy. Steeped as they were in their city's blazoned holiness, the people observed the code of religious law but abused its intent. Lax Moslems were beaten into the mosques by officials armed with a leather strap, and the moment the Russians abolished this practice attendance plummeted. Within a few years of Russian domination, the ferocious hostility to unbelievers had stilled to a mysterious tolerance, almost to lethargy. Travellers wrote that there was no more peaceful populace in the East, and occasionally, as I wondered about the future, I would find myself thinking of this strange flexibility with a faint unease.

Yet nineteenth-century Bukhara seemed remote now. Searching for the bazaars which were the pride of Central Asia, I found them almost gone. Only the market crossroads – lanterned cupolas rising from a nest of semi-domes – marked the lost arcades where the trade of China, India, Afghanistan and Russia had mingled across twenty-four covered acres. Now, in place of the early exotica – the camels' hair and silks, the porcelain and Tartar gold, the suits of chain mail, matchlocks and Khorasan swords (and stray American revolvers) – I saw little but a meretricious clutter of sequin-splashed frocks and slippers. A hesitant free enterprise was surfacing, but the inflation raging through the old Soviet empire had turned everyone poor. Sad traders peered from their kiosks like glove-puppets, or threaded the bazaars with a predatory vigilance. But they had almost nothing to sell. Once the name 'Bukhara' had been synonymous with lustrous dyed silks and the crimson rugs of the Turcomans who traded here; and carpets of Persian design were woven on domestic looms all over the city. But under Stalin, home industries became criminal. Mass production laid a dead hand on all the old crafts. I trudged through the market quarter until dark, but found no trace of handmade silk or rug.

Dusk emptied the lanes. A few street-lamps stood in stagnant pools of light, and a call to prayer wavered on the sunset. Behind padlocked doors, the tulip-shaped columns of a ruined mosque were tottering into the dust. Once or twice, where a view opened, I saw how many domes were crowned not by the Islamic crescent but by a single spike. Around these the migrant storks – a bird of happy omen – used to heap up compacted nests, like urns, until they stood sentinel on half the domes of the city. So long as the storks returned, people said, Bukhara would flourish; but twenty years ago they started to thin away, and were now gone. Some said that the rivers and marshes of the oasis were drying up, forcing the frog-guzzling storks to hunt elsewhere. Others blamed suburban factory-smoke. Yet others I asked, after staring up ruefully at the tenantless spikes, admitted they did not know, but feared only that the storks, by the inscrutable will of God, had flown away with their future.

*

Zelim was an artist who lived with his mother and wife in the alleys south of the Lyab-i-Khauz. A friend had given me his address with a warning that he was silent, and I came upon his house only by chance. Above its doorway a tin plaque read: 'Here lives a veteran of the Great Patriotic War'. But I had no idea who this veteran was, and my knock was answered by a forty-year-old woman with hennaed hair and green eyes. She was Zelim's wife, Gelia, who ushered me down a passageway and into a courtyard which seemed almost empty. Its rooms resonated like cisterns. She was unsure where her husband was, Gelia said. So we sat waiting in a high living-room spread with carpets and lined with classic Russian novels. Faintly embarrassed, she pushed dishes of nuts and sweets towards me. She had a liquid, tender face which might have been European, and she spoke a soft English. But she said her parents were Tartar who had come from the famine-stricken north to Tashkent in 1949, because it was rumoured a 'city of bread'. Her laughter tinkled in the bleakness. She had only been an infant then. Long afterwards she had married Zelim here and given him two sons:

65

gaunt, loose-limbed youths now, who stalked about the compound in silence.

But another, weightier presence brooded in the passages. Massive and watchful, Zelim's mother settled opposite us, cracking sunflower seeds. Her eyes were sorrowful crescents. She sat with her knees splayed in woolly stockings, and listened. The pale oval of her face – smudged with a chance nose and hung with flaccid cheeks – lent her the moon-like gravity of a Chinese.

She was, in fact, one quarter Chinese. In the last century her grandmother had been abducted from Kashgar at the age of six, and sold in the slave-market of Bukhara. Then her grandfather, a rich merchant, had fallen in love with his purchase, and married her. The old woman's eyes watered with remembering. 'She was very small and delicate, with little shoes and tiny hands.' She fumbled a photograph album from a shelf and opened it on a woman wreathed in Bukhara silks. 'There!' I saw a thin-lipped, brooding face, oddly attractive. She had died in her forties. 'They were rich people,' the old woman said. 'My father too. We had a dacha and a garden then, where the statue of Lenin stands now.'

Her father had owned two wives and many children, and her memories were all of happiness, living together in the same house. 'We had servants, many, and when guests came Papa would kill a sheep for them.' Then she spat out bitterly: 'And now we're rationed to a hundred grams of meat a month! And it costs a hundred and ten roubles!' She was starting to shake. She gazed at her father's photograph, high on the wall in the room's centre. 'Papa built this house. It is a memorial to him.'

Swarthy and turbaned, he stared down with a sombre authority. He seemed to inhabit a world long before the age of cameras, but she called him 'Papa' as if he were in the next-door room.

He had fought as a Bolshevik revolutionary, said Gelia – in English, which the old woman could not understand – but he had been too rich to escape the Stalinist purges, and had died in a Siberian camp in 1937. His daughter had fallen in love with a Chechen Moslem from the Caucasus, and they had married; but within a year he too had been banished to Siberia and she had divorced him. She watched us now, uncomprehending, and breathed in long, heaving sighs. A mixture of Tajik and Chinese, she had yet grown one of those awesome Slavic bodies which look born to suffer. 'She left her husband because she remembered her father,' Gelia said, 'and she could not bear to go through all that again.' She had been married just one year, and had born a child, Zelim.

He entered the room like a ghost. He was tall and faintly stooped, although only forty-three. His chest appeared to have collapsed inward, and under his whitening hair the gentle, creaseless face looked out of reach. His speech was blurred and murmuring, and sometimes faded away. I had the deepening impression that the whole house belonged to its dead. Their memory haunted it: that wronged father and husband. By contrast, the living had shrivelled inside its walls.

Yet the old woman remained stoically, violently Communist. Her father and husband might lie in anonymous graves in Stalin's labour camps, but her political faith was pitted deep in her mountainous and immobile body, and would not be shaken. 'She believed it wasn't Stalin's fault,' Gelia said. 'She thought it must be somebody else's. She thought he didn't know.'

Yet even now, when Stalin's role was clear, this schizophrenia continued, so brutalisingly complete had been the woman's indoctrination. She heard the name Stalin in the rustle of Gelia's English, and at once her fists thumped together. 'Stalin was strong! He imposed discipline!' She heaved herself upright in her chair. Her dress strained tight as a drum round her belly and thighs. 'Prices were controlled then. Everything was controlled! It's only after Gorbachev that we had these wars and this inflation .... The Russians need discipline. We can only work under discipline!'

Gelia was simmering with laughter. 'She's a Communist,' she said, as if it were a disease. 'She's famous for it.'

The old lady drew down a hand from her throat to her lap, as if performing open-heart surgery. 'I'm a Communist right through my blood,' she said proudly. 'That was my education.'

I was mutely astonished. I became uneasily conscious of her murdered father watching the room from his enshrined photograph; while her husband had left himself behind in Zelim – 'He's the image of his father!' Yet she sat stubborn as a rock in the chaos of her values. She revelled in memories of her privileged childhood – the servants, the property – but still gave lectures locally which glorified Communism. Each time she saw Zelim, she looked into the face of the husband she had abandoned.

As for Zelim, his eyes were overcast by bushy brows, and his face seemed not to see. But while Gelia and his mother talked, he told me in his faraway voice: 'My father was not political at all. Just a writer who wrote about the countryside. But it was enough to be a writer in those days, to condemn a person.' He looked at me with a kindly, impenetrable gaze. He was older now than his father had ever been. His hair receded from his forehead in two shining inlets. 'I've never read his work. He wrote in Chechen, and I can't read it. He died out there in Siberia ....'

Gelia was saying mischievously to his mother: 'You get it, you get it!'

Abruptly the old woman left the room and returned carrying a military jacket clanking with medals. It was her own. She had fought through the Second World War, and it was in her honour that the tin plaque surmounted their door. She held the jacket up. Perhaps she thought it spoke more trenchantly than words. Her fat fingers coddled the medals. 'This is the highest of all,' she said. 'Look. Gold and platinum. The Order of Lenin!' The discredited head clinked against her thumb. 'I was a radio-operator at the front, reporting the advance of tanks. I helped beat them all – Germans, Americans, British!'

To many Russians, the war was fought only by themselves against the world. Gelia said: 'The Americans and British were on our side.'

'... And I reported the flight of aeroplanes,' the old lady went on, 'and artillery ....'

For a moment the Soviet empire glittered awesomely again in that medal-hung jacket. 'She was a heroine,' said Gelia quietly.

'And all that struggle,' the old woman continued. 'For what? Why? People today, my heart bleeds for them .... Do you know what a television costs?'

Gelia said: 'It's true. Everything's changed here in six months. Our factories produce nothing. People just trade in odds and ends, or buy and sell from somewhere else.'

'It's God's curse on them for all their abortions!' said the old woman enigmatically.

Gelia said: 'But the prejudice is starting to frighten us. When I go to the market now, the vendors sell me the worst cuts of meat, or just stare through me. They think I'm Russian. That dislike never used to be there, not openly ....'

'Four hundred roubles!' the old woman said. 'That's all this television cost a year ago. Now it's eight thousand. And that fridge ... and the carpet ....' She knew all the prices, and everything had gone up ten- or twenty-fold. 'A train to Samarkand used to cost ....'

Gelia said: 'The Uzbeks used to learn Russian. Now they're pulling their children out of the Russian schools and sending them to Uzbek ones. It's they who have the power now!'

'Tomatoes ... thirty roubles ... now they're ....' The old lady's voice had soured to an angry whine. 'Cabbages used to ....'

But Bukhara was a complex city, Gelia said. Many of its people were not Tajik or Uzbek at all, but Russians, Tartars, Jews and a horde of others. The Russian school where she taught English was like a small cosmopolis. 'Even the Tajiks and Uzbeks are muddled up. In some families one brother's registered as an Uzbek and another as Tajik. It's hopeless. But perhaps it'll save us. Maybe people are too interbred to become nationalists.'

But the old woman's litany went on jangling beneath Gelia's

talk like an idiot wisdom. 'Soap …. Oranges ….' There was no telling what people might do if poverty became extreme.

'There's no future for us here,' Gelia said: 'We sent our sons to Russian school, so they speak no Uzbek or Tajik. And they look like Russians. Who will give them jobs now? Who will want to marry them?'

After a while the old woman brought in a platter heaped with mutton pilau, the universal dish of Central Asia, and we dined on this, and drank cabbage soup and sipped her cherry wine. Zelim had turned against his mother long ago, I'd heard, and for years they had not conversed. But now the old woman glowed as she spoke to him, her face quivering, and he would answer in his soft, distracted way, while she went on wobbling and flushing, and sometimes talked on his behalf, so deep were his silences. 'He loves his mother's pilau, especially his mother's …. He's spoken more today than he has for a long time …. He never eats enough, he's too thin ….'

'It's no good being thin,' Gelia said. 'The important people are all fat!' She was mysteriously buoyant in the world disintegrating round her. The household was sustained chiefly by her teaching. Zelim rarely sold a picture now. Only a reticent sadness underlay her jokes sometimes, like a dark instrument in a light orchestra.

Before we parted she said: 'I don't know if Islamic fundamentalism will come here. They've opened small religious schools in every district of the city. They're all learning Arabic.'

I said: 'I thought Stalin wiped out the Arabic-speaking generation.'

'Not quite. People went on learning and reading in the home, while pretending not to know it … and now it's coming out into the open.'

We crossed the courtyard in the dark, under a quarter moon, past its ranges of empty rooms, and said goodbye in the lamp-lit street. Gelia looked at me with a sudden, pained brightness. 'This may be the last time you see our faces,' she said, and raised a screening hand beneath her eyes. 'When you return, we'll be wearing the veil!' She was touched by laughter again; but above her hand the eyes were not happy.

*

On the city's western fringes, the last of its battlements falter and die over derelict parklands. Their eroded towers rootle back into the earth, and their crenellations look as if they would fall at a touch. But just inside them, hidden among trees, stands the tenth-century Tomb of the Samanids. Disconnected in time and style from anything around it, it stands in isolation, without ancestry or heir, as if it had been set down all of a piece from somewhere else.

Its form is modest: a tall cube supporting a dome. Each façade is pierced by arched doorways, and each corner inset with a pillar, while a small, decorative gallery circles them above. But over all its surfaces – friezes, columns, lunettes – swarms a latticework of ornamental brick. No hint of colour touches it except the sandy monochrome of these slivers of baked clay. They are laid with a fertile cunning and variety. Their chiaroscuro of raised and depressed surfaces lends to the whole tomb the absorbent richness of a honeycomb, as if it had ripened in the sun. Brickwork has become an obsession, a brilliant game, so that the mausoleum blooms against its trees with a dry, jewelled intensity.

The tomb is all that survives of the precocious Samanid dynasty, the last Persians to rule in Central Asia, whose empire pushed south of the Caspian and deep into Afghanistan. The tomb escaped the Mongol sack because it lay buried under windblown sands, its builders half forgotten, and it perhaps finds its architectural origins in the palaces and fire-temples of pre-Islamic times. But its sophistication – the lavish, almost playful deployment of its brick – betrays an age more daring, more intellectual, than any which succeeded it.

For over a hundred years, until the end of the tenth century, a creative frenzy gripped the capital. Alongside the moral austerity of Islam, there bloomed an aesthetic Persian spirit which looked

71

back to the magnificence and philosophic liberalism of the Sassanian age, extinguished by the Arabs more than two centuries before. As the Silk Road spilt into and out of Bukhara – furs, amber and honey travelling east; silks, jewellery and jade going west – the Samanids sent horses and glass to China, and received spices and ceramics in exchange.

An era of peace brought men of letters and science crowding to the court, and the Persian language flowered again in a galaxy of native poets. It was an ebullient age. Iranian music, painting and wine flourished heretically alongside Koranic learning, and the great library of Bukhara, stacked with 45,000 manuscripts, became the haunt of doctors, mathematicians, astronomers and geographers.

The short era produced men of striking genius: the polymathic al-Biruni, who computed the earth's radius; the lyric poet Rudaki; and the great Ibn Sina, Avicenna, who wrote 242 scientific books of stupefying variety, and whose 'Canons of Medicine' became a vital textbook in the hospitals even of Christian Europe for five hundred years.

But of all this activity almost nothing in brick or stone survives. The wall which circled the oasis for 150 miles, shielding it from nomad and sandstorm, was allowed to fall to bits in this time of hallucinatory wealth, and Turkic invaders, arriving from the east in AD 999, captured a city already declining into squalor. Only the mausoleum survives among its trees; a lavish, unshining gem. Its centuries-long protection under the earth has left it pristine. Even from a distance the biscuity brickwork lends it a perforated lightness, as if it were clothed in some loose-knit garment.

Yet nobody knows who was buried here. In later centuries, nostalgic for past glory, people imagined that it belonged to Ismail Samani, founder of the dynasty, and its grave shows two holes, where supplicants would whisper their petitions to the emir and a hidden mullah give his answer. Even into the twentieth century, such buried leaders were believed to protect the emirate, so that pious men were bewildered when their vengeful spirits did not rise from their graves against Bolshevik forces in 1920, and massacre them. Now, after years of disinfection as an official monument, the tomb was covertly open to worshippers again. Sometimes a semi-circle of stately pilgrims could be seen praying in its chamber, and occasionally one would place his lips to the perforation in the grave, and whisper.

*

One morning I returned to the Ulug Beg medreseh. The surly guardian had gone, and a group of pale-robed students lingered round the entrance. Their dress lent them a fraternal anonymity, and beneath their snowy turbans the faces all seemed embalmed in the same epicene delicacy. I was assailed again by the feeling that they were the keepers of something cardinal and secret in the country's psyche, and that they knew its future.

But the instant I started talking with them this sameness broke up. A semicircle of disparate faces shifted round me. I arrived amongst them like a virus in a bloodstream. Some cells spun away, fearful of contamination, but a compensating swarm of antibodies nudged closer. They came from all over Central Asia and beyond. Only a tinge of reticence united them, a vague suspiciousness which ebbed away. They had rustic, cloistered expressions, without the acquisitive glitter of the youths who rode motorbikes in the nearby alleys and tried to sell things. There was a hot-faced Uzbek from Namangan, an urbane youth from Tashkent, a sharp-featured Azeri, a Kirghiz, a Turk, even an Afghan Tajik. For five years here they studied the Koran, the Traditions and Moslem law, they said, and they did not want to become mosque imams – 'the imams know nothing!' – but to pass on their learning in the medresehs. They were the future élite.

'How many Moslems live in England? How many in America?' they clamoured. 'How many mosques in London?'

I guessed a figure.

'There are many Moslems in Italy,' said the fervent youth from Namangan. 'Italy is very Moslem.'

'Italy's a Christian country,' I said.

'But I've read it ....' The youth looked at me, bewildered. 'It was written!'

I said: 'You can read anything.'

'But you Christians say Jesus was the son of God, and that Mary was the mother of God. How can that be so? God has no mother or son. God is one.' He was bright with his own certainty again.

I became uneasy. The family tree of God has always amazed the Moslems. It amazed me, a little. I found myself launching a plea for tolerance. Why should one religion hold a monopoly on truth, I asked? Faith was a matter of private conscience .... The clichés left me in gusts of ungrammatical Russian. My evangelism for tolerance began to sound fanatic. In front of me the faces were mild, listening. Several of them murmured agreement; others relaxed into polite waiting. Tolerance, I think, appealed to some modesty in them.

'Yes, Christians, Jews, Hindus ... people should be free,' said the Kirghiz. 'But we believe that in the end everybody will become a Moslem.'

'With the will of God!' they chorused.

'Islam is the last revelation,' the Kirghiz went on. He had a flat, elliptical face, with the shallow-set eyes of a Mongol. 'First came the Jews' book, then the Christians' book, and finally the Koran. The Koran is the last word of God. It was right at the time for Jews and Christians to believe as they did. They had nothing else. But now it is our way which is right.' Yet he spoke this courteously. He was appealing to me.

I said pedantically: 'The Communist doctrine came later than Islam, but didn't disprove it. The last book isn't necessarily the right one. Your own Traditions come later than the Koran, but they don't supersede it.' This coup produced a hum of assent, and the Kirghiz nodded graciously, and I felt, for some reason, ashamed. 'The Jews believe that the first is the best,' I added gently, 'because it's the original.'

Simplified thoughts like these created a profound and uneasy hiatus in them. They were not used to them. They were used to written certainties. They lingered on the edge of such concepts, as if waiting for an imprimatur.

Suddenly the Azeri said: 'What about that other book? *The Satanic Verses?*'

I was taken aback. News of it had filtered even into the bowels of Asia. I delayed. 'What do you think?'

'I don't know,' he answered. 'I haven't read it.' Prayer-beads slithered in his hands.

I looked at the others. But none had read it, and only the Azeri seemed to have thoughts on it, which he did not disclose.

I said: 'It's not fact. It is a novel. Our traditions of the novel are different.'

'Is he still alive?' asked the Azeri.

I tried to read his expression, but could not. 'Yes. Some Moslems wanted him killed, but that is against our justice.'

Nobody demurred, and the moment passed. The youth from Tashkent said: 'We don't like the Iranian model. They are far from Islam, far.' He joined his fingers, then parted them. The simple gesture created an abyss. 'They don't understand the texts.'

'What texts?'

He lifted a teacherly finger. 'Islamic law, for instance, does not prescribe the veil absolutely. If a woman wishes to be veiled, she may. But with us, three parts can be open: the arches of the feet, the palms of the hands, and the face. Yes, the face.' He circled his fingertips close around his cheeks and forehead. 'The hair must be covered, but the face may be open.'

'But best of all is the woman who remains at home,' said the Namangan youth ominously. 'It's written that a woman only has to leave the house twice: once for marriage and once for burial.'

I said: 'What do women think of this?'

They went momentarily silent. The Azeri smiled. But the Tashkent man said: 'The women here are far from Islam. They don't understand, they don't know anything.'

'The veil would have to be forced on them,' said another

youth, 'so it is not possible!'

The Azeri sensed my misgiving. He said: 'When our people see a foreign woman with bare legs or arms, they get inflamed and can't study for hours. But I know that among you it's common, and that you don't notice it or feel anything.'

The others made noises of understanding. They looked a little unhappy. They spoke of the West with mixed repudiation and awe. The West meant licence, profligacy. There was a haunting Westerner in every one of them.

'The people here in Bukhara know nothing of religion,' the Namangan student went on. 'They've been Sovietised. It's a godless place. In the villages they know a little, but here, nothing.'

'Not in our villages,' said a dark Turcoman. 'There's no religion there.'

I looked at them in surprise. Unconsciously I had imagined them the heart of Bukhara, as if they were its unifying essence; but all the time they considered themselves strangers here, just as I was. In this conservative backwater – Bukhara 'the Pillar of Islam' – they felt they walked in spiritual exile, through a sea of unbelief. It was strange.

Soon they said goodbye with the stately Moslem placing of the right hand on the heart, and filtered back into their medreseh. If nobody stirred them, I thought, their natural Islam would be a restrained and dignified one, despite their tyranny to women. Most dangerous was their ignorance – they knew almost nothing of any world outside theirs – and the spectre of economic collapse, which could drive people to extremes. I watched them disappear with mixed respect and misgiving. Compared to the commercial fecklessness of youths in the streets, their questing intensity was archaic, attractive and dangerously innocent.

I ambled away, directionless. The close lanes and squares gave the feel of a city only half unlocked to the light. I found myself brooding over the students, consoled by their slow, Turkic conservatism. The fires of fundamentalism still felt far off.

But as I walked, I lapsed into private apprehension. What

76

would become of the promenading girls whose skirts ascended godlessly to just below the knee, I wondered, and whose legs showed patterned stockings and high heels? I dropped an imaginary veil over every woman I saw, and pictured the world through a gauze of black horsehair. As for the young men wheedling to change money, I turned the passion for dollars into the passion for God, until I had replaced their opportunist faces with others more moral, and more threatening.

In this disquieting daze, I tramped full-circle and arrived opposite the Mir-i-Arab medreseh. On one side spread the huge Kalan mosque, where Genghiz Khan had hurled down the Koran and initiated the slaughter of the city. On the other, the drums of the medreseh shone in complex knottings of Kufic script, and bloomed into sky-coloured domes.

A few students were chatting under the gateway, and I recognised the evangelising Kirghiz youth of an hour before. He approached me shyly. Shorn of his companions, he looked gentler, more awkward, and seemed to wear a faint, perpetual look of surprise. For a minute we talked pleasantries, then he said: 'Don't speak to anyone. Just follow me.'

With the traveller's delight in the forbidden, I followed him unchallenged through the medreseh gate and into the courtyard. It was brimming with life. Its arches were hung with notices in Arabic and Uzbek, invoking sobriety, friendship, integrity. Under the tiled porticoes the students conversed in murmuring conclaves, or sat alone with their Korans propped on chairs, repeating the same *sura* over and over. Above the double tier of their cells, two turquoise domes shed down an astral beauty. The past shone all about them, and seemed to convey a truth. It was the prince of medresehs. For years after the Second World War it had been the only one permitted open in Central Asia, with a mere seventy-five students. Now it housed over 400, and the nasal chant of remembrance filled its walls.

I padded after the Kirghiz, but nobody seemed to notice us. He pushed open a low door into one of the cells. It was tiny: a hermit's den. An unbroken succession of students had studied here for more than 500 years. The air was rife with dogma. Nothing substantial had changed, except that two iron beds had ousted the quilts on the floor, and an iron stove flooded the room with heat. The Kirghiz grinned at me. 'Nobody will see you here.' We sat at the rough table while he dropped a filament into a pot to brew tea, and broke fresh bread. Around us the walls were pierced by banks of niches scattered with belongings: an Arabic calendar, a jar of eau de Cologne, a clock, a box of Indonesian tea, jumbles of bottles, books and pens.

He poured tea into a chipped cup. He came from near Bishkek, he said, the capital of Kirghizstan, the obscure mountain nation on the borders of China. It was the last object of my journey. Yet he was not a Kirghiz by race, but a Dungan Chinese, one of a remote Moslem people who had fled west from China in the 1870s. Crossing the Tienshan mountains in mid-winter, they had left the snowfields covered with their dead. 'My grandparents still speak of what they heard from their grandparents, how people died in the avalanches and on the glaciers. And the Russians shot down thousands....'

He turned his mild face to mine without anger. It was too long ago to resent. And myths had been entwined with history. All disasters were traced back to the Russians, and I told him hesitantly that they had not massacred the Dungans (according to Western historians) and that the native Kirghiz had welcomed the survivors as they stumbled in tatters out of the mountains.

'That's what is good about this place,' said the youth, who was not listening. 'We have no nationalities here, no hatred. Nobody says "You're a Kirghiz" or "You're an Uzbek". They just say "You're a Moslem", and we feel at one.' He mounded the crusts of bread between us in token of community. 'It was the Soviet Union that created nationalism here. Before Stalin, the borders weren't there. It's only since then that people have said they belonged to countries.'

It was true, and I was to hear it again often: the nostalgia for a time before frontiers, for some imagined brotherhood. In these centuries of flux, when the borders of the Central Asian emirates

78

were only transient opinions, people conceived of themselves first by extended family or tribe. The whole region existed in a time-warp, where the tragedy of modern nationalism scarcely intruded. Now people looked back on that era as an age of stateless peace, made not for politicians but for merchants on golden roads. Yet it was this shallow-rooted patriotism that had laid these lands passively under the Soviet heel.

'Our identity is in Islam. Islam goes deeper,' said the youth. 'It's true that in Kirghizstan, where I come from, there's not much religious feeling. But people did pray in secret even in the Stalin years, closed the doors behind them and prayed in the dark, in families.'

I asked: 'Did you?'

'No, my family never did. I came to believe in another way.'

He fell silent, wondering whether to divulge his conversion. I could not guess it. I waited. Maybe some illicit mullah, I thought, had gathered the boy into his circle. Or perhaps an adolescent idealism had led him this way alone.

Then he said: 'It was like this. Near the village where I live was a graveyard, and one year two men were buried there. They were Moslems, but they were drinkers, which is against our faith. Now you know that our dead are buried with the face exposed....' He went silent again and glanced up at the latticed window, which filtered a wan light. Then he said in a cold burst of memory: 'When one man was laid in the grave, his eyes suddenly shot open. Yes, they were wide with fear! White and staring. Terrified.' His own eyes were fixed on mine, and had dilated too, filled with the marvel and terror of the thing. His words were a breathy rush. 'And when they lowered the other man into his grave – what do you think?' His fingers were clutching the edge of the table. 'It was filled with snakes!' He gaped at me. 'Our dead are buried two metres down at least, but even so there were these snakes, dozens of them, waiting for him in the grave. It was dreadful. Everybody spoke of it.' All the calm had left him. 'I know this because my uncle was the gravedigger there. From that time I began to pray and read our

79

scriptures, and I came to understand.'

I stared back into his callow mask of face – the sad arc of its eyes, echoed by the gossamer eyebrows above – and I had the fancy that the blinding moment of his revelation had imprinted itself permanently there, leaving behind a trace of petrified surprise.

'You're European, so I think you're Christian.' He was suddenly urgent, pleading. 'Now Mahomet's uncle, who acted as his guardian, was a Christian too [this was untrue] but he came to believe in Islam. He chose Islam over Christianity.' He caressed the word again: '*Islam*'.

'I know someone who was brought up with no religion,' I said. 'He studied several. And he chose Buddhism.'

This produced a pained silence. Then he said: 'But you *must* believe. When you return home, read our books, read more.' He was looking at me with a hurt, puzzled gaze, where the horror still lingered. 'You see, at the Last Day, at the end of the light, there'll be a parting of the peoples, and only the Moslems will be saved.' He illustrated this separation regretfully, but firmly, with morsels of bread across the table. 'Only the Moslems! As for the rest, the Hindus, the Communists, the Jews, the Christians ....' He swept the unbelieving crumbs on to the floor. 'Finished!'

His eyes were imploring me.

The next moment it was time for prayer, and we trooped back, a little crestfallen, to the gateway. He took my hand sadly in parting. His look of perplexity remained, as he said: 'I think you're a good man.' Some glimmer of another justice, I think, had touched him for a moment. Far inside, perhaps, he wondered why I, who had shared his bread and tea, deserved a fate so different from his own.

'You should study and believe.' His hand lifted to his heart. 'Then you must come back to us.'

4

Lost Identities

One building, and one era, overbear Bukhara like a disfiguring memory. For over a thousand years successive incarnations of a vast palace-fortress, the Ark, have loomed against the north-west walls. Shored up in secrecy, its final, monstrous embodiment is withdrawn out of human reach on a dishevelled glacis, which the binding timber-ends speckle like blackheads, and the ramparts which crown it are forty-foot scarps. Of the ruined buildings inside, only a few cupolas and an arcade can be glimpsed from below; but behind, it disintegrates into a rectangle of rotted bastions which blunder round its plateau in half-pulverised brick. It seems to have slipped down entire from a more savage era. Yet it kept much of its old use until 1920, when the last emir fled, and it is this incongruence in time – it is a museum now, but was a bloodied court within living memory – which perpetuates around it a peculiar disquiet.

As I approached its ramped gateway, this displacement intensified. Two tall towers squeezed the way to a needle's-eye. In the loggia above, ceremonial musicians had once set up a macabre thump of drums and bray of horns. A mechanical clock had hung here, contrived by an Italian prisoner who temporarily bought his life with it in 1851; but it had gone now. A covered passage climbed past the cramped chambers of sentries and janitors, then wound up to a series of sterile platforms into emptiness.

I wandered in dulled surprise. Within seventy years the whole elaborate palace-keep, peopled by 3000 courtiers and soldiers, concubines and catamites, had disintegrated to a jigsaw of blank courts. A few rooms housed depressing little museums where schoolchildren were gawping at photographs (leftovers of Soviet propaganda) recording the emirate's cruelty. But the rest were crumbling and uninhabitable.

I was walking over the debris of all Bukhara's later history. After the Mongol sack, the city had revived under the house of Tamerlane, and when the Uzbeks came south and seized it in 1506, they continued its splendour for another hundred years. But by the end of the eighteenth century Central Asia had resolved into three warring states – Bukhara, Khiva and Kokand – lapped by intransigent tribes of Kazakhs and Turcomans. By now the whole region was in decline, and the nineteenth century in Bukhara was spanned by two vicious and degenerate emirs, products of an isolation which had educated them in little but indulgence.

The atrocious Nasrullah signalled his accession by slaughtering his three brothers, and on his deathbed in 1860 ordered one of his wives stabbed to death before his eyes. His son Mozaffir began his quarter-century of despotism by butchering the heir-designate. At first the poorer classes trusted Mozaffir, dubbing him the 'killer of elephants and protector of mice', for to his ministers and courtiers he was quixotically cruel. But towards the end of his reign one of the few Westerners to reach Bukhara alive described him as a sallow lecher with shifty eyes and trembling hands, whose subjects credited him with the Evil Eye.

I approached his audience-chamber through a ruined gate where a stone lion roared harmlessly, and entered an empty field of paving. The plinths of a lost arcade made orphaned rows of stone. At the end, on a long dais, the canopy of the vanished throne rose on wonky pillars, and touched the dereliction with a trashy pomp. There was nothing else. Even the wealth on which this pantomime rested – the emir's secret gold-mine – was unknown for years after the emirate's fall. Before their retirement, miners routinely had their eyes and tongues gouged out, and travellers were executed on the smallest suspicion that they knew where it was. Only in the 1960s did the Russians locate it and hurry it back into production.

It was the emir Nasrullah who sent a cold tremor through Victorian Britain by executing two army officers on diplomatic mission. Colonel Stoddart was an intemperate campaigner who arrived at Bukhara in the hope of steeling the emir against the advance of czarist Russia. But to this court of touchy etiquette and childish vanities he brought no suitable gifts, and his letter of introduction was signed not by Queen Victoria but merely by the Governor-General of India. Nasrullah played with him like a cat. He either cosseted him under house arrest or entombed him in the *Sia Chat*, the deepest well of his prison. After more than three years Captain Conolly, a romantic and lovelorn officer in the Bengal Light Cavalry, reached Central Asia in an attempt to unite the khanates against Russia, and to retrieve Stoddart. It was he who first coined the phrase 'The Great Game' to describe the shadow-play of British and czarist agents across Central Asia as the Russian frontiers pushed closer to India. He too was thrown into the well.

The prison stands on a dusty spur behind the citadel. I found its cells crowded with dummies chained by their necks to the mud walls. Beyond them a rectangular hole opened in the paving. In the domed pit scooped out below, from which escape was impossible, Stoddart and Conolly had wasted away among excrement and human bones.

I peered down on two decomposing dummies and a glitter of coins thrown in by visitors for luck. A daemonic inspiration had once stocked the well with a mass of vermin, reptiles and giant sheep-ticks which burrowed into the men's flesh. Within a few weeks their bodies were being gnawed away. I descended by a rope ladder, and alighted in dust twenty feet below. The walls were lined with impenetrable brick and every whisper reverberated. Beside me the rag and plaster effigies had rotted to sick apes, their arms extended in supplication, their legs dropped off. I could not tell who, if anyone, they were meant to be. But I looked up at the terrible, hopeless hole in the apex of the dome, and thought about my last compatriots to have lain here. The walls closed overhead in horror. On 24 June 1842 Stoddart and Conolly were marched out into the public square under the citadel, and made to dig their own graves. Then they embraced, professed their Christianity, and were beheaded by an executioner's knife.

Two years later an eccentric and unwitting player of the Great Game appeared in the diminutive shape of the Reverend Joseph Wolff, the Anglicised son of a Bavarian rabbi. Dressed in black gown, shovel hat and scarlet doctoral hood, and ostentatiously cradling a Bible, he rode into Bukhara to discover the whereabouts of the vanished men. He described the city as if it were a heathen Oxford, but by now its trumpeted 360 mosques and 140 medresehs were mostly in ruins, if they had ever existed. Instead of beheading Wolff, the emir became convulsed by laughter. For weeks the clergyman remained a virtual prisoner in the home of the Chief of Artillery (whom the emir years later hacked in two with an axe). From a nearby garden he could hear a Hindu orchestra from Lahore playing 'God Save the Queen' in his honour; and he was continually called upon to answer the emir's queries – about the lack of camels in England, or why Queen Victoria could not execute any Briton she wished. Finally, in bemusement, Nasrullah let him go.

But the brutality and self-indulgence of the emirs alienated them fatally from their people. Imperilled by Russia, they could lead no holy war, and breed no patriotism. Their armies in the field were an absurd rabble. Dressed in random uniforms and harlequin colours, they shouldered a phantasmagoria of matchlock rifles, sticks, pikes and maces. On the march they perched astride donkeys and horses, sometimes two or three to a mount, while a few pieces of camel-drawn artillery brought up the rear.

The czarist armies brushed them aside. In 1868 Russia bit off half the emirate, occupying Samarkand, and reduced Bukhara to a client state. In all their Central Asian wars, between 1847–73, the Russians claimed to have lost only 400 dead, while the

Moslem casualties mounted to tens of thousands.

The ensuing years brought the ambiguous peace of sub-servience. The czarist Russians, like the Bolsheviks after them, were contemptuous of the world which they had conquered. They stilled the Turcoman raids and abolished slavery, at least in name, but they entertained few visions of betterment for their subjects. As for the Moslems, who could stoically endure their own despots, the tyranny of the Great White Czar insulted them by its alien unbelief. 'Better your own land's weeds,' they murmured, 'than other men's wheat.'

Yet there would come a time when they would look back on the czarist indifference as a golden age.

*

The poorest foreigner in Central Asia became a millionaire overnight. The rouble had collapsed. A single dollar might equal two days' industrial wage or a week's pension. The most lavish meal (if it could be found) would not cost a pound sterling, and train journeys carried me hundreds of miles for a few pence. But bankcards and traveller's cheques had fallen useless. Only cash prevailed. Foreigners carrying a few dollar notes were walking treasuries, and people were starting to realise this.

'Things here are different from what you think,' a Russian official confided. 'It's dangerous for foreigners now.' Even the Uzbeks distrusted themselves. Single tourists, they said – those freakish, lonely aliens with their inexplicable innocence and riches – were natural prey.

My solitary status baffled them. Where was my group? But a private invitation from an Uzbek friend had liberated me from the surviving constrictions of Soviet bureaucracy; my visa was stamped with a medley of destinations, and nobody took responsibility for how, or by what route, I reached them. Yet my few hundred dollars exposed me. I was carrying almost the life-time earnings of a factory workman.

I did not know what to do with them. Half of them I had sealed into a bottle of bilious-looking medicine; the other half I

hid in the tinny air-conditioner of my hotel bedroom – an ingenuity which rather pleased me.

But one night I returned late. Nothing definable in my room
had altered, yet I had an uneasy sense of intrusion and
unhitched the frame of the air conditioner. The money was
gone.

It was a creepy shock. Everything else lay undisturbed,
immaculate, just as I had left it. I was reminded of how the KGB
had searched my room in the Ukraine twelve years before:
everything returned impeccably to its place (or nearly), with no
sign of a break-in. This time the motive was not political, but
coarser and less intimidating, and the residue of my money was
untouched in its bottle of malignant medicine.

The hotel summoned plain-clothes police. While two heavy-
weights dismantled the air-conditioner, questioned me and apologised, a third slight, dark man watched them cynically, smiling
a little, and fingered his tie. For a while they attempted to make
out that I was mistaken, then recanted. The size of the sum
seemed to stupefy them. I knew I would not see the money
again. They went uselessly away.

I felt a paradoxical shame, as if I were the criminal. I remembered what Russian friends had told me about the KGB camera
surveillance in tourist hotels, and how blatantly I had counted
out the dollars on my bed the evening before. Yet for a few days
my suspicions fell on half the faces in the hotel, and whenever I
returned to my room I would dismantle the ventilation in case
the money had magically returned.

Then I thrust it out of my mind.

*

One evening I returned to Gelia and Zelim in the hope of seeing
his paintings. As I arrived, I noticed his mother, huge and somnolent, hunched on a bench at the street corner, watching the
world she now hated. The door was opened by Gelia. 'So you
came back!'

We sat in the gaunt room again, waiting for Zelim's return.

She had been teaching at the Russian school all day, and looked pale. 'So many Russians are getting out,' she said. 'There's talk of our school being amalgamated with others.' She began switching on lights around the room. 'Even my friends talk of leaving now.'

'Would you leave?' I asked.

But she answered simply: 'Where to?'

She was a Tartar and Zelim was half Chechen. They had no real homeland. She understood the confused or muted sense of nation which so many of her pupils felt. This week their religious festivals had followed close on one another, and she had set them projects for the rediscovery of their past: the past which had been denied them. Tartars, Uzbeks, Russians, Jews, Tajiks – they had brought back their ritual foods to school: the Moslem pilau from Bairam, the saltless Jewish Passover bread, the Orthodox Easter eggs. The blamelessness of what was once forbidden had touched her.

'But people are bewildered now. A boy came to me yesterday and said, "My father is Ukrainian, my mother Tartar, so what am I? I suppose I'm just Russian." And I couldn't answer him.' She smiled sadly. 'As for these Moslems, they don't feel any identity really. They may call themselves Uzbeks or Tajiks, but it doesn't mean much to them. They were Soviet before, and that was that. We all had this idea that we were one people, that we would melt into one another .... And now we're left with nothing.'

'Or with Islam.'

'Maybe.' She looked doubtful. 'But I think they feel lost, most of them ....'

This lack of nationalism among Uzbek and Tajik had drawn them closer over many decades. A century ago the conquering Uzbeks and the long-settled Tajiks despised one another. The Uzbeks had been nomadic warriors. Many had disdained trade, which they left in the hands of Tajiks and Jews, while farming was done by an army of Persian slaves. An Uzbek (I had read) would introduce himself by race and clan, the Tajik merely named himself by city. But now even this diffused Uzbek sense of race seemed to have dimmed. 'They belong to big families,' Gelia said vaguely. 'Perhaps that is enough for them ....'

Yet in 1924 Stalin, carving out the Central Asian states which had never before existed, often followed ethnic realities with scrupulous accuracy. He was attempting to divide and rule, nagged by the Soviet fear of a united Moslem 'Turkestan'. But sometimes people were so interknit as to defy delineation, and the Uzbeks and Tajiks of Bukhara and Samarkand were the most entangled of all.

Gelia said darkly: 'Perhaps you're right, and they can find themselves only in Islam.' She picked up her spectacles and squinted comically. 'I don't want to think that. I was always frightened of religion. When I was small I once stayed with a Christian schoolfriend, and spent all night in terror that her mother might come in and make the sign of the Cross over me! I've never been to a church.' She smiled at my surprise. 'But I've changed in the last year, I don't know why. Perhaps I'm getting old – my teeth, my eyes are not good any more. Now I think about religion a bit, I never used to.' Suddenly her girlish gaiety was brushed by melancholy. Youth and middle-age seemed to coexist in her. 'I sometimes wonder now if it is not a sin to live without God.'

I heard myself say: 'I don't know about God.' Everyone seemed to be hunting for Him now: God as a means of identity, of throwing back a bridge to the past over the Soviet chasm.

Gelia said: 'Nor do I.'

Her mother-in-law padded in and sat by us, watchful and uncomprehending. Her gaze seemed slowly to inundate the room, until it drowned us. Gelia said, as if excusing her: 'She has nothing to do now. She just reads memoirs by Soviet marshals.' The old woman went on staring. The weak electricity shed a dimness round us. 'Her world has gone away and won't return, and she knows this. But she's loved Zelim all her life, and now my sons, and perhaps she loves me because I love him.'

I said weakly: 'I hope so.'

Her voice roughened in exasperation. 'But she spies on me. She rummages through everything. She wants to know everything. She wants to know what we're saying now.' A mischievous triumph entered her tone, then faded. She said: 'This house isn't mine, you see. It's hers. I'm like a guest here.'

Yet from time to time the sadness of her words was suffused in contralto laughter, and her Tartar cheekbones and auburn hair looked vivid and beautiful in the soft light. Laughter, I supposed, was the only bearable companion to these facts: that she was a guest in another's house, in another's country, probably for ever. And when Zelim returned, murmuring a greeting with his curtained politeness, I was reminded how nobody here truly cohabited, how the old woman occupied a vanished Soviet empire, while Zelim lived in some hinterland of his own.

We went out into the bare courtyard and down a stairway to his studio. I was reminded of a priest entering a chapel: the sanctuary of his mind. He seemed perpetually stooped, not physically but emotionally stooped. We came into a room where hundreds of canvases and sketches were stacked with their faces to the walls. I did not know what to expect as he turned them shyly towards me. They were nightmares: scenes of savage transmutation. Men had become animals, and animals half-men. Even in Bukhara street scenes, the familiar domes tilted vertiginously above lanes where a distorted donkey trotted or a man-vulture flapped. The ordinary had turned threatening, and daylight proportions vanished. A man's turbaned head slept on a mosque cupola, as on a pillow. Flocks of high-coloured sheep grazed nowhere; horses' heads were shriven to skulls.

Gelia said quaintly: 'There's no smile in them.'

Zelim said nothing. They had become his words. Often he had painted lonely sites where a few trees bent over ruins or swaying grass. 'He loves places like that,' Gelia said. 'They frighten me.'

But in a rare oil portrait she had been stripped to a pink doll whose face was annihilated, staring ruthlessly away. Other paintings were abstracts. 'He himself is an abstract,' she said, as if he were not there. 'He does not know what other people do. That's why he is happy.' She looked at him. 'He flies in his dreams.'

Zelim saw my interest. Slowly he turned more and more paintings to the light, but as his racked, vibrant world unfolded, and I asked to buy one, he demurred again and again. One painting, perhaps, was important to his past, to some personal novitiate; while the next belonged to his future and was a blueprint.

I admired a Matisse-like *Madonna and Child* in pink and grey, and wanted it; but this was part of a cycle. 'It has simplicity,' he said. 'I'm aiming for that all the time now. Simplicity.'

'You come and steal it,' said Gelia. 'Perhaps then he'll love something else – maybe me!' She laughed, the lilting, sad sound which came too easily. Zelim turned *Madonna and Child* to the wall.

In the end I found a watercolour of primordial horses which he was willing to relinquish. But he worried over how it would be framed, insisted it be hung in shadow and that it should be set in a grey border, tilted askew. Secretly I wondered if I would ever get it back to England intact. He furled it up gently for my rucksack, and I noticed for the first time his disproportionately powerful hands.

'Oh yes,' Gelia said, as we all emerged into the street. 'He used to carry me on his hands like this!' She held out her palms. 'But now he's too weak – or I'm too fat!'

He smiled distantly, as if she had nudged some remote happiness, and we ambled to the limit of the walled town. A rare shower had turned the lane's earth moist underfoot; it stretched empty under a belt of stars. Where the old town ended and the modern one began, they stopped. For the second time, we parted. I kissed Gelia farewell, and Zelim enclosed me in an embarrassed Russian hug, then I started back to my hotel across the overgrown parklands of the new city. Sunset had pulled a blanket of silence over everything. After a minute I looked back up the lamp-lit lane where Gelia and Zelim were walking home, and saw that he had taken her hand in his.

90

The town's war memorial stood where the old woman's family had once owned a dacha. The inscribed names of the dead – almost ten thousand of them – were faintly legible under the stars, their Islamic surnames tagged with Slavic -*ovs* and -*evs*. Weeds were pushing through the paving-slabs. Nearby I passed the plinth where Lenin had stood. It rose in a ghostly white platform, abandoned, as if he had stepped down from it in the starlight, and walked away.

*

The north-east fringes of the early Islamic empire were rife with alien cults and dangerous forms of worship. Sufism arose in Central Asia as early as the eighth century, and in time the whole region became riddled with mystical brotherhoods centred on the tombs of their founding saints. By the nineteenth century their theology belonged to the distant past, but the holy places were still crowded with devotees, chanting and swooning under matted hair and candle-snuffer hats, while hemp-crazed *kalender* went whirling and prostrating themselves through the streets.

With the advent of Communism the brotherhoods went underground. Official Islam was brutally persecuted and tens of thousands of the religious were executed. Stalin closed down 26,000 mosques, and by 1989, in all Uzbekistan, there were just eighty left. But under this thin carapace of institutionalised worship, whose leaders were forced into compromise with Moscow, there swarmed an undergrowth of unofficial mullahs and holy men. The most fervent centres of worship became not the regulated mosques but the shrines of venerated Sufis, objects of secret pilgrimage. This covert Islam bred paranoia in Moscow. Communists traced the malign influence of the Sufi networks everywhere, and the KGB failed to penetrate them.

Yet everybody I had asked described the brotherhoods as peaceful. Their adepts were engaged on an inner journey, a puritan recoil from the world decaying round them. Sufism became a haven for the spiritually oppressed. In the outer world its *murids* were craftsmen, traders, even soldiers and Party members, but in the hermetic secrecy of their circles they found repose in uncontaminated worship and chanting.

The most powerful of these orders was the Naqshbandi, whose founder had died in Bukhara in 1389. A century ago its warrior-dervishes had fought against the Russians in the Caucasus, and had re-emerged in 1917 to harass the Bolsheviks. The mausoleum of the saint had been closed down under Stalin, then turned into a Museum of Atheism. But widespread memory of it must have survived, I knew, because in 1987, during abortive demonstrations, it was to this forbidden tomb that the Bukhara protesters had marched, as if to the last symbol of purity in their city.

Far on the outskirts I glimpsed its sanctuary clustered round a flaking dome. Two mosques – one for men, one for women – embraced it in faded arcades, and a lopsided minaret tapered nearby. But all around it a fury of restoration had arisen: the drone and rattle of machines rebuilding. It had reopened three years before. Elaborate guest-rooms were going up, and a bazaar. The pilgrims were flooding in. There were several hundred there now, gossiping, feasting, praying. A glow of celebration enveloped them. Infinitely extended families picnicked under the willows, squatting on their divans and delving into hillocks of pilau, carrots and cucumber.

I wandered at ease. The place seemed virgin, unreal. No modern traveller that I knew had ever been there. I came upon a party of gypsies – a people even here despised and unaccounted for – who were crouching in a hollow, butchering one sacrificial sheep while gorging on another. Beyond them a colossal tree seemed to have crashed to the ground in prehistory, and petrified. Its crevices were stuffed with votive rags and messages, and its limbs polished raw by caressing hands. It had been planted as a seed at the time of the saint's birth, said the gypsies, and had fallen the day he died. Now, like him, it had acquired holiness. It induced fertility, and cured backache.

A melancholy trio of men was circling it anti-clockwise. One of them winkled off a splinter with his knife. The whole trunk was flecked with these incisions. After them came a flock of peasant girls, brilliant and chattering. They paced familiarly round the trunk, and stooped beneath it where the greyed body arched from the ground. As they went, they caressed its knobs and fissures like lovers. Then they tied silk ribbons to it, and walked blithely away. Behind them tripped a sad-faced woman in middle-age. She wore a tight skirt and high heels. She ran her fingers over the twisted torso, as if searching for something she had left there, then massaged her belly violently against it, with little cries.

I pushed through a door into the shrine's central court. It was very quiet. The mosque arcades enclosed it on two sides. Their portico ceilings were coffered with deep polygons and stars which were easing loose from one another now, punctured by sparrows' nests, and the blue and gold paint dimming. A line of pilgrims was approaching the grave along a carpeted path. Men and women went together, as if on holiday. The girls paraded in their festival dresses and pantaloons, their plaits scalloped up at the base of the neck under garish clasps, or cascading beneath embroidered caps. They threw coins into the dry fountain whose waters had been holy four centuries ago, and kissed its stones. Then each group settled on its haunches at the path's end, while an austere young man chanted a prayer. Above them a forked mast hung like a gibbet, its horsetail trophy gone. On a terrace beyond, the saint's followers and descendants lay under rough stone cubes. Two women were sweeping away the dust for a blessing. Beside them, a high, imperishable rectangle of grey stone was all that remained of the Sufi's grave.

The faithful went sauntering round it with a rapt, processional dignity. They touched its stones, then bathed their faces in their hands. They knocked their foreheads softly on its walls, and kissed them. They kissed the black slab said to come from Mecca (and sovereign against headaches) encased in one façade. A fusion of sacred and secular lent a mildness to their worship. Their pilgrimage seemed to progress with the ease of a promenade, in which blessing and companionship, the pleasure of picnics and the chance of childbirth, were harmonised in the sanctity of ordinary things – stone, wood, water.

The midday devotees came and went, and the courtyard emptied. The austere-looking man who had conducted prayers under the gibbet-banner turned out shyly accessible. Yes, he said, there were still Naqshbandi Sufis in the city, but he could not guess their number. 'Even they don't know how many.'

Everyone declared the sect's numbers few now. The Soviet fear seemed suddenly absurd. But the Sufis' purity of worship had held up a dangerous ideal, as if they were the people's heart. They had maintained their anonymity even here, in their own Vatican.

'Perhaps the shrine's imam is Naqshbandi,' I ventured.

The man looked momentarily embarrassed. 'Only he knows.'

'But they must have remembered this place all the time it was shut down.'

'Yes, yes. Everybody remembered it. For seventy years. We came here secretly at night and prayed against the walls.' His voice blurred with the wonder of that time, as if it were already long ago. 'Some of us even climbed over in the dark and embraced the tomb.'

'And you, you're a mullah here?'

'No, oh no.' He smiled. 'I'm an ordinary man. I was a carpenter before, but I taught myself the prayers in Uzbek and Arabic, and came to serve here.'

He made it sound simple, and perhaps it had been. But when I asked why he had chosen this, he answered, 'Only God knows.' God's knowledge everywhere overwhelmed his own. He scarcely knew the history of the saint he served, but lapsed into Communist jargon, describing him as a stakhanovite holy man who achieved through work, and planted melons.

Had the black stone embedded in the tomb, I asked, really been taken by the saint from the black stone of the Kaaba, the lodestar of Islam?

But he answered: 'Only the stone knows.'

As we sat under the worm-pocked columns of the faltering mosque, he unfolded a laden napkin and shared his pilau and bread with me. At once a mad labourer ran up, his eyes rolling and his trousers covered in blood. With a democracy old in Islam, he sat down at our meal, seizing rice and bread in crazed mouthfuls, so that the sparrows seethed down to peck up his flingings.

'People bring all their griefs here,' the young man said, as if explaining him. 'They bring them to forget them, to open themselves without secrets before God. Then God instructs them.' He fell again into the spine-chilling Communist argot. 'Without instructions, you can't do anything.'

The builder's eyes, which had rolled to the back of his head, returned suddenly and fixed us with two incendiary black pupils. All at once he stumbled upright and careered away, dragging a club foot. 'He's a little ill,' said the man. 'This place may cure him.'

'How?'

'You find it strange. Perhaps Christians don't have such beliefs.' Ruminatively he folded up the napkin and returned it to his basket. He went quiet. To him the magic tree was less inscrutable than people drinking the transfigured blood of a slain god or believing He had a son. But he said at last: 'We all have the same father and mother, and God knows all we think.'

A few pilgrims had trickled back into the courtyard. The man was embarrassed at being found with me, but only a little. They crouched round him with their palms upraised, not in the secretive closure of Christian prayer but in the ancient Eastern gesture of receiving, as if to catch raindrops. To some Moslems a journey here ranked second in sanctity only to the Mecca pilgrimage. All was tranquil and at ease in the sunlight. The Shia shrines of Iran and Iraq, bitter in their exclusiveness and grievance, seemed far away. Sufism itself, familiar all over Central Asia, is abhorrent to the radicals of Iran and Saudi Arabia. Its survival here was like a pledge of peace.

These thoughts lulled me, perhaps dangerously, in the worm-eaten arcades of the reawakening shrine, until I fell into an ecumenical sleep, tranquillised by the pad of barefoot worshippers, and the burble of rose-headed doves under the eaves.

*

My ramblings in the outskirts next morning led me through a multi-coloured gateway like the entrance to a funfair, and into the summer palace of the last emir. The building was completed in 1912: a bauble confected of East and West. Across its façades the pediments and pilasters were jungled in Turkic plasterwork, which wriggled fatly over every space. Arab arches sat in Chinese porticoes. Burmese domes swooped up from mongrel pavilions.

When I peered inside, I saw that every surface had been tortured into a surreal brilliance. Tiers of niches cascaded down whole walls, while others bloomed into muralled flowers which reared from their vases in spatular sprays. I dawdled down glittering aisles of mirrors and stained glass. Gilded ceilings spun overhead, and Dutch delft ovens loomed out of corners. Sometimes I felt I was sauntering through pure carnival, and sometimes through a playful, jaded refinement: the last niceties of Central Asia sinking under a ton of trivia.

The Hall of Ceremony and the Chamber of Ministers fell behind me in a concoction of delicate plasterwork and looking-glass *kitsch*. From the bedraggled parklands outside arose the crazed scream of a peacock. Here, under Russian tutelage, the last emir Mahomet Alim had governed the rump of his state in tinsel pomp. His lavishly framed photographs bestrode several tables. Even in dress he was the bastard of two worlds. Fabulously sashed and turbaned like his ancestors, he was weighed down with epaulettes and fatuous czarist honours: a stout little sensualist, whose tax-collectors had terrorised the country.

His palace betrays him. It is an intricate, proportionless toy. I wandered about it in shameless pleasure. Outlandish kiosks appeared to have dropped off its body: follies of dazing ingenuity and lavatorial tiles, where cuddly stone lions looked as if they might mew. In one of these pavilions I found the robes of the emir and his wives.

'But I think he had only one wife,' said the girl beside me. She was looking without envy at the cabinets of dresses. 'Or maybe two.' She herself had discarded traditional dress for a lumpy cardigan over an ankle-length skirt. 'Do people have more than one wife in your country? No? They don't with us either.'

I said: 'I've heard that some men keep ... well ....'

She burst into giggles. 'Yes, they call them *sisters*. But it's not allowed.' I looked into a sunny face. She said stoutly: 'I don't agree with it.'

'And the veil?'

Her face turned blank with astonishment. 'Do they still wear that anywhere? *Nowadays?*'

'Yes,' I said. We peered back into the cabinets.

'I hate it!' She turned her back on them. 'I don't feel a thing for that history. Nobody does. It was long ago. That last emir?' She pranced to the door. 'He was rich' – and this seemed to put him beyond her thought.

I went down through orchards to a stone-flagged pond, where an outsize belvedere hovered on gangling stilts. It was reached by stairs in a fanciful tin minaret, and overhung the green pool. From the loggia nearby, it is said, the emir would watch his harem splashing in the waters, and would toss an apple to the beauty of his choice. Or perhaps he wouldn't. He was, it appears, an inveterate voyeur – his palace is riddled with peep-holes and hidden stairs – and he seems to have preferred boys.

Yet he found a moment of power between the collapse of imperial Russia and the advance of Bolshevism. In 1918 he repulsed the Red invaders from his city in a welter of treachery and fanaticism which saw the murder of hundreds of Russian civilians. Two years later, before the advance of General Frunze, he abandoned Bukhara and his 400-strong harem to the Red Army, and eventually fled over the Amu Dariya into Afghanistan, shedding behind him a trail of choice dancing-boys.

He left no affection or regard behind him; but he was a Moslem who did not tamper with his people's customs, and there would come a time when his boorish indifference would be recollected as merciful. Compared to the Communist prose-lytism which followed, his rule was blessedly unprincipled. Mass ideological repression and forced collectivisation were beyond his horizon.

*

Somehwere along drolly named Central Street – a lane which cars could scarcely enter – I found the synagogue of an early Jewish community. It was sunk behind iron gates in the street's wall. Inside hung the old Soviet slogan 'Peace to the world', and the halls beyond were astir with evening prayer. In one I glimpsed the dwarf chair, draped in red silks, where boys were circumcised. In another some twenty men sat cross-legged under walls hung with dedications, and rested their prayer-books on low tables covered with dirty linoleum. Genially they beckoned me in. Under their skull-caps and berets, most were indistin-guishable from ordinary Bukhariots. But others looked sensitised, paler. In another place or time, I thought, they might have been scholars or poets.

Instead they gabbled their prayers with a sunny robustness. They were cobblers, tailors, street photographers. And their hall had seen better days. They sat exposed under striplights, and a skein of dangling wires and bulbs criss-crossed every wall. Instead of flames the seven-branched candlestick sprouted light-bulbs, mostly extinct, and four different clocks hung on the walls, all stopped, as if Time were out of true.

And so it was. Barely a century ago the Bukhariot Jews had dominated the city's banks and bazaars. They had owned the camel-caravans which wended into Afghanistan and over the Pamirs to China, and had controlled the precious silk market. Above all they knew the secret dyes which glowed in the Bukhara rugs. It was they who mixed an intense crimson from the crushed and roasted bodies of insects found on ash and mulberry trees, and squeezed a beautiful, enduring yellow from a species of larkspur. The hands of half the city's Jews were stained to the knuckles with dye.

Now they looked poor. They had tired faces and rough hands. They spoke no Hebrew (and for centuries never had). Foreign Jews had been horrified by the unfamiliarity of their customs. I sat amongst them while they mouthed their prayers out of little books sent from Israel (offering Cyrillic phonetics for the Hebrew words, but no translation). Four or five men eagerly picked up the chain of prayer from one another. A lean-faced youth breathed it at the ceiling in whispered bursts of memory, and a heavy patriarch intoned before the Ark. But while one recited, the rest gossiped, sipped tea and occasionally chatted down a discoloured telephone.

Seated beside me, a tiny, cadaverous cobbler sent up a cloud of furtive questions. 'What food do you have in England?... How much does a middle-ranking person earn?... Here's some tea ... come to my home for supper .... Have your sons been circumcised?...' He gestured at the wall above us. Behind its gold and scarlet silks, the scrolls of the Law nestled in their cupboards. 'How long have there been Jews in England? We've been here since Tamerlane ....'

'Longer! Longer!' a neighbour barged in. 'We came over two thousand years ago, after the Babylonians sacked Jerusalem!'

'More like three thousand years,' said another.

'Not correct,' insisted a pedant. 'I believe we came in 1835, from Persia and Afghanistan.'

'No, no. We came ....'

But nobody really knew. Two hundred years ago Moroccan missionaries had convinced the community that their origins were Sephardic, and they liked to trace their diaspora through Persia and even Tunis. Some scholars believe that Tamerlane brought them from Shiraz or Baghdad, or that they arrived from Merv early in the eighteenth century.

'It was Tamerlane,' maintained the cobbler as we debouched

into the street. 'He moved everyone about. We grew rich after that, I've heard, but now we're all poor. Look at my hands.' They were ringed with callouses. 'Those are a working man's. Most of us are barbers or watch-menders, or deal in clothes.'

He led me into an untraceable maze of alleys. In the dark his smallness made me feel I was following a child. But his talk was a long lamentation on his people's hardships. Half of them had already emigrated, he said: those who were richer or more daring. They had gone to the Americas or Canada or Israel. 'There are only seven hundred of us left now. Most of my relatives have gone.'

'What do their letters say?'

'It's hard out there in America. They thought it would be soft, but it's hard. The government gave them eight hundred dollars a month. *Eight hundred dollars!*' His voice sank into disillusion: 'But that's what a month's rent costs.' He rapped on a low door in a blank wall. 'But they've found work now, and they'll be all right.'

The door opened on a pretty, bird-like woman. I guessed she was his wife: he did not acknowledge her. He and his brother lived in clusters of rooms at opposite ends of a long courtyard. As we crossed it, a shoal of small sons and nephews circled us. The darkness swam with their blackcurrant eyes and wan faces. Inside, the rooms were indistinguishable from those of city Moslems. The walls and floors were clothed in cheap carpets, and photographs of ancestors perched above hangings just under the sitting-room ceiling. The quilts, the black-and-white television, the china cabinet, were all in place. Only on one wall hung a high-coloured print of Moses clasping his tablets, and some prayer-shawls had been sent by an uncle from Canada.

All their windows were barred, but hostility towards them was still muted, the cobbler thought. Far to the north-west in Khiva, anti-Semitism had become so fierce that the Jews had all fled, and it was growing ominous in the Fergana valley to the east. 'Nobody knows what will come.' *Perestroika* had licensed them to worship openly and to start their own schools, he said, but it had also released around them this dark racism, and perhaps it was for this that they assembled in the synagogue every morning and evening now, and searched their scriptures.

As the family settled to supper, drawn in a quiet rectangle round the half-lit room, they seemed already tinged with the bereavement of refugees. The boys were ragged and wary. The fine-boned wife looked preternaturally delicate. A speechless grandmother, whose husband had died fifty years before, huddled like a plinth among the children, while opposite lounged the cobbler's brother, a morose fanatic with bulbous cheeks. They dipped into the pilau with old teaspoons. The grandmother's homemade wine gurgled into tooth-mugs. Only the woman's spoon, after searching out shreds of chicken, never reached her lips but travelled into the mouths of her small sons.

'This is the reason we can't befriend the Uzbeks easily.' The cobbler dangled a scrap of chicken. 'We can't eat with them. Ours is *kosher*. Theirs ....' He dropped the morsel formally into his mouth. 'Our communities have never intermarried. With Russians, occasionally. But with Moslems, never.'

'With Russian Christians?'

'No, just Russians.' A tiny sigh seemed to stick in his throat. 'Life was better then, under the Communists. Now things are happening too quickly for us. Did you see they've taken the statue of Lenin away? I don't think they should have done that.'

I asked in faint surprise: 'Why not?'

He frowned. Everything was more tenuous now. Lenin had signalled a kind of continuity. 'In your country I think they do this: whether a king was good or bad, his monument still stays. It's part of history. You don't demolish history like that.'

But his brother charged in. 'Who wanted that statue?' He spoke in staccato shouts. 'Who wanted anything they did? Look what I got from them!' He flung up his shirt. 'That was in the Afghan war!' Across his hirsute stomach travelled livid, parallel scars. 'Shrapnel!'

Everyone fell silent. These repudiated scars were his dignity. Words were meaningless against them. But the cobbler murmured to me: 'Our local astrologist says that in forty-five years America will go down and Moscow will come up again. You think that's true? He says he knows the future, and that Communism will come back.'

'Not in its old shape.'

'It's rubbish!' shouted the brother. 'That's all finished! *Fooof!*' His nose and cheeks ballooned over his face, squeezing his eyes to hyphens. 'Gone for ever!'

Perhaps it was in reconciliation that they switched on the music they had played and recorded together. It emerged from a cracked cassette-player: sounds of unexpected tenderness. I listened for any strain of Hebrew melody, but could discern none. While the cobbler was playing an Uzbek *dutah*, his brother was singing Tajik folk-songs from Afghanistan. Whatever music their people had carried here centuries ago had been obliterated in the Central Asian vastness. In time, I had read, the Jews became court musicians to the emirs, but their repertory delved deep into an indigenous Moslem music. As the brothers' recorded noises mourned in the room's closeness, they strained to hear, as if it were all new.

> *My soul is a house in ashes,*
> *You are its destroyer*

The cobbler's fingers pattered on his knees, while his brother, seated in sudden melancholy, repeated the words of his recorded voice – lyrical, almost sweet – as it sounded back to him. It was as if only in the insulation of music, in this disconnected passion, could any gentleness come to him.

> *O nightingale of my heart*
> *Sing me that I was right to trust you . . . .*

The young women listened to this abstract love in unreadable stillness, while the small boys lapsed into sleep. I felt unease for them. Subjects of an empire now crumbled into nationalism, their vulnerability sent up unsettling echoes from their people's longer history. Even here, the Jews were set apart. Barely a century ago they had been obliged to wear girdles of common rope and to ride only on donkeys. There had even evolved a sect of crypto-Jews named *chalas*, 'half done', the fruit of forced or pragmatic conversion to Islam. Shunned by both Jews and Moslems, they became sickly through interbreeding and had almost dispersed, but their giveaway surnames were still despised.

Now the Tajik songs had faded from the tape-recorder, and the children were being bundled into their quilts. I got up to go, wishing I could offer something. But as I parted from the cobbler in the pitch-dark street, he only said: 'Don't tell anyone you were here. It's against the law.'

'Not any more.'

He smiled, a little ashamed. The fear still guttered in his eyes. 'No,' he answered. 'But still.'

*

On my last afternoon in Bukhara I drove out with Zelim to a melancholy necropolis which he had haunted as a young painter. His mother levered herself into the car too, ribboned in her war-medals, and pointed out along the road the improvements which Communism had brought. She looked pale, and sometimes trembled, but she gazed through the windscreen with a baleful pride. 'Thirty years ago you'd have seen a hundred horses and carts here for every one car,' she said. 'It was just a filthy track ....'

Zelim said in his faraway voice: 'I remember the horses as a boy. They didn't churn up the mud like cars do.' He loved horses. They crowded his canvases with heavy heads and dissolute manes. He painted them more affectionately than he did humans.

The old woman said: 'These suburbs used to be a disgrace.'

After a few miles we arrived at a graveyard tumbled round a shattered mosque. The building had been raised in the sixteenth century around a three-sided courtyard, but its central structure had collapsed, leaving two magisterial prayer-halls separated in the dusk. Under one arcade stood a blackboard and some benches, where Koranic lessons were starting up.

'Just ruins,' said the old woman, as she heaved out of the car. She hated the place at once.

But a mullah had emerged to greet us – a tall man with a pared, angry face – while a cripple stumbled complaining after him. The mullah remembered Zelim from years before and began to regale us with the history of the cemetery. He exuded a fierce, sweated energy. But behind him the cripple, his white head bound in a frayed turban, followed like a deflating shadow, undermining his talk with down-to-earth asides. As we tramped between mounds of dust and into half-restored enclosures crammed with engraved cenotaphs, the mullah reeled off the names and qualities of the dead in bursts of parrot learning.

'They don't want to hear all that,' the cripple said. 'You can leave that out.'

But the mullah barked on in a harsh monotone, as if he were addressing not us only, but the mosque, the dimmed sky and the surrounding dead. He trumpeted the genealogies of all its buried saints, who had lain here longer than the mosque itself, some of them, and hushed into sorrow at inscriptions worn away or defaced; while the cripple, playing Sancho Panza to his Don Quixote, grumbled and refuted and threw in belittling innuendoes. Often the mullah spoke too fast for my understanding. As for Zelim, he had gone deaf to words, and seemed only perfunctorily present. He was watching the textures and shapes of the cemetery in the painterly twilight, and after a while he drifted away.

The old lady, hobbling after us, grasped my arm suddenly, almost affectionately, in her unsteadiness. 'It's from the war,' she said. 'My spine was broken.' Her fingers hooked frailly over my forearm. She glanced at the carved headstones: their Arabic script had paled to wraiths. 'I don't know whose ancestors these are.' She grimaced and looked away. 'Some of mine', she added

104

vaguely, 'had blue eyes and fair hair. I think they were descendants of Alexander of Macedon's soldiers. Those men intermarried here.' She regarded these later graves with dulled contempt, and after a time she shuffled back towards the car.

I was left alone with the mullah and the cripple. Graves seemed to have dogged my way ever since entering Central Asia. Everywhere they were being restored, reconsecrated, refrequented. Sometimes they were less graves than tribal memories. They were the newly dignified past. The Soviets had tried to amputate history, but now every historical artefact – a tomb, a mosque, an inscription – was a milestone along the half-obliterated road back. The dead had become the conduit by which the living were reintegrating themselves.

The mullah's voice rasped and flared among the tombs. Yet whenever I intruded on this rush he listened with a frowning intensity, and fell quiet. He struggled to disentangle the Kufic script on headstones, but could not. Like many others, he said, he was trying to learn Arabic, but his Uzbek teachers could only read the language haltingly, and did not speak it at all. Around us the earth tossed and heaved beneath its memorials, tilting them left and right. Sometimes it gaped on empty crypts, then closed again where the cenotaphs above had been lugged into shaky order. The mullah pointed down at a warren of breached vaults. 'Those are the tombs of Naqshbandi sheikhs.' His voice lifted in wonder. 'See how big they are! People were taller in those days. Look. Three metres long! All of them. And look at the modern ones.' He gestured at some forlorn mounds. 'Two metres at most! People are small now. We are not like they used to be.'

'Food is rationed,' said the cripple. 'That's why. Even cooking-oil.'

I asked: 'There are still Naqshbandi Sufis here?'

'Yes, yes,' the mullah answered. 'There are many still living in the city. But their dress shows nothing. They are like invisible ones!' He struck his ribs and half chanted: 'What matters is in the heart! It is only the heart that matters!'

I said: 'Perhaps you are one.'

The cripple laughed cynically. But the mullah did not reply, only rushed on with a new genealogy of dead holy men. There had been a time, he said, long before the Prophet, when this place was a shrine of fire-worshippers, and a matriarchy. 'That is why some women still worship fire.'

'Women? You've seen them?'

'You see them often. They pray at tombs. These people are fire-worshippers. When they do that, they are remembering the matriarchy, honouring it.'

He was rabid again, glittering. I could not tell if this supposed heresy outraged or excited him. I asked: 'And you?'

'I can pray only to God, not to tombs. Everything's changing now. We have a class here where forty children come after school to learn the Koran. Our mosque is being restored with the money of ordinary people, although the government gives nothing and it will be finished when God wills.'

He seemed at once exultant and angry. I wondered how to ask him the question which went on rankling in me. But among those cold graves, in the sudden twilight, it asked itself: 'Do you want fundamentalism here?'

He turned to me with dagger-bright eyes. 'No! That won't come.'

'Why not?'

He answered: 'In the Koran it is written that the Jews and Christians are close to us.' He rubbed his fingers together in amity. 'We cannot stand against one another.'

Then he turned and launched into a new encomium on the dead. Always the dead! The whole past seemed to have risen in retribution. But his strident harshness appeared a habit now, just a way of talking. At last he said: 'You must excuse me. I have to pray.'

He entered a hut and re-emerged in a coat and snowy turban. A few bats came whispering out of the trees. Already faint chanting sounded inside the walls of the half-ruined mosque, and through one door, over a brilliant lake of carpets, I glimpsed

106

a rank of kneeling men.

Zelim's mother, the war veteran, was waiting in the dusk. She had been frightened by a rush of doves out of the graves, she said, and had returned to the car. Zelim too had been tramping miserably over the corrugated earth. The loss of the central façade, which had united the two prayer-halls, filled him with dismay. It had stood here only two years before, he said. As a boy he had come often, sometimes on foot, and returned to paint it again and again. 'It was quiet then. Ruined. There was nobody. Just trees.'

What was it he had loved so much, I asked: the melancholy, the wilderness of graves, the silence?

But he said: 'No. You see, the mosque has proportion. The whole building is in one style. I like that. Its harmoniousness.'

He walked away to view it from another angle, as if this might return to him some illusion of its old self. It was almost dark, and a rash of stars was descending the sky. But for a full five minutes he went on staring up at the building, trying to re-create in his head the harmony which he remembered as a boy.

5

The Khorezmian Solitude

The oasis was thinning away. Its fields petered out in formless
swamps, then vanished beneath the dunes. The peasant woman
seated beside me stepped down from our bus near the last village and walked off into emptiness. This whole region west of
Bukhara had been densely populated as late as the eleventh
century, and here and there spectral mounds and ridges swelled
under the saxaul; but it was impossible to tell if they were the
burial-place of forts and villages, or a chance collation of dust.
Our bus clattered and droned in the silence. Only occasionally
the sands hardened to flatlands lightly polished by grass, or
shone with pools of late rain, where sandpipers stood.

Westward along an arrow-straight road we plunged 300 miles
towards the Khorezmian oasis and the Aral Sea. To our north the
pinkish dunes of the Kizilkum, the 'Red Sands', were tossed in
blurred crescents to the horizon, while somewhere to our left
the Amu Dariya, still invisible, wound in a ponderous flood
through the camel-coloured wastes, dividing the 'Red Sands'
from the 'Black Sands' of the Karakum.

Inside my bus the lilt of Uzbek pop songs half obliterated the
shouting of convivial youths; some peasant women slumped in
half-sleep, and two girls were reading romantic novels in
Russian. A student named Rachmon shifted on to the seat beside
mine, and started to talk. Dressed in scuffed shoes and a black
waistcoat, he looked like an apprentice undertaker. A thatch of
hair overhung his forehead like a sunshade, and the eyes
beneath it bulged in adolescent questing. He was returning

home with a low-grade diploma in construction engineering. But he added with a callow charm that his passion was Islam. On his collective farm had lived a secret mullah, he said, and this man had been his guide. But he yearned for more knowledge. Islam was the only way he knew back into his people's past. It promised to enclose him in some lost sense of family. His longing was less a search for God than a quest for self. He asked pathetically: 'Tell me about my country.' I was nonplussed. 'You've read books. What happened here?'

I answered uneasily: 'What do you want to know?'

'*Anything*. You say your shops are fuller than ours. Why?'

Trying to simplify something which I did not understand, I spoke about the discovery of the sea-lanes round Africa, in which power had passed to the kingdoms of the Atlantic seaboard – Portugal, Spain, England – and the Central Asian trade routes had withered away. But Rachmon did not know of this. He thought England lay a little west of Moldavia, where he had finished his armed service. Proudly he showed me his education booklet, which recorded his final exams when aged seventeen. For history – 'Soviet' and 'World' – he had earned 'Grade 5: good', yet of his own people's past he knew nothing at all, and the world's history had reached him distorted by a rigid Marxism. As for geography, I was glad to see, he had received only 'Grade 3: fair'.

His ignorance of the Islamic world deeply frustrated him. He was trying to build something ideal out of fragments. Even his friends on the bus, I sensed, treated him with faint condescension, as if he were a country dolt. He repeated the dogmas of his mullah slavishly to me. He wanted wholeness, a new belonging. He wished he could travel like me. His gaze washed over my rucksack. But he said: 'Aren't you afraid? Aren't the police following you? A foreigner travelling like you in our country! Don't they think you're a spy?'

'I don't know,' I said. 'Do you think I'm followed?'

'I don't know either.' He looked at me, bewildered. 'I'm just an ordinary fellow like you.'

On the horizon to our north a mushroom-cloud of storm had welled up, as if billowing from some supernatural crater, and by nightfall it had covered all the sky except for a crack in the west. Then this too closed, and we were travelling in our own pool of light along the empty road.

By now the passengers' shouting had shrunk to murmurs. The two girls had fallen asleep with their novels in their laps. Rachmon said: 'The Russians brought a lot of bad things here.'

'You want those books banned?' I joked.

'Yes.'

I asked: 'Do women want that?'

But he seemed not to hear, as if it were a question in another language. His mildness, I began to see, was an illusion. He only said: 'Our laws should be Moslem ones.'

The Western clichés of Islamic law had been simmering in my head for days. I heard myself say: 'You'd cut off a thief's hand?'

'Yes. I think Soviet law is too lax with such things. You find that cruel? Really?' His look of boyish surprise redoubled. 'But if somebody steals something, then he can't steal again!' He smiled at me with a ghastly innocence. Brick by brick he was building a tower of absolutes in the wastes of his ignorance, with no creative doubting in between. Learning for him was a process of accumulation.

The two matriarchs behind us suddenly banged on the back of the seat. They had caught the word 'mullah' and wanted to know what we were discussing. Their headscarves wound about their chins in the way Rachmon approved, but their features were whetted to refractory crags, their eyes blazed and their hair curdled round their cheeks in ashen authority. The younger of them knocked Rachmon on the shoulder and let out a jet of Uzbek. I listened uncomprehending while their fusillades pattered to and fro. A final salvo burst from the two women in unison, and Rachmon fell silent.

'What did they say?' I asked.

He shrugged. His boy's face was undented. 'She just talked. About men having two wives. Nothing.'

111

'What?'

'She doesn't like it.'

When I turned to them, the older woman, remembering scraps of Russian, said: 'It's bad, bad, bad,' and her friend puckered and shouted 'Bad!'

'They don't know anything,' Rachmon said. 'What if your wife got ill and was no use?'

'That's when she'd need you more,' I said.

Again there moved over his face the paralysis of listening to another tongue, yet something pained and baffled unfocused his gaze too, as if a discomfort were stirring far behind it. But he said: 'In your country can't you get another wife?'

'Only after you separate.'

He was silent a moment, then said proudly: 'I paid a high price for my wife.'

I was astonished that he was married, he looked so puerile. High bride-prices had been frowned on under the Soviets, but had never been stamped out. He had met his wife by chance two years ago, he said, and they had decided in private to marry. 'It's different with all my friends. Their parents chose for them.' But his parents had been displeased, and the girl had not yet born him a child. Vaguely I wondered if their hostility had thrown him into the arms of a wider family in Islam, but the thought faded.

By now we had crossed the Amu Dariya by a barrage ablaze with lights, and were threading between dark fields tilled for cotton and quartered up for rice, where he disembarked at the gates of his collective farm. Tired with the road's jolting, I thought of him with misgiving. The future suddenly seemed threatened less by the anger of a people's depleted dignity, or the extremes to which poverty might drive them, than by a blinding simplicity. Soon afterwards we were moving through the lamps of the Khorezmian oasis, scattered and dim, and into the centreless town of Novi Urgench and an empty hotel.

*

Isolated from all other civilisations by desert, Khorezm was an oasis-country of mythic remoteness, gorging on the sediment of the Amu Dariya, the ancient Oxus, whose wanderings had spread a treacherous delta of silt north-west into the shrunken Aral Sea. Two and a half millennia ago the oasis became a province of the great Achaemenian empire, where Iranian peoples flourished behind an intricacy of dykes and terraces, and here, it was once believed, was born the faith of Zoroaster.

Only in the seventeenth century, as the ungovernable Oxus changed its bed, was the old Seljuk capital at Kunia Urgench abandoned, and the inhabitants migrated more than a hundred miles upriver to Khiva, near the placeless metropolis where I wandered next morning. Novi Urgench might have crystallised overnight from a sprinkling of villages and fields. It looked harsh and poor. A sterilising grid of Soviet roads had been clamped over the Uzbek lanes. In the memorial to Soviet Power two boys were parading derisively and hacking at the bas-reliefs with sticks.

It was not on this barren metropolis that the government of Khorezm devolved, but on the city of Khiva nearby. By the eighteenth century its rulers, together with those of Bukhara and Kokand, had carved up the heart of Central Asia. Khiva was more compact than its rivals, but poorer, more remote and tortured by Turcoman raids. The whole oasis bristled with fortified farms. Yet in this solitude its khans came to think themselves invincible. They filled their fields and homes with Persian and Russian slaves. Three Cossack expeditions sank against them, and in 1717 a 4000-strong Russian force under Prince Bekovich was deceived by a pretence of hospitality, then massacred almost to a man. In 1839 another expedition, after floundering through freak snowstorms, returned without a blow struck, littering the desert with the frozen corpses of a thousand men and nine thousand camels. Only in 1873 did a three-pronged Russian army under General Kaufmann seize Khiva with scarcely a Russian casualty, and reduced the khanate to a puppet state, which expired in 1920.

Yet when I reached the city, it was as if the air had frozen there. It had been restored under the Soviets pitilessly, its life washed away. Inside its ramparts, I felt, nothing had ever happened, nor ever would happen. The place might have been created on the instant, without a past.

I lingered by a causeway through the battlements. In its corridor a triple succession of eighteen-foot doors swung huge and delicately carved. I emerged into empty streets. Sometimes they wound like canyons between the walls, and lightly tiled towers bulged overhead. On all sides the sculptured doors, wasted and pale, led into gutted houses. They hung light in their sockets, starred with hexagons and lozenges or jungled in sculptured foliage. All the mess of habitation had been cleaned away, and the gates and turrets, the minarets and cupolas, seemed to belong to a civilisation remoter than Byzantium. Everything was tended, sanitised. Over the tawny monotone of the medresehs the green-blue tiles shone rare and sudden. No one was praying in the museum-mosques. Only the flagstones of the lanes, rutted like those of Pompeii by the iron-studded wheels of old horse-carts, betrayed that anyone had ever lived here.

By noon the streets were trickling with tourists – Uzbek and Russian – and booths had opened in the walls, selling cassettes of Turkic pop music and posters of Rambo and Indian film stars. I avoided them down lonely alleys. Once I stooped through a door into the back of a palace, and found myself in the courtyard of the khan's harem. It was quaintly beautiful. On three sides, over every façade, glistened a cool spray of tiles where painted roofs hung over galleries, and little doors showed. On the fourth, a rank of wooden columns tapered like inverted tulips, and scooped deep, shadowed bays from the walls. Every surface was worked into flowers, tendrils, inscriptions. It was as if for centuries, all over the courtyard, a legion of insects had been burrowing nervously across wood and marble, gnawing out, with minute, fastidious appetites, all the intricacy for which the patience of men was too short.

I plunged through the doors into a warren of yards and tiled chambers. Desultory restoration was going on. Through cracks in locked gates I glimpsed derelict courtyards, piled with debris. Nothing betrayed the life of their vanished inhabitants. Even when I walked through the battlements of the citadel, I found myself adrift in a clay field, where the mud-built palaces had eroded to a stark jigsaw of platforms and walls. Here, in the last century, the tyrant khans had reigned in grisly operetta. Even in summer they wore sheepskin caps and boots stuffed with linen rags. Their luxuries were carpets and a few sofas and carved chests. They executed their subjects on whim. The Russian envoy Muraviev, arriving in 1819, described how among the crowds gawping at his entry were throngs of Russian slaves, who whispered to him piteously for help he could not give. The previous intruder Bekovich, he learnt, had been flayed alive and his skin stretched over a drum.

I pushed through a door into the open throne-room. On one side its ceramic dais engulfed the court in a tidal wave of dazzling blue. On the other a brick mound had once supported a felt-lined tent – the herders' yurt – into whose snug fetor the half-savage khans had retired in winter.

It was at this court, in 1863, that the Hungarian traveller Arminius Vambéry, disguised as a dervish, must have received his audience with the khan Sayyid Mahomet. As the curtain rolled back from the dais, the ruler was revealed reclining on a silk-velvet cushion, clutching a short gold sceptre. The sight of his degenerate face with its imbecile chin and white lips, and the tremble of his effeminate voice, were to haunt Vambéry for years afterwards. The slightest mistake would have cost his life.

Later, passing through a public square, he stumbled with horror on a party of horsemen dragging whole families of prisoners-of-war behind them. Out of the sacks that they opened tumbled human heads, which an accountant kicked into piles before rewarding each horseman with a four-head, twenty-head or forty-head silk robe. Soon afterwards Vambéry watched the routine execution of some 300 captives. Most were strung up or decapitated. But the eight grey-haired leaders lay down to be manacled, then the executioner knelt on their chests and gouged out their eyes, wiping his bloodstained knife on their beards. They tried to rise to their feet, but knocked blindly against one another, or beat the ground in their agony. Even Vambéry, whose nerves were of steel, shuddered at these memories into his old age.

I roamed the citadel in mingled awe and gloom. Against its western ramparts, on a pinnacle of natural rock, a last flicker of battlements and stairways upheld a makeshift kiosk. It hung there like a perverted throne, where the dissolute khans sipped sherbet and plotted in the sky, and the whole city fell open beneath them.

Yet in its final years, even before the Russian protectorate, Khiva was suffused by a quiet renaissance. The last khan's progressive vizier (whom he murdered) built roads and schools, and in 1910 erected almost the highest minaret in Central Asia, a stately, tapering pillar belted with sixteen decorative friezes. A previous khan had planned a still more prodigious minaret, but it was never completed. It squats by the main street as fat as a gasometer. Bands of tilework, created for an aerial colossus, circle it in a stilled slipstream of gentian and turquoise, teasing the imagination with its cancelled future.

Islam had returned only thinly to the city. In the tomb-sanctuary of its local shrine, a mullah had taken up residence with his ginger cat. But the nearby caravanserai had been turned into a registry office. Inside, the bellow and slavering of camels had long faded, and their drinking-well was given over to superstitious wishing. History had turned picturesque. On one wall a tin stork dangled a familiar bundle, and a notice listed suitable names for babies. Then the newlyweds would emerge to be photographed under the minaret. They settled into pretty tableaux, framed by the sanitised past. The grooms posed in crumpled suits, the brides in white muslin from which their jet-black hair tumbled in earthy defiance.

But when I entered the Friday Mosque – once the khanate's religious heart – the 200 wooden pillars which upheld its prayer-hall shifted and dimmed in a twilit forest, where nobody prayed.

116

'Turkey is our brother!' The two men raised their hands in an invisible toast. 'Our future is with Turkey!'

We sat cross-legged on a carpeted dais like a trio of Buddhas on an altar, and talked of mutual friends in Bukhara. Shukrat was a slight, pallid man with a thunderous voice. The gates of his house – typical of the older oasis – had opened straight on to this cavernous reception-hall, as if it were a garage. The only other furniture was a black-and-white television, on which the Uzbek president was receiving the Turkish prime minister.

Shukrat and his friend watched this with dark elation. They were in love with an idea of Turkey. They saw it as their country's lodestar. Turkey beckoned from the rich West, inviting them into paradise. But its language and culture were theirs – a Moslem spirit within a secular state – and it lent them pride. On the flickering screen the motorcade glided to a halt and the two stout, bald men entered the Palace of Deputies.

'The Turks have sent us aid,' said Shukrat.

I asked: 'What sort?'

'Just a little food,' replied Racoul. 'But it's aid to the heart.' He was dark and burly, Shukrat's opposite, and his closest friend. A surge of satin hair and beard blackened his low brows and jaw. He looked like the King of Spades. But he spoke in a fluty whisper. He and Shukrat seemed to have exchanged voices.

'Look at that! That's disgusting!' Their eyes were clamped to the television again. The two statesmen had mounted a rostrum and the delegates beneath were clapping with the soulless unity of old Communists. 'Machines!' thundered Shukrat. 'Just like the old days! Like Brezhnev times! They haven't a separate brain between them!'

'I'm ashamed of them,' whispered Racoul. 'What must the prime minister be thinking? They don't have that in Turkey.'

He and Shukrat knew, of course, that Uzbekistan was governed by old Communists under a new name. They both belonged to the small opposition party Erk – Racoul's pockets bulged with its news-sheets – but its activities were circumscribed, and the more formidable dissident parties had been banned altogether.

'Democracy is only a child here,' said Shukrat.

Like urban intelligentsia all over Central Asia, they longed for 'the Turkish model'. Turkey was educating Uzbek businessmen and students, and pushing for a Turkic bloc in the United Nations. There was heady talk of common currencies and flags, and of following Ataturk's adoption of the Latin alphabet. Shukrat and Racoul brushed aside my misgiving at Turkey's poor resources. Their fingers rootled into bowls of sunflower seeds as they announced that the foremost presidents of Central Asia had all declared for the Turkish model. Their talk ascended into dreams. Turkey would become the heart of the world, they said. It had suddenly found a fresh purpose, I knew. It was seeing itself not as a humiliated petitioner on the hem of Europe, but as the paradigm for a Central Asian commonwealth.

'But we have too many poor.' Shukrat was suddenly sombre. 'I think they'll rise up again. Things are getting so much worse here. There's hunger now.' It was the return of Communism which he dreaded. 'I'm not afraid of Islam. Islam has heart.' His face turned bitter. 'But Communists will do anything.'

'Turkey could save us,' Racoul fluted. His gaze returned to the television, but the Chamber of Deputies had been replaced by a dance troupe. He asked: 'Do you think the Turks are European?'

I retreated into pedantry. 'Istanbul is in Europe.'

'Istanbul!' Shukrat cried. 'It's the city I long to see! I know the European capitals must be beautiful, but Istanbul! You've been there? You have?' Their twin stares alighted on me with an almost accusatory envy. 'What is it like?'

I described the stupendous skyline of domes and minarets above the Golden Horn, and the night-built dwellings of a city bursting with immigrant poor. They listened in rapt stillness. The great metropolis – in all its steely glamour, its poverty and stormy energies – was drenched in an atavistic glory for them. Nothing I said could diminish it. A provincial engineer and a schoolmaster, isolated in the wastes of Khorezm, they warmed themselves in its hope, as at a rediscovered faith.

But Racoul was still knotted with worry. He asked suddenly: 'What do Europeans think when they hear the word "Turk"?'

I mumbled uncomfortably, playing for time.

'Yes? Yes?' The two faces were beseeching me now. They were white, hungry for acknowledgement.

'Travellers to Turkey find it beautiful.'

'But ordinary Europeans,' went on Racoul relentlessly, 'what's their first reaction to the idea of "Turk"?'

'They think, well ....' I became desperate. 'They probably think of warriors and sultans ....'

'Ah yes, yes!' They became happy with this fairytale reduction of themselves. It lent them imperial lustre. 'Warriors ....'

Shukrat disappeared into another room and returned with an outline map of the world such as schoolchildren fill in for geography lessons. Across it, in a swathe of buttercup yellow fanning east and north from the Mediterranean almost to the Bering Straits, he had coloured in the farthest reaches of the Turkic world. It was the old dream of Turania, of a Greater Turkey resurrected.

'We're one people at heart,' he said. 'I'm not claiming we should necessarily be one nation, but we could be a kind of federation.' He glowed with prophecy. 'Look .... Look ....'

He laid the map tenderly across my knees, while Racoul loomed alongside, endorsing his words with coos and grunts. Under my hands the whole heart of Asia lay sealed in buttercup yellow. Shukrat's forefinger swooped and darted across it. In the ancient Turkic homelands of steppe and plateau, where mammoth rivers meandered north towards the Siberian plains, the calyx of this buttercup unfolded from the infant nations where I now wandered: the Uzbeks and Kazakhs, the Kirghiz and Turcomans. They were its core. Eastward the visionary empire vaulted the Pamirs to annex China's north-west province of Xinjiang, home of the Turkic Uighurs, then gobbled up Mongolia before drifting north to speckle eastern Siberia – birthland of the

Yakuts – with impatient yellow dots. Westward it flooded beyond Asia Minor to engulf Bulgaria, Macedonia and Cyprus, then leapfrogged north to claim distant kin in Hungary, Finland and Estonia.

I enquired about the capital of this mirage?

'I don't mind!' bellowed Shukrat magnanimously. 'Tashkent or Istanbul or Almaty! They can decide that! Only the frontiers must be down like before. A hundred years ago nobody here felt they were Tajik or Uzbek or Kirghiz. They just thought they were members of families, and Moslems. The borders didn't matter then. You just crossed on your camel and exchanged greetings!' He lifted one hand in a breezy salute, while the other steered an imaginary quadruped over a frontier. 'All that demarcation was the work of Stalin, Brezhnev, Gorbachev! Other people's decisions! It's nonsense. My wife, for instance, is a Tajik, and no different from me!' He glanced guiltily at her photograph on the television, and stubbed out his half-smoked cigarette. 'She hates me smoking.' She gazed back at him from her gilt frame: a handsome face with full lips and wide-spread eyes. He laughed. 'She bullies me. When she's away, like now, I still see her scowling at me.'

His stare returned to the map. 'So I'm not a chauvinist! My wife is Tajik – they're an Iranian people – and we're married. This Greater Turkey has nothing to do with chauvinism! *Nothing!* It is a brotherhood!'

But he ransacked his shelves for books on Central Asia, and ascribed all its civilisation to Turks, winkling out buried references and propounding vertiginous theories. Persian, Arab and Chinese culture withered at his advance. Sogdians were forgotten. Bactria fell. Whole empires were rolled shamelessly back. History resolved into a requiem for a wondrous, lost Turania. He shook his map like a threat. The buttery tide of his empire, I noticed, cynically snuffed out Armenia and his wife's Tajiks; and the survival of Uzbek and Turcoman minorities sanctioned huge land-grabs in northern Iran and Afghanistan. A yellow question-mark hung even over the Tartar-sprinkled Volga and Urals, and

120

the reindeer-loving Samoyeds.

Shukrat demanded: 'Are there Turks in Britain?'

I answered nervously: 'A few, from Cyprus.'

He looked disappointed. Behind his eyes a yellow wave had perhaps reared for a moment, then ebbed away.

Racoul had been silent a long time, restored to a swarthy majesty. But now he cooed: 'Does the West want Uzbekistan to adopt the Turkish model?'

'Yes,' I said, relieved to be truthful. 'It's thought more moderate than the Iranian.'

'Moderation!' Shukrat boomed. 'Yes! We are moderates! Moscow television is always harping on the Armenian massacres, as if Turkic people were all barbarians. I don't understand! Why all this fuss?'

Because in 1915, I said, more than a million Armenians had died, and Turkey had never admitted guilt.

Shukrat grimaced. 'I'm not saying I think it was a good thing. But there have been Armenian terrorists too, you know. These Armenians .... And the Slavs are behind them!' His fingers jittered over the map as if itching to grasp a scimitar. 'But we are moderates!'

*

On 3 July 1881, a colony of German Mennonites, who had settled on the lower Volga to escape conscription in Prussia, heaped their belongings on to wagons and lumbered eastwards on the orders of God. Descendants of Anabaptist dissenters in the sixteenth century, they were pacifist farmers of fanatic simplicity, and refused allegiance to any government. In the end it was the khan of Khiva who offered them sanctuary. Some sixty-four families floated to him down the Amu Dariya in eight hired barges; the rest dismantled their wagons, loaded them on to camels, and marched alongside. So they came at last to the end of the world, where they settled in two colonies and worked the land. The khan valued them as carpenters and polishers. They mended his phonograph, and delighted him by sticking coloured transfers all

121

over the furniture they made for him. And here travellers found them as late as 1933, living lives of classless austerity among the puzzled natives.

They haunted me. I kept wondering what had happened to them. Against all reason, I hoped that some remnant, forgotten in their remote hamlets, had survived Stalin's persecutions. I enquired among taxi-drivers in the bleak spaces round Novi Urgench station, but only one driver remembered their village at Ak Metchet. He had heard of a bizarre German people living there many years ago, he said, but they had all gone. He looked at me with suspicion. Why should I want to see it?

But we drove across a country of misted peace. The whole land lay muffled under the hush of the Amu Dariya, which carried down more silt than the Nile and smeared it for hundreds of miles over the oasis in a counterpane of stiff, pale clay. To either side the soil was tilled for cotton, and a sprinkle of young corn showed. Nothing interposed between us and the horizon, where willows and poplars were scratched in thin lines on an opal sky.

The driver was wincing from toothache. His mouth opened on a blackened stump. I pointed to the Dracula gap among my own teeth, and this perversely pleased him. As our road clattered past mud villages, I scribbled notes idly, then saw in the mirror that he was watching me, his eyes narrowed in distrust. 'What are you writing?'

'Just notes about the land.'

'That won't do. There are too many police. Put your notebook away and just sit and look ahead or they'll take us.'

I did as he said, with despair. A feel of provincial harshness touched every village here. Foreigners never came. We were approaching the most bitter fringe of habitation, where suddenly the desert shone yellow and close, waiting, and the Mennonites had reclaimed Ak Metchet from seasonal marshland.

The driver said: 'It's nearly finished now.'

A few cottages scattered either side of a dead-end. Their doors were lightly carved in the Uzbek way, and their brickwork decorated with Communist stars. The only man we saw knew nothing of the place's history, but directed us to a derelict-looking house where the village elder lived. Still I half expected the porches to fill with the black and white bodices and plaited hair of women at their spinning-wheels, the Gretchens and Dorotheas of sixty years before, and their broods of freckled children.

Instead the old Uzbek tottered to his door and asked us in. A big sheepskin hat thrust forward his ears like radar scanners, and his face was tangled in whiskers. He settled us on the dais which occupied half the room. His voice came thin and high. The Germans had gone, he said, all gone. He spoke of them with distracted affection. Two grandchildren hovered about us, offered tea and broke hard bread among the pots and quilts where we sat. They were desperately poor.

'I remember them,' the old man said, but his voice wavered, as if any meaning was fragile now. 'I worked with them when I was a youth. They lived along the far side of the road, where the Young Pioneers' camp is now.'

'What were they like?'

'Like you!' he piped. 'Their faces! Just like yours!' He contemplated me with a sudden sweetness, and murmured: 'Aach, aach' to himself, and finally: 'You're from England.' England and Germany were becoming fused in his mind. 'They were good people, decent people. They worked hard, because they were Germans. They used to sell their dairy products on the road to Khiva.' He stared at me again. 'Aach, aah. England. Did your parents live here then? Did *you* perhaps live here? No ….'

'No.'

'You were a good people ….' His gaze drifted away and for a moment his canted ears, tufted with white hairs, gave an illusion of listening for something. '… Wonderful carpenters. They were not dressed like us, but the women all in black and white, and their hair ….' His hands trembled towards the nape of his neck to conjure plaited buns.

'Where did they go?'

He closed his eyes. 'They were repressed in Stalin's time.

123

They went away suddenly. In 1935, I think. They were taken away to Tajikistan, to Dushanbe. They vanished.' He opened his fist to the air. 'They left nothing behind. All in the Stalin years. Repressed.'

'There's nothing?'

'Nothing.' His tone drifted between sadness and wonder. 'They took them away.'

A little later he showed us the site of their village. It had been turned into a Communist Young Pioneers' camp, as if to erase their memory. Now the camp, in turn, was falling to bits. Broken swings and seesaws creaked and swung in a faint wind. In the dried swimming-pool, whose tiles were flaking away, a dog had fallen in and died. On one wall a faded mural of glowing youths portended the Communist paradise, and a silver-painted statue of a boy blew a triumphal horn under the trees. But all was abandoned. Only the tree-stumps – pale, split, immense – of two great mulberries survived from their planting a hundred years ago, and looked more durable in the double desolation than anything else.

The old man went in front of me, peering left and right. His craned neck looked so frail, I thought it would snap. Here was a school, he said, over there a meeting-house. His boots kicked up dust. He pointed over a fence to an orchard where a few apple trees blossomed. 'That used to be their cemetery.'

Its ground was chequered with black stubble. Flakes of blossom blew in its aisles. I could see nothing else. It was hard to believe that beneath its untilled earth lay the austere patriarchs and provident child-bearers of Protestantism, who had travelled here in search of a godly peace.

*

Early next morning I selected the most durable-looking car and driver that I could find, and started north-west two hundred miles towards the Aral Sea. Fortified farmhouses sprinkled the town's outskirts – memories of a time when Turcoman raiders tormented the khanate's frontiers – but beyond them the oasis

124

smoothed into a vast, somnolent lake of silt. Under that etiolated sky all life seemed wrung out. Nothing stirred. The land was embalmed in a blank, shrouding pallor. Somewhere to our north, I knew, the Amu Dariya was moving alongside in a red-brown flood, giving birth to a long succession of untidy lakes. But the river was dying. A century ago its forested banks rustled with tiger, wild boar, panther and a host of wildfowl. Now it was bullied by dams and bled by hundreds of pumps whose dipping snouts sucked it away to the cotton-fields, until it trickled at last into the Aral Sea.

My driver was bitter. He could remember from his youth, he said, how rich in sediment the water had been. Now half its silt was trapped behind the great dam upriver, and the water here flowed clear and poor.

I recalled the lament of an Uzbek poet:

> *When God loved us*
> > *he gave us the Amu Dariya.*
> *When he ceased to love us,*
> > *he sent us Russian engineers.*

The driver laughed harshly. He looked sunk in a morose cynicism. His was one of those disruptive faces which I was to meet all through my journey, reminding me of some acquaintance back in Europe. He had ice-blue eyes, so unusual in an Uzbek that I suspected him of Russian blood (which he denied), and under his Gallic beret the broad brows and fleshy nose turned him urbane. He looked like Manet. But instead of discussing the *Salon des Refusées*, he cursed the landscape and the economy together, spitting out of the window.

'We work and work, and don't get a kopek. That's how it is here. No, I don't go to the mosque. I haven't the time. I have to live.'

He echoed the land around us. It was growing poverty-stricken. We went through towns ringed by cement-works, cotton ginneries and factories toxic with dumps and furnaces,

125

where the old Soviet slogans for Work and the Party still hung in the reeking air. Muralled Lenins lifted their wavering hands, and the hammer-and-sickle dangled across the streets in defunct lights, which nobody had dared or bothered to pull down. The people looked jaded and ill. The high-coloured dress of Bukhara had gone. The world seemed at once more contemporary and more wretched.

Soon afterwards there appeared the twin shacks of a new frontier-post, where the Turcomans had eaten into the Uzbek oasis long ago. The Uzbek police demanded two cigarettes before lifting their barrier. The red-faced Turcoman let us through without a word. 'More restrictions!' rasped the driver. 'More fucking borders, bureaucracy, bribes!'

The fields were turning to semi-desert. The sand was tossed into heaps, and occasional salt-flats shone like hoar-frost. Here and there a mole-run of salinated earth marked the passage of a dredged canal, where the water, it was true, ran jade-green, thinned, and a rainstorm had jewelled the plain in pools, lying interchangeably with the watery sky.

Manet's pale eyes drifted over it, accusingly. Things had declined ever since Gorbachev, he said. 'People used to be afraid of the great Russian bear, but now they just spit.' He spat. 'In a year or two we'll be surrounded by civil wars, you'll see.'

'Who will be fighting?'

'How do I know? But look at Armenia and Azerbaijan. Look at Georgia, Moldavia!' A cloud of chaos was brewing up in his brain. 'Khorezm may be quiet, and Bukhara's not too bad, but Samarkand's dreadful, and as for Tashkent' – he swore unprintably.

But he knew little beyond his own, crushed oasis. From here the ripples of his distrust spread out concentrically, growing uglier all the time, until they lapped at the confines of his sense, and created fantasies there: a magic West, a daemonic China.

I said: 'But you must be glad to have freedom from Moscow.'

He answered: 'No. I'm not glad. I wish we were back.'

I stared at him with muted astonishment. Immured in my

unconscious Englishness, I had assumed that nationhood gave identity, belonging. But his nation was young. He said: 'Plenty of people feel like I do. I've never heard anyone say "Thank you!" to Moscow for leaving us like this. We were better off under them.'

Around us the country had faded into desolation. A cutting wind sprang up from the north, and the plains were closed off only by enfeebled ranks of poplars under blackening clouds. Even the fields looked squalid, nearly barren, as if another year would return them to desert.

Then suddenly, without warning, an enormous pale minaret loosened out of the sky. It was huger than anything in the land, solitary and unexplained. Next, a mausoleum appeared, then another – barbaric, conical tombs, like stone tents pitched in the wastes. As we approached, I saw that the land had turned to a sea of graveyards. They rolled in low hillocks as far as my eye could reach, their tombstones half sucked into the dust. The ladder-like biers on which the corpses were carried had been set upright beside the graves, and seemed to cover the dunes with a pathetic hope, as if propped against heaven.

While the driver stopped the car and prepared to sleep, I got out into a howling wind. It thrashed across the plain and levelled the coarse grass over the mounds. I wound my scarf about my face and tramped towards the minaret. Three mausoleums stood among the dunes of dead, far apart. They were almost all that remained of ancient Urgench, capital of a sultanate which had eased loose from the Seljuk empire after 1092. This remote kingdom of Khorezm had stayed independent and powerful for more than a hundred years, and early in the thirteenth century embraced all Central Asia. But in 1221 the armies of Genghiz Khan fired the capital with naphtha; a hundred thousand citizens were marched into slavery, and the rest massacred. Then the Amu Dariya dykes were opened and the city submerged.

The Elizabethan envoy Anthony Jenkinson, who reached Urgench in 1558, found its four-mile walls encircling ruin. By then it had revived under the Golden Horde, been razed by

Tamerlane, sown over with barley, then built again. But in 1575 the Amu Dariya changed its bed and the depleted city was abandoned. Only in the last century was a canal cut and a hesitant new settlement arose, whose Turcoman inhabitants lived beyond the hillocks to the north, and whose dead were buried in the cemeteries around me.

I struggled to the 170-foot minaret. Its pinnacle of lightly decorated brick tapered into a wind which screamed unimpeded across the wastes. Its uppermost bands of script had been chipped away by storm, and its top snapped off like a factory chimney opening into the sky. Whatever mosque or mausoleum it attended had utterly gone.

Beyond, raised on a twenty-foot brick plinth, was the tomb of the martial sultan Tekesh. Its circular body, pierced with bays and crowned by a squat steeple, floated pavilion-like over the wilderness. Tiles still clung to its spire, which had broken open on an inner cupola, curved below like a skull beneath a helmet. The strange, Assyrian shape of this desolate sepulchre found its echo in the Seljuk tombs of Anatolia. Its builders were restless warrior-kings. Tekesh, the sixth sultan of Khorezm, absorbed the Seljuk power in Persia at the end of the twelfth century, before being laid in his steppeland grave, and this, with the smaller cenotaph beyond it, still gave an illusion of nomad impermanence, although it has stood here eight hundred years.

By the time I reached the last of these early tombs, I was craving its shelter. It had been built as a communal royal mausoleum, it seems, but named from Turabek, a Mongol princess. The north wind moaned through its doors. My ignorance of these dreamlike rulers, so powerful in their day, made me doubly a stranger here. I recalled no monument precisely like this one. A tall, twelve-sided sanctuary, it encased a hexagonal tomb-chamber, and was richer, even in decay, than anything in Khiva. Under its blind arches, the honeycomb decorations massed in dense clusters, tiled with a soft brilliance of campanula and grape blue, and a muted, opal green. Exposed and apparently fragile, they hung there in enigmatic strength, while above them the shattered dome cast a shard of turquoise into the sky.

I shivered in the empty chamber. It looked restored. The inner dome was overspread with a mathematic sky of plaster constellations and flowers, like a lost language.

The driver found me here and stared up almost angrily, as if there must be something else to see. A few pigeons flitted among the stucco botany and stars. After a while he urged me on the few miles to Kunia Urgench, where he wanted to eat, and the pavilion-tombs sank behind us into their cemeteries, like survivors beyond their time returning into the earth.

In front of us Kunia Urgench had been resurrected around a kernel of shrines. Its streets were full of fantastical old men. Sheepskin hats dripped strands of wool like dreadlocks over their brows and bulked out a full foot to either side of their heads. Beneath these monstrous fleeces they went in knee-length boots and quilted coats, debonairly sashed, stabbing the ground in front of them with gnarled walking-sticks. Sometimes they rose to a decrepit and fabulous majesty. Their beards forked in twin cascades, or tangled in piebald confusion; and often – if their owner wanted to cut a dash – they fanned down abruptly beneath a clean-shaven chin, as if stuck on like the ceremonial tuft of a pharoah. Only the glint of a war-medal or a wristwatch betrayed that this tribe of hoary and redundant warriors inhabited the twentieth century, and occasionally, between the waterfall of hat and the snowy gush of whiskers, a pair of spectacles gleamed in freakish isolation like headlamps through a fog.

A mosque had just been built, ugly and bright. Its mullah found us walking there, and demanded that we have tea with him. 'A brand new place!' he cried. 'We get a congregation of seven hundred on Fridays, sometimes more!'

In his family compound, littered with rubbish, a car and a motorcycle gleamed side by side. 'Two machines!' he grinned. 'We're rich!'

He was a jovial stalwart, with the beginnings of bearded majesty. On his pullover cantered a pair of idolatrous antelopes, and the walls of his house were hung with calendars flaunting Uzbek film-starlets. We sat beneath them and gossiped. He spoke Russian in the slushy patter of all his country. Two robust and unveilable daughters dropped roundels of bread on our dirty quilts, and brought green tea, and a pair of secular sons in bomber jackets sat with us and enquired about pop music.

It was the mullah's business, he said, to offer hospitality to foreigners, not bigotry. We were all men of God. Laughter cascaded from the next-door room, where his grandson was watching a television cartoon. The mullah wanted to know about America. Where exactly was the Atlantic, he wondered, and what lands did it separate? And Britain?

'Britain is an island,' declared one of his sons proudly. 'And is there Ireland too?'

'Yes,' I said, 'there is Ireland.'

They contemplated this. Then I asked: 'Where is Dev Kesken?'

They went into momentary conclave. Dev Kesken was the mysterious fortress-city where almost five centuries ago the first of the Uzbeks of Khorezm was proclaimed khan. They had heard of it, they said – it lay a hundred miles to the west, some-where in the desert – but they had never been there. It was abandoned.

The mullah peered round at a man sitting quietly nearby. 'Kakajan', he said, 'knows the desert.'

It was the first time I had noticed him. A man of fifty, per-haps, he squatted behind us, self-effacing or dejected, listening. His burnished face was lit by eyes like black searchlights, and his cheekbones bulged raw and high, the flesh beneath them sunk to stark cavities. He nodded faintly at the mullah. A short moustache made a white punctuation-mark under his nose. 'We should go before night,' he said.

The driver drained his tea and we prepared to leave. Opposite the door the most lubricious of the calendar lovelies postured for the month of May. The mullah glanced at her indulgently and caught my eye. 'That is Miss Luxe,' he explained. She simmered back at him.

He left us at his compound gate, his hand lifted to the antelope over his heart; and Kakajan, Manet and I drove west into emptiness. To either side of the potholed road the saxaul filled the distance with a spinach-green ocean. Only after an hour did it start to shrink and the sand spread a pinkish film as far as we could see. It was bitterly cold. Vertically above us the sky was bruised with storm-clouds, but to the south, along a clear horizon, a wind was chafing the sand into a sunlit smoke, and processions of dust-devils were spinning through a yellow, mortuary light.

Manet drove in silence, but Kakajan hunched behind us, watching. He was dressed for action, chipper and trim in polished boots and a white anorak. On his head perched an old trilby hat which gleamed like dented metal. He looked at once alert, detached and sad. The desert was potentially fertile, he said, it needed only water. After the spring rain it came alive with mushrooms, snakes and orchids. 'This is a golden earth!' He talked in a compressed, fast Russian, sucked back in his teeth where he chewed *nass*, a foul-smelling blend of tobacco, saxaul sap, lime and ash. 'There used to be people out there, centuries ago. There were twenty million in the Khorezm alone, it's said, and now look ....'

The humps of camels, apparently wild, were moving above the shrubs in slow motion, Bactrian and dromedary together. Kakajan remembered their herds from childhood. In Kruschev's day, he said, you were only allowed one camel, ten sheep and a donkey of your own, so the camels started to vanish. Yet there was a time when caravans had criss-crossed the whole desert. 'You could go from Kunia Urgench to Ashkhabad just following the wells – and they're still there.' He pointed to a ruffle of hillocks in the sands. 'A three-sided bank means a well; a single bank means an open pool, where you can bring the camels down. That's how they went then. From water to water. Yes, right across the Black Sands!'

He himself had no settled home. He exuded a gypsy hardihood. He represented some factory in Krasnodar, he said, and

131

did a small trade taking vegetables from Kunia Urgench to the Caspian by train. His melancholy detachment made me wonder about him. 'You could travel where you wanted in the old days,' he said; then came the familiar bitterness: 'The borders were created by the Russians.'

Manet asked sceptically: 'But now the borders are here, how will you remove them?'

'The people will remove them,' said Kakajan. He looked suddenly naïve under his curious hat. 'Nobody wants them. We'll make a Turkish Commonwealth!'

Manet's lips twitched. 'And where will be the capital?'

Kakajan looked at him as if he were a simpleton. 'Kunia Urgench, of course!'

'Why?'

He thought. 'In the old days there were only two capitals for Islam. Mecca in the west and Kunia Urgench in the east. Everybody was here.' His mind now brimmed with hearsay and fantasy. 'Omar Khayyám was here! Navoi was here. They invented everything here! It was all right then.'

Manet only repeated: 'Then.'

'And look at the roads!' sighed Kakajan. 'The Russians didn't like us driving, so they kept them bad.' We were crashing across a minefield of craters and corrugations. He turned to me. 'Will you write about our roads? Write that this is a Soviet road, that is why it's so rotten. Now that we're independent, there will only be Turcoman roads and it'll be all right.' He tapped my hand. 'Make sure you write that.'

The car bucked like a stallion at every pothole, while Manet fretted about his chassis and tyres. But Kakajan urged him on with petulant cries, enticing him with the legend of Dev Kesken. It was a place of wild splendour, he said, where a demon had once fought with God ....

For a long time, far to our west, a grey line had crept across the horizon, barely noticeable at first, but gradually rising. I was more than a hundred miles from any place where foreigners were meant to be, but the police had vanished, and the rules with them. We veered off the tarmac and made across virgin sand. The distant pencil-stroke had hardened into a cliff which overspread our whole skyline. Where it turned west, it reared up sheer 200 feet above the sand, crowned by a broken watchtower and a domed tomb. At its foot stood a mullah's hut. While Manet smoked and groaned at the sky, Kakajan went inside to pray. He wanted the mullah's blessing on our journey, he said. Dev Kesken was only a few miles away now, but it was a savage place. 'There was this demon ....'

While he prayed, I climbed the winding cliff-path alone. Desiccated wooden poles stood stiff in the hard earth, and their prayer-rags streamed in the wind. Across the storm-racked summit, where the way levelled to a plateau of shining sand, pilgrims had covered the ground with thousands of small stones leant delicately against one another as memorials to their passage. They surrounded the mausoleum like a fakir's bed.

I stepped hesitantly through its breached enclosure. Beneath the dome was interred an obscure dervish named Sultan Ibrahim, and the wind-blasted graves of three other saints huddled in its fold. Even Kakajan had known nothing of them. It was enough that they were old, and holy, and had performed miracles. Long-extinguished candles and lamps clustered around them. Charred tea-jugs stood in votive rows, and pots stuffed with rags. I walked there in chilled wonder. It seemed a violent, shamanistic place, where Islam had never been. My footsteps crackled in its silence. One grave was inscribed 'The Living Princess'. She lay under a naked mound. The stark light and dry air turned it immortal: the dreaming epitaph and contradictory dust. I felt I was standing at the origins of faith. The wind set me shivering uncontrollably. I stared over the cliff-edge at the desert stretching eastward. Beneath me, in a precipitous curtain, the escarpment zigzagged out of sight through its own shadows and the lowering sun. Its shorn immensity suggested some divide across the map of the world. Beyond here, it seemed to say, everything changes. Far below, the matchstick figure of Kakajan was waving at me to hurry down.

Half an hour later we were weaving under the cliffs in the dying light. They rose like a man-made wall beside us. Far into the distance their veins streamed smooth until the whole escarpment resembled some layered and preposterous cake. Its strata descended through flamingo and coral pink to marmorial white and green, and a procession of caves was scooped along its softer veins. But its summit hung slaty with rocks, like a flaking roof, which had sometimes crashed into the abyss where we drove, split into shale and dust.

At first I could not guess what had created this. Then I glanced at my map and with a shock I realised where we were. We were driving along the abandoned bed of the Oxus river. Three times within historical memory its enormous flood has wavered between the Caspian and Aral seas. No wonder the cliffside strata flowed like water! Above us the Usturt plateau was set in clay for hundreds of miles, while invisible to our south a mosaic of lakes and marshes, some below sea level, traced the dead river almost to the Caspian. As recently as the sixteenth century the Oxus was flowing along the titanic ravine where we now drove, ebbing into distant marshes and leaving the Aral to wither away. Already we had travelled for miles along its floor, while the phantom boats of ancient Khorezm sailed thirty feet over our heads.

Kakajan pointed ahead. 'There it is. Dev Kesken.'

Some way from the scarp, on the edge of the lost river, a line of walls had come into view. Even the driver exclaimed and touched his face in blessing. 'You see, there is a God! If we hadn't had tea with the mullah, we'd never have found this place!'

But a minute later he shrank from the cold with a world-weary grimace, and remained in the car nibbling cubes of toast, while Kakajan and I walked towards the ruin. At first we could see nothing beyond its long outer rampart, which crossed our vision in a ribbon of etiolated yellow under the fading sun. Kakajan had gone quiet. He knew nothing of the place but its name, and his head was full of demons. Our attenuated shadows wrinkled beside us. If this was the place he said it was, it had been linked with a clifftop castle to the north, and had once been a city named Vezir, where the first Uzbek ruler of Khorezm, the sultan Ilbars, was proclaimed khan in 1512. The last Englishman to have seen it was perhaps Jenkinson, who arrived in 1558 to find the river already bending its course back towards the Aral Sea, and threatening the land with wilderness.

Now it was hard to imagine it ever peopled. Dusk was turning the land to amber. The wall looked paltry at our approach. The wind cried faintly in its fissures. I walked through its gate without expectation, and the outer vallum fell behind us. Then, in one of those moments which snare the unguarded traveller, there unfurled before us the ramparts of a phantasmal inner city, whose towers bulged from their battlements, eight to each side, between chalk-white walls. It stood stupendous in its solitude, far from anywhere now habitable. A stricken beauty touched it. Its clay bricks had been smoothed into one substance by the compacting rain and wind, so that all decoration had been rubbed away from them, leaving abstract bones.

We entered between towers over a choked ditch, and found ourselves in wasteland. The rectangle of walls stretched some 400 yards square, but enclosed only tamarisk and camel dung. Yet around them the parapets and walkways rose almost untouched and the loopholes still glared into desert.

Only the melancholy hooting of the driver's horn wrenched me away. He was frightened of the long road back, and refused point-blank to continue to the clifftop castle. It was night long before we reached Kunia Urgench. In the oasis outskirts, Kakajan said, his brother ran a state farm where we could sleep; so the driver started back alone while we trudged there under an icy blaze of stars.

There was no one else about. On the hoardings which flanked the farm gateway, dimly visible in the dark, stately youths and landgirls looked upward to a Marxist sunrise, their arms heaped with fruit and cornsheaves. But beyond, the track petered out among a cluster of mud cottages. It was heart-rendingly poor. All around us in the starlight the salinated earth glimmered like snowfields. Broken wooden steps led into the yard of the director's home, a little bigger than the rest. Some ghostly cattle lifted their heads as we passed, and a tiny donkey stirred.

I had imagined the directors of such places to be heartless engineers of statistics, beleaguered by quotas and corruption. But instead, a bespectacled peasant with a long, gentle face emerged to greet us in his pyjamas. His hair fell lank over a narrow forehead, and gold teeth gleamed in his smile. He did not believe, at first, that I was British. 'I think my brother is joking,' he said. 'Perhaps you're an Estonian.' But thereafter, from time to time, he would gaze at me with a distant, amazed affection at my visit, and murmured 'English, English...' and shook his long head, and said: 'I'm sorry for the poverty here. We have nothing. Everything's very hard. I'm so sorry.'

We had surprised him supping on hardened bread and green tea. A naked bulb dangled from the reed thatch, leaking shadow round walls of mud and straw, which he could not afford to whitewash. Against one wall was a clay stove that only gave out smoke, he said, it was useless even in this cold; and fifteen years before, his wife had brought with her two painted marriage chests, which stood in one corner.

As we settled on the felt carpets, his eldest son came in with a basin, towel and ewer, and knelt while I washed my hands; and little by little the whole family assembled round in biblical formality. Two daughters fluttered in, then vanished, and a row of small sons squatted before me and gaped.

'They've never seen a foreigner before,' the director said.

At once I had an attack of ambassadorial nerves. The boys scrutinised my every movement with bright or stunned eyes. I clamped my lips over my gap-tooth, and offered them sweets. Their fingers wrenched together or plucked at their toes. I became as jittery as they. I was suddenly embodying not only Britain, but the whole Western world. Whatever I did – if I

136

scowled or dribbled or picked my teeth – that was what the West did.

Their mother darted in barefoot and arranged quilts and cushions. She was dark-eyed and handsome, but life had spun her fine. From her flowery dress poked out wafer-thin ankles and long, sinewy hands. Her husband teased her as she worked: 'She's old, she's slow, she can't do a thing any more', and she bustled and laughed at him, banking cushions round us.

Kakajan, meanwhile, sat beside me dismantling and repairing their tiny cooker, which looked rusted away. He had fallen into a quiet, solitary place as elder brother, respected and indefinably sad. Only now did he take off his trilby from flattened hair, which caressed his mahogany face in a shock of premature whiteness. After a long time the woman carried in a stew of apples, marrows and a little mutton, scalding in its oil. This had taken two hours to prepare, its ingredients gathered in panic from other houses. The children filtered away, one by one, and we three men ate alone – but it was bitter to eat what they could not afford.

Hospitality here could blind the traveller. Lulled by its traditional language, I used often to forget the squalor – sometimes the brutality – of my hosts' lives, and think: these are a good and happy people. But in this desolate farm the signs were of a benign unity. They examined my passport incredulously, running their blackened fingernails along its crest. '*Dieu et mon Droit* ….. Her Britannic Majesty's Secretary of State requires ….' The director gaped dumbly at its visas. 'And I thought my brother was joking.'

Then mortification overtook him. 'I am ashamed to be offering you so little. Our life here …. The land is hopeless. Even if we fulfil our quota, the government scarcely makes a return to us. We have no machinery. We gather everything by hand. And the cotton doesn't grow properly – barely this high!' He levelled his hand at knee-height.

I said: 'Can't you grow vegetables or fruit?'

'The soil is too bad. It can't bear it. You've seen it. It's just salt.'

'Salt,' repeated Kakajan. 'Everywhere.'

Yes, I said, I'd seen it. I had grown aware of it insidiously, as if it were the bitterness to which everything reduced: salt along the canal banks, salt in every hollow, salt crusting the fields, in the air, the water, the lungs. Legend ran that it was the dried tears of the despairing inhabitants.

I could understand now why the director looked hopeless, broken. All his defeat seemed compressed in his self-mocking mouth. 'And you in England have everything. I'm sorry .... I'm ashamed, Mr Colin.'

I had heard that the fields could be rejuvenated by scraping off the saline topsoil and piling it up for the rain to leach. But the director shook his head. 'Even the rain is salty here. I've seen it lie in pools after a fresh downpour, and when it evaporates, there's salt. It's because of the Aral Sea drying up. The clouds collect its vapours and deposit them here.' He looked almost contrite, as if what was happening were his own doing. 'So the clouds rain salt.'

'The Aral will disappear one day,' Kakajan said. 'There used to be rest-houses and beaches there, but now you have to go farther every year if you want to find water at all. And the fish have almost gone, it's so polluted, or they're very small. When I was young, we used to catch monsters ....'

It haunted their minds like a despair: the delicate Aral, withering to our north. All evils were attributed to it: from the whinging tears of their sick children to the changed weather-patterns. 'The air has become cold,' said Kakajan. 'It never used to be like this.'

Already a hundred years ago the sea was so shallow that nomads waded with their cattle to an island eight miles from the shore, and a strong wind might blow the waters back from its bed for as far as the eye could reach. But now the two great rivers feeding it were being bled away down networks of canals, seeping and wasting. More than half its water was gone, and the main port lay stranded sixty miles from its edge.

138

'There's no future here,' Kakajan said. 'People in this region get everything, Mr Colin. Skin rashes, stomach problems, problems with hearing and sight. My brother, too. His eyes are failing now.'

The director dropped a sad smile. 'I can see during the day, but not at night, I don't know why.' He took off his thick-rimmed spectacles and his eyes shrivelled. 'And now even in the day it's getting hard. Everything's blurred at the sides. I can only see straight in front of me.'

He turned to me to test them, and I imagined myself suddenly at the antipodes of his fogged tunnel, and smiled at him. 'The doctors can't do much,' he said, 'and the mullahs only pray. Nobody can prevent the salt. All our water is contaminated with it.' He laughed cynically and picked up his bowl of tea. 'Now let's drink!'

Then, as if hunting for someone to toast, I enquired after Kakajan's family. I should have known better. No man voluntarily wanders his country homeless here. Instantly his face became hard – like the intensification of a hurt which had been there all the time – and fixed the floor without speaking. 'It was in a road accident,' the director said. 'The car overturned. My brother lost his wife and only son.'

Kakajan remained motionless. I found nothing to say, only placed my hand on his knee while his brother pulled a *dutah* from its cover, and began to play. So this, I thought, was why Kakajan led his mendicant life, passing from brother to sister, or sitting with the mullah like a mercantile gypsy in his shiny hat and boots, always a guest, surrounded by other men's children, making himself useful. The *dutah* whined and twanged. The director was agile-fingered, but would not sing. The notes arose as if from far away, miniature and lonely, like distillations of fuller and more passionate sounds being played somewhere else. The director smiled at my listening with a loose-lipped smile and heavy eyes, and shook his head a little, while Kakajan sat upright, his palms lifted on his knees as though praying, and the night wore on.

We slept in a row on the floor. For a while, in darkness, the brothers conversed in the soft, disconnected voices of people who lie close but cannot see one another.

Once I said to Kakajan: 'At least you have a family of brothers and sisters ....' The words floated bodiless in the night.

He murmured stoically: 'Yes. Many.'

At last their voices blurred into sleep, and I lay listening to silence. Out of the thatch a few insects dropped metallically on to my hair, and I brushed them away until I slept.

In the grey morning Kakajan was contemplating something, sitting bolt upright with his trilby set whimsically on his head. This soiled hat, and the black eyes shifting beneath it, dissolved his melancholy to an entrepreneurial watchfulness. We ate the hard bread together, with some tasteless jam. His brother had already gone. After a long silence of considering, he said: 'Mr Colin, would it be possible for me to accompany you to Nukus?'

'Of course.' Nukus was the capital of the Karakalpakia region where I was going. (It turned out grim and characterless.)

Silence. Then: 'Mr Colin, would it be possible for me to accompany you back to Novi Urgench too?'

'Yes it would be possible, but perhaps boring for you.'

'I will not be bored,' he smiled sadly. 'I have today free, and tomorrow free ....'

Guiltily I thought of this life, and agreed. Perhaps to him any companion was better than none, and I had the novelty of foreignness, and seemed kindly. But after another pause, in which his fingers curled no longer prayerful on his knees, his sun-blackened face looked up and said: 'I have a brother in Novi Urgench who collects dollars. He needs them for a car he wants to buy. Mr Colin, if I was to accompany you to Novi Urgench, could you perhaps afford ....'

'I need all my dollars,' I said, with the traveller's ruthlessness. The idea of this nagging presence suddenly palled. I could not tell what he was thinking. The mournful widower was fading in my mind, and somebody more resourceful and sly was emerging.

140

He said neutrally: 'Then I will accompany you to the bus station.'

I parted from the family with a sense of desertion. The older daughters appeared suddenly at my going, then disappeared in embarrassment, leaving their mother to wave farewell from an undertow of small sons whose future nobody knew.

At the bus compound, where I prepared to take the long road through Nukus to Bukhara, Kakajan said: 'The bus drivers always cheat you. Give me three hundred roubles and I'll bargain. He won't cheat me.'

Five minutes later he gave me back a ticket and a pitiful handful of notes, and it was obvious what he had done. I forgave him without speaking, a little sadly. He had almost nothing. But now his burnished head wobbled and shone on its neck like a sunflower in delight, and his eyes poured out something like love to me. I had covertly given him perhaps a week's wages. 'Oh Mr Colin! It's been so … oh ….' Then he could not resist asking this inexplicable foreigner: 'When you get back to England, could you send dollars to me?'

I said: 'Only through Ashkhabad. Then they'd be stolen.'

His face fell, but recovered as I clambered into the bus. 'Goodbye, Mr Colin. Really, you ….' He wanted to thank me, but could not. 'I'm so very glad we met!' And the next moment he was gone.

But a few minutes later, as my bus lumbered into the street on its way north-east, we overtook him. Jaunty in his dented hat, he was prancing along the roadside, counting my money.

141

6

Samarkand

By early May I was moving east from Bukhara through a land gentling into fertility, among villages of whitewashed clay, towards Samarkand. At last the deserts and plateaux which glare for a thousand miles east of the Caspian were falling away, and I was following a river basin towards the foothills of the Pamir. Behind me the Bukhara oasis paled into fields where the water sidled green along thinned canals. In scattered villages the only signs read 'Shop' or 'Baths' or 'Food' in the heartless Russian way. They looked like frontier-posts. Black cattle plodded across wastelands slung with pylons and telegraph poles. Once or twice the arch of a ruined mosque appeared, or a minaret stood in emptiness.

My bus crashed through the conurbation of Navoi. Hot-water pipes swarmed across its scrub, and its rundown factories throbbed and retched unabashed, as if still trumpeting Socialism. The effluent that had poisoned children, orchards and livestock all over the republic, and filled its water with sulphates and aluminium waste, blackened the sky from an antiquated sprawl of chemical plants and power stations. The air reeked.

The next moment we were out in the bleakness of cotton-fields, but now tractors were trawling them in plumes of dust, and there unwound along the road a feel of leisured and untidy life. Orchards thickened. Under wind-breaking belts of trees the banks had turned green, and cows were grazing in the ditches. The horizon ahead of us hoisted faint, sky-coloured hills.

'You be careful in Samarkand,' said the man beside me.

'Bukhara's a quiet town, but they're violent in Samarkand. They all live on the black market.' He was old and he came, of course, from Bukhara. 'Everything's getting worse. Our people are changing. Young people don't work any more, and nobody can afford anything. You watch out ....'

On my other side a Russian geologist was making for Tashkent with his two children. Among these dark people his blondness turned him raw and guileless. His upper lip let fall a Viking moustache. For years he had worked excavating gas in the south, he said, and his Uzbek friends had begged him to stay. But the future was too uncertain, and he was heading for the Ukraine. 'I've never been out of Central Asia before.' He was gazing at it through the window in passionless farewell. His children lay against him, fair and sleepy, with bubblegum dry on their mouths. 'My wife's Ukrainian, and I'll work there as a labourer, just to stay alive. I'll build a house, and give my boys a future.'

Around us the hills were starting to squeeze the valley, while a sharp wind curdled the unsown fields. We were following the arc of a river which trickled down from its high glacier in the western Pamir. The flecks of gold which sparkle uselessly in its water lent it the name Zerafshan, 'the gold-strewer', and even the ancient Greeks knew it as Polytimetus, 'very precious'. A hundred years ago, travellers described orchards blossoming all along its course: almond, peach, blue plum, cherry, fig and apple, and the finest apricots and nectarines in Asia.

Now the trees were split by vast cotton-fields, and the river meandered through its shallows to our north, depleted by irrigation-canals. Sometimes last year's cotton harvest still bulged in hills above the yards of collective farms. It had been the hope and bane of the whole country: cotton. A hundred years ago the Russians introduced an American species, and the Soviets rushed into its expansion, increasing the yield per acre by almost two-thirds. They became the largest cotton producer in the world. Moscow bought it cheap and raw from Central Asia, and turned it into clothes.

144

Under Brezhnev, who rose to the presidency from his power-base here, the corruption of local officials grew outlandish. The routine inflation of statistics, and the diversion of cotton on to the black market, poured subsidies into the lap of the Uzbek supremo Rashidov. Some of his henchmen ruled like feudal lords, with their own estates, prisons and concubines. The mafia embezzled more than five thousand million pounds in fifteen years. Only after Brezhnev's death did a spy satellite by chance photograph vacant fields where cotton should have been, and the more flagrant mafiosi were brought to trial in a welter of executions, suicides and imprisonments.

Meanwhile, the cotton itself was failing. Deep-rooted and thirsty, it was leaching the soil and the rivers, and growing feebler. Defoliants and pesticides were spreading disease among the harvesters: cancers, anaemia and hepatitis. Infant mortality rose. Only now, gradually, were people starting to talk of imposing limits and diversifying crops.

'Rashidov's still a hero to these people,' the Russian said. 'He cheated Moscow. He even built football stadiums with some of the money. They love that.'

*

'Samarkand' conjures no earthly city. It is a heart-stealing sound. Other capitals of Islam – Cairo, Damascus, Istanbul – glow with an accessible, Mediterranean magnificence. But Samarkand inhabits only the edge of geography. It rings with a landlocked strangeness, and was the seat of an empire so remote in its steppe and desert that it only touched Europe to terrify it. For centuries after it slept under obscurity, it shimmered in people's imagination. It was the fantasy of Goethe and Handel, Marlowe and Keats, yet its reality was out of reach. Even in the famous verse of the diplomat-poet Flecker, who travelled no farther east than Syria, its merchants took the golden road as if to a perilous mystery.

Over an ocean of fields and half-connected townlets, my bus made landfall at last in a nondescript depot, but I glimpsed to the east the surge and glitter of another city, circled by snow-lit mountains. For the last few miles I approached it sentimentally, on foot. I went through motley suburbs and an upthrust of flat-blocks and public buildings. A mountainous statue of Lenin was in place in a jaded square, where the slogans still bleated unread from the rooftops: 'The affairs of the world are in the hands of the people.'

From these surburban heights there opened below me a flotsam of red and grey rooftops – tin and asbestos wreckage floating on a swell of trees – studded with turquoise domes and minarets. Beyond them a long spine of snow-peaks glimmered with an unearthly radiance, and seemed to mark some ancient protection.

I went down through lorry-clogged streets. The way became sordid and ramshackle. A new harshness was in the air. An old man was praying among rose-beds on a traffic island, but had forgotten the direction of Mecca. Then, rounding a corner where buses clamoured under a flyover, I saw above me a sheaf of shattered domes and pinnacles. It started up in intermingling fawns and blues, as if a whole secret city had died within the modern one. Even in decay, it was huger than anything around it. The stubs of its entrance-gate and spring of broken arches hung above the lower town as if in another ether. It was the mosque of Bibi Khanum, built by Tamerlane the Great.

I circled it in purposeful delay, past big, dim shops down avenues of plane and chestnut trees. The people looked rougher, more secular, than in Bukhara. The city was more expansive, less uniform. The wreckage of its past hovered close against its present. While Bukhara had been a warren of obscurantism, Samarkand still owned the ghostly structures of an imperial capital.

Round its old market square, the Registan, three medresehs ranked in near-perfect symmetry. It was almost deserted. Once the centre of the world, it was now the centre of nothing. Even foreign sightseers had gone. Over the bare flagstones where I went, its enclosing majesty broke like a flood. In each of the

146

three façades, a mammoth *iwan* made a gulf of shadow, and was flanked by walls tiered with shallow bays. Gate for gate, minaret for minaret, they echoed and confirmed one another. They overbore the square with an institutional solemnity, sureties of royal power and the immutability of God. To the Western eye the minarets, whose flattened tops were under-hung with honeycomb decoration, conjured stout Corinthian columns supporting nothing. Earthquake had set them leaning with a crazed, plastic ease, which had teased nineteenth-century travellers into theorising and dropping plumb-lines from them, and never quite believing it.

The tilework of their façades does not drench the eye in a faience curtain like the mosques of contemporary Persia, but splashes the brick with cool, rather cerebral designs. The colours were familiar: grape blue, turquoise, wax yellow. The buff brick interknit and sobered them. Only here and there did a ceramic frieze blaze out complete. Beneath the entrance to the fifteenth-century Ulug Beg medreseh, the oldest of the three, some of the panels resembled lustrous carpets, and across the *iwan* of the seventeenth-century Shir Dar a pair of heretical lions chased white does across a field of flowers.

The doors still swung over polished thresholds, but when I entered the courts the only noise was birdsong. In the arcades the student cells had been locked behind their doors for decades. Some peasant women were wandering bemused over the flagstones. They followed me listlessly about. For religious students the treasures of these courts must have been the beautiful ribbons of Arabic script – always pure white against peacock blue – which overswept the arches of the *iwans* or rippled beneath their vaults. But I could not read them. Their Kufic epigraphy seemed locked away in some exquisite battle with itself.

Yet it is in these courtyards, too, that the illusion of the square evaporates. Here, suddenly, I was backstage. The grandiloquent façades, I now saw, were little more than that: an overbearing theatre-set. They had no depth. Their backs were only lightly decorated, or not at all. Their duty was over. These were not shapes to be viewed in the round, but bullying stage-flats which loomed over the square below in heady propaganda.

Some deadness of restoration, too, shadows all this with emptiness. The Soviets found the Registan collapsing, and began to repair it with the same diligence as they bestowed on their czarist palaces in the west. Here a dome was reconstructed wholesale, there a minaret jacked upright; while over every dilapidated surface swept a meticulous veneer of new tiles and bricks. The interior of the central mosque, in particular, is mesmerising. From the centre of its ceiling, in spectacular *trompe l'oeil*, a shower of gilded leaves and flowers radiates down a dark blue sky, while the vault above the *mihrab* unfurls a fan of stalactites in coral and gold.

Only when I entered the medreseh of Ulug Beg did I realise what had been lost. He was the most attractive of the grandsons of Tamerlane, a scientist and astronomer who urged his pupils into secular learning. Here, in a courtyard more intimate than the others, the original decoration was still in place. It kept a subtle, broken beauty. The jigsaw of its tiles was shedding pieces everywhere, fragments easing loose from their ornamental whole, petals dropping, tendrils breaking. But for the moment it was suspended in a sweet opulence of decay. Its threatened restoration was necessary, of course; but something vital would disappear for ever. These bricks and tiles betrayed by their ageing that they belonged to the first creation: to the piety and flare of their conceivers, not to the duty of a later time. They belonged with the past. Even if the restoration were identical (and some of it is suspect) its purposes would be modern, and would leave the imagination cold.

I wondered what would happen now that Soviet rule had ended. Such mammoth reconstructions would perhaps stop, or go forward more cautiously, piecemeal. I sat for a while under the arcades, and thought ungratefully of this, while the birds were screaming in the courtyard trees, and the tiles silently, unnoticeably, were easing from their plaster and dropping into dust.

*

Inflation and instability were on everybody's lips. Everyone feared the future. In the streets the drab men and high-coloured women coalesced into crowds which consorted only asexually, men with men in shoulder-hugging embraces, women sauntering together with linked arms. Tajik-speakers, their faces yet showed every permutation between the Turanian and Iranian worlds; blunt features and eagle features, full mouths and tight.

In the government emporia, where bags of rusks, noodles and bottled fruit were stacked, almost nobody lingered. Everywhere, free markets were stirring. Yet even in the central bazaar there was no bustle, but a cautious, ambling passage in which an hour might pass in the purchase of a few carrots. It was oddly quiet. Farmers heaped their rented stalls with pomegranates, radishes, mounds of liquid cheese. But nobody had any money, and every quoted price elicited hissing and upturned noses. In the courtyard stood a blank-faced giant with a Chaplin moustache. Stripping his shirt from a massive beer-gut, he lay down sacrificially under a pair of planks while a bus drove over him, then got up again, still expressionless, and circulated a money-can.

He was fuller employed than many. The pavements were dark with knots of loitering youths. They were the new unemployed, and there were over a million of them in the country. They wore T-shirts inscribed 'New York' or 'Chanel'. If I were carrying my rucksack, they would eye it like psychopaths. They thought I was Estonian. 'Didn't you bring anything to sell?' they demanded. They tried to work me out. 'Why are you here?' If I were seated somewhere, one of them would be sure to perch beside me like a shrike and nudge my knee or jolt my shoulder with every question, as if I had to be tormented into answering.

'Where do you come from?'

Wearily: 'Britain.'

'How is your life there? Do you get plenty to eat?'

'Yes.' I would remember, as if down a long tunnel, a race obsessed with slimming and cholesterol.

'How much do you earn?' Prod. 'How much is meat?' Prod. 'How much is a car?' Bang on shoulder. 'Will you get me a visa to Britain? How much …? How much …?'

Affectionately I would recall the old men in mosque court-yards, who greeted one another with a sober hand on the heart, and with only dignified enquiry. Then I would remember remorsefully that these youths, with their lost past and precarious future, their restless eyes and talk of dollars, lived in a new void, and what did I expect of them? On and on the inquisitors would nag, while I halved or quartered my income and tried to explain a world of tax and mortgage. But nothing stopped them. My prodded knee would become psychosomatically inflamed. So would my temper. And however shrivelled my earnings or qualified my answers, this dialogue always left cupidity glittering in the hard young eyes.

'They don't believe in working. They don't produce. They just buy and sell things.' The stale complaint slurred on the Russian's lips. He was peering at the announcement of a dog auction to be held in the Spartak football stadium. 'And they're getting more nationalistic by the minute. But how do you leave here?' He gazed at me with the smeared eyes of the perpetually drunk, and the uninvited monologue. His fingers were ochreous with nicotine. 'I've been here all my life. My father was killed in the battles round Smolensk during the war, and this is my mother ….' She was staring vacantly at the market. 'She's never known anywhere but here. We've nowhere to go in Russia. Her and me, it's too late for us …. I haven't enough left.' His orange finger-tips trailed over the notice. 'We'll die here.'

The old woman shuffled up beside us, her face withdrawn inside a tattered shawl. 'What are you saying?' she piped. 'What's happening?'

'We're talking about the dog auction.' She drifted away again. 'Look at her. She's already ending her days. But what do we do? We have no homeland now.'

So he was buying a dog.

Watching his creased face, I realised how deeply my concept of the Russians had changed. Suddenly everything which they had achieved here – in education, welfare, administration, however corrupt and limited – was threatening to collapse. The old, bullying propaganda – the Marxist invocations to work and unity – all at once looked like benign common sense, a plea for the future. The familiar certainties were in retreat. Russian arts – literature, music, ballet – which had once seemed the treacherous tools of colonialism, now resembled instead the rearguard of a gracious civilisation, fading away before my eyes.

Even the Soviet sops to local custom had changed. Not a moment ago, it seemed, the oriental street-lamps, the tulip domes above restaurants and police-posts – even the mock-Islamic latticework in the tourist hotels – had sent up a sinister smokescreen behind which a people's heart was being stolen away. Now, instead, these *kitsch* concessions seemed innocently integral to local life, like a lifted curse.

Only plastic tiles coated my restaurant, whose floor was littered with crusts and fish-bones. Beggars limped from table to table. They had torn coats and split boots. They hovered above the tables as if no one was sitting there, picking at the customers' bread and drinking their tea, while the conversation went on obliviously below. As I left, one of them shambled over to my place and emptied my bowl of its mutton-bones.

I went out into the ruins of the Bibi Khanum, feeling an obscure self-reproach. Even in desolation the mosque seemed to tower out of an era more fortunate than my own (but this was an illusion). Tamerlane had built it as the greatest temple in Islam. Thousands of captured artisans from Persia, Iraq and Azerbaijan had laboured to carve its marble floors, glaze its acres of tiles, erect its monster towers and the four hundred cupolas bubbling over its galleries. The emperor flailed its building forward. He considered too small the gateway completed in his absence, pulled it down wholesale, hanged its architects and began again. But the mountainous vaults and minarets which he envisioned crushed the foundations, and the walls started to fracture almost before completion. People became afraid to pray there. It towered above me in a megalomaniac reverie, raining the sky with blistered arches and severed domes. Cracks pitched and zigzagged down the walls. Tiles flaked off like skin. The gateway loomed so high that the spring of its vanished arch began eighty feet above me, and completed itself phantasmally in empty air. Gaping breaches had split the prayer-hall top to bottom, and the squinches were shedding whole bricks.

Everything – the thunderous minarets, the thirty-foot doors, the outsize ablutions basin – shrunk the visitor to a Lilliputian intruder, and peopled the mosque with giants. In the court's centre a megalithic lectern of grey Mongolian marble had once cradled a gargantuan Koran, but its indestructability, and per-haps its isolation in the mosque's wrecked heart, had touched it with pagan mana now, and it had become the haunt of barren women, who crouched beneath it as a charm for fertility.

As I sat nearby, three young worldlings, urban and confident in high heels and tight skirts, went giggling and nudging towards it. Their shrieks rang in the ruins. Then, separately, they dropped on all fours and crawled in and out between the lectern's nine marble legs. At first they ridiculed one another at this place where fun and superstition merged. But once unseen by their companions, creeping through the marble labyrinth, an unease descended. Covertly they touched their palms to its stone. One of them kissed it. Then they emerged, straightening their stockings, and tripped away.

*

Sitting by a mosque under silver poplars, Tania had inherited the gross, maternal look of Russian peasant women in poor lands. Her ginger hair dangled corkscrews round a slovenly, vegetable face, whose nose and eyes had capsized in the fatness of her cheeks. We had fallen into conversation by chance, and only as we walked together under the trees did she start to surprise me. She pointed out the grave of a Naqshbandi statesman, which stood still honoured on its mound. It was unlike a Russian to know this history, and I glanced at her in puzzlement. 'I'm mar-ried to a Moslem,' she said.

She looked so rooted in the earth of her own people that I

152

blurted out: 'Isn't that difficult?'

'It's always difficult.' She stopped and contemplated the calligraphy on the gravestone, as if it might yield a solution. 'Moslem men are more patriarchal than us. But I don't fight with mine. He manages the money, I manage the house. But he's a wonderful cook!' She gave a hoarse, burbling laugh. 'Yes, I boss him a bit. I've stayed independent. That's why I understand my cat.'

She started to walk again, wavering fatly on her high heels. Her body conveyed a torpid, Russian strength. Her marriage was obsessing her at present, she said, because her husband was not happy. He could not relinquish his past, the memory of his first wife, who'd been a harpy. 'After she left him he sat five years alone, sulking and drinking, and he's still affected by her. He can't deny their daughters a thing.' Her face puckered in revulsion. 'They're our chief source of argument, those daughters.' She splayed out her fingers, which were stubbled in garish rings. 'And there's the cat. We argue about that. He can't accept that animals are really humans, which of course they are.' She sighed unlaughing. 'A Moslem, you see.'

I could salvage no insight from this rush of detail.

'I know other Russian women married to Tajiks and Uzbeks,' she went on, 'but each one is different. Even the prejudice. Some of my husband's family feel so violent that they can hardly bring themselves to see me. But others have been kind. There's no pattern to it.' Yet her voice was tinged with recklessness. I realised there was something I did not understand at all. 'It's hard for any Moslem's wife. But sometimes the men may start to recognise a Russian woman's intelligence. Native women are often lazy. They just sit and gossip while their children run wild. They can prepare meals, of course, but often they can't even sew. No wonder Moslems need several wives.' She was striding beside me now, with colonial self-confidence. 'Yes, I know Tajiks who keep more than one wife – they celebrate second or even third marriages in secret with some mullah. It's hard on everyone.'

We had reached a side-gate of the mosque, whose guardian

recognised her. He said quaintly: 'Guests and good men are always welcome here,' and we entered a courtyard murmuring with old men in blue turbans who leant on their sticks under the trees and dozed or hobnobbed on weathered benches. A balm of companionship filled the air, of past ways returning.

'I wanted you to see this,' Tania said. She spoke a halting Tajik with the mosque officials. They asked her where we came from, and looked pleased. Islam had always been tolerant in Central Asia, she said, without accuracy, but I knew what she meant. She did not fear religion, but politics. 'It's the politicians manipulating for their own ends – that's what frightens me. Clans. We're overrun by cliques like extended families.' Their rivalries and subterfuge crept up to the highest levels of government, I knew, and created a delicate power-axis between Samarkand, Tashkent and the Fergana valley. The country's apparent unity splintered apart as you thought about it.

'But young people sometimes talk as if they had a nation now,' she said. 'They talk of being Uzbeks or Tajiks. It never used to be like that.'

'You think they feel it?'

'I don't know, I don't know.' She sounded suddenly harrowed. Some distress welled up in her whenever we touched on the future. Perhaps the old concept of a family of peoples, with Russia at its helm, was too painfully entrenched in her emotions.

We went back past a medreseh, and peered in. It was the largest in the city, but it seemed deserted. The student cells were locked, and pigeons massed undisturbed under the porticoes. No caretaker emerged to greet or deflect us.

Only days later did I learn the reason. According to hearsay, one of the clerics had raped a pupil. While news of this whispered through the city, the boy's relatives had assembled to tear the man to bits. But instead, after negotiations with him, they had watched while he hanged himself.

Unknowing, Tania and I walked in bewilderment through the school's silence. 'You will come and visit me soon?' she asked. Her high heels rang on the cobblestones. 'Yes. Come to us.'

The north-east suburbs break against a grassy plateau which undulates for miles. Colonies of ground squirrels stand sentinel at their burrows, and a shepherd drives his black flock over the cemetery-like ground with sharp cries. Its abrupt banks and mounds betray an earlier Samarkand decaying into the grassland. The earth seems to writhe underfoot. Sometimes it splits open on abandoned excavations. The glittering mountains stare in. Wherever the bricks rise exposed, their tamped clay has reverted to earth. The walls have become natural cliffs whose fissures had once been gates, and the ground is ripped by gullies where streets had gone, or tossed into shapeless citadels.

From the sixth century BC this ancient Samarkand, named Maracanda, was the capital of a refined Iranian people, the Sogdians, who traded along the Zerafshan valley and beyond. Alexander took the city in 329 BC, and here, in a fit of drunken hubris, transfixed his favourite general 'Black' Cleitus with a spear. But the Sogdians outlasted the fragile dynasty of Alexander's followers. Famous for their literacy and commercial cunning, it was they, perhaps, who taught the Chinese the art of glassmaking. The Romans reported that their city walls ran seven miles in circuit, and they endured here until the Arabs conquered them in 712. Then, little by little, they dwindled away, until Genghiz Khan wrecked Maracanda in 1220, and put the past to sleep under the loam-filled earth. Later peoples named the site from the Giant Afrasiab, a mythic king of Turan: after failing to take Maracanda by assault, they said, he had buried it in the sand.

In a museum nearby, the Sogdians falter back to life. Russian archaeologists pulled their corroded swords out of the compacted dust, their bangles, their buttons and bone clothes-pins. They seem to have worshipped early Persian gods, at a time of resurgent Buddhism. Monolithic altars and carved ossuaries emerged, and some precious fragments of seventh-century fresco, in which the Sogdian king (if it is he) receives embassies

155

from as far away as Tang dynasty China.

They advance to meet him against a hyacinth-blue field in cavalcades of dignitaries mounted on dromedaries, horses and elephants. In airy perspective they ride harmlessly above or beneath one another, but the plaster has dropped from them in obliterating grey flakes, as if they processed through storm-clouds. The lumber of elephants' feet and the prance of hooves emerge fitfully out of the decay, while a file of egrets parades inexplicably behind. The Chinese tribute-bearers carry goblets and wands in a humbled cluster of girlish eyes and close-plastered hair, and their starched dresses, embroidered with wolves' heads, seem to have hypnotised the painter. The king, meanwhile, walks forward to honour the image of his people's god. His prodigiously pearled robes woven into lozenges, his dripping ear-pendants, his soft, jewelled headdress and the necklace which dribbles nervously from his fingers, invest his kingdom with an effete strangeness. Yet his subjects' slender noses and delicate hands may have left behind their shadow in today's Tajik people.

I stumbled all afternoon over the indecipherable city, and emerged at evening by a tributary of the Zerafshan. Perched almost inaccessibly above it, under five grassy domes, was a half-forgotten tomb. An aged caretaker, slumbering nearby, opened its door in mumbled confusion, and there burgeoned before me into the gloom a monstrous mound. 'This is the tomb of the prophet Daniel,' he said. Tamerlane, he added, had brought him here from Mecca.

Like the graves of other half-legendary figures revered by the Moslems – the tombs of Noah and Nimrod in Lebanon, the sepulchre of Abel near Damascus – it was built for a titan. Local people had believed that Daniel went on growing even after death, and they lengthened his grave every year until it stretched over sixty feet. Through the decades of Russian persecution it had been silently remembered. Its walls were still black with candle-flames.

I must have cut a weary figure as I trudged back along the

road to Samarkand, because after a while a young Tajik in a clattering Moskvich offered me a lift. Shavgat was returning from a three-week job as a driver, and invited me home to meet his little son and old father. He was handsome in a slender, Iranian mould. Alert, candid eyes gleamed in a long head smoothed by jet-black hair. But an Islamic maleness overbore his home. He had been away three weeks, but when his young wife came to the door – a wide-eyed girl who was not quite pretty – he extended no greeting to her, only ordered her to hurry up a meal. I never saw them exchange an intimate word. Yet she was smiling and proud; for she had borne him a son.

They lived in a traditional suburb, and made me welcome. I was growing used to these compounds now, whose gates clanged open on to a family courtyard where the father and his married sons each owned a stuccoed cottage, and gardens of roses and vegetables straggled in common. Inside, the walls and ceilings were painted in pale flower-patterns, and the crimson silks of newlyweds still flamed round the doors. The bride's dowry was piled up inside cupboards and cabinets in mountainous quilts – fifty or sixty of them – and pyramids of unused tea-services. Dangling above one wall, two roundels of hardened bread – a mouthful bitten out of each – had been preserved from the farewell meal for Shavgat's younger brother, who was serving as a soldier in Poland, and they would not be touched again until he returned.

Shyly Shavgat's wife carried in their infant son for my approval. A canary stuck like a toy to her shoulder. The baby clutched a papier-mâché dog sprinkled with glitter-dust. With them came Shavgat's sister-in-law, a tallow-haired Russian girl dressed in native gown and silk pantaloons. They clothed her like a submission. She was pregnant, yearning for a son of her own. But the flamboyant dress only threw into crueller relief the sallow plainness of her face. She looked slightly bitter. I longed to ask her about her situation – questions which had eluded me with Tania – but it would only have been possible alone, and soon Shavgat was parading the baby in his arms.

157

'Does he look like me?' he demanded. 'Does he? Does he?' I hunted in the tiny face for any resemblance, but it only reflected – as in some simplified cartoon – the wide gaze and cusped mouth of the mother. She might have produced him alone, by parthenogenesis. 'Tell me. Does he look like me?'

But the moment was saved by Shavgat's father, a gross, wily-faced peasant. He seized his grandson – the family obsession – and dandled him ferociously on his shoulder, while the child screamed and plucked at his Brezhnev eyebrows. The old man sobered only to pour scorn on modern times. 'Everything's terrible now. In Rashidov's day the shops were full and everything was cheap!' He flung his arm across their supper-table. 'This would have been covered then. Covered! Meat was only three roubles a kilo, and now it's ninety. And vodka, three roubles a bottle. Now it's a hundred!'

Their luxuries in these bare rooms were few and cherished. A cage-full of canaries fluttered and sang; a little stock of Marlboro cigarettes collected in a niche; and before sleep Shavgat rubbed hand-cream delicately into his palms, as if it were magic. We slept under quilts along the floor, he with his hands folded carefully over his stomach, while his wife went into the bedroom, her hair released down her back. The canaries fidgeted to a standstill, then never stirred all night, as if stuffed.

In the silence I asked about the photograph of a woman hung in honour on the wall above us. A weak bulb dangling over the door lit up an unreadable sepia face. 'That's my mother,' Shavgat said. 'She and my father have been separated many years.' His voice fell away. 'Yes, it's unusual with us Tajiks. But she's a fine woman.' He said nothing more, except that she was living in Chimkent – a beautiful town, where he sometimes visited her – and that she had never married again.

*

For two thousand years Central Asia was the womb of terror, where an implacable queue of barbarian races waited to impel one another into history. Whatever spurred their grim waves –

158

the deepening erosion of their pasturelands or their seasons of fleeting unity – they bore the same stamp of phantom mobility and mercilessness.

Two and a half millennia ago the shadowy Scythians of Herodotus – Aryan savages whose country was the horse – simmered just beyond the reach of civilisation, like a ghastly protoplasm of all that was to come. Then the Huns flooded over the shattered Roman Empire in a ravening swarm – fetid men clothed in whatever they had slaughtered, even the sewn skins of fieldmice – and they did not stop until they had reached Orleans, and their rude king Attila had died in unseasonable bridebed, and their kingdom flew to pieces. But the Avars followed them – long-haired centaurs who rocked Constantinople and were eventually obliterated by Charlemagne at the dawn of the ninth century. Soon afterwards an enfeebled Byzantium let in the Magyars, and the fearsome Pechenegs rushed in after – Turanian peoples, all of them, who evaporated at last in the gloomy European forests, or settled to become Christian on the Great Hungarian Plain.

Then, at the start of the thirteenth century, as Christian Europe ripened and Islamic Asia flourished, the dread steppeland unleashed its last holocaust in the Mongols. This was not the random flood of popular imagination, but the assault of a disciplined war-machine perfected by the genius of Genghiz Khan. Unpredictable as a dust-storm, its atrocious cavalry – neckless warriors with dangling moustaches – could advance at seventy miles a day, enduring any hardship. Only their stench, it was said, gave warning of their coming. In extremes, they drank from the jugulars of their horses and ate the flesh of wolves or humans. Yet they were armoured in habergeons of iron or laminated leather scales, and they could fire their steel-tipped arrows with magic accuracy over more than two hundred yards at full gallop. Consummate tacticians and scouts, they soon carried in their wake siege-engines and flame-throwers, and around their nucleus of ethnic Mongols rode a formidable mass of Turkic auxiliaries.

159

By Genghiz Khan's death their empire unfurled from Poland to the China Sea. Within a few years his sons and grandsons came within sight of Vienna, laid waste Burma and Korea, and sailed, disastrously, for Japan. Meanwhile, in their Central Asian heartland, the *Pax Mongolica* was instilling administrative discipline, commercial recovery, and a frightened peace.

Tamerlane, the Earth-Shaker, was the last, and perhaps most awesome, of these world predators. Born in 1336 fifty miles south of Samarkand, he was the son of a petty chief in a settled Mongol clan. He acquired the name 'Timur-i-Leng' or 'Timur the Lame' after arrows maimed his right leg and arm, and passed as Tamerlane into the fearful imagination of the West. By his early thirties, after years of fighting over the splintered heritage of Genghiz Khan, he had become lord of Mavarannah, the 'Land beyond the River', with his capital at Samarkand, and had turned his cold eyes to the conquest of the world.

From the accounts that are left of him, he emerges not only as the culmination of his pitiless forerunners, but as the distant ancestor of the art-loving Moghals of India. Over the terrified servants and awed ambassadors at his court, his eyes seemed to burn without brilliance, and never winced with either humour or sadness. But a passion for practical truth fed his unlettered intelligence. He planned his campaigns in scrupulous detail, and unlike Genghiz Khan he led them in person. He clothed his every move with the sanction of the Islamic faith, but astrology and omens, shamanism and public prayers, were all invoked to serve his needs. An angel, it was rumoured, told him men's hidden thoughts. Yet he assaulted Moslems as violently as he did Christians and Hindus. Perhaps he confused himself with God.

No flicker of compassion marred his progress. His butchery surpassed that of any before him. The towers and pyramids of skulls he left behind – ninety thousand in the ruins of Baghdad alone – were calculated warnings. After overrunning Persia and despoiling the Caucasus, he hacked back the remnants of the Golden Horde to Moscow, then launched a precipitate attack on

India, winching his horses over the snowbound ravines of the Hindu Kush, where 20,000 Mongols froze to death. On the Ganges plain before Delhi, the Indian sultan's squadrons of mailed elephants, their tusks lashed with poisoned blades, sent a momentary tremor through the Mongol ranks; but the great beasts were routed, and the city and all its inhabitants levelled with the earth. A year later the Mongols were wending back over the mountains, leading 10,000 pack-mules sagging with gold and jewels. They left behind a land which would not recover for a century, and five million Indian dead.

Now Tamerlane turned his attention west again. Baghdad, Aleppo, Damascus fell. In 1402, on the field of Ankara, at the summit of his power, he decimated the army of the Ottoman sultan Beyazid, and inadvertently delayed the fall of Constantinople by another half century.

Between these monotonous acts of devastation, the conqueror returned to the Samarkand he cherished. At his direction a procession of captured scholars, theologians, musicians and craftsmen arrived in the capital with their books and tools and families – so many that they were forced to inhabit caves and orchards in the suburbs. Under their hands the mud city bloomed into faience life. Architects, painters and calligraphers from Persia; Syrian silk-weavers, armourers and glass-blowers; Indian jewellers and workers in stucco and metal; gunsmiths and artillery engineers from Asia Minor: all laboured to raise titanic mosques and academies, arsenals, libraries, vaulted and fountained bazaars, even an observatory and a menagerie. The captured elephants lugged into place the marble of Tabriz and the Caucasus, while rival emirs – sometimes Tamerlane himself – drove on the work with the parvenu impatience of shepherd-princes. The whole city, it seems, was to be an act of imperial power. Villages were built around it named Cairo, Baghdad, Shiraz or Damascus (a ghostly Paris survives) in token of their insignificance. It was the 'Mirror of the World', and the premier city of Asia.

Tamerlane himself confounds simple assessment. He kept a

private art collection, whose exquisitely illuminated manuscripts he loved but could not read. His speech, it seems, was puritan in its decorum. He was an ingenious and addicted chess-player, who elaborated the game by doubling its pieces – with two giraffes, two war-engines, a vizier and others – over a board of 110 squares. A craving for knowledge plunged him into hard, questing debates with scholars and scientists, whom he took with him even on campaign, and his quick grasp and powerful memory gave him a working knowledge of history, medicine, mathematics and astronomy.

Yet at heart he was a nomad. He moved between summer and winter pastures with his whole court and horde. Even at Samarkand he usually pavilioned in the outskirts, or in one of the sixteen gardens he spread round the city: watered parks with ringing names. Each garden was different. In one stood a porcelain Chinese palace; another glowed with the saga of his reign in lifelike frescoes, all long vanished; yet another was so vast that when a workman lost his horse there it grazed unfound for six months.

In such playgrounds were held the *fêtes champêtres* witnessed by the Castilian envoy Ruy Gonzalez de Clavijo. At the wedding of six royal princes (including the eleven-year-old Ulug Beg) he described how 20,000 tents covered the meadows near Samarkand for a month. The central pavilion alone accommodated 10,000 guests. Its forty-foot mountain of silk cascaded from a dome woven with eagles, billowed down above 500 vermilion guy-ropes, then reared up again to turrets crested with silk battlements. In the banqueting tents a gluttonous feasting and drinking took hold. Enormous leather platters were dragged in, heaped with sheep's heads, horse-croupes and tripe in balls the size of a man's fist. After one such feast came a ceremonial presentation of gifts, and Clavijo writes with pride that his Spanish tapestries were outshone only by the Egyptian delegation's presentation of nine ostriches and a giraffe. The city's guilds threw themselves into sumptuous displays of ingenuity. The linen-weavers constructed an armoured horseman in pure linen, 'even to the nails and eyelids', while the cotton-workers erected a hundred-foot minaret in flax, crowned by a cotton stork. The butchers dressed up animals as humans; the furriers disguised humans as wild beasts.

But among the tents, in black warning, there dangled from gallows the bodies of the mayor of Samarkand and the emirs who had bungled the gateway of the Bibi Khanum mosque, with the corpses of merchants who had overpriced their wares.

At last, as the autumn nights darkened towards winter, Tamerlane ordered the tents rolled up and turned his ageing eyes towards the richest quarry remaining: China. With an army quarter of a million strong, he marched north towards the Jaxartes valley, planning to strike east with the first hint of spring. But the winter was the coldest in memory. The rivers froze and blizzards howled out of Siberia. Men, horses, camels, elephants struggled through deepening drifts. 'Seared by the cold,' wrote Tamerlane's Arab biographer, 'men's noses and ears fell off. They froze to death as they rode .... Yet Tamerlane cared not for their dying, nor grieved for those who had fallen.'

Soon after they reached their base-camp, the emperor fell into a shivering sickness. Wine laced with spices and hot drugs had no effect, so his doctors laid ice-packs on his chest and head, until he coughed up blood. Then they despaired. 'We know of no cure for death,' they said. Towards nightfall, while a thunderstorm raged outside, Tamerlane called together his family and emirs, and appointed his successor. Then to the sound of imams' chanting in the neighbouring room, and the crashing of the tempest, the monster died.

He was buried in Samarkand in the mausoleum which he had prepared for his favourite grandson, dead of wounds two years before. The college and hospice which once enclosed it have been effaced by earthquake, and it rises alone among alleys intimate with mulberry trees, whose fruit crunched underfoot at my approach. Its courtyard gate stood up in fragile solitude. Ruins made a phantom geometry inside. Amongst them a marble platform, carved with flower-tendrils, had been the coronation-stone of the emirs of Bukhara.

But beyond this, above a façade to which broken minarets and a few tiles stuck, a ribbed dome swelled like the calyx of an unearthly flower. Chance had stripped bare everything around it, so that it floated pure above a high drum, on which 'God is Immortal' blazed in white Kufic letters as tall as a man. Above this, a belt of recessed corbels lifted the dome through its faint but seductive swelling towards the elliptic. It was a dome peculiar to Central Asia, grooved like a cantaloup melon. Up each of its faience ribs, against an aquamarine field, went diamond lozenges in lapis blue. I had seen it in picture books as a child, redolent of desert farness.

I crossed the courtyard and found myself in a bare passageway. At its end, on either side of a low door, hung a broken Kufic frieze, huge, as if displaced from somewhere else. 'This is the resting place of the Illustrious and Merciful Monarch, the Magnificent Sultan, the most Mighty Warrior, Emir Timur Kurgan, Conqueror of all the Earth' ran the original inscription; but it had gone.

I peered through the doors and into the chamber. The latticed windows let in diffused sunbeams. High above me, across the whole summit of the dome, fanned a net of gilded stucco, which twined upon itself in mathematic delicacy. It dropped its golden creepers over the enormous spandrels, bays and pendentives, and shed a soft blaze of light on to everything below. Beneath it the walls were coated in alabaster – hexagonal tiles, still translucent – and circled by a jasper frieze carved with the deeds and genealogy of the emperor. Beneath this again, within the low balustrade at my feet, the cenotaphs of his family lay side by side in rectangular blocks of marble and alabaster. And at the centre, stark among their pallor, the grave of Tamerlane shone in a monolith of near-black jade. It was disconcertingly beautiful: the largest block of jade in the world. Its edges were lightly inscribed. A vertical split showed where Persian soldiers (it is thought) had hacked at it two and a half centuries before.

I stayed here a long time, at once moved and unsettled. A man entered and prayed for a while, then went away. The cries of children sounded faintly outside. Under the decorated brilliance of the cupola, the simplicity of these gravestones was dignified and rather terrible: a recognition of the littleness even of this man, and the passage of time. Beside him lay his gentle son Shah Rukh; at his head, his minister; under a bay, his sheikh. His grandson Ulug Beg was at his feet. Others were gathered round.

At last the young caretaker, pleased by my interest, ushered me out of the chamber and led me round the back of the mausoleum. He unlocked a tiny carved door. 'Here is the real grave,' he said.

I descended a steep, ramped passage beneath the building. In the blackness I sensed the sweep of vaults low overhead. Somewhere behind me, the man turned a switch, and a bare bulb made a pool of dimness in the crypt. Each cenotaph in the chamber above was mirrored in this darkness by a flat gravestone. They lay secret in their dust and silence. The air was dry and old. I knelt by the emperor's graveslab and touched it. Beneath, wrapped in linen embalmed in camphor and musk, his shrunken body had been laid in an ebony coffin. I could not imagine it. The living man was too vivid in my mind. For a year after his interment, it was said, people heard him howling from the earth.

In the dull light I saw that every inch of the marble slab seethed with carved Arabic, as if even the words were waging a battle across his stone. They traced his ancestry back through Genghiz Khan (a claim he never made in life) to the legendary virgin Alangoa, ravished by a moonbeam, and at last to Adam.

The stone was split clean across in two places; but when Soviet archaeologists opened it in 1941 they found undisturbed the skeleton of a powerful man, lame on his right side. Fragments of muscle and skin still clung to him, and scraps of a russet moustache and beard. An untraceable story warned that if Tamerlane's grave was violated, disaster would follow, and a few hours later news arrived that Hitler had invaded Russia.

But the investigations went on, and from the emperor's skull

165

the Soviet scientist Gerasimov painstakingly reconstructed a bronze portrait-head, before sealing Tamerlane back in the tomb. Under the sculptor's hands there emerged a face of hardened power, compassionless, bitter and subtle. Perhaps some Slavic prejudice heightened the epicanthic cruelty of the eyes; perhaps not. A hint of the emperor's youthful truculence tinges the full lips, but that is all. Cord-like ligaments scoop the cheeks into harrowed triangles. Ancient muscles knot the cheeks, and a heraldic flexion of the brows seems to signal the sack of a city.

'He was a hero,' said a voice behind me. I jumped. The caretaker had entered noiselessly and was looking down at the tumult of calligraphy on the slab. 'What a history!'

'Perhaps he should have done less,' I said.

'Less? No. Timur turned us into one country.' He seemed lighthearted, but a reticent evangelism tinged him. 'Yes, he was cruel, I know. People come to this grave from Iran and Afghanistan and they hate him. They say, "He destroyed our land, he enslaved us!" And of course it's true. He smashed Isfahan and Baghdad.' He smiled charmingly. 'He was ruthless.'

I said: 'Ulug Beg might be a better hero for your nation.' My eyes drifted affectionately over his graveslab. It was richly inscribed too.

The caretaker laughed. The sound made a soft insult in the silence. 'He was only a teacher.' He squatted beside me above the stones. 'But Timur was world-class! If I was an Iranian, I'd hate him too!' He was laughing at himself a little; after all, it was long ago. 'But Timur was not a savage. He knew about Alexander of Macedon, and the slave leader Spartacus and ....'

'Spartacus?' This was a Soviet cult leftover. 'Did he?'

'... and he'd read the great Persian poet Firdausi, who claimed that the Iranians were natural rulers and the Turks were natural slaves.' He cocked his head at the gravestone, as if trying to read that tremendous obituary. 'Our two worlds have always been at war. And when Timur overran Persia and came to Firdausi's tomb he shouted: "Stand up! Look at me! A Turk in the heart of your empire! You said we were slaves, but look now!"'

His words rang in the dark. We both fancied, I think, that the dead were listening. He glowed with vicarious triumph. Tamerlane for him was the unifier and recreator of his notional fatherland, of the Pan-Turkic dream. He said: 'The Persians were here once, you see. You've been to Afrasiab? You've seen those Sogdian paintings, Persian things? They were our conquerors.'

'Those paintings are extraordinary ....'

'So Timur avenged us. He created a Turkish empire!' His voice had whetted into a funeral oration. He had the northerner's scorn for the soft, dark people of the south. 'He's our hero.'

I said: 'But he was a Mongol.'

'No, Timur was not a Mongol, he was a Turk.'

I stayed silent. Everyone was claiming Tamerlane now. Uzbeks and even Tajiks whom I met would debonairly enrol him in their nations. In fact Tamerlane had been a pure Mongol of the Barlas clan, infected by Turkic customs. But this pedantry could not staunch the caretaker's sense of ownership or belonging.

'I may be an Uzbek,' he said, 'but above all I am a Turk. Most people have forgotten their tribes now, but I know my father was a Kungrat, my mother a Mangit – these are Turkic tribes.'

'They're Uzbek tribes too.'

'But you can't *feel* Uzbek.' He was losing the infant Uzbek nation in a Turkic sea. 'Look at our ancestors! We have Navoi, we have Mirkhwand, we have ....' His list spilt into the unknown for me. In fact his people were ethnically too complex to shelter under any name. Even his Turkic umbrella was full of Persian holes. The hero of Uzbek literature, the fifteenth-century Timurid poet Navoi, had written of Uzbeks only to disparage them. Yet his name and image were as ubiquitous in Uzbekistan as Makhtumkuli's in Turkmenistan. Young in their state, Uzbeks and Tajiks were suddenly annexing poets or scientists out of the past, steeping their nation in the magic of great men. The Tajiks were even appropriating Saadi and Omar Khayyám, any Persian at all. To challenge such claims was to wander an ethnic labyrinth until the concept of a country became meaningless.

The caretaker got to his feet, still reeling off names, and we started to return up the passageway. '... And we have Timur!'

He switched off the sad bulb and locked the narrow door behind us. In the sanity of daylight he relented a little. 'Well,' he said, 'occasionally somebody *does* feel quite strongly "I'm an Uzbek"' – he feebly thumped his chest – 'but you don't hear it much.'

We walked round the mausoleum in the sun. Some ease and lightness had returned to us. Uzbek independence had freed him into pride, he said, instead of condemning him to some Slavic sub-species. 'Of course I'm pleased by it. Everyone I know is pleased. You've found some not? Well, those are the uneducated.' He spoke the word without regret. 'Some people don't know what to feel. They can't see beyond their faces. They just know that things are bad now. But I'm thinking of my children, and the world they'll grow into. I want it to be their own.'

We stopped at the mouth of a shaft descending through grilles beneath the sanctuary. When I set my eye to it, I descried grey rectangles suspended far down in the blackness, and realised that I was gazing into the crypt. It was a vent for whispered prayers. I straightened and moved away, shaking off the notion that some dreadful authority lingered in those shreds of gristle and calcium under the stone.

The man went on eagerly: 'How can anyone regret the Soviet Union falling to bits? They bled us. In the old days they gave us five kopeks for a kilo of cotton. Just *five kopeks*. One factory in Russia used to make two shirts out of a kilo and sell them for *forty roubles* each. Moscow said we were partners, but what kind of partnership is that?' He clasped my hand in illustration. 'Partnership should mean friendship, shouldn't it?' We had circled the building now, and the handclasp turned into farewell. As I walked back across the courtyard, his shouted optimisms followed me to the gate. 'Enjoy our country! Everything will get better!'

Above him the great dome made a lonely tumour above the ogre-king.

168

To the White Palace

I wandered one Sunday morning among suburbs blooming with chestnut trees, where birds sang in the unaccustomed stillness. All around clustered those brick cottages which seem to cover the old Soviet empire in petrified log huts. It might have been a suburb of Novgorod or Oryol. But nobody was about. In front of me a brick cathedral thrust up its gaudy spire where the bells had hung silent for seventy years. In the aftermath of *perestroika* a few women in bedsocks and slippers were begging near the entrance, and now the belfry sent up a hesitant, rusty clanking.

Inside, where a congregation of a thousand might have worshipped, some eighty faithful stood in broken ranks. Old women cowled in headscarves, with a few children and lanky young men, they belonged in the Belorussian fields, not here in the heart of Asia. But they kissed and embraced each other as they ambled among the icons, and slowly a feel of family security brewed up. This, after all, was their transposed homeland: the mystical body of Christ, where the massed contingents of saints, Church fathers and attendant angels – the whole hierarchy of Orthodox holiness – mounted the walls and pillars in arcs of candle-flame. Across the iconostasis they unfurled their white wings and fingered blessings. St Basil the Great, St Nicholas, St Theodore, St George on his white charger – their Slavic eyes and brandished swords and books encircled the faithful with the comfort of an immemorial truth.

But my heart sank. The people looked beleaguered. Their singing quavered and whined in the void. A few acolytes in pale violet drifted back and forth like disconsolate angels, and in the balcony a little choir set up a shrill, heartbreaking chant, whose verses lifted and died away like an old, repeated grief. Beneath them, where a verse should have come, the people seemed to let out a deep, collective sigh. They had survived the blows of Communism only to face nationalism and Islam, and they seemed now as remote to this land as the time when their saints were flesh, and God was in the world.

Then the doors of the iconostasis burst open on a huge, gold-robed priest, who raised his arms in prayer. Where Western prelates beseech God with an alto sanctimoniousness, Russia turns out these booming giants who seem to understudy Him. The whole church at once filled up with a Chaliapin thunder, and the liturgy went forward in a deafening, homely pomp. As the incense spurted from the thurible, each sweep of the priest's arm could have felled a tree. The coals grated and the sweet smoke rose. A domestic balm descended on the worshippers. All was familiar, theirs, right. From time to time one of the old women would trundle away to kiss a saint or calm a baby or top up an oil lamp. But she would return to cross herself again and again, while the groves of candles blossomed beneath favourite icons.

Meanwhile the processions of the gold-embossed Gospel and the elevated Sacrament, swollen on the voice of the priest, brought on a fresh flurry of self-blessings, and at last the silver Eucharist spoon, dipped into the chalice beneath a scarlet napkin, administered the body and blood of Christ like a wholesome medicine. Even I felt a sense of remission. For this hour, at least, all seemed well among the dwindling faithful, as they and the priest and the dim-lit saints watched and nurtured one another into the unknown future.

It was Tania, married to a Moslem, who had told me about the cathedral, where she sometimes prayed alone. I had kept her address in my pocket for days, but now I pulled it out and it pointed me down streets where pastel façades cloaked a motley

170

of dwellings behind. I peered through her gates into a bedraggled courtyard. Four shabby cottages with lean-tos and padded
doors confused me. Some half-washed stockings lay trampled by
a tap. Somewhere the voice of a woman seared up in fury. Then
a haggard youth emerged from a door and swivelled his back on
me, smoking furiously at the sky. I glimpsed a woman in the
window behind: a slackening face with high-painted cheeks.
Her hair bunched above her head in an impertinent tuft.

The next moment Tania came to a window opposite, and saw
me. Her mouth opened in a soundless oval, and a second later
her stout body was wrestling through the door-frame, and her
ring-encrusted fingers patting my cheek. 'You found us!' She
pulled me inside. 'Ignore that woman!' She slammed the door.
'Half the men who come here are her clients.' She stood before
me in the cramped hall, trembling a little. Her high heels had
been discarded for woolly bedsocks, and she looked squatter
and coarser. 'Prostitutes! I suppose there've always been such
women. People without education or skills. So they do that.'

She lived in a nest of chaotic warmth and colour. Her walls
gushed scarlet draperies and shelves of disintegrating books.
Cheap silver and Russian crystal crowded every surface, with
Lithuanian dolls, Moldavian honey-pots and wooden dishes
from the Urals. Orange hangings partitioned off the stove, yellow
silks shone sluttishly over the bed. She tugged a curtain across
the window – 'Block out that woman!' – and plunged me into
the chair where she had been watching television across a tray
littered with half-eaten biscuits. Then she mounded herself
opposite me, glowing and disconcerted. The prostitute had
shamed her. Her cat arched against my shins. 'The system
before the Revolution was better,' she breathed, 'when those
women lived in brothels and carried yellow cards and everybody knew who they were.' She was still quivering. 'But there's
no law against them. They can carry on a business as they like.
So they live among decent people and cause disruption.'

'That happens everywhere,' I said, to soothe her.

'Does it, does it?' She dropped her hand to her cat, which

171

stalked away. She did not want to be driven from this house, she said.

It stood in a region still called the Garden of the Winds, after a palace laid out by Tamerlane. She'd found fragments of old porcelain and glass in her vegetable patch, and liked to think they might have touched the monster's lips.

'In any case, where would I go? I'm rootless, like my cat.' She laughed. 'That's what I like about her. You say "Come here" and she leaves you, like a man.'

In all this she barely mentioned her husband, the elusive Moslem whose suits hung dowdily in a half-open cupboard. It occurred to me that they were not married. But she addressed the cat as if it understood, ending half her sentences with the saccharine diminutives of Russian sentiment. 'Where would we go, my Katenka? Who would take us in, my little Katya, my Katooshka?... I've told you before not to walk on the table. Don't you ever listen?... Yes, we have to stay here ....'

'You won't return to Russia?' I noticed the icons above her bed. The cat had taken to chewing at the refrigerator door behind the curtain.

'Return? I was never there.' She fell into a frowning distress. 'My parents were sent from Moscow to Tajikistan to teach. They didn't ask to go. They had no option. But they gave their lives to it.' She sounded angry. 'They were dedicated, and their pupils loved them. And I too, I've taught here for thirty-three years. And suddenly this ....'

She stopped, perhaps challenging me to ask if her whole life, with her parents' lives, had been poured into an abyss. I began: 'So you feel ....'

'Do you really want to know what I feel?' she demanded. 'Do you really?' The anger flushed her cheeks into pink roundels. 'Well, I feel humiliated. *Humiliated.*' The ginger curls shook round her cheeks. 'And betrayed.'

I asked gently: 'By the failure of Communism?'

'No, by the failure of the Soviet Union. We could have demolished the Party but kept the Union. Why not? We gave people here so much. Why shouldn't we go on? But now they're saying Moscow bled them, and Moscow says Central Asia gave nothing back – and neither is true. But everybody's showing his wounds now, shouting "Look at my damaged eye!" or "See this cut on my neck", or "Look at my leg, I can't stand!"' She mimed these wounds in a stormy sadness. 'It's true we took their raw materials. But people like my parents gave everything to this land – it was a desert before – and now they're saying it was all mistaken.' Her body was shaking like a girl's. 'Yes, I feel debased.'

Hers was the old, unfathomable belief in Russia's holiness, in her civilising mission. It had been the bedrock of her dignity. Hers, too, was the inborn colonial expectation that people be grateful for what they had never requested. My own nation had made the same mistake. I said cruelly: 'Moslems have a saying that your own country's weeds are better than foreign wheat.'

But Tania had stopped listening. She was inhabiting a timeless Russian theatre of self-pity and helplessness. Now that she did not want it, the cat had returned to her, and she plucked harshly, absently, at its coat in her distress. 'And so we're left with this ... this nothing, overnight. Nobody should suffer that. If you want to move house, you first build another, don't you? But instead we find ourselves without anywhere, the roof fallen in and the rain pouring through!' Her laughter did not reach her mouth. She disgorged her feelings and swallowed them back simultaneously, savoured them almost, like a painful possession, in the mournful Slavic way. She seemed to be voicing what the old lady, Zelim Khan's mother, would have voiced, had she been able.

'We Russians don't know what to believe in now,' she said. 'So we're turning in to our families – that's where our belief goes now, close to home.'

'Perhaps that's better,' I said.

Yet I pictured the huge religious energy of her people raging like disconnected horsepower across the continent, hunting for an object, some reconciling love.

But as if to illustrate her newly domestic affections, Tania

173

stooped under the bed and tugged out a basket mewling with kittens. She seemed suddenly exhausted. 'Look. My Katya has children. When they were born my husband said "Drown them", and I replied, "You drown them" and put them into his arms, and he couldn't. He is a good man.' She lifted two out, and coddled them with -ooshas and -oolyas. They almost vanished in her plump fists. 'How often do I have to tell you to wash them, Katooshka, my Katenka? Look at their bottoms ....'

She dropped them back into the basket. She could not keep them long, she said; but it was growing harder for her to get rid of anything now, even cats. She had already lost too much. Especially she had loved her father: a gentle scholar from Moscow. After one of the earthquakes his house had been demolished, she said, and he had never recovered, simply wasted away so the doctors thought he had cancer, and he'd died from a misjudged blood transfusion. 'It was more than five years ago, and I still weep.'

It was he who had taught her to love books, and among the ragbag of veterans on her shelves (Fielding, Aldous Huxley, Dale Carnegie) I noticed Russian translations of once-banned works, even *Animal Farm* published in Moscow. 'But I'm sick of all that,' she said.

Sick of all what, I asked?

Then her bitterness resurfaced and shook the words from her in spasms of vehement regret. She wanted to believe in her country again. 'Up to a few years ago I always received *Literaturnaya Gazeta* from Moscow,' she said. 'But when all those things started to be published about what Stalin had done, the numbers killed – I felt sick, physically sick. Soon I couldn't stand it any longer, and I stopped reading those articles. Some of my friends too, I think one or two were literally killed by it. They just gave up.'

'Hadn't you suspected?'

'No, it wasn't that. In my family we always knew. My father loathed Stalin.' Her voice filled with a desolate truculence. 'But to read all that, on and on... there was so much of it, the sheer quantity. Stalin, Brezhnev, even Chernobyl.' Her features retracted into nausea. 'I took to reading detective stories, science fiction, anything ....' After a while she calmed and said in vague wonder: 'I suppose I could imagine, before, that it wasn't so. I knew it was true, but perhaps ... I did not really face it. And when day after day, month after month, our papers were printing such things, after all we had already suffered, the millions who died in the war ....'

She stopped in a confusion of shame and recoil. She was trying to understand how with exposure her country's sins seemed suddenly enormous, which before had lain known but anaesthetised in half-concealment; how the fantasy of national innocence could vanish overnight. Somehow, for years, she had seen her nation bifocally. She was a woman of long, tenacious passions, and this dishonour went to her heart. So she clung to an outrage at the world's ingratitude, and to her own and her parents' sacrifice. Sometimes I felt that the dying of her father and of her country had become knit together in one loss. He had been a Christian believer, she said, and had bequeathed to her the icons which hung above her bed. Their eyes gazed blindly over the cluttered room. Someone at that time had given her a Bible too. 'I wished I had thought before about that verse,' she said. ' *"Let no man be your teacher, only God" ....'*

She asked me to return to her for lunch on Victory Day. 'Then you will meet my husband,' she said, 'and we will honour our country's dead.'

*

On the north-east outskirts of the city a sunken trajectory of domes and gates traces a funerary way up Maracanda's ruined ramparts. In this secret glade, through the late fourteenth century, the women and warriors of Tamerlane were laid in sepulchres whose precious tiles, carried on camel-back from Persia, were fitted round the tomb façades in a cool splendour.

In early morning, before any tour-groups arrive, you may walk up this avenue undisturbed, while the dawn leaks a thin

175

light over its walls. At its foot a mullah waits in a newly working mosque; but beyond, the screams of swallows ricochet among the domes, and the way ascends over hexagonal flagstones between the mausoleums. Their cupolas do not swell and bloom, but complete their graves modestly, like a wardrobe of antique hats. A few plane trees lean over the path. Here and there a building has vanished, leaving an anonymous hump.

Then the first pilgrims appear. Peasant women mostly, gleaming in gold-splintered scarves and iridescent leggings, and trailing picnic bags, they toil up to the entombed saint who casts over this place a halo of miracle. But on the way they squat inside the chambers where the half-pagan Mongol aristocracy lies, and smooth their palms over the stones, and murmur Allah, Allah. Methuselahs with sticks and flaking beards, and dowagers whose shawls pile their heads like the wimples of medieval burghers, they ease themselves upwards in an aura of pious holiday.

Half way along, the ascent bends through an overhanging gateway, and there opens up a zone of disciplined brilliance. The acres of lightly patterned brick which covered contemporary mosques contract to an aisle of private piety and grief. To either side its walls and high entranceways are clothed in waterfalls of pure faience. Sometimes the façades converge across the way with barely twelve feet between them, echoing one another with the lustrous intimacy of miniatures. Two sisters of Tamerlane are buried here, and a young wife, Tuman, all of whom pre-deceased him. Inside, the chambers are nearly bare. Here and there a smashed tile sticks to a grave or a shadow of fresco lingers, but the cenotaphs are simple cubes and rectangles, mostly uninscribed. It is the entranceways which give voice to the distinction, and perhaps the belovedness, of the dead. They are tiled vertically by eight or ten different friezes in turquoise and gentian blue, powdered with stars, wheels, flowers: a whole lexicon of motifs. They hang there in ravishing detail. Sometimes white inscriptions twine them. Occasionally a touch of oxblood or pale green intrudes. Many panels are raised in deep relief, as

176

if wrapped in a veil of loose knitting, so the sun glitters over them unpenetrating. They are an aesthete's paradise.

But pilgrims steer for the avenue's end and the tomb of the legendary Kussam ibn-Abbas, cousin of the Prophet, who carried Islam to Samarkand, it is said, and was martyred here in the seventh century. 'Those who were killed on the way of Allah are not to be considered dead; indeed, they are alive,' runs the *aya* on his grave, and it is perhaps from this that the necropolis takes its name of Shakhi-Zinda, 'the Shrine of the Living King'. As late as the 1920s, before Stalin stifled religion, its underground cells were full of devotees fasting and contemplating in enforced silence for forty days at a time. The martyr, they said, lingered here unseen 'in the living flesh', waiting to expel the Russians. Beyond the shrine, all along the sunlit heights of the vanished ramparts, thousands of graves still spread within the sacred force-field of his tomb.

A pair of deep-carved walnut doors lurches open on its antechamber. Dust-filled beams of light hang in the dark. Glimpsed through its grille, the porcelain grave is delicate and small. It unfurls in four jewelled tiers upon the bare floor.

'It was the fire-worshippers who killed him. Persians, you know. They cut off his head.' The burly, soft-faced man who dispensed prayers here touched his neck with a karate chop. 'But then what happened? The saint didn't die, no. He picked up his head and jumped with it into a well!' He tucked an aerial head under his arm, like a Tudor ghost. 'And there he waits to return, in the Garden of Paradise.'

Crouched along the walls beside us, ranks of village women let out bleating hymns, their scarves dropped over their faces, their legs doubled under them, their shoes off. Sometimes they turned their furrowed hands upwards while old men led them in half-sung prayer. A bevy of town girls came in and squatted opposite self-consciously. They were necklaced in seed-pearls over their high-ruffed dresses, and their hair drawn tight under nacreous clasps in the style of the day. They fell silent almost at once, listening to the unfamiliar words. They seemed to be

177

sucking nourishment back out of their past, learning from these ancient peasants who they were, or who they might yet be.

From time to time the burly man went out to pray with other pilgrims in his cell – a converted tomb – where I would hear him chanting in a plangent, musical voice before he returned to sit in the sun. The whole sanctuary was resurrecting now, he said. Its mosque, closed down since Kruschev's day, was open again, and the pilgrims returning.

And what of the saint, I asked? Had there been miracles?

He could not answer for others, he said. 'But I myself...I used to have high blood pressure. It got up into my eyes some-how, and into my kidneys. I thought I might not have long to live, and the doctors couldn't do a thing. So I came here to clean the dust round the saint's tomb.' He gazed at the walnut doors with rested eyes. 'And now I'm well again.'

Then a younger man sat down beside us. I saw, beneath the cap of a medreseh student, a white, possessed face. He wanted to know what we had been saying. The burly man went silent. Under the student's hot, arid stare our conversation spluttered up again, then died.

A medreseh had opened recently in Samarkand, he said coldly, and he was there. I remembered it, of course, and the rape and the mullah's suicide, but said nothing. 'The top gradu-ates', he went on, 'will complete their studies for a few months in Saudi Arabia or Iran or Pakistan.'

I tried hopefully: 'Doesn't your Islam differ a little from theirs?'

He hooked his forefinger into a knot of indissoluble union. 'We are all one. The Koran is one. Our faith is one.'

I sat there a long time, touched with alarm, before he went away, irritated by my questions. The burly man remained seated in silence beside me, relaxed in the sunlight. Now the Russians had gone, I asked, what enemy was left for the Living King to expel? Couldn't he rest?

'I don't know. You'd have to ask others things like that. But the saint expels the sorrow in people. That's why they come here.' An old woman was kissing the door-jambs in front of us.

178

'And eventually he will return.'

'You believe that?'

'Yes, I believe it. He'll return at the end of the light.' A millennial fatalism overtook him. 'Perhaps if we live long enough, we'll see it.'

I went back down the funerary way, wondering about the nature of its dead. (Who, for instance, had been the niece of Tamerlane laid under a dome decorated pathetically with faience tears?) As I passed the grave of the astronomer Kazyade, teacher and friend of Ulug Beg, my thoughts turned to heresy and science, and a confused train of history flooded in.

All through the fifteenth century Central Asia was filled by the quarrels and luxuries of the Timurid princes, successors of Tamerlane, with their poetry and miniatures (and weakness for wine and catamites). Hedonism and science ran free. Tamerlane's son Shah Rukh reigned – a mighty prince – from Herat in Afghanistan, where years before I had seen his wife's college toppling in ruin, while their own son Ulug Beg governed as viceroy and then sultan in Samarkand. A century later a great-great-great-grandson of the emperor, Babur, ruled here in brief happiness before fleeing the Uzbek invaders south, and left behind him an autobiography of entrancing humanity. It was he, years later, who founded the Moghul empire in India, and carried into its rice-deltas the vigour and epicurism of Central Asia, whose bulbous domes were to fruit in the Taj Mahal. Here the schizophrenic spirit of Tamerlane survived (or so I fancied) among the imperial chess-players and refined Moghul gardens, and lingered too in sudden, often intimate acts of cruelty – that terrible divorce of aestheticism from compassion which was to trouble all his descendants.

In Samarkand meanwhile, the empire of the dead conqueror was disintegrating. Its economy was too shallow to support it. The city workshops still produced their rich cloths and metal, and the finest paper in the world – a skill taught here by the Chinese seven centuries before – but the Silk Road was dying. Tamerlane's wider conquests, which settled no government in

179

their wake, were now revealed only as the megalomaniac raids of a brilliant predator.

Ulug Beg, his grandson, ruled with a different glory. In the 100-foot observatory which he built on a hill outside Samarkand, frescoed with embodiments of the celestial spheres, a caucus of astronomers and mathematicians fussed over azimuths and planispheres, traced the precession of the equinoxes and determined the ecliptic. Here he discovered two hundred unknown stars, and recalculated the stellar year to within a few seconds of that computed by modern electronics. But the pietists, of course, hated him, and in 1449 he was killed by reactionaries led by his own son. His observatory was damned 'the cemetery of the forty evil spirits', and levelled with the ground.

In 1908 a Russian schoolmaster, Vladimir Vyatkin, after calculating where the observatory must have stood, dug down and hit the arc of what appeared to be a primitive escalator. Now sheltered under a modern vault, its twin marble parapets swoop side by side through the excavated earth. Meticulously jointed and calibrated, they are the section of a titanic 180-foot quadrant along whose rails ran the astrolabe by which Ulug Beg bearded God and identified the heavens.

*

The Victory Day celebrations were muted that year. For the first time, there was no parade. Down the memorial avenue red flags still mingled with the national colours, and groups of Russian and Tajik veterans were hobbling separately, their chests ablaze with medals, towards the temple which sheltered the eternal flame. But a mournfulness of anti-climax hung about them. The ragged line of police had nothing to supervise. On either side, Second World War tanks and anti-aircraft guns stood on their plinths like relics of prehistory, and martial music sobbed from the loudspeakers. Inside the red-stoned cube of the temple, lilies, peonies, carnations and irises were banked around the sacred fire. 'Nobody must forget', raged the slogans. But young Tajiks and Uzbeks with their families were strolling about on holiday, and glanced curiously at the shuffling mourners, who looked suddenly redundant as if – in this empire of long memories – the war were at last receding.

'I was at Potsdam and Berlin,' confided one man. His lapels dripped with medals. 'Look.' He bowed his head to me. Under its powder of hair the skull was dented by a cavity empurpled with veins. I would not have thought anybody could survive such a wound. 'I got that a week before the war's end!'

'I'm amazed you're still alive!'

'Alive? I've marched every year in the parade.'

'I missed it.'

'Well, there wasn't one. There's only this now.' He jerked his chin at the silent veterans trudging about the flowers. He looked belligerent. 'It's because of that Gorbachev and everything he did ....' He scanned me with filmy eyes. 'Were you in the war?'

'No.' I wondered how old I was looking. 'But my father fought in North Africa and Italy.'

'North Africa ... Italy ....' The words fell experimentally from him. After their appalling sacrifice, Russians often forget that anyone but they confronted Germany. But suddenly he squeezed my arm in a brotherhood which overleapt the continents, and kissed my cheeks, so that I was moved by a vicarious pride, and I wished my father there.

'Next year, I tell you,' he said, as if to comfort me, 'there'll be a parade again.' He opened his arms like a boasting angler. 'A *huge* parade!'

I wandered away into the memorial gardens. Tajik and Uzbek veterans were walking there too, and an old woman in full decorations was posing for her photograph. In their remembered war they converged – native and Russian together – at a point where time had superseded race. I went down glades lined with the busts of Heroes of the Soviet Union.

'Look at them,' one of the Uzbeks said. 'The heroes are still there, but the Soviet Union's gone!' A delta of smile-lines flowed from his mouth and eyes, but he was not happy. He had the face of a wizened monkey. 'I tell you as an old man, as

181

a veteran of the Great Patriotic War, that it's a bad thing. Absolutely a bad thing.'

'You don't want independence?'

'No! Everything's got worse. And it'll go on getting worse and worse.'

I stared at him, still touched by a vague wonder at the gap where nationalism might have been. A pair of policemen shambled by, their hats tilted back on their heads.

'Only young people are glad,' he said disgustedly, 'because they don't have to do any work. Look at those police! They just play-act and take bribes.' He bent his arm in a mock salute. 'Nobody works any more.'

This, I knew, was more than the perennial complaint of the old against the young, the lament for uninherited beliefs. A gulf of unshared experience gaped between the generations. The world was slipping away from him. 'And you wait,' he said, as we circled back to the eternal flame. 'In a minute hooligans will come and steal the flowers.'

I loitered until noon while the crowds thinned. The soulful music throbbed and tramped in the loudspeakers overhead, as if the dead were on the march again, accusing. Then I remembered that I had promised to share Tania's Victory Day lunch, and walked to her home down streets which were almost deserted.

In the courtyard two sallow youths squatted by the gate, awaiting their turn with the prostitute, while a neighbour harangued them from his window. They looked sheepish, but did not budge. When I knocked, a middle-aged man opened Tania's door, and from the photograph by her bed I recognised Petya, her husband. He was slim and dapper, with black hair and gold teeth. He looked almost designed. Despite his Russian name, any Slavic blood in him was subsumed by a Tajik darkness. He appeared younger than Tania, more delicate.

Inside their love-nest, the drinking had already begun. Clustered round a table strewn with cheeses, pickled vegetables, brandy and wine, and facing a mammoth television, we watched a favourite Russian war-film *The Warriors* relayed from Moscow. 'Today we remember our great dead,' said Tania – already the brandy had curdled her speech to a squelchy aria – 'all our millions killed in the Great Patriotic War.' We lifted our glasses. Her gaze swivelled towards mine. 'This was our time of greatest suffering, and today we remember all that. . . . Petya had an uncle killed, and I too.' She added formally: 'It went from 1941 to 1945.'

'Ours began in 1939,' I said.

But they were not listening. A Russian platoon was charging across the louring skyline with fixed bayonets, and their brandy-bright eyes had turned moist with emotion. 'So many gone ... and what for? What for? I'm glad they cannot see us now. I'm ashamed ....'

Only once these maudlin celebrations were interrupted. Petya's son-in-law, a jobless youth who was hoping to start up some business, but did not know what, arrived nervously and sat down near the door. He looked haunted. 'He's useless,' said Tania, as if he were not there. 'All these young people, they just want to do business. They don't want to sweat. He lost his last job because his wife's having an affair and he kept leaving work to spy on her.'

The young man got up and went away. Neither Tania nor Petya seemed to notice. Across the table the Germans were advancing towards us through a thicket of tank-blocks and barbed wire. 'And to think our soldiers sacrificed themselves for a better world!' Tania tossed back another brandy. 'And what now? What now?' Her eyes languished over Petya. 'We were told we would achieve perfect Communism by 1980, and what did we have? Now we must build up our house again from nothing. On the old foundations? Or new ones? And how?'

'How? How?' echoed Petya, uncorking the wine.

She said bitterly: 'I realise now we have to do everything alone. You can't trust anybody. People are just out for themselves. And I too, now.' She turned up the noise of the television. '*Let no man be your teacher, only God....*'

Petya stumbled from the stove with dishes of dolmades and meat-balls which he had cooked. He was already drunk. His face had loosened into a slovenly grin, and the eyelids hovered over his gaze like portcullises. Did I love his cooking, he demanded? I must love his cooking. He had cooked just for me. Black locks straggled about his neck from a thinning hairline. And did I not love his Tania also, his Tanoolya? Where would he be without her? He had no other homeland. The wine gurgled into our glasses.

'I have five kinds of blood in me!' His head knocked against mine. 'You, you're English – was it? – so you feel a homeland. But I, I am not Tajik or Russian or Uzbek, quite. I am nothing. Where do I belong?' It was the fearful Russian cry of self-humiliation. 'Before I was a Soviet man, but what am I now?'

Nobody answered. This betrayal, they both felt, had wrecked their lives. The Soviet Union had been their natural state, in which they could shelter and identify, enrolling themselves in a nationless empire of the future. But overnight it had vanished. It had proved itself less potent, in the end, than the maze of fragile-seeming nations which it had sought to absorb. And it had gone with bewildering suddenness, like a genie from a broken bottle, leaving them no time.

I said: 'Perhaps you can be your own nation.'

'That's all right for you in the West,' he groaned. 'But for us here things work differently. People need support, a clan, a network. But what have I . . .? Do you love my cooking? I have cooked just for you!' He flung his arms about me and demanded kisses. I felt miserably Anglo-Saxon as I skimmed his bristly cheeks and eulogised his cooking and tried to resist the procession of toasts which was mounting around me. To victory, to the future, to the past, to the war dead (mugs are never clashed here), to friendship – glassful after glassful disappeared down our slackly gaping throats. A moment's solemn silence for the dead punctuated this revelry, then we were off again.

By now Tania and Petya were surfing along on waves of self-pity. Their twin gazes meshed adoringly over the table. The wine trembled and slopped in their hands. Again and again she leant across to fondle him, or he her, fastening their lips on each other's necks or noses or mouths, their stomachs and chests knocking over brandy bottles and jars of preserves. Sentimental diminutives burbled and multiplied. She was his Tanishka, his darling Tanyoosha, his little Tanoolya. And was he not her Petenka, her everlasting Petrousha, her faithful Petyulka? Yes, yes! They extolled each other, reproached then forgave each other, in an antiphonal euphoria which was at once slatternly, touching and absurd.

As for me, I might have arrived from another galaxy. They knew, and asked, nothing about me at all. I was simply the occasion for festivity. I became irritated and self-reproachful as they descended into their oblivion. 'Come! Come!' crooned Tania. 'Get drunk and I will lay you out with Petya on the bed. You can sleep the afternoon with us, and drink again this evening.'

'No ....' I was starting to hate myself.

But as my stare reeled from Tania's face to Petya's, I wondered at their arrogance, and felt my last compassion veering away. I was thinking of the quiet dignity of Moslems at their prayers. Who were the Russians to teach the Uzbeks how to live? I thought drunkenly: perhaps a decade of Islamic fundamentalism, with its war on maudlin self-indulgence, would serve everybody right. I was starting to sympathise with the prostitute in the courtyard outside, who had earlier yelled at a Russian client that his self-righteous people had taught hers how to drink and fornicate.

At last Petya succumbed backwards on to the bed, and lay like a baby with his forearms curled against his face, and started to snore. He looked thin and somehow desolate. Now and again an arm or a leg clunked on to the floor. Across the television screen the Russian infantry was massing for victory, unnoticed.

'He's gone,' Tania said. She herself seemed no more nor less drunk than when I arrived. 'But he'll come round in an hour or two. He's always been like that.'

185

'How long have you been married?'

Her voice dropped into monotone. 'Actually, we're not married.'

Somehow I had known this. 'Can't he get a divorce?'

'His wife doesn't want to. She thinks it bad for her daughters' status. She's a vulture. I knew them early in their marriage, and she never spoke well of Petya, just called him "that alcoholic".' She glanced down at Petya. His snores had stilled to a distant growling. 'He's still obsessed by her. Some people say she's attractive, but I don't think so. Perhaps I'm just jealous because I am not a pretty one, but you judge.' She pulled a folder from a shelf and plucked out sheafs of photographs: Petya as a pilot, Petya on his premature retirement being presented with a gilded clock. ('It's there by the bed. It's stopped.') And Petya's wife: a strong-boned Slavic blonde, not beautiful. 'What do you think?'

'Not pretty, no.' But I understood the woman withdrawing herself and her daughters from the inebriate ex-pilot. 'Perhaps she's ambitious for their children.'

But Tania said: 'I could have had a child too.'

A little drunk, I asked: 'Have you no children?'

She replaced the photographs on the shelf. Then, as she turned and looked at me, I saw her face transfigured by a kind of crushed and harrowing sweetness. 'Last year I conceived a baby .... It was so grotesque somehow, at my age .... I'm fifty ... and unmarried.' Her eyes dropped from mine. She added in her sombre monotone: 'I had it aborted.'

Then she sat down and sighed with curiously mixed relief and despair. I touched her arm, unfelt. I wondered how many other lives here would darken into confusion if more deeply known. Petya was stirring on the bed, and sat up with a rootless moaning.

'Petooshka?' Her voice had regained its jellied solicitude. It was Petya, not alcohol, that made it drunk.

He propped himself beside me. I imagined that he was selecting a role to play. He said confusedly: 'We will drink again and you will stay the night. And tomorrow ....'

186

'Tomorrow I go to Shakhrisabz,' I said curtly. It was a town to the south, where Tamerlane had built his country palace.

'Stay with us!' Tania burst in. She had returned to her voluble, domineering self. 'You don't want to go to Shakhrisabz tomorrow! Or go for two hours – there's nothing to see there! – and come back. We will wait for you.'

Petya planted a kiss on her ring-studded hand. 'Yes, we will make love together and wait for you.'

Neither idea was appealing. 'I want to stay there,' I said.

'You do not want to stay there!' Tania broke in. 'You want to be here! Come back tomorrow. Or don't go at all. We'll drink....'

Petya curled up on the bed again, but she went relentlessly on, ignoring anything I might really wish. She demanded and cajoled and insisted in a melodrama which sensed nothing beyond its own outpouring. In my mind her blindness to myself became fused with her blindness to her adopted and ungrateful country, to her spent life. Because she would not grant autonomy to any recipient of her giving, she seemed condemned to be hurt. Its separateness from herself, once she had embraced it, was unendurable to her.

An hour later I said goodbye with her demands for my return still ringing about my ears.

*

South from Samarkand a broad road ran fifty miles to Shakhrisabz, over an outlying finger of the Pamir. Beyond foothills rose a wraith-like curtain of mountains whose pelmet was lost in cloud. As my crammed taxi started to climb, the crags surged unsteadily about us in the mist. Everything paled, until the web of our splintered windscreen overlay only a watercolour softness beyond. Sometimes the road reverted to a cracked causeway unchanged since Soviet tanks moved down it to Afghanistan in 1979. All around, the mountain-scarps hung in diseased-looking palisades of flaking rock. Then we topped the pass and stared down through haze. A sandy fox watched us from the mossed rocks. Nothing else stirred. Half an hour later we had arrived in Shakhrisabz.

It was a cool, harmonious town. To either side, the porcelain mountains herded it into its lush valley, and hung the sky with disembodied snow. The tea-houses along its main street were leisurely with old men, and the parks soft under willows. Tamerlane had been born a few miles to the south, and an after-glow of imperial patronage tinged the place. In later centuries it had enjoyed semi-independence from the emirate of Bukhara, and had flourished with more grace. Slavery was never allowed here. Even at executions, a traveller recalled, a criminal's throat would be mercifully cut before he was hanged.

Ruins still scattered it. The tomb of a son of Ulug Beg shone against the mountains, and a fifteenth-century congregational mosque survived in gutted dignity. Nobody guided or stopped me as I waded through poppies and cow-parsley into the wrecked mausoleum of Jehangir, Tamerlane's oldest and favourite son. Carved doors swung into a rank and sickly desola-tion, where only a slung canvas protected the grave against the pigeon-droppings and bricks raining down from a disintegrating dome.

But the glory of Shakhrisabz, dwarfing all else, gleamed in dereliction above its own parklands. Here the White Palace of Tamerlane had stood on the caravan-route to Khorasan and India, and had left behind a gateway so immense that nothing – not even the Bibi Khanum – could equal it. Such buildings were expressions of political power. The terror and grandeur of their appearance was crucial, for few ever entered them, and their gateways, like awesome warnings or advertisements, were huger, more portentous, than anything inside.

But I saw, as I approached this one, that it occupied a mega-lomaniac dimension of its own. It belonged among those dazing gargantuas of ruin – Karnak, Angkor, Baalbec – which might have been built by another species. Its central arch had long ago collapsed, but on either side a cylindrical tower merged into a nine-storeyed complex of buttresses and chambers, so that each jamb rose in a self-contained citadel 140 feet to a skyline of naked brick. The patina of tiles ripened as the entrance went deeper, edged in bands of peacock blue, packed with white script. Exposed for centuries, they hung precariously in veins of cobalt and gold high up – an inexplicable delicacy of calligraphy and flowers.

The place was deserted except for a dreamy girl sitting on a ruined wall. She fell into conversation with the spontaneity of Turkic women when they feel unwatched. Tamerlane was definitely an Uzbek, she said, and from this I guessed her race. She walked naturally beside me. The ground was lightly paved inside the gate. High on either hand the piers were lanced by fissures and screamed with swallows, as if we were trekking through a canyon. Here the past was channelled to a narrow flood, and I sensed before us the limping tread of the monster over the grass-ringed stones, and the tramp of Shah Rukh after him, and of Ulug Beg and his patricidal son.

The girl talked with the childlike candour which perhaps only a stranger could release. She had the rosebud mouth and almond eyes beloved of Timurid miniatures, but already the flesh was loosening around them, and at twenty-nine her life was full of sadness. Her father had died young of a heart attack, and her brother too, at twenty-five. 'My mother still cries in the street.' The girl was the youngest in this decimated family, and felt in debt to them, as if she had somehow failed. 'I was accepted into university to study German without paying, because we were poor. My four sisters all got married, and helped me to live while I was there, since my stipend was so small.' She smiled sadly. Her mouth was already full of gold teeth. 'I had just two dresses, but they were enough.'

Beyond the gates we had entered a haunted void: a few brick foundations, some sunken steps and straggling trees. It was here that the Castilian envoy had been conducted in astonishment round a maze of reception halls, galleries and council chambers faienced in gilded blue, and saw under construction the banqueting-rooms where Tamerlane would feast with his princesses.

189

'It didn't matter having no money at university,' the girl went on. 'Everything was exciting then. I wore my hair down to here.' She trickled her fingers down her breast. Now she had a perm. 'What's hard is to love something, then find nobody wants it. And nobody much wants German.'

So in the end university had been a dazzling entrance to nothing, like the palace in which we walked. She stared hopelessly at the ground. 'I need to work, my husband earns so little. He's just a jeweller in crystal. We live in two rooms.' The unhappiness in this marriage needed no saying. 'I don't know what to do. I suppose I should start some business, but we've no money.'

'It should be easier to start a business now,' I said, but sounded cheerless even to myself. I seemed to be contracting her despair.

She shook her head. 'This isn't the West,' she answered. 'It will never be the West.'

She had seen American drama on television, and the West now appeared to her as delectable as it had once – under Moscow's censorship – seemed sordid. She looked at me with a faint, bovine hope and asked: 'How much do flights to Britain cost?'

I modified the price, but she sunk her head in resignation. I might have been talking of another cosmos. 'How much do apartments cost?' she enquired. 'How much is a refrigerator?' But now she was asking me not in aspiration but with the wan amazement of someone enquiring after another faith's paradise. Behind us the shattered palace had fallen from sight, and in front the streets of Shakhrisabz were closing in again.

*

A pang of childhood excitement surrounded the 'Veiled Prophet of Khorasan'. Perhaps I had read of him in Moore's *Lalla Rookh*, but more likely in the schoolboy vulgate of adventure stories and comic books. I have forgotten now. But the impossible romance, with its nimbus of messianic mystery, had remained obscurely with me, so that when I discovered that this phantasmal figure had died in the mountains around Shakhrisabz, I felt a tremor of boyish curiosity.

Even in history Muqanna, 'the Veiled One', is enigmatic, but from a conflation of old accounts – all of them hostile – he emerges as a sorcerer of seductive power, who raised the standard of revolt against the Arab conquerors of Central Asia in AD 776. At night he could summon up the moon from a deep well, it was said; and he covered his face with a golden mask, or a green veil, to spare men the effulgence of his countenance. Once a humble fuller at Merv, he proclaimed himself the ultimate incarnation of God, last and most sacred in the line which passed from Adam through Noah, Abraham, Moses, Jesus and Mahomet. He appears to have preached a blend of Persian Mazdeism and Islam, and promoted a primitive communism, even the sharing of wives.

His Arab foes ascribed his power to trickery. Deep in the well he refracted the rays of the sun in a great bowl of mercury, they said, and he covered his face because he was hideously deformed. He was one-eyed, bald, dwarf-like; he stammered. The claims and counter-claims only added to his mystique. But his white-robed followers raged across Transoxiana, subverting all ancient Sogdiana and the Bukhara oasis. The pagan Turks flocked to him, with a miasma of religious and political dissidents. They threatened to overwhelm the whole land. He himself crossed the Amu Dariya north into the heartland of his self-made faith, and for years defied the Arab armies from a fabled castle in the mountains near Shakhrisabz. Within its outer bastions spread orchards, a river, and cultivated fields, and high on a hill, in a massive keep, he lived alone with his harem and a single slave, a focus of scandal and awe.

But at last, in 786, a vast Arab army surrounded the walls. Thirty thousand of Muqanna's men deserted him, and opened the outer gates. Immured on the heights of the citadel, and realising that his position was hopeless, he kindled a white-hot oven and incinerated all his possessions, even his animals. Then he commanded to follow him anyone seeking heaven, and with his

191

family, harem and remaining followers, leapt into the furnace. When the insurgents entered the castle they found nothing at all, and at once the rumour started up that he had vanished into paradise and would one day return.

The whereabouts of this castle obsessed me. In my empty hotel the tremolo of frogs kept me awake as they mated in the pool outside, and for half the night I pored over my large-scale maps of the region in search of a clue. But the Arab historians situated the castle only vaguely, close to Shakhrisabz on the heights of Sam, or Siyam, which was probably no more than a generic name for the northern Hisar mountains of today. My pen-tip dithered uselessly among the little villages. 'Zamas' raised a momentary hope, destroyed by its second-syllable stress. Tashkurgan – the ubiquitous Turkic word for a 'stone tower' – sent up a feeble promise. Otherwise, nothing.

For two days I bullied drivers to launch their derelict taxis along tracks and defiles in the neighbouring ranges. The late spring rains gushed and rustled through the clefts. The foothills bristled into counterfeit donjons and barbicans, which would disintegrate at our approach with the teasing monotony of mirages. In the Uzbek hamlets of mud and thatch, under roofs scarlet with wild-sown poppies, village elders shook their gnarled and fur-capped heads in ignorance of any vanished castle. One trip petered out at a pass where the driver refused to go on because of wolves. Another ended when a lorry skidded on a loose-stoned track and crashed into us. After some explosions of self-righteousness, the two drivers settled down to debate for an hour in a measured unravelling of pride. Then we limped home.

On the third day I found a tough, bad-tempered driver, so crippled that he was bound to his taxi like a centaur to its hooves. We moved east along a newborn river towards the village of Siyon (the name augured well) between terraces sprinkled with apple blossom. In front of us storm-clouds rolled beneath the mountains, liberating their crests to float in solitude. The hills were all uncrowned; but sometimes their summits smoothed and spread like mesas, as if planed away for walls.

Suddenly, beyond Siyon, a mountain spur came thrusting into the valley. It reared up like a natural citadel. At its foot, where I imagined outer ramparts, the slopes were littered with crashed-down debris. Above, for some eighty feet, their scarps lifted sheer, fissured geometrically as if they were hewn blocks, before levelling out to a tatter of shrubs over the summit. It was impossible to tell which stones were carved, if any, and which natural. But the simulacrum was all of a mighty keep. It was hypnotic. Grey battle-clouds were storming down the valley in collaboration, and had twined ornamentally along the upper bluffs. It was a forbidding and mysterious place, uninhabitable perhaps, I did not know.

I paid off the driver. It was only noon, and I reckoned on a three-hour climb. I marched across the intervening downland in reckless elation. Sapphire and cream flowers spiked the grass underfoot, and the spires of wild tulips gone to seed. I crossed two gullies heaped with black stones, like incinerated rivers, and scrambled up the crevice of a third. A four-foot snake erupted under my feet and flashed away through the tulips in a barbaric gleam of bronze. In front of me the castle (if that is what it was) rose ever more formidable. I strained to identify squared stones, but could not. In the silence an eagle rose and circled the summit on stiffened wings.

Many versions were told of Muqanna's end. It was said that before the Arab armies closed in, 50,000 of his subjects gathered beneath the castle and begged him to unveil his face to them. He prevaricated, warning them that the blaze of his countenance could kill them, but they insisted piteously, so he commanded them to return at sunrise. Just before dawn he ordered his hundred-strong harem to line the parapets, while his followers waited below. As the sun rose, and his slave called on the people to behold the prophet's face, the odalisques canted their mirrors against the sunbeams and refracted them in a blinding conflagration of light. His followers hurled themselves on their faces in terror. Then, said the chroniclers, they took to

Muqanna's cause with renewed zeal, and boasted that they had seen God.

This drama replayed itself easily on the clifftops in front of me. Labouring up a goat-track through an airy dust of thistles, I left all doubts behind me. My reddened eyes swam with the past. I reached the saddle which joined the great spur frailly to the ranges behind it, and dropped exhausted on its rocks. I was pouring sweat. Around me russet butterflies twitched and dark birds sang in the cliffs. I had no idea what I would find.

Some historians wrote that Muqanna's body was rescued from the furnace, and that its head was hacked off and sent to the caliph in Aleppo. But the starkest story was told long afterwards by a crone who claimed to be the last survivor of his harem. As the besiegers closed in, she said, the prophet feasted his women and ordered them to drain their goblets. But she sensed that the wine had been poisoned, and poured the drink unseen into her collar. As her companions died around her, she only feigned death. For a moment, she said, Muqanna surveyed the carnage, then she saw him go to his slave and strike off his head. Finally he removed his robe, and leapt into the furnace. 'I went over to that oven,' she said, 'and saw no trace of him. There was no one alive in the castle.'

Now, stumbling through the indigo flowers which swarmed across the summit, I could imagine a whole city here, or none. The porous rock had been split and polished into the sleekness of sculpture by millennia of exposure to the rain. I traversed it in a madness of indecision. It was impossible to be sure if the stones which balanced on top of one another had been lain by men or fragmented by wind, or if the runnels were those of water or chisel.

I struggled from natural terrace to terrace. Sometimes the storm-gouged outcrops seemed to have been slotted for posts and rafters. Dwarf oaks blurred every shape, with wild apricot trees wreathed in caterpillars. Once I came upon a plateau quartered and squared like a parquet floor. But it was a quilt of natural stone. In one place only, a vallum of boulders had been raised too regularly for chance, and I found traces of dissolved clay: a bandit's lair, perhaps.

At last I sat down bewildered on the cliff-edge. Below me the valley made a vista fit for any reincarnate god. The threatened storm had gone, and the river threaded through mist in a silver torque, from which the far calls of goatherds ascended. All around, the slopes deluged with the white scented buds and violet pods of shrubs unknown to me, and I gave up wondering if I was seated on the ravaged castle, and listened, without history, to the river.

8

Tashkent

A familiar Soviet gloom permeated Samarkand's railway station. Its gangways clanged to the trudge of labourers, and the air stank with diesel and steam spurting from vents under the platform. Everything was being rebuilt, groaning with old cranes and trucks, but nothing complete. The backs of a women's road-gang were bent over gravel-heaps in the sidings, and a pair of bare-chested Goliaths, gouging holes along the rail-track, might have muscled out of a Socialist Realist poster. Everything – the grey-faced passengers, the engines blazoned in hammer-and-sickle, the steel bridges rigged with searchlights – conspired in a Stalinist film-set. All that was needed to complete it was a lank-haired waif with a battered suitcase, and the next moment she had arrived, haggardly pretty, her skirt muddied and her head circled in a red hair-band. I never discovered what she was doing in Uzbekistan, although she rested a moment beside me. Her father was a Czech, she said, but she had been born in the Baltic, so there was nowhere left for her now. 'The Czechs won't take us back,' she said, and wandered on down the platform, trailing her one suitcase, and faltering occasionally from some pervasive tiredness.

North to Tashkent my train moved under a mottled sky. Between the punctuation-marks of messy towns and mud hamlets, we pushed across miles of pale earth ploughed for cotton, where farmers scratched the topsoil with hoes, or a lone tractor turned. My carriage was thronged by fattening Uzbek traders with their soft, jewelled wives. In the cubicle opposite, the

Russian waif curled under a blanket, reading, and talked of herself in a lacklustre, musical voice. Although she worked as a
clerk in a town on the Lower Volga, she said, she had trained as
an actress, and an instinctive theatricality stained her cadences
and tilted her profile as she said: 'It is so hard a profession!' or 'I
have never married.' She spoke as if any chance of marriage
were over, although she was only thirty, and she did not have to
act the sadness which crowded behind her tone. Now she was
reading Chekhov to perform in the people's theatre in her home
town, where amateur players starred. So for a few hours a week
she became somebody else. Next month, she said, they were
staging his short story *The Fiancée*.

I dimly remembered it, and imagined her the heroine.

'Oh no,' she laughed, but faintly. 'I play the old woman.'

Ahead of us brown hills steepened and closed in round the
track, then we were thundering through the Gates of Tamerlane,
whose slatey cliffs reared to either side, split into mounded
cubes and pyramids. Through this breach in the dwindling
Pamir, Turkic and Mongol tribes had for centuries descended out
of the steppes into the Zerafshan valley; Uzbek khans had battled back and forth and left their sanguinary inscriptions on the
rocks, and Tamerlane stamped the cliffs with the record of his
five-day forced passage, forbidding anyone to follow without his
permit. Among rashes of modern graffiti, these early testimonies
remained neat and clear and within a hand's touch as we
passed, and a few moments later we were out into pasturelands
under a stormy sky.

*

I looked with awe at Tashkent. I had flown here briefly the year
before, and had thought it a backwater. But now, after so long
in the deprived south, I felt surrounded by the sweep and
grandeur of a true capital. It was a cosmopolis of over two million, the industrial giant of Central Asia. Its streets were broad
and ordered. Its institutes and ministries withdrew soberly
behind their railings. Double ranks of chestnut and chenar trees

channelled its avenues between big, plain buildings, and its citizens had lost the look of intruding peasantry, and seemed almost urbane. Nearly forty per cent were Russian. Scarcely a trace of native costume showed. The manicured Uzbek secretaries looked as worldly as the ex-Soviet officials with whom they mingled.

But I searched for remnants of the czarist city almost in vain. The Russians had captured Tashkent in 1865, not on orders from St Petersburg but by the adventurism of local generals. Within a few years it became the capital of Russian Turkestan, and there grew up beside the native town a pleasant, nondescript cantonment, where water channels trickled and great trees bloomed. Its first governor-general, the vain and chilly Kaufmann, ruled like a petty emperor. His army and administration were filled with exiled bankrupts and adventurers. Far from home, local society became inward-looking and licentious, while beside it the Uzbek community continued almost unstudied, as if it would one day fade away.

The homely administrative buildings of those times, washed in buff or white, had been swept away by the triumphalist concrete boulevards and palaces of Bolshevism, or shaken down by earth tremors. After the earthquake of 1966, which gutted almost half the city, builders were rushed in from the other Soviet republics and resurrected whole suburbs which still bear their names: the 'Kiev' or 'Riga' or 'Ashkhabad' districts. The inflated monuments and halls of the Rashidov years followed soon after, and the unstable earth was tunnelled with seventeen miles of grandiose subway. Its stations still gleam in pink-veined marble and ceilings gushing with triple ranks of chandeliers, where Uzbeks and Russians build socialism together in hectoring bas-reliefs: heroes of an already bygone age.

As I tramped the city, the enormousness of its spaces – the swirl of six-lane avenues fringed by trams and trolleybuses, the opening out of parks and vistas under the watch of statues – oppressed and disquieted me. The city's heart seemed numb with lessons and memorials. People faded to shadows here.

199

Only their tiered balconies betrayed human variousness: a line of washing, a pot of violets, a cat. Under a superficial diversity of style, their flat-blocks erupted in the same prefabricated brutalism – often thousands to a block – that barges across all the old Soviet Union from Minsk to Vladivostok.

But suddenly the dogmas were being unlearnt. The rooftops which once clamoured with Communist propaganda now webbed the skyline in vacant scaffolds, or had been filled by traffic advice for pedestrians. On the crest of the Ministry of Construction the red star had fallen off its frame on to the roof below. Outside factories and offices the boards of honour were blank where the grim portraits of local exemplars had hung. The whole city was hesitating, as if waiting for something new to think.

Tired with hours of walking, I succumbed to a taxi and watched the passing streets across a smashed windscreen and a dashboard where no needles worked. The driver yelled above his motor's din: 'The Russians will get out soon, and good riddance! We were rich here before. We had melons, nuts, everything. Then the Russians came and we just had these bloody trees.' He waved at the beautiful avenues. 'When it's all Uzbek again we'll cut these down and grow proper ones which give you something – oranges, olives.' We went grinding from the Palace of Friendship past the monument to the earthquake victims. 'It's OK, life. It's like this, as a driver I can earn two hundred roubles a day. But in the factories they earn only two thousand a month. That's lousy.' We crashed round the inverted soup-bowl of the state circus. 'But the factory-workers take stuff, you know. On the side.'

We passed a statue of Alisher Navoi, the national Turkic poet, fingering his beard and open book in a park by his museum. He had been promoted by the Russians as anti-clerical (his Islamic piety censored out) and the driver reeled off a harsh fusillade of his verse. Then the familiar complaints started up. 'You know, meat here used to be two roubles a kilo, and now it's *a hundred*. And sugar ....'

I walked into Karl Marx Park and made for the anonymous square once named after Lenin. A bust of Marx, aswirl in a hurricane of hair and beard, still glowered down my path with the ridged brows of a Mongol warlord. Someone had laid a red carnation beneath him. Beyond, the way was lined by shashlik and pilau vendors, doing poor business, and empty restaurants which in Moscow would have lain under siege.

I crossed the swollen canal which had divided the czarist town from the native one, and entered the void which was once the largest square in the Soviet Union. A thin drizzle descended. It was less a square than a formless plain dotted by dwarfed monuments, ministries and gardens, and bisected by streets. A bridal couple circling the Tomb of the Unknown Soldier on the far side was almost invisible. Only the god himself, the biggest bronze Lenin in the world, threatening from his fifty-foot plinth behind belching regiments of fountains, tried to dominate these tremendous acres. But his gestures were meaningless. The clenched eyes, everybody knew now, were gazing into nothing. The scroll he clutched contained a terrible mistake. The tarmac in front of him had been scored for the May Day march of soldiers twenty-three abreast, but the tribune at his feet was walled off and labelled 'Closed for repairs'. 'They'll take him away soon,' the driver had said. 'But nobody knows what to replace him with.'

A man was lying among wet rose-bushes nearby, the rain falling on his face. I wondered if he were ill, but as I bent down to him he only murmured 'Comrade ....' and closed his eyes again, drunk.

I settled on a bench under the trees, while the rain thickened around the great statue. In the blank square, all the certainties had gone. It was emptier than it had ever been. A few women tripped between puddles under bright umbrellas, and a policeman was reading a sodden newspaper. I turned up my shirt collar in a gesture of self-protection, while the rain began falling on me steadily, inexorably, out of the trees.

A month later, the statue of Lenin was gone.

*

It had become a city of unemployment, nerves, locked doors. In my hotel the drains blocked and the electricity faltered; dawn light flooded in through wafer-thin curtains, and the black-varnished furniture was falling to bits, its drawers spilling to the floor at a tug. In a night-club across the road, louche young Uzbeks drank with their innocently rouged girls, while a cabaret of half-veiled odalisques wriggled to gutted pop music. In this temple to their lost civilisation, complete with prostitutes and bouncers, the clients sank into a counterfeit of the West: raucous, extravagant and forbidden.

The hotel guests were mostly on business. An Israeli foreign office agent was scouting to open an embassy, but everything belonged to co-operatives, he said, and nobody would sell. Two Chinese delegations were trying to nose out trade (but falling ill on the Uzbek cuisine). An American Mormon had started a food-processing plant, he said, and the KGB, who had once harassed him, were now pestering him to sell them things.

Someone had given me the address of Jassur, an *apparatchik* who financed business initiatives. But when I reached his institute it was half-inhabited. Its receptionist slumped asleep with her hennaed hair loosed over her knees. I padded past her. Two dyed-blonde secretaries were gossiping at the boardroom table, and Jassur was sitting between them. They scattered to a sofa as I entered, while he retired importantly to his desk.

His hair dusted back from a creaseless forehead and a face which looked oiled and rather child-like. The desert of his desk-top was broken by a bottle of champagne and three pieces of paper. On a table behind him, the attendants of activity – an electric typewriter, a word-processor, a fax machine – stagnated beside three telephones. A guitar stood in a corner. A map of America hung on one wall.

'I was awarded this post last week. I am the director here.' In the amber-skinned oval of his face the eyes and slight moustache made an unreadable code of black dots and dashes.

202

Beneath them, when I enquired about his work, a pair of fleshy lips budded like an anemone, and soliloquised in English with formal smoothness, as if he were addressing a panel.

'I dispense money to various companies for projects. I've been in many foreign countries, and understand them. I have started a joint stock company with one of our gold corporations and with Saudi Arabia and Syria. I was two weeks in Israel and changed my position very much on the Arab question. I was two years in Moscow in the military academy there, very close to things ....' I listened to him, unspeaking. The anemone lips seemed to move independently of his face, like an oracle. 'I've been in the States, and I speak almost perfect Spanish, better than my Russian or Uzbek. Uzbek' – he dismissed it with a pout – 'is just a language for the family. I was at Harvard University for a month. And I have a speciality: the Soviet view of the Western world. I'm told that it is interesting ....'

I was glad, I said, to find somebody optimistic about the economy. But I stared bleakly round the office, then back at the goldfish face. Its lips were moving again.

'Optimism? Well... I am trying to set up contact with South Africa for the purchase of gold-mining equipment. Theirs is the best in the world. But our government here doesn't help with this. They are afraid to make contact with South Africa, I think. But I believe it is a great country, a fine country to work in.' He said in the same anointed voice: 'I hope to go there to live.'

'*For ever?*'

'Yes.' So after all his trumpeting of status and possibility, he was getting out. 'South Africa has a great future.'

I said I thought its future more uncertain than Uzbekistan's.

'You think so?' He looked at me as if I had propounded something extraordinary. For a moment he was silent. I gazed back into the nurtured face of an infant, at once self-adoring and disappointed. Then his voice turned petulant, as if he had found it for the first time. 'But I don't want to go on relying on other people. Here everyone is dependent on someone else, and nobody does anything. I want just to rely on *myself.*' He pointed narcissistically to his brow. '*Myself!*'

This was precisely what a Westerner should have wanted to hear. It was odd how futile it sounded. 'What about your work here?' I gestured foolishly round the office.

'It's hopeless. My job is to dispense money. But I have nothing to dispense.' He looked like an angry cupid. His hands opened in a gesture of helpless deficit. 'I want to get promotion somewhere. We're starting embassies around the world now, and I want to be in one of these. But you have to know somebody.' His voice dwindled into naïvety. 'People's sons get these positions. Perhaps my joint stock company' – he savoured the words 'joint stock' as if they conferred some talismanic stature – 'perhaps that will give me the opportunity to travel.' But this company was dwindling to a paper idea, or perhaps a fantasy. 'I want to work at an American university, where I can use my Spanish .... they use a lot of Spanish there, in administration.'

His imagination was roaming at will now. He inhabited a cloud of dreams. He did not see that the Uzbek provincialism which he so despised was also his own. 'I want to sell my military expertise to South Africa. That's the country. East Germans are doing this too, selling their knowledge there, I know. You can do what you like now. It's all open.' But whenever his secretaries' chatter fell silent on the sofa opposite his voice dropped into confidence, and now he was almost whispering: 'But I can't get through to South Africa ....'

The world was beginning to bewilder him, a little.

'Then I'd try somewhere else,' I said.

'I applied to UNESCO for a fellowship, last year. I heard there were very few applicants. I made a breakdown of my project about Soviet concepts of the West, and word-processed it myself on this' – he pointed to the god-like machine. 'But that was months ago, and I haven't had an answer. I don't understand this.' He fumbled in a drawer. 'There was a man going to help me in England ... his name was Stewart Davis. Do you know him?' He handed me a crumpled card. 'I haven't heard from him. We get no information here. If I want to telephone someone in

England, I must wait three days.'

Yet this man, I reminded myself, was the head of a government institute.

'You must excuse me.' He suddenly stood up. 'I have to see my wife in hospital. She has just given me a son, but she is producing no milk. That is the problem with our modern women.' He repeated his gesture of hopeless shortfall. 'Shall we meet tomorrow in your hotel? I have a publishing project I wish to discuss ....'

I agreed to this with foreboding, wondering what favours he would ask. But I need not have fretted. Next day I waited for him at the arranged time, and for a further three hours, but he did not come.

*

For a long time, immersed in the challenge and strangeness of a new country, I imagine I am missing nothing of my own. Then an intruding memory – a chance thought, a facial resemblance – ignites a transient but overwhelming homesickness, like some unacknowledged weariness, and I try to return for a moment into my own mislaid tradition. So, after weeks of hearing only Turkic folk music and pop song, I went nostalgically to the state playhouse where the Russians had once planted opera and ballet as the ambassadors of their empire.

It was a hefty, mongrel building, raised half a century before by the architect of Moscow's KGB headquarters and of Lenin's tomb in Red Square. Its charmless façade had been truncated by lack of funds, and instead of rising to a skyline of victorious statuary, it petered out in a row of apologetic turrets. But an icing of Islamic decoration frosted all its surfaces, and continued over the auditorium and lobbies in a wintry beauty of white and pastel stucco. Along the upper hall, busts of the Turkic poets mingled coldly with Tchaikovsky, Borodin and Moussorgsky, and dish-shaped chandeliers of latticed plasterwork mottled the ceilings with a net of fractured Islamic light.

This patina of native culture, usually devoted to the mosque,

205

had been subtly enrolled into the Communist scheme of things. Secularised, it had thrown a superficial sanction round the propagandist dramas and ballets of the day, and in return it had lost its soul. So I wandered round the halls in guilty pleasure. They had a snowflake delicacy. I was almost alone. A few Russian matrons were promenading with their daughters, but they looked lost and dowdy. Their high heels echoed over the wooden floors. And when the curtain rose on *Esmeralda*, an old ballet hectic with gypsy child-stealers, distraught heroine and murderous priest, the auditorium was barely quarter full.

Yet habits died hard. Over loudspeakers the dancers were still announced by their grandiose Soviet titles – 'People's Artist of the USSR .... Honoured Artist of the USSR ....' – and the ballet unfurled in a shameless melodrama underscored by sub-Tchaikovskian music. At its end a limping beggar triumphed over religious despotism by tossing the lecherous priest over the battlements, and the auditorium sent up a splutter of applause.

As we trooped out into the vestibule I saw, of course, that the spectators were mostly Russian. They were cooing and purring. Perhaps this theatre, with its fleeting, sentimental ceremony, was all that remained to them for a shrine. But they were so few in its gaunt spaces, they seemed embattled. The Moslem decor looked newly liberated around them. Where once it had appeared tainted, even sinister, it had now entered into its own.

*

Ludmilla had been to *Esmeralda* too, and had thought it beautiful. At the age of thirty she lived with her mother in a cramped flat near the city centre, and her life was devoured by books and music. Russian friends introduced us, but I might as well have met her in the pages of nineteenth-century literature. She was suffering from a nameless allergy, which often made her faint, and she shook my hand frailly. She had Polish, Ukrainian, Tartar and even Uzbek blood, she said, but she looked wholly Russian. She talked about books while her fingers writhed in her lap. She had contracted a synthetic, Slavic charm, whose veneer had eaten inward, like acid, until its lilting voice seemed to have become her own. A fountain of auburn hair dangled about her shoulders and sprouted in a mauve-ribboned knot on the crown of her head; and from the centre of this cascade watched a white, pinched face with intelligent eyes and delicate, enquiring lips. Yet she swayed and wriggled her shoulders in shock at anything she said, as if it must be foolish or betraying.

'No, I never studied literature. It's just ... a passion.' Her tone at once embraced and repudiated such a thing. 'My father thought the only proper professions were medicine and engineering. I wasn't interested in either, but when I was seventeen I went to study construction in Leningrad. All the time I really loved the arts, but of course nobody asked *me* what I wanted.' She laughed ornamentally, without bitterness. 'I just did as my father said.'

'You don't regret that?'

'No ... no. Then I went to Kiev and studied to teach computer technology. It's a safe job.' She said wistfully: 'It's the future.'

'Your father wanted that too?'

'Yes.' She tilted her head with the charm which was not quite hers. 'But he died seven years ago.'

Her passions revolved around sporadic concerts of Vivaldi and Mozart, and flowed into the privacy of her reading. She nursed an aberrant love for Dostoevsky and an indifference to Tolstoy – she fluttered with embarrassment at this – and had read European classics in the old translations of Russian Parisian immigrants: 'They wrote a cleaner language.' She had long ago devoured Pasternak and Solzhenitsyn in *samizdat*, and had developed an obsession for science fiction and fantasy.

'But it's strange,' she said. 'Nobody seems to read any more. Before, Tashkent was full of cultured people. But not now. Maybe life has become too hard, I don't know.' As a young girl, perhaps, she had entertained the illusion of a world run by cultivated men, and it had left behind this melancholy afterglow. And when she said 'No, I've never married,' she did so as the waif on the train from Samarkand had done, as if at thirty all

207

possibility were gone. 'My parents were very strict. It wasn't easy to meet men.'

Yet she announced this coolly, unsoured. As the veil of stylised sweetness slipped a little with the ease of conversation, I thought I discerned in her the scrupulous, rather particular and intelligent nature which some men might fear. It was a gentle but not a generous face, the eyes alert and only conditionally giving: a face discreet and a little sad.

She toyed with her dress collar. Five friends were precious to her, she said: women who had cherished her during her elusive illness. 'But many others have gone away, and live in Israel or even Spain. I had a lot of Jewish friends, and now they've gone. They were the most interesting here. My best friend left a year ago for Tel Aviv, and for months I wept ....'

Into this circle of female comradeship, I thought, the intrusion of men could be coarsely disruptive. I asked: 'Will you leave too?'

'No, I'm happy here,' she said, 'although it's growing harder. If you're honest here, you're poor. It's becoming difficult for decent people to survive at all. You have to belong to a mafia. But I don't think the future will be very good anywhere.' A flutter of her hands dispersed it. 'I think the whole Revolution was a mistake. We could have improved ourselves gradually, steadily, without that chaos. And now everything's hopeless with us, poor Russia. We've become an example to the world of what not to do, how not to be!' She smiled with ornate irony. Here Russia's spiritual mission had reached its tragic obverse: its failure had taught the world only a negative truth. 'And think of the blood ....'

But it was hard, sitting beside her, to realise that the Revolution had happened and been undone at all, because she seemed to predate it. In her bleached, old-fashioned dress and reclusive frailty, she belonged in the country houses of Chekhov. Her Ukrainian ancestors, she said, had arrived here with an eccentric cousin of Czar Nicholas II, whose palace still decorated the city's centre. She should have been reclining there. She kept touching her wrist to her forehead. Perhaps convalescence was her nature, I thought. Talking with her, I had the fancy that the Revolution was still brooding below the skyline, that Lenin was waiting in Switzerland again, and the czar still on his throne.

*

The advance of suburbs and boulevards had eroded the old Moslem quarter, and left it under siege. Its insanitary tangle of clay walls and twisted tarmac, the tunnelled entranceways and secretive yards and roofs where spring tulips grew, had always been anathema to totalitarian rulers, and were often threatened with demolition. It was too hidden from them, too various and unaccountable. But the 1966 earthquake which ravaged the modern town had left this subversive warren eerily intact. Its beams and walls had merely shuddered a little, shed a skin or two of dust, then subsided.

I explored it fitfully. Its derelict mosques were starting into life again, but humbly. In cemeteries murmuring with willows and doves, the gravestones were inset with photographs of a severe, portly people, who flaunted Soviet service medals but were buried under the Islamic crescent.

I strayed into the courtyard of the Imam Bukhari medreseh, the highest seat of Islamic learning in the country. It was soft with apple and persimmon trees. Three years before it had been permitted twenty-two students. Now they numbered 300 youths who devoted their days to the Koran and the Traditions, the study of Arabic and Islamic law, with a little mathematics and English. I peered through the classroom doors. Arabic grammar was scratched over the blackboards. In the language laboratory the cassette-players were all broken, and the desks tufted with snapped wires. Poppies sprouted through the concrete of an abandoned volleyball pitch.

But a feel of leisured study prevailed, steeped in old certainties, the rhythms of a life denied for seventy years, and instead of apprehension I was filled by a fleeting nostalgia for this half-lost faith in the scented garden, for the shy students with their clasped books who talked pleasantly with me under the arcades, for their conviction in an overseeing Father. There was no breath of the excluding anger which I had once encountered in pre-revolutionary Tehran.

By evening the men had gone away, and 500 women students flooded into the courtyard. Thin veils snowed their hair and shoulders. It was the end of term. One girl – a pretty teenager whose veil slipped from her curls – incanted a prayer of thanks to God and to her teachers, while her father stood beside me and wept with pride.

In the residence of the Grand Mufti, the galleries murmured with wimpled secretaries and delegations. A throng of several hundred men and women crowded the central hall for the announcement of their pilgrimage to Mecca. Thousands would go eventually, where a few years before barely a pilgrim had been released.

I lodged a plea with the Mufti which I feared would be refused. In his library, I knew, was reputedly the oldest Koran in the world. It had belonged to the caliph Othman, third of Mahomet's successors. In AD 655 he was murdered in Medinah, and it had fallen blood-stained from his hands at the *aya*: '*And if they believe even as ye believe, then are they rightly guided. But if they turn away, then are they in schism, and Allah will be thy protection against them.*' Soon afterwards the adherents of the fourth caliph Ali, the cousin and son-in-law of the Prophet, were bloodily overthrown and the kinsmen of Othman succeeded him, and from that time there began the deep Sunni–Shia rift in Islam.

I waited uncertain in the library courtyard, where children were shaking mulberry trees. After three hours the squelch of the young fruit underfoot announced the librarian, a middle-aged man with a spade beard. 'You have a camera?' he demanded. 'You have a recorder?'

He relaxed when I shook my head. He led me into a reading-room of baroque charm, where gilded pillars upheld a little gallery with a crescent of desks, and a staircase spiralled up. The painted ceilings shone delicate under a lanterned skylight, and in showcases along the walls glowed Koranic manuscripts of minuscule beauty. I admired them cautiously. The librarian's stare scoured me. Under his robe I heard the telltale clink of a key. Shamelessly I let drop my scant knowledge about the caliph's Koran, and translated the blood-stained *aya* into stumbling Russian. He said gruffly: 'You know this?' But he was looking pleased, almost genial. Then he just said: 'Come.'

An iron door opened in the wall, and we entered a tiny room. Behind us crept an old mullah from Urgench, whom I had befriended in the courtyard. The librarian backed away. In the wall before us hung a massive copper safe, fronted by thick glass. 'Our holiest book.'

And there it was. It resembled no other Koran that I had seen. It bore no illumination, nothing exquisite at all, but was strong and utilitarian, with the beauty of something primitive. It lay mounded on itself in separate pages: thick, deerskin leaves. The script flowed long and low over them, like a fleet of galleys going into battle. The strokes were broad and strong. They belonged to the harshness of history, not the embroideries of faith.

'Ali took it away to Kufa,' the librarian said, 'and when Tamerlane conquered Iraq he brought it here. It is stained with blood, but I cannot show you.'

We stared at it through the glass a long time, while I imagined its leaves slipping from the fingers of the eighty-two-year-old caliph as he fell, and schism fanning out into half the world. Over a century ago, a traveller claimed to have seen it lying on a lectern in the tomb of Tamerlane, where mullahs chanted from it day and night. But by the time the Russians conquered Samarkand there was not a native in the city able to decipher it. The imams of the mosque where it was kept, it is said, sold it to the Russians for 125 roubles, and it remained in the Imperial Public Library in St Petersburg until the Bolsheviks returned it.

In the dim light of the cramped room we gazed at it with

separate thoughts: the white-robed librarian, myself and the mullah under his soiled blue turban, who began hesitantly to pray.

*

I met Bachtiar in a tea-house off Navoi Street. He wanted to practise his English on me. Under a T-shirt blazoned 'Commandoes' his chest and shoulders swelled like a bodybuilder's, and he folded his forearms in self-conscious layers of muscle. He was pure Uzbek. A basketball cap skewed backwards on his head, and beneath it the blunt, boy's face, still peppered with adolescent spots, confronted the world with a look of stunned belligerence.

He spent his time on the streets and in the gym. He had built up his body by boxing, he said. It had become his life. 'But I think your memory goes. My best friend was a champion, but he forgets everything now, he got hit so many times.' He bunched his fists threateningly against his jowls. 'But being a boxer, you feel better in the streets, you walk differently.'

He did too. After we left the tea-house, he straddled beside me with the bow-legged threat of a prize-fighter. He was an open challenge. Military service, he said, had taught him self-reliance, solitude. 'I don't trust anybody. Not my parents, no. Maybe my three closest friends. But nobody, in the end.' He spoke of his conscription in a string of tense, unresolved memories, his voice pitched higher than natural. It made a harsh, tuneless music, as if petrified into one expression, like his face.

'The army was meant to bring us together – Russians, Balts, Uzbeks. But the Russians were bastards. They thought because I was an Uzbek I must be some kind of wild man, you know, come in from the desert. We were out in Brandenburg, in freezing winter. The officers would punish you by pouring cold water on the floor and giving you a rag to mop it up. It took hours, while your hands froze. And then we'd fight. Russians against Ukrainians, Uzbeks against Russians.' His tone was one of long, harsh grievance, still breathy with rage and surprise. 'Then one day a Ukrainian fellow attacked me because I didn't lend him my boot-polish. Another held my arms while he punched me. When an officer appeared and stopped them, I hit the Ukrainian so hard I broke his nose and he fell down under a canteen trolley in a pool of blood. I thought he was dead. And the officer took out his pistol and fired bullets round my head. I was so terrified I just stood there, staring at him, frozen. For a year after that I used to stammer ....'

We stopped under parkland trees, where he turned with his odd, glazed stare unfocused just above my eyes. I was beginning to understand it. I asked: 'What did you do when you got out?'

'I made a street-gang with my three friends – Uzbek, Korean and Tajik. We used to go up to the race-course where black marketeers sell their stuff on stalls – leather jackets, dark glasses, stuff from Europe. I'd pick something up as if I wanted to buy it, then hand it to the friend behind, who'd hand it to another, who'd disappear with it. The seller would yell "Where is my goods gone?" and maybe he'd grab me. Then I'd hit him ....' His voice, normally hard and toneless, suddenly faltered. He said: 'I hope you don't think badly about me for this. I think it's more honourable than taking bribes, like lawyers do, like everybody else does.'

I did not know how to answer. He was engulfed by an obscure rebellion. I could not fathom it. The chaos of his values seemed to stem from outrage at any world he knew. His father was not some petty gangster but a high official. 'We don't talk together.' In his hunt for self-esteem, he was full of quaint chivalries and taboos. He rebuffed my attempts to pay at the next tea-house we entered, and recoiled from exchanging my dollars.

Irked by my silence, he asked again: 'Well, do you despise me?'

He was like a hurt child, desperate for good opinion. I said: 'No.' But I could not judge him. The mafia here, tangled in ties of clan and family, had deepened into a labyrinth more complex than anywhere else in the old Soviet Union. Russians who

213

attempted to penetrate it had either been excluded or enrolled. The illicit businesses which mushroomed in the seventies, the private cultivation of opium, drug-trafficking and prostitution, had bred a shadow-world of extortioners and protection rack-eteers, with legions of predatory gangs compared to which Bachtiar's was small fry. These mafias fanned down from the highest reaches of government to the poorest shopkeeper or policeman, and because they battened on Moscow they had acquired a halo of spurious patriotism, which united all classes in accepting them. Between 1984 and 1987 almost the entire top echelons of the Uzbek Ministry of Internal Affairs was arrested and purged. But nothing changed.

I asked: 'Have you ever done anything else?'

'My father makes me study English now, at an institute.' Snatches of Western pop song began to spangle his talk, culled from *Pink Floyd, The Who* and a host of others. 'You think I'm talented? "*Sweet Impressions* .... *You mean a lot to me*" ....' The songs held a lodestar magic for him: America. 'Our gang split up four months ago. The police caught one of us and beat him senseless. They're all bastards. They use rubber truncheons with steel inside. You may come out of the station an invalid for life, and nobody can do a thing. "*Maybe it's the end of the road*" .... The police just get witnesses against you. It's easy. You'll come out trembling, your whole body ....'

We were out among trees again. Bachtiar swung idly on the ball of one foot, practising karate-kicks. 'The police beat me up once. They tried to pin a theft on me, which I hadn't done.' He lashed casually at the air. 'But I hit back and cracked some-body's head against the wall. If he'd got a hospital certificate, I'd have gone to prison. But it didn't reach the courts. It just reached my parents.'

'What did they do?'

'I don't know.' A pop song faded on his lips. The karate went still. He lumbered beside me, suddenly deflated. 'I've never asked my father about it. I don't want to know. I don't want to hear he paid money to get me out.'

We crossed a bridge over a canal in angry spate and peered down into the cinnamon water. He said: 'I want to give up that sort of work.'

'Haven't you?'

'No. The tea-houses here are all in the hands of two mafias, which divide up their protection. I work as a bodyguard for one of the mafia bosses sometimes. It's not much. You just have to look tough.' He turned to me as if about to ask again 'Do you despise me?', but saw my expression and glanced away.

This assignment, I thought, was uglier than the other, because these bosses might do anything. They were petty kings. In the Rashidov years the notorious Akhmadzhan Adylov, who claimed descent from Tamerlane, had governed part of the Fergana valley like a separate country. Only after his arrest in 1984 did the details emerge of his slave-labourers and concubines, his estate furnished with lions and peacocks, and of his underground prison and torture-chamber, where he sprayed men with icy water in sub-zero temperatures until they died. His subjects had bowed to this without a word, just as they had done more than a century before under their khans. Rashidov himself, the Uzbek Party chief, a lisping sybarite whom Brezhnev had loaded with honours, had been judged a national paragon and entombed splendidly in Tashkent's Lenin Square. In Gorbachev's time his body was quietly removed. But now, in an ugly signal of his country's principles, the Uzbek president had restored this god-father to honour and proclaimed him a hero.

Bachtiar was gazing into the muddy waters, singing '*Sweet Impressions*'. 'I think my boss is in the prostitute racket too,' he said. 'The other day I saw some pimps who'd brought two tarts for the Pakistani businessmen I was dealing with. I didn't understand what was going on. I just heard them say, "You've seen the merchandise. What about it?"'

Then the credulous Bachtiar had trudged over to look at what goods they had brought, and saw two girls in the back of the car. 'They were quite pretty, but I went numb. It was the first time I'd seen that trade.' A high, smarting hurt was in his voice. I

215

anticipated one of his incongruous chivalries. 'The girls opened up their blouses to show they had no skin disease. I just felt sick. I told the Pakistanis that if they took them, then our own deal was off, and they let them go.'

He sounded bewildered. 'I'm going to stop this bodyguard work,' he said. 'You see, I've never beaten a guy up. I've seen what they're like afterwards – covered in blood and shaking, everything shaking. I don't think I could do that to anyone ....'

My gaze drifted over the cumbersome scaffold of biceps and deltoids which had become his self-esteem. He had built up his muscles and his pride together; but it was all bravado. He had no heart for it. He did not seem to know whether to applaud or despise himself. He went on peering down into the water. Then he fastened me with his look of aghast blankness – the same look, perhaps, as he had fixed on the officer whom he thought about to take his life in Brandenburg – and just said: 'I think I'm rather a pathetic person, really ....'

*

Nobody is quite as you remember them. Oman seemed younger, more ebullient and less predictable than when I'd met him the year before and we had planned to travel together. He was compact and stout, like a soft toy, with short arms and legs, and a crumpled face. Perhaps because of his grey-flecked hair, I had imagined him more mature than me, and it was with a shock that I realised he was ten years younger. He had grown up in post-war poverty, he said, assigned with his family to a single room in the mansion of a long-dead Russian count. As a youth he had worked in a factory producing bodywork for cars, then became a foreman in a lorry depot, and now, bubbling with free enterprise, he transported goods in two small vans of his own. Unexplained blanks yawned in this biography, I knew, but how important they were I could not guess, and his family affairs were rife with silences which he did not fill.

He lived in the farthest outskirts, where Uzbeks had built their traditional houses in suburbs around Russian flat-blocks. Skirted

216

by verandahs, the big, half-empty rooms were laid out for summer round a court of apricot and cherry trees, and cooled by vine trellises. Their decor dithered between cultures. Pilasters and flowers were painted lightly over their walls and ceilings, and the quilts and china of a long-ago dowry heaped the ill-jointed cabinets. The dados were hung only with rugs; but from roundels in the carved ceilings fell miniature chandeliers, and a video and colour television tyrannised the sitting-room.

All this Oman threw open to me with tycoonish pride, his eyes moist with welcome, and exploded little grenades of optimism around him in fluent Russian: 'This is my son! That's my wife! Those are my dogs!'

Yet they barely responded. His wife, Gulchera – a heavy, silent woman who never ate with us – pushed forward a charmless ten-year-old son to take my hand. The boy looked like the disenchanted daemon of Oman. I had the eerie feeling that he was older than his father. He walked already with the straddle of a Turkic adult, and beneath his dulled eyes the mouth sagged in seasoned disdain. Oman's eldest son was an angry-looking youth of twenty, who lived with his bride in a range of rooms on the far side of the courtyard. His middle son he never mentioned at all.

But for the moment, he was jubilant. On a table cluttered with festive dishes of mutton and cherries and pyramids of nuts and caramels, we balanced my large-scale maps and traced our future journey with meat-stained fingers into north-east Uzbekistan. Eased by vodka, we vaulted over the Tianshan foothills to Kokand. 'No problems!' Oman's cheeks bulged with sweets like a hamster's. 'We can go anywhere now!'

Soon a betraying trail of gravy was meandering among the towns of the Fergana valley and along the headwaters of the Syr Daria. I had visas for none of these places, but Oman blew this aside. I was his guest. Travelling on obscure roads in his tough Lada saloon, we would drop out of authority's sight. The police posts were unconcerned with passengers, he said. They just took bribes. So our greasy fingers jumped the border into

Kirghizstan and turned towards the Pamirs. Beyond the Alai mountains we moved south-west along a distant tributary of the Amu Dariya, and approached the Tajikistan border. But here Oman faltered. Tajikistan was in civil war. In the capital, Dushanbe, mobs were rioting.

'We won't get in,' he said.

But on the map the road crossed the north-western Pamirs in a glittering trajectory which was impossible to resist. 'Let's try it and see.'

'We should take a third person,' he said seriously. 'A guard. Three will make a proper gang.'

'I don't want a proper gang.'

But his stubby fingertip remained at the border. He said with an uncertain smile: 'I've read that soon a monster will rise up, another Tamerlane. It's predicted in Nostradamus. Did you know that Nostradamus foretold the fall of czarist Russia and the fall of the Soviet Union? To a month!'

Sortilege and clairvoyance had flourished all over the Soviet Union, but I had thought Oman a sceptic. Now he said: 'Nostradamus foretold three great tyrants – Napoleon, Hitler and a third – a man in a huge turban. And he's coming this year!'

I scowled in disbelief. 'We're still going to Tajikistan,' I said.

His vodka-softened eyes flickered over the map in vain search of distraction. Then he murmured without conviction: 'You're the boss,' and his finger nudged over the frontier and followed mine down the wild road to Dushanbe, jinked south to the Afghan border, and traced a long loop home.

By the time Gulchera marched in with bowls of strawberries, his rumbustiousness had returned. 'We'll try it! Let's see!' He smote the air with self-mocking gallantry. 'My wife won't mourn me ....'

A smile started on her face, like a crack in concrete. 'He's a monkey,' she said. 'He was born in the Chinese year of the monkey, and in the Moslem year of the lion. What kind of an animal is that?'

I laughed. 'It sounds effective.' But this confused beast was

218

closer to Oman than I knew.

We enshrined the map among a debris of dishes, and tucked into the strawberries. A month's sybaritic travelling shimmered across the simplified geography in front of us. The emerald sliding of the valleys one into another, and the whitening contours of the mountains from which glacial rivers dribbled and great peaks ascended, filled me with longing. Here were some of the highest summits in the world. It was a region almost untouched. China, Afghanistan, Kashmir hovered just off stage. Oman, too, had contracted my infection, and was remembering his war-service in the early seventies behind the still-quiet Afghan frontier. We sealed our plan with a glut of cherries and sweet liqueurs. It would be a walkover, we decided.

After a while Oman's daughter-in-law entered and flitted round him, adjusting his napkin and pouring out coffee. 'She's a fine girl,' he said, 'but my son's hopeless, a playboy. I tell her all the time to be tough on him, to grab him by the ears and shake him.'

But she did not look as if she could be tough on anybody. In her narrow face the eyes were soft almonds. She had been brought up gentle, he said, the daughter of his best friend. He played a video of her wedding four months before, while she watched with a sad half-smile. Across the screen the ritual bouquet-laying at three or four war-memorials, and a banquet in a bleak hall, were followed two days later by a Moslem wedding and an orgy of pilau-guzzling in the courtyard of their home. After the video ended, she slipped away.

But by now Oman had weighed anchor on a sea of vodka. We drank to peace everywhere, to our looming journey, to British–Uzbek concord. He said: 'Tashkent has just been twinned with Birmingham! Oh Colin, there is a bigger difference than they know!' His dark eyes were watering. 'I don't know what will happen in this country, but I'm afraid everything is on the brink. Things are like they were in Germany before Nazism in the twenties. I'm afraid Communism will come again by December, or Fascism.'

'Or Islam?'

'Those people only pray to God, I'm not afraid of that. God expects honesty and right behaviour. It's these other people ....' He drained another glass. 'We may have civil war one day. Then my neighbour who wants Communism will shoot me, who doesn't, and so on ... and on ....'

His spirit was draining away. He looked older again, and touched by a sombre authority. Some latent bitterness, too, shook in his voice's loneliness. These bouts of pessimism, often followed by a savage self-unfurling, would soon become familiar to me, but that evening I only watched in surprise while he levered himself to his feet and said good-night.

For a long time I lay awake in the silence of the spare room and of the suburb outside. It seemed unnaturally still. The street lights printed leaf-shadows on the curtains, and occasionally one of Oman's wire-haired dogs yelped itself awake on the verandah. At last, in this filtered light, I fell into a confused sleep, hypnotised by Oman's shelf of European books and their arcane Cyrillic authors hanging above me: Jek London ... Aleksandr Dewma ... Artoor Heyli ... Jems Hedli Cheis ....

For the next four days, birthdays among Oman's friends delayed us with an outbreak of parties round the city. In my memory they have blended into a single guzzling revel, which roisters through the cramped rooms of high-rise flats and dappled suburban courtyards. The tables creak beneath the same glut of side-dishes: the chocolate-coated biscuits in their paper wrappings, the bowls of raisins and walnuts and apricots, the heaped and saccharine confectionery.

Then the people dance. Their upcurled arms seem to free the swaying bodies below into a celebration of erotic power. But the men are already a little drunk, and begin to filter into other rooms. It is their wives who want the music. Sturdy Uzbek and Tartar women, they kick off their shoes and thump the floor with feet fringed by gaudily varnished toenails. Their frizzed hair bounces round features concertinaed in flesh, and their eyes

220

glint out from mascara pools. The mood is at once dreamy and ebullient, tinged by the sentimentality of Russia and by a stirring sensuousness.

There is rarely a Russian present; but the Moslem Tartars, whose language lies close to Uzbek, often look indistinguishable from Slavs, and stretch a tentative bridge between the cultures. 'The Tartars just took the Russian women when they invaded,' Oman said, 'and this is the result!'

The men, meanwhile, have reconvened around the vodka bottles, where old comrades pledge their love in bouts of clannish connivance. They were in college together, perhaps, or in business, and somewhere a marriage has cemented the families. They clamp their wrists together where the veins bulge – 'Blood brothers!' – and pour out advice, trust, knowledge. 'My true friend!' Nothing, for the moment, is more important, more overwhelmingly real, than this male fidelity. The vodka gurgles and the eyes gleam with replenished belief in the world before they become overcast by drink and the phrases dither into platitude. Then the circle of love expands to include anyone present. Soon all barriers and differences are declared void, and only emotion valid, as if benign drunkards everywhere are doomed to slip into the same language. Vaulting insights are asserted with the heat of discoveries just made, until every declaration becomes a sodden *Eureka*! from the heart. All around, the heads nod sagaciously, as if testing some mighty truth; a zealous celebrant takes it upon himself to fill the glasses of the rest; and the next toast blunders on its way in a jumble of metaphors and goodwill. 'We are many farmers, but we till one earth ....'

Eventually the foreigner, too, stumbles to his feet and blurts out his gratitude and love, while a bonfire of benevolence ignites around him. But outside, the town has gone still and the stars are shining, and at last the guests depart in a clamour of tenderness, leaving behind only a few party bores, elderly men mostly, too drunk or important to move. For a while an inebriate litany continues in the starlight: 'What difference does it make ... black, white, Asian, American?... People are just people ....

221

What matters is the heart .... There is no difference in the sight of God .... We are all one .... God is One ....'

But at these parties, too, sit surly men and shy women who sink out of notice and are the first to slip away. Social and dynastic rivalries simmer beneath the chatter. Perhaps that was why Oman's wife shunned such gatherings, and he himself sometimes looked isolated. Once his hostess turned on him and hissed: 'Tell Gulchera this is the last time I ask her to a party if she won't come!'

The people eating and dancing beside me might turn out to be lawyers or restaurateurs, carpenters or businessmen, who chattered democratically together. They inhabit my memory now in raucous isolation, vivid, sentimental and open. Once I found myself gazing into a face of rare Turkic beauty. Over her cheek-bones the bronze skin stretched tense and fragile, lit by a pair of hazel eyes. She was an economist whose government institute had foundered for lack of funds, and she was married to a fat, wordless lorry-driver with chest-hair bushing between his shirt buttons.

On my other side a jolly Tartar woman in a candyfloss pink dress had dismissed her drunken husband after ten years of battering marriage. 'I told him I didn't want any maintenance. He couldn't hold down a job anyway. I just wanted him to go. So he went.' She was bringing up their two children while operating an elevator on an eleven-hour shift.

Once, too, as I danced among the stout legion of my contemporaries, Oman's daughter-in-law appeared in front of me, confident in her young beauty, the bride of four months. In my drink-dazed eyes she danced like a reborn Salome. It was impossible to relate her to the women lumbering around me, to the matron she would one day become. The music thumped and howled. Her arms swung above her with a rhythmic violence and her belly wriggled bare between a pruriently modest skirt and a little jacket. Then she was gone.

Somewhere else an old man buttonholed me with melancholy evangelism. Parties like this, he said, crooking a finger at our lavish table, would soon be extinct. Things had been declining for forty years, and would go on getting worse. A pair of quizzical eyebrows tufted him in comic bewilderment. He could remember a heaven, he said, when Stalin's law prevailed, and crime was unknown. 'There was justice then. You didn't escape prison by knowing somebody-or-other. Vendors in the bazaar would just cover their wares in a cloth and find nothing disturbed next morning!' A perverted truth clung to this. 'The canals were so clean you could drink from them. The air smelt good. Most people had a room or two, and enough to eat, and clothes. People were not rich, but they were honest. Buses were enough transport, and some horses. And I had a first-rate bicycle' – his hands lifted in delight – 'made in Birmingham!'

Then he dwelt on the mystery of creation and its irreversible decline, on how God had designed a man and a woman and given them fruit trees – 'and there were some cows too' – and everything had grown up from this radiant simplicity. His eyes began watering. He deployed walnuts across the table to illustrate the triple rotation of crops, and mimed the waking up of the earth in spring, and its snoring in winter. But then there became too many people, he said – again he crooked his finger at the gluttonous guests crowding our table – and bosses and kings had appeared. His upturned eyebrows floated in airborne sadness. 'And now people think that after this life they'll just go into the earth. So why should they be honest? Why not grab what you can? Nobody cares any more.' He let a pinch of raisins trickle from his hand. 'Because afterwards they'll be dust ....'

9

Into the Valley

Dawn had not broken when we moved east out of the last suburbs of Tashkent. Our headlights swung over an empty road. We were keen with the journey's start, Oman singing to himself as he steered around the potholes, while I sat awake in high spirits, and the faintest apprehension.

After a while, as if some deeper shade of darkness had overprinted the night, I became aware of the cones and triangles of mountains standing on the blackness of the southern horizon. One by one they detached themselves into three dimensions, and within a few minutes the sky was lightening and the stars were peeled away.

But Oman said: 'It's still dark ahead.'

At first I imagined storm-cloud. But then, as the sun rose and dangled like a weak bulb, I realised that from end to end the earth ahead lay under a leaden ceiling of smoke. Desolating flat-blocks, pylons and allotments of withered sunflowers appeared, and the next moment we were in the coal-mining town of Angren, whose deposits had been torn open in 1942 to feed the Soviet war-machine.

Nothing might have changed since then. In front of us a landscape of primitive horror had opened up. It belonged to Britain's collieries in the thirties, or to the Pennsylvania coalfields of the Depression. Under that sky of cruelly filtered light, the whole plain was littered with industrial dinosaurs: coal-fed power-stations and factories like old Meccano sets, strangled in their own chutes and pipes, and chimneys belching yellowish waste. Their windows were smashed or blank. Some were dead on their feet, their turbines and gangways left to rot unremoved. Murals of Lenin flaked from their walls. Others looked derelict, yet had only just been built. Silver water-pipes wriggled for miles between them, sloughing their lagging here and there, and overarched the road like abandoned gateways, while on the town's eastern limits yawned the amphitheatre which tyrannised it, ringed with pink rock. We got out of the car and gazed down hundreds of feet. It plunged beneath us in a black stairway. It looked less like an open-cast mine than a canyon, in whose centre the waste-tip surged in a crumpled mesa. Trains and dump-trucks tinkled and whined far below, while the town teetered and smoked on the excavation's lip, and the first peaks of the Tienshan, the Chinese 'Mountains of Heaven', glittered in the polluted sky.

In this wasteland a depleted colony of Germans remained, deported from the Volga by Stalin in 1941. Among cottagey suburbs, an old man, dozing in his courtyard under a Homburg hat, could still speak a stumbling, lonely German although his ancestors had lived in Russia for over 200 years. Ever since Catherine the Great had ushered in her countrymen as farmers, they had settled on the lower Volga, and the old German could remember from his childhood its modest prosperity. He had the Stoic face of a man whom huge events had misruled. His working hands rested on his knees, and his big shoulders were bowed a little. He spoke in husky Russian.

Everything had been all right until the war, he said. 'But on August 28th 1941 – that was the blackest day of our lives – Stalin deported us all within three days. My family were taken to northern Kazakhstan, where we worked in military construction. The people hated us, because they knew who we were. A year later my father died, broken, and I was sent to an arms factory in the Urals. We never saw the Volga again.' He spoke all this placidly, as if its history were long ago. 'After the war I married a German and worked as an agronomist for the rest of my useful life. Then we came here where my sons and daughter are. It

226

was difficult out there in Kazakhstan on our own. We're old.' He straightened his back against the chair as if resisting this. 'But of course people here don't understand how we came. Some of them think we're ex-prisoners-of-war ....'

'Even now?'

'Even now.' He clambered to his feet and returned with a wooden box. 'But you see I served the Soviet Union well.' He opened the lid on a row of work medals, and pinned one to his lapel. 'You see.'

So even he, suffering the immigrant's split identity after eight generations, had sheltered under the blanket impersonality of 'Soviet'. I asked tentatively: 'Have many gone back to Germany from here?'

He looked vaguely troubled. 'Yes, many.'

'What do they write back?'

'They say they're sad. The shops have everything, but they're sad.' A few words of German had strayed into his Russian. 'I have relatives who've gone to Hamburg, and it's very tough. After all, they were born here. They barely speak German. But at the beginning it's always difficult. It's like that everywhere.' He looked at me as if he had read my thought. 'No, I won't go. Who wants me there? No one needs me. I'll stay here with my old woman. Or perhaps we'll return to the Volga ....'

'You think that will happen?' Even now, I knew, politicians were deliberating the revival of the autonomous German region there, and Germany itself was lobbying for it, in a bid to deflect a tide of immigrants from its own borders.

'I think it may happen,' he said. 'And if the republic's established there, many will go.' He smiled for the first time. 'I, too. I don't want to lose the feeling of belonging to my nation.'

I said: 'You can't lose that now!' But I did not believe that this Volga republic would be recreated, and a few weeks later Moscow refused it. Perhaps the ingrained fear of Germany, or vested interests in the old republic, had proved too strong.

'The Uzbeks have been fine with us,' the old man said. 'But it's not the same as your own land.' He folded the medals back

227

into their box. Engraved with Communist stars and portrait-heads of Lenin, they already looked like museum exhibits. 'And I want to speak my people's tongue again.'

A few hours later our Lada was circling into foothills. Beneath us the Chirchik river made a wild corridor through the rocks, while the road above us corkscrewed into treeless passes. Erosion had flayed the slopes to powder, spotted with shrubs and gashed by scree-filled ravines. These were the last gasp of a massif which had swept west more than a thousand miles from the borders of Mongolia.

Now, over a pallid membrane of grass, the heights were scarlet with tulips. Once we blundered over the rubble of an avalanche which had shaken loose after earth tremors two days before. Then we were spiralling upward through tightening circles, where crags burst in black fists, and the mountain-crests wheeled overhead in shining parapets of snow. Cloud and rain gusted across the road. The next moment we were over the pass and descending a valley where a stream slithered down a thread of villages. Maple, apricot and silver poplar followed one another in a long brilliance of yellow, crimson and green, while isolated scenes unfurled like a Chinese scroll: a horse grazing under a footbridge, a house decaying, an old woman munching bread on a scarlet mattress. When we wandered into the hamlets of mud and poplar-wood we found farmers and silver miners, Uzbek and Tajik mingled, who fed us fruit and new-baked bread.

At intervals along the road a police-post would flag us down and Oman trudge off to present his papers and return often deprived of some petty bribe: a few cigarettes or a ten-rouble note. 'We never used to have all this! Never! So why? Why?' Then the festering anger would erupt and his thick arms pummel the steering-wheel. 'Ninety-five per cent of our people are poor – how does a peasant live on twenty dollars a month? – and five per cent are rich and corrupt. No wonder people are starting to call for a Stalin! The Mafia in Sicily are a kindergarten compared to ours!'

An hour later we were crossing the Syr Dariya, the old Jaxartes river. Legend claimed its valley to have once been so populous that a cat could stroll from wall to wall, or a nightingale flit from branch to branch of its orchards, all the way from Kashgar to the Caspian. Now a 300-yard pontoon bridge moaned and clanked under us. Beneath it the river poured west in a silt-heavy flood, leached by cotton-fields, before curling north to cross the Kizilkum desert and vanish in the Aral Sea.

By evening we were nosing into Kokand. The old town looked young now, nondescript in its grid of Russian streets, but its past drenched it black, and suffused its most innocent inhabitants for me. It had been called Khoh-kand, 'town of pigs', from the boars which infested its marshes, but in time the name grew other connotations. By the start of the nineteenth century, together with Bukhara and Khiva, its khanate had carved up the core of Central Asia, ruling from the rich Fergana valley to the steppes beyond Tashkent. Its citizens were known for cowardice and cruelty. Their khans were murderers and debauchees. Even their subjects loathed them. Their land was stubbornly fruitful – it exported wool, silk, fruit, hides and opium – but within its eight-mile battlements the town eventually became an arsenal shrunk among fields and cemeteries, and its diseased waters turned the inhabitants cretinous with goitre. The Russians absorbed the khanate in 1876, after routing an army of 50,000 for the loss of six dead, and abolished it wholesale.

Yet a moment of tragic distinction visited the town in 1918. In the chaos of the Revolution a Moslem congress assembled here to set up a rival government to the Bolshevik soviet in Tashkent. It was a unique sign of united national sentiment in Central Asia, and a first and last attempt to achieve democratic unity by peaceful means. Claiming that it spoke for the masses, Kokand appealed to Lenin in vain. The Tashkent Bolsheviks attacked the ill-armed town, slaughtered some 14,000 citizens, indulged in an orgy of rape, and burnt or mined every house and mosque. Then a tremor of fury and realisation surged through the

Moslems, and within a week the whole region was in flames. It was from this moment that the *basmachi* guerrilla movement arose to plague the Red forces – and continued fighting for another five years – and that Moslem faith in Communism was lost.

It was hard to forget this as we strolled among the brick and stucco houses of the Russian streets, and entered the Moslem lanes behind, although they looked idle in the failing sun. Here and there a mosque was reopening, and the flash of women's silk made a dark fire in the alleys. Oman found a half-empty bookshop and bought a Russian translation of *The Castle*, available here at last seventy years after Kafka's death. He loved Dostoevsky, he said, and had heard that Kafka too was a painter of inner worlds.

He found a hotel where we settled for three nights. It was the best in town, but Spartan, rowdy and haunted by black marketeers. We shared a fetid room, and were visited by rats. Oman barely noticed them, nor the stained bedsheets and toxic plumbing. Yet he indulged in fastidious vanities. Every morning he dabbed his thickened neck in eau de Cologne and often visited the barber for a hedonistic shave, and his shabby suitcase was packed with scrupulously clean shirts. Sometimes he would gaze for long seconds into the mirror, as if hunting for somebody who had gone, his shallow-set eyes separated by a double-groove of knotted flesh.

But each evening I returned from exploring the town to find the vodka bottle lowered by his bed, a mound of cigarette-stubs and *The Castle* still unread. Then he would clamber to his feet, and a fearful anger release itself from him. 'I just bought some lint. Four roubles! It would have cost less than ten kopeks two years ago! That's the mafia for you!' His voice flew up an octave. 'That's why this country's being ruined! If you start any business they're on to you in a wolf-pack. Everything you buy is old or broken. It's got to end sometime. One day the people will get on their feet like they have in Tajikistan!' Then he would seize a shirt or a razor or a packet of cigarettes and yell: 'You know

230

how much this cost only a year ago? Yes, only ... and now ....'

Increasingly I realised how little I knew about him, and I came to dread these sessions. Suddenly all his features would contract into a bitter defensiveness, as if the short nose and blunt chin had been ingested back into his skull. It might have been the face of a boxer, were it not for its compact, fleshly softness, and the hazel eyes, which touched his features with a damaged gentleness.

At last he would go to bed in a pair of crimson underpants, and sprawl above his sheets in the humid dark; but his snoring changed key all night, sometimes pulsing in a deep, body-filling respiration, sometimes gargling and shallow like a death-rattle, until a burp or a cough changed its chord. But by morning, immaculately shaven and spruce in a white shirt again, he would be off to hunt for bargains round the nearest bazaar, jaunty and game in a whiff of eau de Cologne.

*

The royal palace, built in 1860 by the repulsive Khudayar Khan, stretched a long façade above parklands of weeds and roses. Its blank arches and walls were sheened in a medley of garish tile-work, but its rectangle of ramparts had gone, blown up by the besieging Russians to the stupefaction of the townspeople. A heavy ramp still mounted to the gates in a baleful path of unwelcome, and entered between narrow towers. Inside, the 113 rooms had been completed only three years before the Russians sacked them, and their survivors spread round the porticoes of empty courtyards, where I walked in solitude. The whole palace was infected by a grotesque dilapidation which cruelly suited it. In one range of rooms a natural history museum was decaying unvisited, its stuffed animals tottering into dust under the intricately painted ceilings. The inner court, once interlaced with verandahs, stairways and pavilions, had dropped into a lake of rubble, and in the park a children's playground was disintegrating. Schoolboys splashed naked in the preposterous fountains, and a defunct Aeroflot jet had come to

231

rest among the birch trees. Seated under the weeping willows, a few lovers gazed away from one another in awkward unison, the girls flushed and coy in their earthy silks, the youths silent, their interlaced hands lying guiltily between them on the bench.

The last khan had distributed his harem among his friends as the Russians closed in, then fled to Mecca. But some of his ancestors lay in a cemetery near the Friday Mosque – a wilderness of the dead, dense and secret with trees, where Oman and I found them one afternoon. In a high, turreted enclosure, their graves stood peeling and half-abandoned, with those of their prematurely dead children and a holy man. The courtyard was strewn with branches where worshippers, in pious servitude, brushed away the dirt from the floor. Two pilgrims, praying there, rolled over and over in the dust before the holy man's tomb, then went on to worship robotically at the royal graves.

All around the mausoleum, among the cubes and headstones of the dead, a flock of lesser holy men – sightless ancients, frosted in scanty beards – dispensed medicinal magic. These were the spiritual descendants of the dervishes who had always infested Islam – holiness and charlatanry inseparable, even in one heart. Their clients sat before them in the dust while the old men, swathed in tattered coats and turbans, breathed over their faces in spitting puffs, and murmured spells. There were masseuses, too, who stretched out passing worshippers fully clothed on benches or stones, gabbling enchantments, and in five perfunctory minutes would slap their arms and legs, tug at their finger-joints and rummage over their heads.

Under the mausoleum's gate I stumbled on four blind patriarchs crouched round a young couple. They breathed first over her, then over him, on and on, in a crossfire of whistling spittle. The lean husband strained fiercely forward. His young wife, her lips thin in a bitter, withdrawn face, kept her eyes averted from him. Beneath her jacket, close against her breast, she cradled a live chicken, a charm for fertility. For hours, it seemed, the old men swayed and incanted, their eyes shrunk to white slits, while their gusts and spits sought out the couple through their darkness, directed by the man's nervous shifting on his haunches and the smothered clucking from the woman's coat. She stared about her with a shamed hope. Sometimes she seemed to wince in terror. She was praying for new life, but was surrounded by death; and these blind sages seemed coeval with it, their second sight coiled unimaginably behind their eye-sockets.

On a bench nearby a sickly boy was being blessed in his mother's arms. His two sisters were giggling uncontrollably, but the child gazed back at his benefactor aghast, his face frozen and staring, and I thought how years later, if he lived, he would remember this terrifying blessing, and the strange old man with blanks where his eyes should have been, and the mausoleum looming behind. At last the woman got up and gave the man two roubles. His fingers fondled them and he mumbled something to her. Inflation had hit even holy men. So she handed him five roubles more, then went slowly away, cradling her sick son, between the graves.

*

Oman had a friend in the town, an actor named Jura who was famous there. He was a master of *askiya*, the theatrical exchange of insults which could still be heard in tea-houses. His face was a mask of polished flesh, where the features were only sketchy afterthoughts, but humour fidgeted chronically beneath, and broke open a mouth fabulous with gold teeth. He had spent forty years on the boards, or bandying tea-house abuse rife with sexual innuendo, surrounded by the toothless hilarity of old men.

His house was as prodigal as he was, thrown round a majestic courtyard overswept by fourteen varieties of vine. He shared it with four married sons, and had fifteen grandchildren scattered round Kokand. Even his gait was a study in amplitude – a kind of rollicking waddle. He wore a baggy, grey-blue suit, like a crumpled Chinese, but when we sat down to lunch its jacket strained to bursting, and his arms bulged like columns.

233

We ate monstrously in his garish dining-room, sitting beneath a tapestry of damsels cavorting on a barge. Dish after dish arrived in gluttonous procession, all carried in soundlessly by one of those daughters-in-law who seem touchingly enslaved: a thin, frightened girl in flaming silks. She fluttered in and out, and barely raised her eyes.

Jura spoke in a dead-pan monologue. Sometimes in his face I discovered only the cruel oval of the Mongol steppe; then a twitch of plastic flesh would presage a joke, or the mouth open in a second's gleaming banter. 'It's in the blood,' he said. 'Humour. I was an only child – an odd thing with us – and my father taught me *askiya* from boyhood. My grandfather and great-grandfather were court jesters to the khans. And their ancestors before that. All jesters. I don't think it was a very safe job.' I pictured, for a moment, a line of Mongoloid hunchbacks and wise simpletons rigged up in cap-and-bells. But he went on: 'These jesters were most like wits and story-tellers. Sometimes there were many of them. In my great-grandfather's day, my father told me, there were forty, and he the oldest.'

'Forty of them ....' Oman echoed his words from time to time in dreamy sycophancy. 'The khan was hard to cheer up.'

'The last one was like a wolf, you know, savage,' Jura went on. 'He told the forty one evening that if they didn't make him laugh he'd have them executed. This was his own joke, I suppose, but perhaps it wasn't. Then he sat in front of them, looking grim.' He depressed his mouth and shoulders in surly xenophobia. 'And one by one they all failed – thirty-nine of them – until at last he came to my great-grandfather. The khan said, "Make me laugh." But my great-grandfather just yelled at him, "You mother-fucker, why haven't you already laughed? What's wrong with you?" And the khan rocked back in astonishment and started to guffaw!'

This hoary jot of family history coaxed a smile from him, which instantly faded. He said: 'But the line of humour dies out with me. My sons don't act. And audiences are smaller now, much smaller. People stay at home watching television.'

In the town's theatre they acted classics too, he said – Schiller, Sophocles, Shakespeare. He had just played Iago in *Othello*, and it might have been a chilling performance, for the neutrality of his face seemed capable of erupting into any nature, and I wondered vaguely what other selves might lie beneath it.

He and Oman went on eating long after I was exhausted. I watched them in awe. Fistfuls of potato and sheep's fat vanished down their throats with a smacking of lips or a carnival burp. They plunged their spoons into the mounded pilau, plucking out choice gibbets of mutton or wedges of scented rice. Sweets and raisins disappeared in a trice. Vodka came and went. 'And I have wine! From our own grapes!' Jura flashed his science-fiction smile. 'We'll taste the oldest!'

The gentle house-slave brought it in a jug, and we drank. It was pure vinegar. Oman, who had tossed it back like vodka, was racked by gasping coughs. Even Jura looked angry as he sent it away. But their spirits revived with the arrival of sugared sweetcorn and dried apricots, and the vinegar was exorcised in the renewed gurgling of vodka. Only after an hour did Jura lie back on his cushions, sharpening a toothpick with a gilded penknife, and regale us with descriptions of the towns where we were going.

The citizens of Margilan, he said, were delicate and obsequious – his hand fluttered sweetly to his heart in corrupt invitation. 'They'll ask you to their home and then go out by the back door!' Next he brought his fists crashing on to the table to illustrate the coarse robustness of the people of Andijan. And as for those of Namangan, he said ... well, the men slept with one another. But the people of Kokand? 'We're the humourists! That's our reaction to life. We laugh! The Margilanis simper, the Andijanis bluster, but ...' – his face puckered – 'we laugh!'

This thumbnail scenario was to haunt us during the next week's travel, when time and again, as if by telepathy, townspeople reproduced Jura's mannerisms with unsettling accuracy. As we said farewell, he announced with sudden grace: 'This is not a Margilan man speaking, but my door is open to you whenever you come again ....'

As we crossed the courtyard, his daughter-in-law waved to us shyly. I wondered about her – as I often did about such women, living in the extended family of strangers, under the rod of their mother-in-law. But now her look of fear had gone. She was cradling a baby son in her husband's doorway, and as we went she lifted him up to our view like the badge of her honour, and was smiling.

*

Next day the long, alluvial corridor of the Fergana valley began to steer us east. It scooped a festering cul-de-sac out of the mountains on three sides: a land more enclosed and volatile than any behind us. It was the easternmost limit of Uzbekistan. The icy tributaries of the Syr Dariya tumbled down from north and south to feed it, netted by dams and ordered through canals, and all about us the waters were sucked away by cotton-fields glossed with green.

Across their giant plantations, and all along the roads, the mulberry hedges had been hacked back to writhing trunks as provender for silk-worms, and now filed across the fields like ghosts. Here and there, where electric cables intersected them, an ungainly stork would be hunched on each pylon above a ramshackle nest and two unsteady fledglings, their beaks ungratefully open.

Half a millennium ago the emperor Babur, who was born here, wrote of the country's flower-filled meadows, and of fruit so plentiful that melons were given away free on the roadsides. As a youth he had hunted wild ass in its hills, and loosed his hawks to bring down pheasants so plump that the broth of one could feed four men. But he was driven from these lands of his youth and never returned, and their lost paradise haunted him long after he had founded the Moghul empire in India. Even in the last century, before the Russians imposed cotton, travellers described the indolent beauty of brimming orchards, and the charm of tea-houses perched above cold rivers.

236

While my mental map of the land was starred with historical leftovers and formidable mountains, Oman was travelling another country. His was dotted with promising bazaars and restaurants. He slowed the Lada to a watchful dawdle at any wayside market, then would march in to haggle over a pair of socks or a sliver of silk, for resale in Tashkent. These minor purchases put him at peace. He hummed tunelessly to himself. At every lift of the ground we would look out on a misted plain of orchards and whitewashed villages lanced with poplars, while far to the south the Pamir mountains were trailing their snow-summits across the blue.

Fergana, the industrial core of all this valley, had been founded by the Russians only a century before. It was a centre of textiles and oil refining, but already it looked old. Avenues of plane trees tunnelled through its heart, dappling façades washed in a seductive peacock blue. So its poverty of shops and offices was tempered in this veil of splintered sunlight. Uzbeks and Russians still mingled, and files of blond and black-haired schoolchildren made mongrel undercurrents in the streets. But when I tried to find my way with a two-year-old map (Oman had vanished into the bazaars) half the road names were unrecognisable to me. Karl Marx St had transformed to Fergana St, Communist St to Samarkand St, Kirov to Constitution, Pushkin to Navoi.

I sat down in the central mall. Beside me a man of eighty trembled faintly, continually, with Parkinson's disease. He was trying to pull liquorice tablets from his pocket, but could not, and turned to me with a shiver of helplessness. Two maple leaves had settled undisturbed on his shoulders. He had worked all his life in the cotton-fields, he said, but did not know if the sprayed chemicals had infected him. He lived on a pension of 1100 roubles a month. I wondered how he survived. Meat alone cost over 100 roubles a kilo. But he had not eaten meat for many years, he said. 'I live on eggs and bread. Pensioners do.'

'And what do you do all day?'

'When the weather's good, I sit here and watch everything

changing.'

He did not see the sun-gentled city of my imagination. He saw threat. He could not fathom it. In 1989 the region's youths had gone on the rampage against its minority Meskhetian Turks, who had been transported by Stalin from the Black Sea and never returned. Nearly two hundred were killed. The whole valley, dyed with a deeper Islam than the country's west, was angrier and less predictable.

'But it wasn't because of nationalism or Islam,' Oman told me later, 'although the Meskhetians are Shiites. It was because of the Turks' mafia!' All evil, as usual, was rooted in the mafia for him. 'The ordinary people had had enough. They said "Get out!"' He chopped the air triumphantly. 'Out!'

Yet the reasons for these upsurges were enigmatic still; an imponderable mix of economic distress and racial bigotry. In 1990, some three hundred people were killed in the Kirghiz town of Osh, where natives and Uzbeks battled over housing; and in the past few years half the large cities had grumbled with separate crises.

Whenever this happened, Central Asia trembled. The frontiers of its states still ran almost as Stalin delineated them in October 1924, trying to follow ethnic realities. Sometimes they divagated nervously to join mountain headwaters with the plains which they nourished. The results were freakish. Turkmenistan and Uzbekistan sliced up the Khorezm oasis bizarrely between them, while Tajikistan was crowned by a horn of lowland reaching almost to Kokand. Kirghizstan (which was shaped in 1926) straddled the Fergana valley like a snapped wishbone; and even now – as I conceived of Uzbekistan as a crouching dog – we were travelling along the creature's preposterously jowled and bobbled snout as it thrust into Kirghizstan.

Yet despite these convolutions, the peoples of each nation were helplessly interleaved. The Uzbeks overlapped their Kazakh borders, and were numerous in every other state, comprising one quarter of the population of Tajikistan. But the Tajiks formed the bedrock of Uzbek Samarkand and Bukhara, while

238

the little Karakalpak nation, ethnically close to the Kazakhs, lodged discomfitingly in the dog's groin. Russians littered every nation, of course, especially Kazakhstan, alongside Tartars, Ukrainians, Germans, Koreans, Chinese, Uighurs, Arabs and a host of others.

It was this potential ferment which licensed the diehard government in Tashkent to limit democracy. And the chaos did not end here. Turcomans and Tajiks circled the Caspian into northern Iran; Afghanistan was rife with three million Tajiks and over 1,500,000 Uzbeks, heady with dreams of forging unified states; and in China the remnants of Kazakhs and others still formed petty communities in the grimly beautiful mountains of Xinjiang.

Even now, one of these quirky frontiers faced us as we drove south out of Fergana at evening. The tiny Uzbek enclave of Shachimadan lay isolated in a rift of the Pamirs, just inside Kirghizstan, and was circled on my map by a conscientious international boundary. Even as we drove, the green of our valley ended as precisely as if it, too, had been inscribed across a map, then we were pushing through desert hills along a nervy river, into the Pamir. Clouds and rain descended together. The colour had drained from the world. For twenty miles the road jittered through Kirghizstan, but only a few sodden herdsmen signalled this, swarthy under their peaked hats, and the mountains showed nothing but gnarled and befogged foundations, like the claws of great birds hidden in the clouds.

Then we were out again in chastened sunlight, on the edge of Shachimadan, and were soon lounging in a tea-house under willows by the river. Oman ordered up *lagman*, a soup which he loved, thick with noodles and treacherous flecks of mutton fat. He had never been to Shachimadan before, but he had heard of it for years, he said. Everybody had. It had been renamed Khamzabad by the Russians, and was sacred to a Communist saint, Khamza Niyazi, a poet and playwright devoted – as propaganda ran – to the ideals of the Revolution. Moscow had canonised him as the founder of modern Uzbek literature, but he was murdered here in 1929 by reactionary mullahs (it was said) and entombed gloriously in the town's heart.

'But that Khamza fellow ....' Oman slurped dismissively at his soup-bowl. 'My uncle was at school with him, and everybody knew how he chased girls. A playboy.' He flickered his hands back and forth, regulating a procession of eager women. 'History may say one thing, but people remember another. He was talented all right. I've read some of his stuff, and heard his plays. But not *so* talented.' He did not qualify for Oman's pantheon, alongside Dostoevsky and Jack London. 'Middling, I should say. His characters are black and white, as the Soviets wanted them to be.' He went on robustly: 'But in their hearts people know that reality is not like that, that life is different. When it's true, they recognise it. There are many people in all of us.'

These thoughts fell from him not as learnt platitudes, but urgently, like personal discoveries, with a kind of warm ruefulness. 'We are both black and white, aren't we?' He dug his thumbs into his twin shirt pockets, as if exhibiting himself. 'There are two Omans.'

'Many Omans,' I said. I had already witnessed six or seven: the inveterate merchant, the embittered drunk, the tea-house philosopher, the poignant friend, the sentimentalist, the hedonist.

'Each of us is too many people.' He tipped the last noodles down his throat, as if this might homogenise him. He asked suddenly: 'Are you an atheist?'

The word always hurts. 'I don't understand about God ....'

He said: 'Nor do I. And how can we know?'

'But you're a Moslem.'

'Of course!' His culture, he said, was Moslem, and in this person he prayed to God. But another Oman was cynical, and could not locate Him.

We talked with sudden abandon about the inability to know, and I realised that at some time he had suffered over this. Then grandiose clichés turned into confidences. If we had been drinking, this would have explained us. But there were only the dregs of the *lagman* soup, and cups of green tea, and the whispering river. We ruminated sentimentally over the limitations of the five senses, and the possibility of there being hundreds or thousands more. We complicated Time into different stereotypes. Perhaps it was not linear at all, but circular, or could be opened anywhere like a book, and so on. But the mystery, we agreed, was that we were here now, with the eternities of death and prenascence in front and behind us, and that we were conversing under these willow-trees, drinking green tea (which was getting cold) and munching some suspect meat pancakes.

Oman had a theory that the best of our thoughts and feelings survive us, and go to heaven. 'Heaven is a bank,' he announced. 'What isn't put in gets spent and vanishes.' He saw my look of doubt. 'Well, when we die, we'll know ... or perhaps we won't know.' He sighed. 'And I will look up from the Moslem hell and say Colin, help me, and perhaps you in the Christian heaven will tell God something, and He'll say Come up, Oman ....'

This unlikely script filled us with lugubrious affection, smiling at each other over the chasm of faith and race. We poured each other the cold tea, and drank to some future. A few bats darted in the failing light.

'But perhaps we aren't immortal,' Oman rambled, 'and only our sons will continue us.' He stopped. 'But you haven't got one.'

'No,' I said.

'And mine are useless.' The light had suddenly gone out of him. It was as if somebody had thrown a switch. 'I tell my eldest, if you don't work you'll have to do manual labour, and he just laughs. I say I'll chuck him out, but he doesn't believe me.'

And what of his mysterious middle son, I asked. Where had he gone?

I had no time to regret the question, although an instant's silence fell. Oman's face had taken on its punch-drunk defensiveness. 'He was by another wife. He lives with her. We separated years ago.'

241

'You had two wives together?'

He stared expressionlessly into his tea. 'Yes, with us that happens. I was rich. I kept two. Our Moslem law sanctions it. My marriages were celebrated and blessed by a mullah. It's nothing rare.' But he spoke with distant regret. 'In Tashkent our mosques were never really closed. They went on working secretly. People were buried by mullahs too. The Communists here just copulated with Islam.' He gestured obscenely. 'Most of our officials were Moslems at heart, after all.' He said almost in afterthought: 'I married neither woman for love. I married because my friends had. I was already twenty-six when I took Sochibar, and my parents favoured it, and I wanted children.' He sounded tired. 'But not for love.'

It was almost night. The lights of Shachimadan winked along the river ahead of us. Oman said: 'I think our law will come to authorise polygamy. It already turns a blind eye. Our women wouldn't stand for the veil, but in marriage law they'd be offered a choice of contracts.'

I enquired if the choice might include several husbands.

But Oman did not smile. He sensed some buried criticism. He only said, for some reason: 'The world is soiled.'

After nightfall a caretaker took us into a deserted holiday camp, where beside the rustling stream, under overhanging mountain-flanks, a few damp huts stood, and lamps tilted in the grass. In the suddenly cold night, sitting out on a broken-down verandah, we shared a biblical picnic of bread and fish. The caretaker was young and cheerfully defamatory. People came here in late summer, he said, with their vodka and shashlik meat and Russian mistresses, to escape the lowland heat, and nobody thought about Khamza, the mediocre playwright, any more.

'People still climb the hill where he's buried, of course, but they'll demolish that grave in time.' He wiped it away with one hand. 'I saw a film once portraying how he was stoned to death by mullahs. But the Communists made it up. He wasn't stoned to death at all.' His cigarette flared in the dark. 'There are plenty

242

of old men in the town who remember those times well, and they say two men came up to Khamza in the street and put a knife into him. They were the brothers of a girl he'd violated, I think ....'

He gave a heartless chuckle. For a while we gazed down towards the sound of the river, while he and Oman shared a cigarette. A gaunt moon rose, and shed a mortuary pallor into the camp. The glade was littered with decayed ovens and latrines, decomposing tables and stools, and the drunken lamps. Above the torrent I could make out a range of wooden kiosks, like parodies of Moghul water-pavilions.

'There are two graves for pilgrims on the hill now,' the caretaker said. 'There always were, but the other was secret. Stalin levelled it. They say it's the grave of Ali, cousin of the Prophet Mahomet, and are rebuilding it.'

I asked: 'You think that's true?'

'Oh, yes.' He gave a cynical laugh. 'It's true for the moment.'

A clear dawn polished all the shapes which night had blurred. The mountain angled in the valley above us forked down in a razor pyramid to the river. Its snow looked a hand's touch away. In the town's centre two streams glittered out of their heights and collided at the base of the hill where Khamza was buried. A carnival frivolity was about. Bazaars had broken out along the banks, and photographers had set up fanciful canvases of the hill, against which they could snap your picture with a live peacock. Oman, sighting the markets, cried in self-parody 'Business, business!' and laughed light-heartedly, as if he were returning to somebody he had been years before. Then he disappeared to bargain, while I made the ascent alone.

A flight of monumental steps scarred the hill from base to summit, ascending out of a faded park of street-lamps and weed-sown fountains. I wandered up uncertainly. Beneath me, a naked rush of mountains filled the valley, and nut-brown houses bunched along its river. The stairway lifted into quiet. Far below, from a children's playground, a ferris-wheel rotated against the snow-peaks.

Directly above me, at the head of the steps, sprang up a Soviet memorial to victory over the *basmachi* in 1921: a hectoring cluster of brandished rifles and fists. Cynically insulting, it had been raised here in the heartland of the conquered, to wring out gratitude for their own defeat. And it had been sited, with cruel bravado, to extinguish the memory of the tomb of Ali, which Stalin had demolished just behind.

But he could not demolish a myth, of course. Even during persecution the tomb had been covertly rebuilt, destroyed again by Communist officials, clandestinely rebuilt again, destroyed again, on and on. Now a gang of bricklayers was replenishing it with a domed enclosure, where the great plastered grave was waiting under sheets, and across the hill-crest a multitude of old men perched on tea-house divans, proffering blessings, and praying.

One of these, the historian of the place, spread a quilt for me and motioned me beside him. He was benign with authority as he muttered a brief prayer. Ebony beads twined in his fingers. Then he recounted to me the biography of Ali, how he had been favoured by the Prophet with the hand of his daughter, and become the fourth of the caliphs of Islam. But after this, the old man meandered out of history. He never mentioned that Ali had been murdered by a heretic at Kufa, or how the powerful Ommayad clan secured the caliphate to themselves and slaughtered his younger son; and he ignored the tragic schism which had flowed from all this – how the Sunni had adhered to the Ommayad line of caliphs and almost thirteen centuries of their successors, while the Shia clung to Ali's martyred inheritance with a sleepless, rankling outrage to this day.

Instead the old man branched into a kindlier story. Somebody brought us bread and cloudy tea. He watched me with teacherly concern, assessing my attention. I stared back into a face swept by white bristles and smudged with a nose netted in red veins. But out of this steppeland visage the eyes shone out disconcertingly young. He spoke of Ali not with the harsh exclusiveness which I had encountered years ago in Iran and Iraq, but with reverent laughter and collusion and wry smiles. Ali had indeed been murdered in Kufa, he said, but blamelessly. Besides his own two sons, he had adopted a third, a little orphan. His palms patted the air at the height of a three-year-old. 'Already God had told Ali that he must die while he was reading the scriptures, so when he wished for heaven he paid this boy to kill him in the mosque.'

The old historian beamed with the simple beauty of this, in which nobody was at fault.

I asked: 'How did he come to be buried here?'

'Well, the orphan made a poor job of it.' He shook his head in regret. 'Ali lay dying for four days, while seven pall-bearers descended on Kufa, all wanting to carry the body to separate parts of the empire. Each one was told to dig a grave and pray, and that in the morning one would be favoured. And in the morning all seven graves contained his body!' The old man's mouth gaped open at this multiplication of Alis. 'So each pall-bearer took him away to different destinations, and he is buried in all these places.'

He recounted this untroubled, with an easy acceptance of miracle, secure in the imprimatur of half-remembered books. So Ali, he said, was buried here, and in Jidda too, and Afghanistan and Kufa and Almaty and Najaf and … he could not remember the last.

Then, as if shifting into some other element, he said: 'But personally I know that the real body is here. In 1918, when the tomb was desecrated, a villager witnessed it – I heard this myself from that man's son. He saw the shin-bone of Ali sticking out of the rubble, and it was twice as tall as a man!'

Out of his wintry bristles the eyes sparkled artlessly. He was filled now by a gentle irrefutability. I smiled back at him. I wondered where his strange learning had come from, and who he was. These saints' tombs attracted an underworld of Sufis, I knew. The Communists had feared them. Sufism posited a world which they could not touch: a migration back into the heart. It was, in its way, profoundly subversive. But the old men scattered across the hillside might have been typical of it: private, benevolent, introverted.

I asked: 'Is this a place for Sufis still?'

Outside cities, the word had usually evoked bewilderment. But the historian's mouth quivered in a crescent of disordered teeth. 'Yes, it always was. There are still Naqshbandi here.' He saw my quickened interest. 'If you were a Moslem, I would teach you how they pray and what they do, and how we tell our prayer-beads.' His grammar had slipped painlessly into the truth. The beads fidgeted in his hand.

'So it's secret ....'

'It is not exactly secret, but we don't speak of it.' He said apologetically: 'Only if you become a Moslem, I could tell you about these things. But ....' – he suddenly roared with laughter – 'first, you'd have to be circumcised!'

We guffawed uncouthly together. He looked uncannily as I would have expected of a Naqshbandi: a timeless innocent, lit by those unsettling eyes. For a while we sat there while storm-clouds dragged over the mountains, and the blue sky was ripped away. Then I got up and thanked him. He said: 'This place is holy now. That's why they call it Shachimadan, "King of Men", again. There is no Khamzabad any more. Khamza, who was he? I don't know him.'

I crossed slowly to the poet's tomb: a temple built in the same red granite as Lenin's mausoleum in Red Square, but coated in Islamic plasterwork and pierced by Arabic arches. The devotional benches spaced around it were all empty. Dandelions pressed between the steps. Inscribed on the gravestone, one of Khamza's verses suggested that Oman's verdict on him had been accurate ('Not quite as good as Jack London'). Nearby stood one of those old-style Soviet museums which are collections of photographs and propaganda. The manner of his death was clouded over, but laid at the door of 'the evil forces of obscurantism'.

'Only three or four people saw him die,' a man told me in the derelict camp-site that evening, 'and my father was one of them.

246

It happened after Khamza had announced that the tomb of Ali should be demolished. Then the mullahs and the people gathered to protest, and a great anger started up. But he wasn't stoned to death at all. He ran away down an alley and collided with a blind beggar, a giant, who just strangled him with his hands. My father saw this with his own eyes. But there are barely twenty men left who know of this first-hand, because the Communists shot a hundred and ninety people in retaliation for that one death, and the village was scattered. But that is the truth of it.'

Under louring storm-cloud I started to descend the hill past the grave of Ali, where the workmen were still tapping the bricks. Who really lies buried here is unknown: some early holy man, perhaps, or a pre-Islamic chieftain. Ali himself was probably entombed at An Najaf in Iraq, where the caliph Haroun er Rashid was supposed to have rediscovered his grave in 791.

By the time I reached the bottom the three monuments clustering the summit had paled back into their contending strangeness. They would not coexist for long, I guessed. The old divinity was returning, and all the works with which the Russians had hoped to stamp it out, or steal its power, must soon be swept away. The war-memorial, perhaps, would be the first to go, followed by the museum and tomb of the lecher-poet, leaving alone on the summit the grave where the stout, rather naïve Ali of history was being turned into a saint.

At the hill's foot, photographers were still buttonholing passers-by to pose before their canvases, while the peacocks screamed alongside. Each backdrop showed a fairy-tale version of the hill. Toy mountains sprouted behind the domes floating on its crest, while steps cascaded beneath it to a jungly Eden of outsize tulips and an azure river. The real-life hill, meanwhile, stood in full view opposite: a mess of concrete and dead fountains. But nobody was being photographed near it. People were posing instead against these gaudy dreams. And perhaps it did not matter, I thought, as the first rain began to fall. Because the monuments on the hill were as dreamlike, in their way, as any

247

picture could make them, and as little troubled by fact. They were memorials, rather, to the manipulation of minds and the corruption of history.

It was a hill of lies.

*

Next day the river accompanied us back into the Fergana plain, and by afternoon we were driving between blue-stuccoed houses into the silk town of Margilan, whose inhabitants had been so cruelly lampooned by Jura. I sensed a deepened Islam. But the little I knew of the town proved out of date. Where was the old fortress, I enquired? Its rubble lay under the central square, a man said. And where was the famous statue of Nurkhon, the first Uzbek woman to have cast away the veil (for which she was killed by her brothers in 1929)?

'Oh, Nurkhon,' said the same man: he complied mesmerisingly with Jura's honeyed parody. 'She was taken down a few weeks ago.'

'Why?'

'So that everything will be more beautiful.' His hand fluttered up to caress his heart. 'You see, our times have changed. We used to have nothing. Now we have our freedom.'

'So you pull down statues of women?' I was brewing up a Pygmalion affection for Nurkhon. 'I thought the people of Margilan were milder ....'

'Ah, we are.' Effete smiles suffused him. 'We're a sweeter people than the others. We are more feeling. We believe more strongly in Islam. We wish everybody well.' His voice was a sugary glissade. 'We make no distinction between one race and another. We welcome everybody.'

'Then why ...?'

'Because we need order,' he lilted. His smile was like make-up. 'Stalin, I think, was a good thing, whatever anybody says. My father fought through the war for him and even took his picture. We need somebody cruel here now.' He went on in the same fastidious, courtly tone: 'Cruelty is good for people.'

248

I said: 'Your mosques would be shut down again.'

'We don't need the mosques. I learnt my Islam from my father, and from old men in the tea-houses when I was a child. It was alive then, and we all listened.'

'But ....' I faltered. This was like handling water, or the slithery local silks.

'Our families here are everything,' he simpered. 'We are each a little dynasty, all merchants.' His fingers touched his heart again. 'They say we can sell anything.'

*

An enormous family of merchants and teachers, to whom a Turkic friend in England had given me an introduction, lived near Namangan in the countrified suburb of a town famous for its craftsmanship in steel. Oman and I arrived unheralded, and found ourselves peering into a labyrinthine courtyard, thronged with fig and persimmon trees and traversed by a rivulet where roses bloomed. Somewhere in this compound's heart lived an ancient progenitor, whose sons, grandsons, nephews and their families inhabited the households all around in a maze of kinship which I never unravelled.

A suave English teacher named Hakim, the youngest of this brood of sons, ushered us into his reception-room, where a rosy wife bustled and children marvelled at us through beautiful, dark-lashed eyes. Hakim spoke a bookish English. My friendship with Fatima – a distant cousin whom he had scarcely seen – and my penetration to his home filled him with fitful amazement. Periodically his face would loosen into a rather sensuous concourse of alert eyes and mobile lips, and he would breathe out: 'How remarkable!'

All day and far into the night Oman and I sat in one of those big rooms whose pastel-painted walls and ceilings were familiar now, while a procession of relatives, flushed out by the news of our coming, trooped in to share our pilau and tea. Grave, open-faced men, flecked by moustaches and accompanied by silent wives, settled around us in ceremonious enquiry, dignified in

249

their dark jackets and skull-caps. Sometimes they resembled a
meeting of shy farmers, their thick hands splayed over their
knees or tunnelling discreetly into the pilau. Their eyes shone in
passive scrutiny. Formally they asked about Fatima, who began
to take on a half mystical presence among us. To many of them
she was only hearsay, but they grew sad when I told them she
had parted from her husband, became intrigued by her car and
flat, and revived when they heard she was succeeding in jour-
nalism. Sometimes, under the pressure of their questions, I
found myself reinventing her to please them. I expressed her
enthusiasm for returning to Uzbekistan, but I did not know
when this might be. I enquired after babies and school diplomas
on her behalf. They answered with sober pride. But yes, I said,
she was well, she had not forgotten them – and their faces split
into ranks of silvered teeth.

For a brief half-hour I slipped into the courtyard under the
persimmon trees, where a niece of Hakim found me, and we sat
on one of the throne-like Turkic benches. In the branches above
us a tame quail sang in a cage. The girl was seventeen, and
physically adult, but her face looked empty of experience, like
an infant's. She was studying to enter university, she said, and
wanted to specialise in English, but she was too shy to speak it
to me.

What would she do with this English, I asked?

'I'd like to be an interpreter,' she replied, smiling at me, 'for
the KGB.' Her legs swung childishly. The prismatic trousers of
Atlas silk had eased a little up her slim, unshaven calves. 'I think
that would be interesting work.' The KGB was just a job, an
institution which had always been there, like the army or the
local collective farm. 'But I think they don't often take women,
they prefer men.'

'What else could you do?' I asked anxiously. 'What do you
enjoy?' It was like talking to a ten-year-old.

'I like tennis.'

'*Tennis?*'

'Yes. You know, at a table. And I'd like to travel. I love

travelling.' But she had not ventured beyond Bukhara, and when she asked where I had been her gaze settled on me with a soft wonder. 'That's what I want to do: travel. I don't want to marry before I'm twenty-five. Twenty-five is late, but I won't sit at home all my life.'

'Not a good Moslem wife!' I was beginning to believe in her future.

She wrinkled up her nose. 'I don't go to the mosque. That's only for men. I don't like that sort of thing.'

'You wouldn't wear a veil?'

'*No!*' It was a hushed, violent monosyllable. 'I think that's revolting.'

At nightfall, from every house in the compound, the men converged on our reception-room. While Oman and I occupied the place of honour opposite the door, they circled out from us in a cross-legged ring, like a pow-wow of tribal elders, and a time-honoured banquet unfolded. No woman was present, but even the young boys ate with us, and from time to time Hakim rocked a wooden cradle where his infant son lay tied with scarlet sashes. From a makeshift catheter attached to the baby's penis, a potty in the cradle's base was filling with urine. He lay there immobile as a mummy, howling.

The men, meanwhile, touched their faces in self-absolution, and launched into drink. More insidiously than any propaganda, I thought, vodka had leaked into their culture and undermined their Islam. They toasted in the Russian way, the cups emptied wholesale down their gullets – pledges to peace, to Fatima, to their arrival in London one day (I tried vainly to imagine this), and to my safety – before dipping their *lepeshka* bread into bowls of oily mutton, or seizing handfuls of strawberries.

Then the conversation darkened. They spoke of troubles in neighbouring Namangan, where women had been browbeaten to accept the veil and self-appointed vigilantes had administered Islamic law, parading petty criminals. Recently the police had moved in and arrested fifty of these zealots, they said, and a good thing too.

251

'They were only a few hundred,' said a young man. 'A lot of them were people without work, I think, bitter people. Youths.' He looked only a youth himself.

'They wanted to create their own power-block,' said a merchant, 'their own mafia.'

'Just mafia!' Oman cried. The word always electrified him. 'We don't want them! What we need is business. Freedom to do business!' I dreaded this. Vodka turned him voluble almost at once. Two or three toasts, and he was throwing his arms about and discharging a battery of theories and platitudes. 'Islam wasn't meant to be like that!' he clamoured. 'Where is it written in the Koran that women have to wear veils? It isn't, it isn't!' He started punching the air. 'It's not appearances that matter but the heart!'

The others began to look embarrassed while his voice mounted and his eyes swam with a fevered glitter, as if he might weep. They all agreed with him – they were nodding in stately unison – but he was snowballing into an uncontrolled passion which they mutely repudiated. They fingered their spoons and cracked nuts and looked a little away. Only when he subsided did they return to life. Then, with homespun decorum, they rejected fundamentalism and 'the Iranian model'. They would follow 'the Turkish model', they said. Their Islam would be their own, temperate and hospitable.

'Our people aren't like the Iranians,' somebody said. 'We think in a different way.'

They tacitly despised them. All that emotion, they implied, was unmanly. They settled back on their cushions.

'In time we'll create our own system,' boomed a giant. A short beard fell from his chin like a tattered bib. 'But at the moment, you see, we have no feeling about ourselves as a nation. History is the key, and the Soviets took ours away. We were sold a mass of Bolshevik stories, and nothing of our own. In secondary school, where I teach, the text-books devoted only two lines to Timur, the world conqueror. *Two lines*! And they just described him as rotten.' He spoke with gruff irony. He clenched his fists and said: 'But now our books are being rewritten by Uzbek historians, who have proper access to the archives!'

I wondered how much truer these would be. The past here seemed to change all the time. It was impossible to foretell it. I wondered, too, how he had felt, teaching a certain truth one year, then overturning it the next. After *perestroika*, I asked, how had he faced his students?

It was a cruel question, but his jovial smile remained. 'I just explained to them that the facts were unknown to me too! I hadn't known them either! But that now it was possible to know the truth, so we were starting again. What first opened our eyes, you know, was the invasion of Afghanistan. They say that nearly half the Soviet force came from Central Asia, and I believe it. Moslems ordered to fight their fellow-Moslems, Uzbeks against Uzbeks, Tajiks ....'

Had they been sent, I asked, on some mistaken propaganda notion, or out of simple ignorance?

'Ignorance,' a gaunt merchant intruded. His eyes flickered back and forth, as if he were missing out on some deal. 'The Russians never learnt anything. Not from anybody.'

'I don't know,' the history teacher said. 'I'm afraid I don't know. But they were still sending us in long after the start. It made a terrible bitterness. My brother was one. Many just deserted, and are still living over there. And in the end people started refusing to fight.'

'Refusing?' I asked. 'Here in Central Asia?'

For the first time his face fell, and his smile vanished. In a tone of puzzled shame, he said: 'No. Sadly, there were none here. The conscientious objectors were all Russians. They demonstrated in Moscow. But we ... we just did as we were told.'

Then I thought of the paradox in these people: their mixture of rustic sturdiness and fatal acquiescence. Even in the last century travellers had remarked how they took on the protective colouring of whatever power was dominant. As my hand came to rest on the edge of the stilled cradle, I found myself wondering

253

about this helplessness in which as babies they were bound for months, and a herd of Freudian dogmas lumbered into my head, drifted away ....

'We have far to go,' the teacher said simply. 'We haven't moved as the Russians have. We don't have democracy here at all. Just a sham. They talk about it all the time, of course, but do nothing.'

'At least you're ruled by your own people,' I said: so one layer of repression had been peeled away.

They nodded approval. 'Yes ... yes ....'

Oman was rocking the cradle. 'This is our democracy!' he cried. 'It's just an infant!'

The baby started bellowing again; but his father released him and stood him on his feet, while everyone watched and applauded. He looked like a young Hercules. He was stroked, kneaded, saluted, lectured and kissed. Then Oman seized him and lifted him up and down above his head like a trophy. 'This is the future Uzbekistan!' he cried. Tears shone in his eyes. He was dangerously drunk. 'Here is our country! Look how fine he'll be!'

He was playing to the crowd, I knew, ingratiating himself. Yet at the same time he was subtly condescending to these provincial teachers and tradesmen, and soon he began preaching against people in Tashkent who thought themselves superior to other Uzbeks. It was absurd, he claimed. Why should they think so? He entirely disagreed with it. But his denial came with a drink-loosened suavity which belonged to the theatre of another civilisation. As he flaunted the baby on his shoulder, the others looked back at him with mixed deference and unease. He engaged and slightly awed them. But they did not trust him.

And now Hakim stretched up and eased away the child from Oman's alien and uncertain hands. Somewhere, it seemed, he had gone too far.

Our voices leaked into an unhappy silence. Hakim strapped the child back into his cradle, then touched my arm in embarrassment and in his quaint English changed the conversation: 'I am unable to make known if my English language is good or not. I wonder if you in your office can give me a blank with on it a stamp?'

'A blank?'

'Yes, a blank. If I have a blank, I can show to authorities.'

Oman was shifting beside me, drunk, wretched.

'We don't have such forms,' I said. 'I'm just a private writer....'

'But if out of your position you would write that I'm good with English, and say you famous English writer, even without the blank, would maybe help.'

So I promised to send him a reference from England (and wrote this shamelessly on my return) and he relaxed again, and went back to rocking his howling son.

The next moment everybody rose in respect. Tiny and frail in the doorway, wrapped in a dusty coat caught round with three sashes, the family patriarch hovered, still light on his feet. He was ninety-four. Under the coil of his turban a pair of light, leprechaun eyes glistened shallow in their sockets, and an ashy beard jutted spryly in front. As he alighted beside me, a semi-circle of earnest, deferential faces turned as one man to listen. My presence became the occasion of his history, which his progeny must have heard a hundred times, but nobody uttered or stirred.

He had been a Silk Road merchant in the old days, he said, carrying gold from the Fergana valley into China's far northwest, and returning with silk on eight camels across the Pamirs. He had weathered the tracks which the Chinese graded 'big headache' or 'small headache' passes, but on his last journey, as relations worsened between the Soviets and Xinjiang in the early 1930s, the border bridge was dropped into the Ili river and he'd been stranded on the far side.

'But the Chinese governor was a man of honour,' he said: his silvery voice belonged to a faraway age and place. 'He exchanged our gold for wool and ferried us back across the river. But that was the end of my travelling. I couldn't go back. So I became a butcher in Almaty, and married there.'

As the men strained for every note of the treble voice, I thought how hopeless had been the task of Communism here – its suppression of the past and hurrying-in of the new. For the past was seated amongst us, innately respected, in its triple sash and worn coat full of years. The true country of these people had been their genealogy, which they used to memorise through generations back into myth (tracing themselves to Adam), and dignity still lay in age. The health and longevity of the old man was a subject of clannish marvel and pride among his descendants, and as his history dwindled away in the abattoirs and domesticity of Almaty, and his offspring warmed back into conversation, he buttonholed me with health tips.

'I've never been ill ….' He was sitting bolt upright, his legs supple under him. 'I used to drink a bottle of vodka with every meal…and my meals have always been the same: one kilo of mutton, one kilo of rice, and half a kilo of sheep's fat. That's how I've lived on. Remember. I recommend it. I've had a little trouble with my left knee this last year, I don't know why …. But that's all there's ever been wrong with me.'

His digestion was perfect, he said, but he had no teeth. One grandson shredded cucumber for him, while another cracked and crumbled some hazel-nuts. I hunted in his face for any clue to his endurance, but found myself staring into a visage of uncanny agelessness: clear and almost featureless, except for its goblin eyes. The bridge of his nose sank untraceably into his cheeks, leaving only an isolated flare of shell-pink nostrils. He had outlived most of his seven children, but his youngest daughter, whom he had fathered at sixty-four, still visited him.

'But everything was better,' he began, 'in the time of … of … that man Nikolai ….'

'Nikolai II?'

'Czar Nikolai, yes …. Those were good years. Nobody bothered you. There were just camels and horses, plenty of horses, yes, and quiet …. And then the Soviet Union came and everything got collectivised and rearranged.' He shook his head. His neck trembled with wrinkles, like a lizard's. 'And it was a lot of trouble ... for nothing ....'

Towards midnight he got up – 'I'm going to visit my nephews! I'll be back!' – and by the time we had clambered respectfully to our feet, he had tripped away.

An hour later the last guest departed, Hakim unfurled quilts over the floor, and Oman rolled himself up, his voice turned maudlin and tearful: 'I'm sorry, Colin. It was not me that was talking, it was the vodka.' Then he snored sonorously, horribly, for hours, shifting an octave whenever he turned over, while Hakim made a lighter, nasal moaning beyond. Finally the patriarch returned at an early hour of morning and lay like a statue on a catafalque, wheezing, with his fingers laced over his stomach, and his beard pointed at the ceiling. Their wind trio rose and filled the room.

At a time before anyone in the town could remember, an itinerant holy man had struck water from its ground and been buried where the cold streamlets descended a hillside. Now acacias and chenars plunged its terraces into a subaqueous light, and teahouses spread their divans among ornamental pools, where men drank discreetly – for this is a holy place – and women played with their children round the tomb.

A posse of Hakim's younger relatives took me there in the morning. A few nights before, the town's Lenin statue had been pulled down ('they always go in the night,' somebody said); but the holy man's tomb was under restoration. All around us, as we squatted before our mountainous breakfast, the tea-house habitués were deep in confabulation, and had hung up their cages of pet quails in the branches overhead. Sometimes, Hakim said, they pitched the birds against one another in a bloodless battle of nerves, and laid bets. But now the aviaries, each one cowled in a black hood, dangled in silence among the leaves, while the quails sulked underneath.

Relaxed in the young sunlight, and freed from the polite reserve of their elders, the young men pummelled me with questions. The West shimmered in an El Dorado beyond their reach, but their black eyes settled on me as its exemplar. Back in England, did I own a house, a car? What did it cost to marry? But the price of a Honda or a flat reeled into meaninglessness. Inflation had already turned their own prices into bedlam, but the disparity between the dollar and the dwindling rouble laid waste all comparisons. A plane ticket to the West would alone have cost them over a year's salary.

But there was one thing that baffled them entirely. Why wasn't I married? Later they confessed that they had all been aching to ask me this, and now it sprang from the lips of an open-faced youth who had listened to everything in silence. Here, after all, every man married automatically. Even Hakim looked at me with bewildered charm. 'You miss all the sweetness of life!' he cried, and the others gazed at me in mute accord, while the shadows splashed over our half-forgotten meal, and the blacked-out quail cages shifted in the branches, and they waited for a reply.

'Where is this sweetness?' I asked. The question held a Socratic quaintness. 'With the woman or the children?'

Hakim answered at once: 'With the children, of course, with the boys!'

But in the West, I told them, it was more often the woman who inspired the longing to marry. I could not convey to them a world in which the preciousness of one person might change a life's course, or the chances of love refute the ordered programme of matchmaking and childbirth.

The callow man echoed: 'Just the woman?' He was frowning.

'Yes.'

They started munching their food again in perplexity. Whatever secret yearnings might rankle in them (and I'd met several who had seduced other men's wives), there was too much of market-place practicality and clan responsibility in their hard lives to allow of understanding any other. A woman was only a woman, after all. But a child was a descendant, bone of your bone, who would carry on your blood and memory, and secure your continuance in the chain of things. I, as far as they could see, was a cul-de-sac, an unaccountable exception to natural law.

They ranged about for other explanations of me. Women and commerce, they presumed, were the motives for travel. What were Arab women like, they wondered, and the French? Was it true that Japanese women were made differently *down there*? Had I ever had a Chinese?

In me, I realised, they were being left with an ungraspable paradox; yet to them I inhabited such riches and freedom that perhaps the secret of my solitude lay somewhere there.

The sweetness of life. I saw myself in their eyes, and was touched by a fugitive melancholy. They gave me cherries in parting, and a small knife. Their questions posed an innocent challenge, and to some I had no answer.

*

For a few days Oman and I dawdled east through a country where cotton-fields were interrupted by alfalfa, wheat and rice paddy. In Namangan we saw no trace of the veil now, and drove on towards the old capital of Andijan where Babur had been born 500 years before. Even its people were beautiful, he wrote, and its meadows, sweet with violets and tulips, would tease him far into his exile. But now, as Jura had intimated, Andijan was rougher and less pastoral, an oil and cotton town whose streets were sober with yellow stucco. So at last we slipped over the Kirghiz border into the town of Osh, and prepared to move south to the Pamirs.

In these towns the hotels were baffled by the arrival of a foreigner. Some accepted us, but quadrupled the price. Others telephoned the police asking what to do, but the police did not know either. The rules had all gone. Then Oman, growing irritated, would stump into the police-station and cry out at every official hesitation: 'Hasn't the Iron Curtain come down yet?' or 'I thought Stalin was dead!' and the officers would look foolish and acquiesce, or angrily refuse. Eventually we would succumb in some cramped room reeking of urine, where I

259

would try to write notes under a weak bulb and Oman would smoke and read Arthur Hailey. (He had abandoned Kafka, who scooped about in himself too much, he said.) Then I would return from a night ramble to find him overcome by boredom or sleep, his shapeless body thrown down among his sheets as if by somebody else.

By now we were barely seventy miles from the Chinese frontier, separated only by a neck of mountains where the Tienshan and Pamir converged. It was from the Chinese that the Fergana valley people had learnt precious metallurgy, paper-making and the sinking of wells, while the cultivation of vines and clover had travelled the other way, along with a breed of horses different from the stocky battlers of the steppes. Over two thousand years ago these Fergana horses came to the ears of the Chinese emperor Wu Ti, who coveted them for his new-fangled cavalry. They were said to sweat blood and to be of celestial descent. In 104 BC a Chinese invasion left its dead strewn along the deserts and mountains of a 3000-mile route-march; but the tribute of horses was secured – beautiful, high-strung creatures, akin to the modern Arab.

But in Osh we sensed nothing of China. The frontiers had been sealed for sixty years, and were only reopening far to the north-east. The first blades of intervening mountains rose from the outskirts. Legend ascribed the town's foundation to Solomon, and by the twelfth century it had become a holy place. Its inhabitants were pious and a little mischievous. When travellers rested in its meadows, the local urchins would open the river sluices and drench them. Now earthquake, decay and Soviet rebuilders had conspired to emasculate it.

I walked here weakly in the morning after a poisoned supper of noodle soup, and left Oman moaning on his bed. He was, in any case, afraid of the town, where riots between Kirghiz and Uzbeks had left 300 dead eighteen months earlier. The Uzbek rumour-mill had placed the killed at over 1000, and he'd seen amateur video-film of the massacres which still drained his face. The agents of these horrors, I knew, must be walking in the streets about me, and the dominance of the Kirghiz – a pastoral race of recent nomads – edged the town with a ruffianly freedom. They were burlier than the Uzbeks, blunter, more secular. Their white felt hats, jaunty with tassels and upturned brims, touched them with an incongruous comedy. Beneath this headgear you might expect to glimpse the blond complexion of a Russian fairytale prince. But instead, an arid plane of Mongol cheeks appeared, and an innocent, unfocused gaze. 'They're just shepherds,' Oman had said, and waved them nervously away.

But the town seemed deceptively at peace. I saw no sign even of the earthquake whose epicentre had trembled here two weeks before (and had rattled the crockery in Tashkent). The cracks in our hotel walls had been there for years.

On the western outskirts a rocky spine of mountain, named the Throne of Solomon, must have given the town birth. Here, pilgrims believe, the king viewed the city which he founded, and on its summit descended into the grave. Solomon's tomb became a haunt of Sufis, of course, and for decades the Russians tried to halt the secret pilgrimages there. Officials railed against the 'sectarian underground' and 'reactionary Muslim clergy' with paranoiac anxiety, and in 1987 tried to neutralise the site by encouraging tour-groups of East Europeans there.

Now the spur hovered open above me, tufted in shrubs and grasses. At its foot a stone plinth still trumpeted the dictums of Lenin. Nobody had bothered to remove it. On a municipal hoarding superscribed 'The Best People in Osh', the empty boards were dropping apart. Crowds of local sightseers were climbing the path in funfair mood: boisterous youths, and schoolgirls in white-aproned smocks, like truant parlour-maids.

I trudged up after them. Concrete steps zigzagged askew along the mountain's rim. Bushes and trees were speckled with telltale rags. But all zealotry – Moslem or Communist – seemed past. It had gone under the trampling feet of sweaty weekend vacationers slung with cheap cameras. Flocks of sturdy women had kicked off their high heels to grip the steps barefoot, and seemed to wear their silks not as a national statement but a pretty fashion. On the crest, the Sufis, shorn of their bogey status, remained as they had probably always been: a handful of elderly men in search of peace.

A light wind brushed the summit. The tomb of Solomon was a rebuilt chapel facing Mecca. An old man dispensed blessings, assisted by his son in an Adidas tracksuit. Some say that Solomon was murdered here, and that his black dogs still lurk in the fissures of the rocks, where they lapped his blood and ate his body. In the last century, invalids would press their heads into the crevices as a cure. But now the tomb was screened off by the coarse, flushed smiles of Kirghiz families lined up to photograph themselves, their women's faces dashed in sweat and rouge. Below us, Osh curled among its trees in a foetal crescent, while beyond surged the nakedness of the Pamirs, whose cloud-coloured peaks infiltrated the sky, then vanished.

I yearned to travel these mountains, but Oman was losing his nerve. On my descent he reported that the road I had chosen into Tajikistan was snowbound. He had been talking to lorry-drivers. He had heard of passes over 10,000 feet, he said. He did not want to go near Tajikistan at all. The country was in civil war. On our hotel television he came upon a blurred news bulletin which reported shooting on the roads around the capital. When I remained obstinate, he started to look miserable and to tramp about with a boyish, hurt air. But he spent the afternoon locating bread, mineral water and soggy strawberries. He made a few bargains. And soon the buoyancy and slight fatalism which I liked in him resurrected, and he cried: 'Then we'll go! Let's try it! We'll know when we arrive!'

My wanderings in Osh, meanwhile, came to an end in the upper room of a defunct cinema. I had noticed young men loping furtively through a door labelled 'Cosmos Video Hall', and had followed them up a dank stairway. At the top I paid five roubles and entered a curtained room. Some fifty men were seated on plastic chairs, leering in rapt stillness at a television hoisted on to the wall in front. As I came in, the screen flashed and up came *Blondie*, produced by 'Svetlana' and filmed by 'Mr

Ed'. It was a hard-porn movie purveying clichés of fantasy sex –
multiple, oral, underwater – between four tireless studs and a
stable of dyed blondes. Its stock American dialogue had been
dubbed slackly into Russian, and its garnish of sports cars,
yachts and private swimming-pools suggested a synthetic paradise somewhere in the idle West. From the darkness the men
gaped up expressionlessly. Their hands strayed to their crotches.
The gulf between their reality and the profligacy on screen
yawned so hopelessly that they might have been watching
science fiction. They huddled before it like impotent conspira-
tors. How would it seem, I wondered, when they returned to
their plain suburbs, to the swarthy, unpampered bodies of their
own women?

An hour later they slunk out, shielding their eyes against the
sun or the world, where the Throne of Solomon thrust against
the sky. I asked one youth what he thought, and he said the film
was OK, but expensive at five roubles. Already its gross, deper-
sonalised dream seemed to have dimmed out of his face, and he
was returning to other cares and to the qualifying daylight.

*

The day before we crossed into the Pamirs, Oman and I drove
north through poor Kirghiz hamlets to the little town of Uzgen.
At roadside police barriers brutal-looking officers flagged down
anything that passed, but viewed me with hospitable surprise,
and let us go unsearched.

Uzgen clustered below a pass of the Tienshan in a green valley; and here, beside a field damp with poppies and clover, all
that was left of an early capital of Mavarannahr lay mouldering
in the sun. Three mausoleums and a minaret, raised in the confident simplicity of patterned brick, marked the site of a city
whose empire had straddled Central Asia. For a century and a
half, between the year they overran the Samanids in 999 and the
time they vanished under Mongolian invaders, the obscure
Karakhanids ruled here in unreachable splendour at the
antipodes of the world. Who they were, I scarcely knew: a

Turkic people, I had read, whose loose-knit federation was constantly in flux. Yet their dominions spread huger than India.

I waded through grass to the mausoleums. They appeared to have been restored, and then abandoned. Their portals were scooped from a single façade: tall frames of decorative brick flanked by engaged pillars. Within them, the doorways to the chambers were encrusted with bands of terracotta foliage and colonnettes, from which the colour had long ago been washed away. Columns, friezes, vase-shaped capitals – all were covered with the same perforated blanket of relief work: dry, subtle, exquisite.

One doorway, in particular, stood almost free of restoration, and in that desolateness shone with a honeycomb intricacy. Under a whole gallery of geometric patterns carved foliage oozed and crept, and a sensuous wriggle of calligraphy overswept half the gateway. But the arches led from nothing to nothing. Their dead had gone. Outside, from the ruin's height above the valley, I imagined the capital poised schizophrenically between cultivation and wilderness. For the Karakhanids were the first of the Turkic dynasties in Central Asia – hesitant precursors of the waves to come – and their site looked pastoral and impermanent even now, cramped on its hill beside the graves of their nomad kings.

10

The High Pamir

The first foothills folded round us under a cloudy sky. Horsemen overflowed the road with flocks of mud-clogged sheep and goats, descending to drink at a distant tributary of the Syr Dariya which meandered beside us. We were entering a half-pagan country of summer nomads. Once or twice we passed a wayside grave speared with horsetail banners and rams' horns, and here and there a herdsman's yurt crouched like a dirty igloo on slopes spotted with cattle.

Then the valley narrowed. The earth-built cowsheds of winter villages appeared, deserted now. The river cut through the earth in a silty torrent, and flash-floods spinning down the gulleys had torn off chunks of tarmac and dropped them into its valley. Thunder-clouds rolled from every defile and rose from the summits as if they were steaming. The lowland heat had gone. Ahead of us arteries of snow trickled down the mountain-flanks, and the earth darkened to a sooty shale where wind had broken the ridges into blackened spikes. Oman let out bleak noises of foreboding. The snows had withdrawn late this year, he'd heard, or not at all.

Then our road mounted into a stadium of white peaks which shook out black streamers of cloud thousands of feet above us. Crows flew in the valleys like blown ash. The river turned green. Wherever the road had torn a cutting, it exposed a stark magenta earth, which sometimes splashed bloodily to the snowline. Below us I glimpsed red and white crags tossed up through the clouds. Then the road turned to dirt and for an hour no vehicle passed us. The police posts were all deserted. As we spiralled above the snowline, clouds plunged across our track and we entered a monochrome void. A harsh, blurred light refracted from the snowfields. The road hung in disconnecting whiteness. Once we brushed past a gang of shepherds – black-faced men with forked Mongol beards – and the headlights of a solitary lorry glowed out of the pall. Then we emerged from the clouds into a planetary upland without sun or shadow or colour. The rounded hills and mountains looked exhausted and disembodied, as if the land had grown ill, and flowed before us unbroken into a white sky.

The Alai range – the northern bastion of the Pamir – was behind us now, and soon we were descending into a wide valley. Here, at over 10,000 feet, the headwaters of the Kizylsu, the Red River, gathered to slide westward 400 miles, until they had swollen to a raging force which deluged into the Amu Dariya on the edge of Afghanistan. But in the silent valley the river was only a shallow twine of streams. Herds of chestnut horses cropped their banks. As we turned west, the mainstream, crimson with silt, was wreathed about with ice-green tributaries, running side by side. The grass twittered with invisible birds. Their sound – and the weak patter of the rivulets – deepened the silence.

But we had crossed some indefinable divide. The air was utterly still, and the whole sky transfigured to a vivid, artificial blue. The snow-peaks to our west stood in Tajikistan; those to our east were glittering out of China. In front of us, in a glacial palisade which shadowed the valley for a hundred miles, the Transalai mountains – the Pamir heart – shone in the sky as if formed from some rarer element than ours.

We stopped by the shingly streams, and gazed. Along our whole horizon the mountains made a frozen tumult of spires and ridges, erupting to over 23,000 feet. Seven centuries ago Marco Polo recalled that even birds did not survive here. The plateaux are sprinkled with frozen lakes and lie under so intense a cold that their stones crumble away and the earth unlocks its

266

plants for only a few summer weeks. The impact of the Indian subcontinent, pressing into Asia's underbelly, still squeezes up the Pamir at a rate of two-and-a-half inches a year; but the ranges to the south-east are rising even faster, and over the millennia the monsoons have dwindled away. They have left a region of mummified emptiness. In the permafrost of its high valleys even the snow is only a dust and the wind blows not in storms but as a nagging, sandpaper restlessness in the starved air. Against this awesome cold, some of the bulkiest mammals on earth have developed: the yak, the Marco Polo sheep, and *Ursus Torquatus*, the world's weightiest bear. Even now, in late May, icicles fringed the river banks, and when a west wind sprang up it cut like a scythe.

A young shepherd, riding up on a brindled colt, shared our bread with us, resting in the saddle. Winter kept its snows for the valleys, he said. Sometimes they reached above his shoulders – he raised his hand eloquently to his neck – then his people coralled away their herds and fed them by hand. They called this valley paradise, yet suffered the highest proportion of still-births in the world, I'd read. He glanced along the road where we were going. Two days earlier, he said, it had been severed by a torrent of red mud....

For an hour we drove west along the ghostly causeway of the valley, arrow-straight down a gravel track. Once we passed a faded hoarding which still read: 'Glory to the Defenders of the Soviet frontiers!' Beyond it a cemetery streamed with horsetail standards. And always to our south the mountains kept pace in a phantasmal counterpoint of scarps and pyramids, where cloud-shadows spread a dim commotion, and hawks wheeled.

Less than thirty miles from the Tajik border we reached the village of Darvat Kurgan, and found a lorry depot where we downed a meal of noodles and cold soup. It was from here that in 1871 the Russian explorer Fedchenko had looked across with longing at the Transalai, and had given his watch to the Kokandi garrison commander as a bribe to let him proceed. But at once the watch stopped – the commander had childishly wound it to

267

death – and permission was withdrawn. Only later did Fedchenko return and discover the glacier – almost the largest in the world – which sprawled out of sight for fifty miles in the massif across our valley. Now the Kokandi fort had become a warehouse and was crumbling away, its towers half collapsed and its loopholes blocked with mud.

Three miles farther, in the impoverished village of Chak, our track disappeared among mud alleys. They looked abandoned. A few bald-headed Bactrian camels stood among the hovels, and did not stir as we nosed our way through. We splashed over a gulley, and found the only path out of the village. Ahead of us hung a wooden bridge whose struts stood thin as sticks in the river. My heart sank. It was the only way west. I thought we might edge on to it and test its strength. Then suddenly Oman shouted 'We'll see!' and set the car at it headlong.

For a second it crackled like dry biscuits under us. Then we were over and charging up a precipitous bank.

I yelled: 'Weren't you afraid?'

'Of course I was!' he yelled back.

Now the mountains engulfed us. Their flanks crowded the track in vertiginous gulfs and spurs. Through their flaccid earth the river had dropped sheer, opening up purple veins, and soon it was winding in a blood-coloured trickle a thousand feet below us. Our route was a maze of ruts and stones, and we went in clouds of reddish dust which clogged our hair and eyes.

Oman settled at the wheel with a strange, sombre glee. I had misjudged him. It was not hardship or challenge which turned him morose, but the emptiness of ordinary living. But now crisis freed him into near-recklessness. His only sign of nerves was a dangerous urge to smoke, and once, glimpsing the track fringing the precipices in front of us, he blessed himself. He never paused before a new wave of congealed mud or stones, simply drove his twelve-year-old Lada at it full tilt, and bullied us through or over.

But we had entered a deepening wilderness. Beneath us the river plunged unseen through a corridor of chasms and gulfs barely forty feet wide, while we wandered along its rim high above. Across our track the snowfields poured down shale and melted ice, turning it to a sepia rink. And it was these mud-slides which most threatened us. Set loose by shifting glaciers or rains, they descended in noiseless slicks which sometimes engulfed whole villages, leaving nothing behind. A few days earlier, unknown to us, a Tajik hamlet of a hundred souls had simply vanished from sight under an avalanche of liquid earth.

All afternoon we laboured on. Once only the liver-coloured slopes which walled us in burst open on a white gallery of mountains, brilliant and untouched, peak piled on peak, and desolately beautiful as they shone down on the wastes through which we blundered. At last a landslide turned our path to quagmire. Oman set the car at it again and again, but we dropped axle-deep into an ocean of red mud. We clambered out and piled stones round the wheels, but nothing moved. Bit by bit, we were sinking. I imagined enduring the night here, our doors locked against wolves, while we waited for any help. But after an hour a truck-full of Kirghiz shepherds arrived from the other direction, their bedding and chattels mounded about them – wild men with flayed cheekbones, who heaved us clear with a rope.

We pushed on through fallen rocks and snow, and somehow we never stuck again for long, but wove and charged our way out, with no man or vehicle in sight, and the light failing. At sunset we came to a stream under an alpine meadow, where cattle grazed, and we washed, exhausted, and Oman eased the car into its ford and swabbed it tenderly down. In the ageing light above us an eagle circled. There was no sound but the boiling of the distant river in its canyon.

Somewhere we had crossed unnoticed into Tajikistan. No military or police post marked the border. 'They think there's no road through,' said Oman, with a glint of pride.

But this was a country in civil war. It was the poorest and least urbanised of all the republics of the old Soviet Union. It endured the highest birth-rate, but its population was barely five million. Alone in Central Asia, its people were not of Turkic but Iranian stock and language, and some made common cause with their fellow-Tajik *mujahedin* over the Afghan border. Now, in the capital, an incongruous alliance of Moslems and democratic liberals was confronting the ex-Communist government. Their schism was heated by clan rivalries and by the dichotomy between an industrialised north and an impoverished south; and within a year war was to claim some 20,000 dead, and set loose a torrent of refugees.

But this evening, at sunset, nothing disturbed the mountains which circled our sky. As we eased west into the night the crowding slopes receded, and we descended into a broad valley. My map disclosed a few villages on the north bank of the river, and in the first starlight we crossed a bridge over a tributary among apple and cherry orchards. As Oman negotiated a room in a bleak inn, curious faces multiplied round us. In this region, at least, a tenuous peace prevailed. But nobody believed we had come from the east. The track was impassable even to horses until May, they said, although a heavy lorry might get through. Who were we really, they seemed to be asking? And from where had we actually come: an Uzbek and an Englishman?

As we sat in our room, opening a celebratory tin of tuna fish, we were joined by a Tajik and an Uzbek who owned a bus for transporting village wedding-parties. Sherali was a copybook Tajik. His fierce, Iranic features were drenched in a silky black beard and set with rapier eyes. Yet often he looked indefinably bewildered, and his suave courtesies seemed to have been borrowed from somebody else. His Uzbek partner was a near-dwarf named Sadik, who proffered a curved arm in handshake, as if he had suffered a stroke.

In the cool night we huddled round a table and exchanged road and war news, and a little food, and dim philosophies. The villagers here were still quiet, Sherali said. It was the mountains that should be feared. 'People don't understand them. The mountains can be very sensitive, very terrible. A man may go

270

hunting and fire off a shot and it sets the whole valley moving, or people shout to one another, and even the reverberation of their voices is dangerous, and finishes them.'

'We've seen those avalanches.' Oman had swelled like a bull-frog. 'We crossed six or seven.'

'Last year,' Sherali went on, 'in those mountains where you were, forty-two climbers disappeared. They were caught in a mud-slick and buried. Only one was separate from the rest, and got back to tell us.'

The dwarfish Sadik, meanwhile, was insinuating his lit ciga-rette between the others' dangling fingers, allowing each a puff before he retrieved it. From time to time he stared into my face with the half-evolved eyes of a lizard, then nudged me with a question. But his voice came always in a venal near-whisper as if everything he said must be secret or ugly. I at first thought him a little imbecile. 'Who are the most famous footballers with you?'

My mind went blank. I'd been cut off from England too long. A few months earlier, I was sure, I could have named several.

Sherali continued with a kind of fiery sadness: 'Those moun-tains have claimed more lives than any war ....'

But Sadik's saurian gaze was still on mine. Perhaps he was doubting if I were English. He said resentfully: 'England is the birthplace of football ....'

Then, in a fit of recall, I said: 'Gazza!'

He had not heard of him. 'He must be young,' he said, and went on questioning me. 'I knew an Englishman once who gave me a coat. What clothes do you have?' He reached through my jacket flaps and fingered my pullover.

But Sherali broke in: 'Look! We're just back from a party!' He delved into his bag and lifted out something wrapped in news-paper. 'We drove two soldiers back to their village after service in Siberia. Their family killed a sheep and gave us some!' Jubilantly he unwrapped a steamed head, complete in its skin. 'I've never met an Englishman before! We'll celebrate!' The skull had been sliced laterally, shearing off its mandible and exposing

271

the meat inside the cranium and upper jaw. He dangled it in front of me. 'Delicious!'

I stared at it uneasily. Its eyes were closed under dark lashes half steamed away. Its ears stuck out delicately, like a deer's.

Sadik said: 'This Englishman gave me a suit .... What will you give me?'

But Sherali had stripped away the sheep's skin in a flash. Its yellow skull ogled the ceiling. 'Eat!'

I heard craven excuses dropping from me. 'It's not my country's custom ....'

'You don't eat mutton?'

'Not like this ....'

I felt a hypocrite. These men gluttonously acknowledged what they were eating, whereas my sensibilities had been manicured. But they did not mind. Sherali opened another bag and poured out a mound of moist, rather bitter *haloumi* for me. Then they upended the sheep's skull and dug their fingers into the cheeks and brains. It was grey, soft meat. They sucked their hands luxuriously. Even Oman, after fruitlessly offering round our tuna, settled down to cram his mouth with filmy morsels. Sadik tried to dig out the eyes with his penknife, and snapped the blade. Sherali levered one up with a fork and popped it joyfully into his partner's mouth. I heard Sadik's teeth crunching the eyeball. 'These are wonderful!'

'I've heard.'

Within five minutes the head was stripped to a *memento mori*. It looked hopelessly reduced, like a fossil. Its spirit seemed to have transmigrated into Sherali and Sadik. Their tongues caressed their lips in remembrance, and they grinned collusively at one another, as if they had shared the same woman. Their business partnership was rooted in childhood friendship, which the war had not yet disturbed. Uzbeks still numbered one quarter of Tajikistan's populace. Uzbek troops, alongside Russians, had even been called in to shore up the *status quo*.

'Me and Sadik never faced anything like this before,' Sherali said. 'Some people resent our friendship now. Nationalists.

But we'll keep on together.' Yet they were starting to feel threatened. Their self-conscious pledge of comradeship might be the first sign of its disintegration. 'Who would ever have thought the Soviet Union would fall the way it did?' The war brought on Sherali's look of bewilderment. 'Just one man brought it down....'

The searching sharpness of his features still prejudiced me to believe him more intelligent than Sadik with his pancake cheeks and dead eyes. But now Sadik said: 'No, that empire was ripe for falling. Its own system did it. It was rotten.' Then he turned to me with his corrupt whisper. 'What will you give me? You see my knife is broken. Do you have a knife?'

'Only from Fergana.'

'That will do. Anything from you ....' His stare never changed. He said: 'Tell me, who takes more drugs, do you think, England or Tajikistan?' He injected his arm with a phantom needle.

'I don't know.' But I wondered what was in his cigarettes.

'I'm telling you, England does ....'

I snapped: 'But Tajikistan grows and exports them.'

'That's just business.'

I was starting to hate him. I turned to the others, while his eyes tormented the back of my head. He began: 'Who fucks more ...?'

But Sherali was lamenting his country's deepening crisis. He did not understand it. Nothing but a quiet pragmatism fell within his understanding. 'I'm a working man. I just want to feed my family, and get on with my living.'

Oman nodded. 'Lenin at least said one good thing: "Politicians are all prostitutes!"' The vodka was out, and his eyes had started their sweating. 'Just think. Here we all are – Uzbek, Tajik, English – and we're all friends! Why can't it always be like this? Why can't ...?' Then the fatal bottle passed between us, and the toasts started their rounds, and set in train grandiloquent musings. So, in this close room under the cleansing mountains, we dropped into the recurring lament of travellers who find themselves released from race and class and context, and momentarily

273

entered a heart's region freed from all differences.

But in the morning I found my knife had gone.

*

For 200 miles, as we made for the capital Dushanbe, the river prised apart the valley where streams of scarlet and ice flowed side by side. Nothing seemed natural. Fluffy clouds dangled in the mountains, as if hung up for a court masque. The snow-peaks stacked above green hills, and the crimson gash of river-beds drew us through a country of white, emerald and synthetic red, as if the national flag (a similar confection) had bled over the landscape. From time to time our track still disintegrated into a rutted causeway where an avalanche had passed, and tilted up putty-soft scarps or squeezed to a sliver under cliffs. But little by little the snow withdrew, until only the Pervogo ranges far to the south shone white.

In their villages of clay and brushwood, the Tajiks walked in harlequin colours and a touch of defiant grace. Longest settled of all the Central Asian peoples, they had been driven from the Zerafshan valley and into the mountains by Arab and Turkic invasion almost thirteen centuries ago. They had intermarried with Mongoloids, but an Iranian physiognomy prevailed, and from village to village the faces changed. Some were inbred and delicate. They showed long, European features and heavy noses. Sometimes the hair curled russet or auburn above their high brows, and their faces shone with blue or green eyes. All the colour which had drained out of the Kirghiz towns returned on this side of the mountains. Even the old men glittered in gold-threaded quilts and bright-hued skull-caps: biblical patriarchs with dripping beards, who crouched still limber on their haunches by the wayside. Children sported embroidered shirts and dresses, and the lean, handsome women walked in fiercely brilliant gowns with their headscarves tied piratically around their foreheads.

Within a few months, during open war between Moslems and the old Communist regime, this secluded valley would be

274

invaded by its clan rivals from Kulyab to the south, and swept by Russian tanks, and the refugees would be pouring from the villages in their thousands on the way to Afghanistan. But for the moment the land dropped westward in hushed apprehension. Beneath us the river inscribed idle hieroglyphs over its flattened bed. Sometimes now it measured half a mile across, while a hundred tributaries meandered to meet it, carving up the hills like cake. Then the flow would narrow to a flood, slapping itself into rapids, until it left our road altogether, plunging south, and we followed a milder river towards Dushanbe. The country softened round us. Its lower slopes were tinted with vetch and rock roses. Their scent gusted over the road. Orchards filled with yellow grosbeaks and the darting of blue-green rollers, and a booted eagle coasted across our path.

We limped towards the outskirts of Dushanbe, nursing two broken brake-discs. Vigilantes and armed police flagged us down as we entered, and searched us. Armoured cars waited in the alleys nearby. Beyond them the city had gone unnaturally quiet. Scarcely a car moved in the streets. Ranks of plane trees muffled and darkened every avenue, where a few trams and taxis jittered. Fear of earthquake had built the city low, and its offices and apartments lined the boulevards with three-storey façades washed in faded buff and blue. Here and there some sop to oriental taste had sanctioned a rank of pointed arches or a filigreed balcony. But there was an old Russian feel of life rotting away behind appearances. The municipal rose-beds seemed to be blooming in solitude, for themselves, and the pavements looked too wide for the pedestrians. In this half-Moslem ambience, the sexes walked separately, and the slender women still wore their native brilliance. But people hurried in preoccupation, mostly alone. Nobody raised his voice. When men met, the eloquent language of Moslem handshakes – the cordial double-clasp or the perfunctory touch, all the graded signs of friendship or distrust – was magnified in the tense streets. The hovering mountains bathed them in cold air, and turned the avenues into gleaming culs-de-sac.

This was the ghost-city which the Russians were leaving. Before 1917 it had been a small village, but with the arrival of the railway in 1929 the Bolsheviks had made it their own, and until recently only half its people were Tajik. In common with all Central Asia, its factory workers and the bulk of its specialists had been Russian. But every month they were streaming home in their thousands, and now, during an armed stand-off between government and opposition, a paralysis had settled over the city. Its appearance of peace was only the stillness of suspense or the stagnation of closure. Along its avenues, in the serenely banked façades of flats and businesses, windows were boarded up or blocked, balconies sagging and crevices leaking weeds. In half-abandoned newspaper kiosks the familiar Western icons – posters of karate and bodybuilding heroes, Pink Floyd, prints of Solzhenitsyn selling for three roubles – looked foolish or redundant.

I walked along the old Lenin Prospect (renamed Rudaki Prospect after the Tajik national poet) which made a dog-leg through the city's core. It was suffocated in chenar trees eight deep, but empty of traffic. In Independence Square, the previous month, a huge demonstration of Moslems and liberals had threatened to assault the Supreme Soviet in session. After a four-day protest, fluttering with green Islamic flags, they had forced the resignation of the whole Presidium. Close by in Freedom Square, two days later, a counter-demonstration had seethed round the president's office shouting pro-Communist slogans. The pink and white government buildings still shone surreally in front of us, flying the national flag; but opposite, the Lenin colossus raised in 1960 had left behind only a plinth of shattered marble.

Within a few months the old regime would reassert itself; but already it was dressed in Tajik colours, and paid lipservice to a mild Islam. The certainties of doctrinaire Communism were gone. Instead the city was sinking into a chasm of nationalism and tribal feud. I wandered it in ignorant misgiving, and occasionally, where a Marxist memorial or a slogan remained, was touched by foolish nostalgia. In the contemporary chaos, these statues immortalising work and learning seemed invocations to a more enlightened time, and the heraldry of Communism – the slogans urging men to paradise – imbued with some lost knowledge and even a moral sweetness.

In the windows of the Firdausi Library busts of Pushkin, Tolstoy and Gorky mingled with those of Persian and Tajik classical writers. A few years before this would have smelt of insidious colonialism: the absorption of native heroes into the Russian body. But now they looked innocently ecumenical, and echoed with ruined ideals. So I forgot for a while the corruption and evangelistic cruelty of the old empire, which had handed these people the poisoned chalice of a split identity, and understood those who wanted the Soviet Union back.

In the library next day, I roamed among the deserted stacks where old, permitted titles mingled with fledgling new ones. Lenin's *On the Defence of the Socialist Motherland* and *Can the Bolsheviks retain state power?* nestled beside D.H. Lawrence's *The Rainbow*. Only Lenin's hypocritical tract *The Rights of Nations to Self-determination* rang with irony.

'All this will go up in flames soon,' said a Russian teacher hunting the card-index beside me. 'These people are ripe for burning books.' She was stout and bitter, with cropped hair. She worked in a small town in the hills, an enclave of mines and factories which had once been full of Russians. 'The Tajiks are hopeless,' she went on. 'They just trade and trick. All merchants. Our Russian technocrats have already mostly gone, and the others are following – factory-workers and teachers. Everybody.'

'You have no Tajik friends?'

'I do, but this nationalism is growing every day. You can feel it all round you.'

'And your school?'

'Our classes are down from thirty to fifteen, and all amalgamating. Everybody's planning to go. And I'll go too, in the autumn, back to the Ukraine. People work properly there.' Her face quivered with memory, perhaps too rosy. 'It's good in the Ukraine.'

In my hotel the only other foreigners were Afghan merchants and students. Oman said they were trading in opium and heroin, which would find its way through the Baltic ports to the West. On the tarmac outside, a drift of youths was selling bootleg brandy and French (they said) champagne, and fraternising with a slovenly troupe of police. From time to time they moved in and out of the lobby in a tremor of secrecy and suspicion. Their eyes raked the doors for custom, while the handshakes and embraces rose to a crescendo. Friends or rivals would be plucked aside for a sudden confidence, and Oman would catch fragments: '... seventy roubles ... I can manage ... ninety ... as a favour ....' Then the restless circles and pairs would reconvene, and their conspiracies start all over again. 'My friend ... tomorrow ... *dollars* ...?'

The sight of the hotel terrace made Oman sick. Twenty years before, he had finished his military service in Dushanbe as the building was being completed, and a tile had dropped off the roof and killed his closest friend.

While I was rambling the streets, he would set off to view the tea-houses and barracks of his past, but always returned a little melancholy. There was nobody left whom he knew, and the friends he remembered were mostly tragic. One had shot himself; another was killed when his tank tipped over a ravine. Then there was the Polish woman he had loved: a ravishing creature, he said, but married. Every night, while her husband was away, he had escaped the barracks to visit her, and returned before dawn. Even now her memory turned him maudlin. 'I still know where she lived. Perhaps she's still there. She was so beautiful, like a dream to me. I was just twenty-two.' His fingers clasped and unclasped the remembered body. 'But she would be fifty-three now, and our women don't last like yours do. So I think I'll not go. I'll keep her memory.' But he looked miserable.

In the evening he would often winkle out scraps of meat from some half-closed shop, and would grill them into tough kebabs

278

in the hotel yard, and brew up tea. But at other times I returned to find him slumped in tousled gloom among discarded newspapers and cigarette stubs, drunk. Then we would open our iron rations of tinned fish and calamary, and I would reassure him that we would soon be gone, for he was growing bored.

After dark, when the traffic drained from the streets, the city went silent and a rash of stars glittered in our window. Then, from some distant suburb, we would hear bursts of automatic fire, which Oman recognised as Kalashnikovs, and hundreds of awakened dogs would howl from alley to alley in a mournful counterpoint. Morning brought news of men killed by random skirmishes in a city filled with armed civilians.

These disturbed nights goaded Oman into vodka-loosened ramblings about the mafia, his troubled parenthood, or the whereabouts of God. His past was scarred by loss and hardship. His mother's father had been a wealthy man, he said, and had owned a restaurant and a small factory, and was shot in the Stalin years simply for being what he was. Oman's mother was only seven then. His father had been wounded in the Russo-Finnish war, and invalided out to Novosibirsk where he met and married her. Oman was the lone result. His father never truly recovered, and died when his son was ten. Oman posthumously adored him. It was this dimly remembered father who had built their family home at the epicentre of the 1966 Tashkent earthquake: a traditional brick-and-timber house which had survived when all around it the Soviet buildings crashed. 'They were built inflexibly of concrete,' he said. 'So they just disappeared overnight.'

On one of these distracted evenings, when the crash of small-arms fire kept us up late, the question of national identity nagged at me again, and I asked him if he were proud of being Uzbek. No Latvian or Georgian would have responded tepidly to such a question, but Oman answered: 'It's hard to feel it much.' He looked a little bewildered. 'Yes, I suppose I'm proud ... but I'm proud of being Moslem too.'

Yet I knew he was not a believer. Rather he felt part of the

Umma, of the wider family of Moslem peoples: a generous but vague identity. Staring at his smoothed face, as at a cryptogram, I realised that this absence of national clothing did not seem a lack to him, only to me, soaked as I was, unthinking, in my own. His true nation was his extended family. It was this which surrounded him with the comfort of belonging, the womb-like flesh of his own kind.

'I can trace my people over two hundred years,' he said. 'It used to be common among us, but it's dying out now. So I'm teaching my youngest son the same.' Then the old, stubborn hurt darkened his voice. 'I don't want to be forgotten after I'm dead.'

I said exactingly: 'Is it so important? A name?' I was wondering what it really meant: the transient survival of some syllables in the collective memory.

But he did not understand this. 'I want to be honoured,' he said. 'I want my place back.'

'Back?'

'Yes, back.' A fusion of anger and self-pity burnt just below his words. 'I've been wronged in this life.'

I said: 'How?', and at once regretted asking. He was seated at our table like a sulky child. Vodka swam in his voice and heated eyes, and I anticipated one of his generalised tirades.

But instead he looked down at his hands on the table and said: 'Nine years ago I was sentenced to seven years' imprisonment. For something I never did.' He gazed at me for my reaction. I don't know what he saw. But I was aware, beneath shock, of unexplained things slipping into place. And now the words gushed helplessly from him, as if they had long been waiting: his terrible inner anger and sadness. His face tightened with inconsolable memories. 'In those days I was director of a big combine, and somebody wanted my position. So he rigged a case against me, said I'd agreed to accept a bribe. There was nothing I could do. It was a mafia job.' His voice pulsed to a rhythmic crescendo, as if he were singing himself into fury. 'So I was sent to prison on rigged evidence' – he caught at the scruff of his neck – 'and half a year later that man had a heart attack, and soon afterwards was sent to prison himself for something. Where he is now, only God knows.'

I asked softly: 'What was prison like?'

But he turned quiet. His face convulsed. 'I can't even talk about it.' And this silence was more potent than anything he could have said. He started pacing the room as if it were a cell, while his creased vest and trousers touched up the illusion of a convict. 'I was already forty. But when they took me I just went into shock. I remember standing in that place dazed for almost three minutes. I just went on repeating, "*There's no sun, there's no sun, there's no sun.*"' He glared upward. Then his words came in declamatory hammer-blows. 'The cells were two metres by five ... with six convicts in each one ... three bunks to each wall. And sometimes another six were shoved in too ... and they slept on the floor. We were cattle.'

He struck the room's wall with his fists. His eyes had filled with water. 'Then after a year and a half I was sent to a labour camp not far from Tashkent, and in some ways it was worse than prison. We worked in the fields all day, and sometimes in that region, you know, the temperature climbs to forty degrees Centigrade, and we just laboured under that sun, so that our necks and ears swelled to twice their size ....'

As he went on, I realised that for a long time inarticulate questions had been rankling in me, because all at once he seemed resolved. His air of private hurt and self-reliance, all his rancour and solitude, appeared natural now. It was a rare Uzbek official, I thought, who had never accepted a bribe, but I believed in Oman's innocence. The rage which came riding out of him was too intense for show.

'I wrote letters to everybody, on and on,' he said, 'even to Gorbachev and Lukyanov. And in the end the state procurator came down from Moscow to review my case, and asked me why I was so outraged and writing all these letters. I told him I was angry because I wasn't earning anything and so was depriving the government of income tax' – this joke momentarily ironed out his forehead – 'and he asked me off the record what had happened, and I told him – just as I'm telling you now – and because of him I came out of that place after three years, and I thought: so after all, there is a God, and He is watching me.'

He dropped into his chair again, his anger withered away. 'Do you know, when I got out the policeman who had arrested me came and apologised and said "What could I do?" although he'd known I was innocent.' He crossed his arms over his chest in ironic penitence. '"I'm sorry," he said, as though he'd dented my car, "I'm *so* sorry!"'

He cradled the vodka bottle against his chest, then one plump arm came up and covered his head in remembered despair. 'After that I didn't want to see anybody – not my old friends or work-mates, nobody. I took to working on the railway as a mechanic – I'm good at that – mending the refrigerators on trains.' His voice rose again in a momentary, pathetic outrage. 'I did that alone for three years!'

I began: 'You've started again now ....'

But he was not listening. 'Somebody should write my story. Why don't you write it? I couldn't write it.' The vodka trembled into his glass. 'I've got a stack of papers and documents. It would make a bestseller! Like Solzhenitsyn's *One Day in the Life of Ivan Denisovich*!' The drink was overwhelming him. 'Did you know that one in thirty of our population goes to prison? And I reckon half of them are honest men, blackmailed.'

I said: 'But you've a fine house now, and good work. And your son's married well ....'

'Yes, but ....' He gestured hopelessly. 'I can't enjoy them. I can't be happy there. Not in my real heart.'

In some vital part of him, I realised, he was broken. However much he travelled with his vans striking lucrative deals, this lesion would not heal. He looked flushed and spent. I did not know what to say. My arm around his shoulders brought his head half sobbing against mine, while the dogs began barking all over the city in the wake of new gunfire.

282

In the 1930s, at the height of Stalin's persecutions, a pious citizen of Dushanbe opened his house for the secret prayers of Moslems, and around this modest building there grew up the country's central mosque and the residence of its spiritual leader, the Qazi. Now the Qazi's faction, in alliance with the Islamic Renaissance Party (soon to be banned), was tasting a precarious power. But no delegation clogged the doorways, and nobody barred me from entering the courtyards, where a few builders were cutting sheets of marble at a lathe. The 160 medreseh pupils had just dispersed for the summer vacation, and an air of dereliction was about.

But one student had been left behind. He could not afford the train home, he said, and was waiting for a cheap bus fare. 'My father's just a mechanic. He hasn't the money to pay for me.'

So we sat together under the sleepy porticoes. He was half Tajik, half Uzbek, and across his open face I fancied that the two worlds did battle, and that periodically the sturdy Turk in him was being sabotaged by a volatile Iranian. But he was callow and earnest. 'We have to live on a stipend, you see,' he went on. 'Three hundred roubles a month. It's not much. It gets paid by our brothers in Iran. Our government gives nothing for religion. They hate us.'

I glimpsed a spark of anger, which was snuffed out at once by his enthusiasm. 'But it's all changing now! You heard about our demonstration? People came from everywhere! From the factories and collectives and state farms – old, young. When the police blocked the roads, they just went in on foot. And they were half starving. Some of them hadn't received pay for six months, and there was nothing in the shops: no sugar, no meat, bread. Nothing.'

But he was jubilant with the certainty of future triumph. His had been one of the thousands of faces massed in Independence Square a month before, and he had seen and felt their power. 'This government is still run by old-time

Communists,' he said, 'and that system was atrocious. Nobody could speak or believe as he wished. Now our law gives freedom of belief, but Islamic law will be better.'

'Why?' I asked. 'Will it also give freedom of belief?'

He began: 'Yes ....' But he sounded subtly dissatisfied, as if Islamic law should magically unite everything, and cleanse it. 'It will come. Perhaps in five years, perhaps in ten. But it will come like it did in Iran.'

This chill certainty fell mildly from him. It seemed to him, after all he had witnessed, that an irreversible wave were gathering. Only five years ago barely twenty mosques were open in the country. Now there were 2500. He said. 'I think the Iranians are the best Moslems.'

'But they are Shia,' I said, sowing discord. The Tajiks were almost all Sunni.

'There may be a few Shia,' he answered quixotically, 'but most are Moslems.'

I gazed at him in wonder. Iranian propaganda must have evaded all grounds for friction. He seemed infinitely manipulable. I asked: 'You think there will be a revolution here like Iran's?'

'I pray God not. I believe it will happen gently.' His fingers sieved the air, as if welcoming a breeze. 'Some of our women are fearful, but the Ayatollah Khomeini said that women might work – and why not? – for five or six hours in the morning, and that afterwards they should tend the house. But look what they endure now! They slave from dawn to dusk in the collectives and get paid a pittance a month! As for the veil, that should just cover the head.' He outlined a wimple, and smiled at me for approval. All this seemed decent to him, even free. Only his freedom was not mine, and I was scowling ungratefully. I was familiar with this recipe for cowled servants by now.

I said: 'Perhaps women should decide what women do.'

'But that's what they wear in Iran,' he rushed on. 'They cover the head and they look very attractive, the women, dressed like that.'

'You've seen them?'

284

He looked incredulous. 'Of course not! I've watched it on television.' He grinned at the simplicity of this. 'Maybe I'll study in Iran one day, or in Saudi Arabia' – the possibilities filled him with awe as he spoke – 'they give students a hundred dollars a month in Saudi Arabia! I couldn't earn that in a lifetime! They have Islamic law there, but the biggest millionaires in the world!' His eyes glittered. 'That's the place!'

In his face the Turk and the Iranian had momentarily made peace, hypnotised by lucre. 'But some of us will go to Pakistan after our four years here,' he went on. 'They have the best colleges there, because they teach English. Next year we will be learning English in this medreseh too ....'

'Why?'

'It's the world language. It's the one you have to know. But Saudi Arabia would be best!'

Somewhere in his imagination there shone a paradise of Islamic justice and gross riches. It restored his native pride, yet promised dollars.

But wasn't Islamic law hard on money-making, I asked? It condemned usury, limited private property and amputated thieves' hands.

'Amputation?' He looked astonished. 'Our law wouldn't do that! No, no, it's not like that at all. Only if you steal something *big*. A car, say. But if you steal something small, or steal for the first time, they'll just cut off a fingertip.' He held up his splayed hand. 'Just a little, a very *little*.' He laughed in depreciation, charmingly. 'And the second time you steal, they'd still only cut off *that*, and then *that* and *that* ....' He sliced off an imaginary sheaf of fingers. They dropped soundlessly on to the portico floor, until his hand was a stub. He was smiling at me now. It all seemed irreducibly logical to him, beautiful even. 'Only then would the hand come off!'

He was not really cruel, I knew. He simply belonged to a harsher world: the poor mechanic's son.

'You don't agree with it?' He looked astonished. 'Why not?' His face was a childlike question-mark. 'But it works!'

Among the racketeers and bootleggers adrift in my hotel lingered a lecturer in the department of physics at Dushanbe's university. He supplemented his breadline income by siphoning off hotel guests into private lodgings. When Oman had bargained at the reception-desk, this delicate figure had emerged from the lobby's shadows, offering a list of private rooms – but they all lay too far from the centre. With a pucker of deference he had not pressed their merit, and returned to the shadows.

But four days later I met Talib again, walking near the university. The fervid face, gentled in shelving hair, had been changed by its location from diffidence to self-esteem, and he invited me home. He lived in one of those flat-blocks whose tiers of splintered stairs and padlocked doors scarcely vary all the way from Minsk to the Pacific. But inside, his apartment had been prettified with alcoves and little chandeliers. His wife was cooking supper for their eight-year-old son in the kitchen, and his daughter, perched in the sitting-room, was playing on a Cyrillic typewriter.

She was the perfect type of those lissom girls who chattered in flocks along the boulevards, holding hands and flaunting *Atlas* silks. She had the slender face and alert eyes of her tribe, and ran barefoot about the flat on long feet with prehensile toes, giggling and flirting a little. Out in the streets these urban shepherdesses, speaking their mysterious Tajik, seemed touched by enigma. But in the house Sayora suggested some international teenager, by turns sulky, warm and abruptly independent. She was reading economics to become a book-keeper.

'Maybe she'll marry and it'll be hard for her,' said Talib. 'It's always hard for women working. But I don't believe Islam will change things for her. We'll make our own Islam here. Can you imagine our women wearing the veil?'

Sayora levelled a playful hand across her nose. Her black eyebrows converged at the centre in the way the Tajiks admire. She played on her beauty like an instrument. Her portly mother, bustling about us with sweets and nuts, made me at home with domestic questions which she answered herself. 'Are you all right?... No, you're not, here's another cushion .... You will eat with us? Yes, of course, there will be pilau in a moment ....'

'Things will get better in this country,' said Talib, infected by her homely commotion. 'I don't just think this, I know this. I even delivered a lecture to my students about it. It's up to you, I said, you're young, it's your world. I'm an old man, I told them [but he was my age] and I can't do much. But you can.' He raised a frail fist. 'And nobody dissented.'

This belief in the future was ardent and mercurial, like him, rooted more in his desires than in reason. He burnt with patriotic longings. He belonged, I guessed, to the fragile alliance of democrats and Moslems which opposed the old government. 'I used to be a Party member,' he said. 'You had to be, in the university. But hardly any of us believed in it, although a few did, and their world crashed overnight. Now we've had seventy years of Communism to mitigate our Islam, and perhaps it's been civilising. I'm a Moslem like any other, but there comes a time when you feel: It's enough!' He thrust out his palms in repudiation. 'Islam can be mild, you know.'

Then his little son ran into the room firing a space-gun. He was thick-set and boisterous. He shot us all dead, twice. Talib, who was teaching him the poetry of Rudaki, disarmed him and tested him on an opening *rubaiyat*. The boy pressed his knuckles to his forehead, dislodging himself into duty. Then he stood to attention and chanted:

> *Many a desert waste existeth*
> *Where was once garden glad;*
> *And a garden glad existeth*
> *Where was once desert sad ....*

Talib turned to me. 'You hear how beautiful the words are! And that was a thousand years ago!'

His bookcase brimmed with Tajik poets, and he annexed all

Persian culture to his nation, from Hafiz to Omar Khayyám (who had been a formidable mathematician). 'And we knew about Communism long before the Bolsheviks came! Listen to this ....' His eyes went dreamy as he quoted the poetry of Abdulrachman Jami, on how Alexander the Great was astonished to come upon a city in Sogdiana where everyone was equal, and all houses and gardens held in common, and poverty unknown.

I asked: 'And what did he do?'

'He thought that they should have a czar,' said Talib, 'and he destroyed them.' But this denouement did not trouble him. What mattered was the pre-eminence of the Tajik culture. More than two millennia ago his people had known and absorbed Communism. What could the Russians ever teach them?

'But they've already taught you,' I said. 'Even in your university.'

'Of course, of course.' Talib tacked to this graceless wind. 'But it's good they're getting out now. So long as they were here we could sit back and let them do the work: in administration, in the factories, everywhere .... But now we'll be forced to learn ourselves, and that's right. We're losing our nurse and we'll have to grow up.'

He spoke with rueful warmth and only muted optimism. Perhaps, I thought, I was listening to the birth-pangs of his nation. For him, I slowly realised, it was a deep-set mission: the returning of his people to their own heart and tongue. He had already published six works on chemistry in Tajik for secondary school and university students. They were the first of their kind. And now, he confided, he had completed a dictionary of physics terminology, converting each concept from Russian into Tajik. It had taken him fourteen years.

'But nobody will publish it. My publishers promised, but they have no paper now.' He gathered up the typescript to show me. It was formidably long. I recognised the protective way his fingers riffled and stroked the paper. 'It's not the money I care about. It was something I had to do.'

'Of course.' This detraction of money touched me with affection.

It was the first time I had heard anyone here say he disregarded money. 'Someone must publish it.'

'They will, in time,' he said. But he left the typescript in his lap like an orphan. Sometimes, he said, he had gone back to early Tajik manuscripts, hunting for synonyms where the modern language had none; at other times he had been forced to invent them himself, struggling to conflate existing Tajik roots and suffixes. A single neologism might consume a week.

Fourteen years! And at last this Casaubon-like enterprise teetered on the brink of the light. 'But nobody's interested in things like this now,' he said, 'just in demonstrations and in shooting one another.' Abstractedly he weighed the book by sections on his palms, as if assessing its value or meaning, or its chance of surviving at all.

His doubts were to be justified. Within a few months pro-government insurgents from the south would rampage through the city killing Moslem sympathisers, and I never discovered what happened to Talib, or his gentle family, or to the painstaking book which was to coax his people towards civilisation.

*

Next morning in our hotel room an ancient black telephone sprang to life, and Oman started flirting with an unknown woman at the other end. She had dialled the wrong number (she said) but he would not let her go. He joked, cajoled and teased her, flattered a little, and reeled her in. She was a teacher, was she? How strange! He had thought of teaching himself .... Wasn't that a Tashkent accent he heard? It was! Might he meet her in half an hour, then? Yes! His would be the green Lada parked outside the Lakhuti Theatre on Rudaki Prospect. He very much looked forward .... Wonderful!

He replaced the receiver with an anticipatory 'Oooh!' Who was she? He had no idea. 'They're usually tarts telephoning from outside,' he said, 'but she sounded genuine ... with a pretty voice.' He writhed into a clean shirt. 'I think she just wants a man!'

289

He scrutinised the Oman in the mirror, patted his hair for several minutes, and spent a long time in the broken-down bathroom. Then he emerged to dab his 'Moscow-Paris Eau de Cologne' around his neck and on his chest, and made for the door. 'I'll see you this evening!' he called, and added from the corridor: 'She sounded young!'

I trailed off puritanically to the Orthodox church of St Nicholas, brushed by a transient loneliness. Momentarily I invested the siren voice with an ondine's body, then promptly forgot her. Under the church's vegetable dome and blazing cross the women in the gardens were old, and had turned themselves to God. Shuffling among the terraces in rubber boots and worn-out slippers, sipping water from a holy well, begging, praying, waiting – one of them stark mad – they seemed to be dying piecemeal and contented.

But inside the church a mass christening was in progress. Some 200 Russians crammed into a side-chapel while a garrulous, whirlwind priest anointed their children and babies – on foreheads, eyes, wrists, chests, hands and feet – with a phial of oil and a wispy brush. He looked overworked, and had run out of pomp. But he dabbed crosses on the elder children as if touching up masterpieces. Then a batch of babies was slipped from its underclothes and plunged one by one into the font water, which he scooped over their heads in a gabble of names and a triple blessing.

For an infant or two, this ceremony passed in stunned silence. Then there broke out a terrible, contagious howling. It spread from baby to baby in a bush-fire of unappeasable terror. Even the stoutest broke down. As each baby was returned wailing and sinless to its parents' arms, it was instantly enveloped in shawls and kisses, but bawled remorselessly on. Dummies and bottles were rushed unavailing to the rescue. Cooing and burbling fell on scream-deafened ears. They urinated miserably over the floor or down their mothers' arms.

A few adults, meanwhile, reaching Christianity after the years of its persecution, bowed their heads over the font. Then, as the hubbub shrank, the priest marched among the babies and sliced off a damp tress from every whimpering head with a pair of kitchen scissors. Each curl he passed to the old woman following him, who kneaded it into a paste, while I watched with the bewilderment of any intruding Moslem.

I imagined that these embattled Russians were experiencing a resurgence of faith. But when I asked another priest, walking in the overgrown gardens that evening, he said No. 'Our congregation used to number two thousand or more. There was scarcely room for them. But they're less than five hundred now, and the baptisms, as you saw, were only fifty today, when there used to be twice as many.'

He strode beside me in a gold soutane and hobnailed boots. But under its purple cap his face was fretted with lines, and his peppery beard turning white. 'Our people have gone back home – plane-loads and train-loads of them.' He thrust out his arm at the setting sun, and I sensed in the gesture a homesickness, out of this deepeningly alien land, for the refuge of once-Holy Russia. 'I've served here twenty years and I've never seen so few believers.'

But now that the other religion, Communism, had died overnight, were people not renewing their identity in this one?

No, he said bluntly, they were fading away. 'Only after the troubles earlier this year a few grew afraid, and came to be baptised because of that. Fear is a great baptiser.'

As we passed the church's shop, stocked with a few pamphlets and icons, he burst out: 'But people can read about their faith now! At last, after so long! Look!' He pointed in the window. It was still a luxury to him. 'The laws of God!'

At first he had reminded me of those East Mediterranean priests who smelt of incense and garlic and mild corruption. But now I was starting to like him. I asked: 'What about the future?'

His stride did not falter. 'I just go day by day. I'm not thinking about it.' We passed the enclosure where the priests before him lay buried, remembered under flowers. 'So long as there is just one old woman left in my congregation, the church will be open, and I'll be here to serve her.'

They were sitting, four or five *babushkas*, in the warming sun of the courtyard as I left. But by the time I reached the hotel, it was dusk, and Oman's Lada was parked smugly in the yard behind. I remembered the siren voice of the schoolteacher, and felt a pang of irritated envy. Oman was seeing life!

But I opened the door on a crestfallen back. 'She never turned up,' he said. 'I suppose she was just joking.' He saw my face and fell into rueful laughter. 'Yes, there I was, running after her like a besotted boy.'

But the indignity went on rankling. Why had she not come, he wondered? Did she never intend it? Perhaps something had delayed her. Or had she lost her nerve? 'I've never had any trouble finding girlfriends in Tashkent. No, they're not prostitutes. Some of them are married. We just meet in a dacha for a little holiday – half a day, perhaps, a day ....' His lower lip jutted out like a child's. 'Why didn't she come?'

I couldn't tell, of course. But one explanation did not occur to him, and I never mentioned it: that the young schoolmistress had glimpsed the stout and ageing Oman waiting there, and had walked past him without a sign.

*

One morning I woke early after a night jolted by gunfire and Oman's snoring and, in the thin light trickling through the window with the call to prayer, felt suddenly that we should be on the road. For a while now a mood of jaded restlessness had descended, and a sense of being trapped. The passes to our north were blocked by late snow, deflecting us towards the Afghan frontier before we circled back to Tashkent, and Oman too wanted to be gone: idleness provoked his demons.

The moment we were on the move again, his ebullience returned. He smote the air and declared the Lada ready for anything. Its brake-discs had been mended and the red mud sluiced from every crack. So where would we go now?

'To the grave of Enver Pasha,' I said, 'but I don't know where it is.'

'Nor do I. But we'll find it!'

So we started on a tortuous search, in the wake of a story seventy years old. Enver Pasha had risen from humble origins (his father a railway worker, his mother an undertaker's drudge) to become a leading architect of the Young Turk revolution in 1908 and head of the triumvirate which ruled Turkey during the First World War. Proud, glamorous, ruthless, he was a master of conspiracy and an erratically ambitious general. No one could predict him. An avowed republican, he married an Ottoman princess. He was rumoured the finest swordsman in the empire. But by 1918 he was in flight from his country, and under sentence of death. Lenin welcomed him in Moscow as a revolutionary tool, and in 1921 despatched him to Central Asia, where the *basmachi* guerrillas had been tormenting the Bolsheviks for three years. Lenin seems to have hoped that the reputation of the charismatic Turk would entice rebels into the Communist fold.

But Enver was dreaming something different: a *jihad* which would rouse the Turkic regions of Asia and weld them into a Pan-Turanian empire from Constantinople to Mongolia. The moment he reached Bukhara he escaped the city, went over to the *basmachi*, and proclaimed a full-scale holy war against the Russians. Messengers rode out to every guerrilla leader, urging their unity. He secured the support of the exiled emir of Bukhara, and arms and personnel from King Amanullah of Afghanistan. Thousands of recruits poured in. A shock of early victories, and the capture of Dushanbe, swept him to a brief glory. He declared himself 'Supreme Commander of all the Armies of Islam' and kinsman of the Caliph (through his wife), the legate of the Prophet on earth.

But now the battle-tempered Bolshevik war-machine steam-rollered east against him. The ill-armed and disunited *basmachi* could not halt it. One by one their strongholds were overrun, and they melted away, while Enver's little army fell back on the Pamir foothills. His position was hopeless. He might have fled into Afghanistan, but flight was not his nature. Ten days before the end he wrote a farewell letter to his wife, saying that his men were being mercilessly pursued and could not adapt to defensive warfare. With it he sent a twig from an elm tree on which he had carved her name.

On 4 August 1922, while the Bolsheviks closed in, he celebrated Bairam with a handful of his closest followers in the village of Abiderya. Soon afterwards, as his outposts opened fire on the advancing enemy, he leapt into the saddle, drew his sabre and charged the Red machine-guns head on, followed by twenty-five companions. They drowned in a rain of bullets.

The Russians did not know whom they had killed. One of the dead, spattered by seven bullet-holes but still dapper in a Turkic jacket and German field-boots, was carrying papers and a small Koran. These they sent to Tashkent for identification, and left the bodies where they had fallen. Two days later a passing mullah recognised the corpse of Enver Pasha. The news spread. The villagers of Abiderya streamed out to bring his body back, and thousands of mourners appeared like magic out of the hills. He was buried in a nameless grave under a walnut tree by the river. He was just forty. Even now, it is said, on the anniversary of his death, the descendants of his comrades-in-arms come from as far away as Turkey to pay homage at his grave.

But confusion surrounded this story. Three years after his death an Austrian carpet-dealer, Gustav Krist, claimed to have spoken with the commander of the Red attacking force, who told him that Enver and his adjutant had escaped to a nearby spring, where Russian agents murdered them. Scouring my maps, I could find no trace of the old names. No Satalmis, where Enver wrote his last letter. No Abiderya, where he was interred.

For two days Oman and I threaded roads across the bare hills. In Kurgan Tube, soon to be war-ravaged, we came upon a giant mosque half-built. Its work-force of Moslem faithful, who had given their labour free, had sensed the coming storm and trickled away in fear, leaving the architect alone there, boasting of its future size, while it disintegrated round him. He had never heard of Enver Pasha.

The commander of the Red force had apparently told Krist that Enver was cornered near the town of Denau, and killed at the Aqsu spring nearby. We found the Denau fort circling its mound in a breached ring, and goats grazing in the town streets; but when we blundered up a track to the nearest Aqsu (the common Turkic word for 'spring') its inhabitants met our questions with baffled frowns.

We took to badgering tea-houses along different roads. Every twenty miles or so we would stop off and question their habitués. Satalmis? Abiderya? Old men listened to us in puzzled confabulation, sitting comfortably in their tattered beards, and fingering scraps of bread. In the Tajik tea-houses our questions sometimes started up a gale of answers and counter-claims, which cancelled each other out. But in the Uzbek ones (for we were weaving between the two countries now) heads were scratched, moustaches tugged in sober rumination, and looks of honest vacancy appeared. Many claimed to know where Enver had fought. 'But nobody knows where he was killed,' they said. 'Somewhere up there in the mountains ....' Then tea-cups would be raised to pursed lips, brows would corrugate in surmise, and everybody's gaze drift to the east.

In a cloud of frustration, as we were driving south of Denau towards the Afghan border, we stopped at the local military commission. 'These fellows know everything,' Oman said, and we marched brazenly in. A surprised Russian captain received us, grew interested, and telephoned an old comrade, who asserted that, yes, Enver Pasha was buried in the nearby village of Yurchi, with other *basmachi* in an unmarked grave.

We drove there in high hopes. On the edge of a deserted football-pitch dotted with cattle, we came upon the tomb of the regional Bolshevik commander: a concrete mound under an iron star. It was simply inscribed: 'Licharov 1889–1924'. He had been killed two years after Enver.

Then we reached a hill overgrown by graves, with a tiny

mosque below. Its ancient caretaker, lean and bright in a sky-blue gown and turban, ascended the cemetery before us on noiseless feet. A breeze sprang up and nudged white butterflies out of the scrub. A pair of rams' horns, old companions of prestige and death, curled on a post in shamanistic sorcery. To the west the mountains shone like Christmas decorations. The village spread below, and a thin canal.

We came to a pit on the lip of the hill. Thorn bushes were crowding into it. The old man stood on its brink. 'I'm too young to remember that time,' he said. 'I was only seven. But the people who guarded the graveyard before me told me what happened here. After Enver Bey's last battle the captured *basmachi* were shot at the foot of the cliff below.' We peered over the hill's edge on to an empty track and a sprawling fig tree. 'Then their bodies were thrown into this well. It was a hundred metres deep, so you can imagine how many of them! And they said that the body of Enver Bey was among them. That's what they said.'

Wind-blown thistles rasped against the headstones. 'Do pilgrims ever come?' I asked.

'People come.'

'On the anniversary of the battle?'

He looked baffled. 'I don't know when the battle was.'

I waded over the hill-crest through shin-high grass and cow-parsley droning with bees. Nothing fitted the official story. No river skirted the grave, and the only walnut tree shaded the mosque. The village, above all, had always been named Yurchi. Here was only the memory of an execution-ground. Enver Pasha, I now felt, had died farther east, in the Beljuan hills near Kulyab. But we could not go there. The region was sinking into war, swept by the killings which the Kulyab tribesmen would soon visit on the capital. As for the Yurchi mass grave, it only added another layer of enigma and confusion to the story.

I asked the man: 'There was never a river below?'

'Ah yes,' he said, resurrecting a phantom doubt, 'there was a river here twenty years ago, instead of the canal. It forked beside the graveyard then.'

A call to prayer rose from the mosque below in a throaty wail, to which nobody answered. Then the only sound was again the scratching of the thistles against the stones.

*

As we neared the Afghan frontier, the mountains to our west and south sank into haze, and desert hills glared in their place. The air shimmered in a 110°F stillness which blistered the fields. Gangs of women were breaking the soil with spade-headed mattocks, or culling the cotton in blackened hands. Just north of Termez, where the Russians had built their bridgehead into Afghanistan, we swung into a sordid scrubland crossed by pylons and wasted canals. Beside us the Amu Dariya moved through a sliver of green, and Afghanistan lay flat and yellow in mist beyond. We turned north where a crimson river wound between mud-flats. The slopes reddened into angry mounds and ridges, and the yurts and pens of goatherds appeared. But after an hour we crested a watershed, the river had gone and a clear stream was flowing with us where cornfields dribbled round champagne-coloured hills.

Since leaving Dushanbe we had described a frustrated loop almost to Samarkand. The euphoria of being on the road again had evaporated days ago, and hours passed in silence. Our differences were suddenly exacerbated. Oman longed to speed home with the car radio yelling. For him only occasional bazaars punctuated the barren stretches in which his inexplicable companion contemplated scenery, talked with somebody useless, or wandered a ruin. He was pining after other companionship. Yet whenever we reached a hotel he regarded my desire for a separate room as wasteful and a little insulting, and I rarely achieved it. He did not want to be alone.

As for me, a long-festering irritation had risen to the surface, and Oman was suffering for it. The remorseless cupidity which surrounded me day after day had brought on intolerance. In the town streets the eyes raking over me saw only an assemblage of material possibilities – a watch, a pen, a chance of dollars – and

I began to long for any disinterested curiosity or pleasure. And now this misanthropy spread to Oman. I bridled at his habitual cheeseparing in restaurants, and the monotonous cataloguing of inflation. He could not resist economy. Although I had given him a gift worth several times the cost of our journey, he was subtly absent whenever a bill had to be paid. The sums were always paltry, but they left me resentful.

In penitence now, belatedly, I record how costly life had become within two years: the price of a chicken had risen from four roubles to 300; a sheep from 300 to 5000; even a box of matches from one kopek to 1.30 roubles. Petrol had gone up 150 per cent in less than a year. Flour, cooking oil, butter and sugar were all rationed. Money was on everybody's lips, except mine.

Meanwhile, as Oman and I sipped *lagman* or munched *samsa* meat-balls in streamside tea-houses, our rambling talks, conducted in a clash of disorganised Russian, became sparser and more abstracted. And Oman's impatience to be home had been exacerbated by the gradual failure of the car. For over 200 miles between Termez and Shakhrisabz he nursed an overheating engine, until we were topping up the radiator with spring water every quarter hour. This deepening setback fired him into a new round of invective against crime – he thought he had been cheated by mechanics – until he burst out in favour of Islamic law.

'Yes, I think it would be good here!' His voice had tensed to its self-hypnotised sing-song and his hands flew about the steering-wheel. 'People don't understand anything else! You in Europe say that it's uncivilised, but civilisation is a *process*. It's gradual.' He lifted his levelled hand in a jagged procession of generations. 'These people need to *fear*.' He was almost shouting. 'It's the Russians who brought in this thieving and prostitution! I remember my father telling me that in his day nobody stole. Doors were left unlocked everywhere, even by jewellers! Then in the thirties thousands of Russians came down from Samara during the famine and ever since then Tashkent's been full of robbery.'

So it was all the Russians' fault. I felt the legend of his nation's purity growing before my eyes: the conviction that evil does not erupt from within, but is imposed from without. 'Islamic law may be cruel,' he said, 'but it wasn't that cruel. In the reign of the last emir of Bukhara, I've read, only eight or nine people were executed by being thrown from the Kalan minaret. I know it wasn't very nice, but it wasn't many.' Yet his face remained foolishly merciful. Once or twice he swerved on the road to avoid killing sparrows. 'If only there were a thousand honest, intelligent and energetic people in Uzbekistan – just one thousand out of twenty million! – we'd be all right. But where are they? Where?'

As we ground to a halt in Shakhrisabz, where I had been happy two months before, he discovered that the engine was exuding water. 'I think the cylinder block's gone,' he said. 'It's a big bit of trouble.' He peered under the bonnet. 'I'll have to find a lorry to tow us back to Tashkent.'

'But that's over two hundred miles away.'

'Yes.'

I watched his face for violence, but none came. Petty expenses and boredom turned him stingy or sad, but this disaster seemed to release something in him, as if he needed it. A strange calm welled up. He grew carefree, even buoyant. When I asked him how much the repair would cost, he shrugged and puffed across his palm, dissipating a mountain of roubles into the air. 'Don't worry! It's not your problem. To hell with it. Let's eat!'

He was his old self. He paid for a lavish supper and talked about his pantheon of writers: Maupassant, Jack London, Rousseau, James Hadley Chase .... He spoke of happier, commercial travels, before the days of his disgrace: how as a young man he had taken ten lorries packed with melons into Siberia, and made a killing. Once he had flown 250 tons of fruit and vegetables to the Kamchatka peninsula. There hot geysers created natural saunas, and many Russian women, whose husbands

299

were away fishing or with the battle-fleet, languished uncontrollably.... But all this, he said with a nostalgic sigh, happened in the golden Rashidov years of corruption.

We left the car in a yard labelled 'Autorepair No. 35', and strolled at sunset under the gates of Tamerlane's palace, where Oman became lost in astonishment, and talked about the building's splendour without once mentioning its cost, and traced the swoop of swallows round the broken arches. Swallows had nested in the lamp-brackets of his home in Tashkent, he said, and Sochibar had planned to expel them. 'But I threatened to expel her first!' He laughed like a boy. 'And look how they built in those days! Six centuries ago! Our hotel will be gone in a few years, but this ....' He paused and glanced up. 'But I think it needs repairs.'

I could not blame him for having repairs on his mind. 'I prefer it unrestored.'

'But imagine it completed! It would be magnificent! If I were a Rockefeller ....'

*

The damage to the Lada turned out lighter than we had feared: only a worn-out gasket. Next morning Oman bullied five languid mechanics into replacing it, while I rambled irresponsibly along a nearby river, planning a last sortie into the Pamirs.

But that evening I returned to our hotel to find that Oman had been arrested. Apparently he had come back drunk an hour before me, and had instinctively identified a KGB officer in the lobby, and insulted and tried to assault him. My heart sank. I had no idea what they would do with him. By old Soviet standards, his behaviour was insane, and the Uzbek KGB had not changed with independence.

I tracked him down to a pavement police-post near the hotel. The door had been left momentarily ajar, and I glimpsed inside. It was like viewing an old, ugly lantern-slide. The cramped room was lit by a single bulb, which cast an orange glow on the circle of uniforms and plain clothes. Oman stood in the centre – small, stout, intransigent – while a sleek-faced man in an anonymous suit was questioning him from behind a desk. Above hung a photograph of Felix Dzerzhinsky, founder of the Soviet secret police. In Moscow his statue had been toppled by chanting crowds the year before. But here he presided undisturbed. I heard Oman's voice rising with its impassioned hurt, and saw his arm starting to lift in fury or helplessness. Then the door slammed shut.

I sat on a wall outside. Two or three other men were loitering in curiosity. 'They'll probably beat him up,' one said. But Oman had not seemed afraid. Instead, drink had blinded him, and dropped him into a pit of anger and self-pity. I was afraid he might antagonise them further. In his sudden aloneness, engulfed by humiliation and memories, all the old, wronged bitterness would be welling up in him. Perhaps it would inhibit them, I thought, if they knew he was with a foreigner. It might be harder to treat him as they wished.

I pushed open the door in assumed naïvety. He was seated now. The plain-clothes officer was haranguing him. The others stood above him like clichés: square-built, expressionless, out-of-date. Dzerzhinsky glowered from the wall. Oman was my driver and friend, I said to his interrogator, and I would be responsible for him .... A second's bewilderment passed. The officers' eyes all turned on me. Oman's head suddenly bowed. For a moment the cross-examiner looked baffled, then a big, pale-eyed officer loomed against me, pushed me back without a word, and closed the door softly in my face.

I lingered outside for what seemed a long time. I could no longer hear the voices of either Oman or the police. The loiterers grew bored and drifted away. A few cars passed down the warm street, and a half moon rose. Then the door burst open and Oman emerged alone. His shoulders were hunched in fury. He was hopelessly drunk. He turned round and bellowed at the emerging officer. 'I'm a man, I'm not a sheep! I'm – not – a – sheep!' His fists shook in the air. It was faintly ludicrous. I pulled him away along the pavement, while the big, bland officer stood and watched. Oman turned and bawled: 'I'm not afraid of you, sonny!'

'Don't you call me sonny,' the man said wearily, as if this had been going on a long time.

'Sonny! Swine!' yelled Oman. 'Swine! Sonny!'

I flung an arm round his shoulders and propelled him away. 'They called me a sheep!' he cried. 'They said, "You're just a sheep, a Soviet sheep!"' He was close to tears. Soviet was a term of abuse now, it seemed. To be Soviet was to be a traitor. 'Well, if it's true, for the first time I say "Glory to the Soviet Union!"' His fists whirled in the air again. 'Glory! Glory!'

*

Eastward, where the Zerafshan river descends from the north-west ranges of the Pamir, a splintered road followed it under a mottled sky. At first it crossed empty flatlands. Then the mountains grew out of the horizon, lit by isolated sunbeams, and gathered along a valley corridor which led us unnoticeably up. Oman was overwhelmed by posthumous shame, and nothing I said could lift it. He drove in a sombre oblivion. We were climbing back into the westernmost spur of Tajikistan. As we neared the border a platoon of Uzbek soldiers stopped and searched us, but there was no other sign of a frontier.

It was up this causeway that the Tajik ancestors, the Sogdians, had fled from Arab invaders in the eighth century. For more than fifteen hundred years they had lived along the Zerafshan in a loose-linked galaxy of oasis princedoms. These, with Bactria to the south, were the cradle of the Iranian race. But Turkic and Arab incursions at last confined them to the great cities, where their Tajik descendants survive, or drove them deep into the mountains, and the valley which we followed still seemed to echo their desolate migration.

Near modern Penzhikent, one of their last towns stood in ruin above the river. Rain and wind had compacted its clay brick to yellow bones, so that houses, streets, gates, temples all traced themselves over the earth in a sleek cipher. The modest compass

302

of its ramparts, half sucked back into the ground, exuded domestic peace. Its people had been craftsmen and Silk Road merchants, above all, and ingenious farmers. It was the Sogdians who gave wine to China, and apricots to the world.

I left Oman brooding in the car, and entered the city. A sea of wild flowers overswept the battlements – purple heliotrope, pink vetch – and through the roofless passages and breached rooms spread a lake of poppies. I blundered between enigmatic doorways and culs-de-sac, then out along avenues to where the ruler's citadel crested its mound in a cluster of chambers and towers. Even in ruin, a feel of private opulence survived. The mansions, many free-standing, had crashed in two storeys about their pillared reception-halls, but here and there an early *iwan* – the vaulted porch of a later Persia – showed in some façade a little grander than the rest.

Among the debris of roof-beams, stairs and carbonised wooden statues cluttering the courts, archaeologists had uncovered fragments of fresco: pigments faded to damson, maroon and a backdrop of smoky blue. They portray a rich, ceremonious people at banqueting and war. In their idealised faces the features show delicate and small. An unearthly luxury pervades the nobles seated cross-legged as they feast. They converse unsmiling in a flutter of thin white hands. Their embroidered tunics are caught in at the waist, and beneath their tiaras the hair is immaculately trimmed, or falls in black sidelocks. Swords and daggers droop ornamentally across their laps. They carry wands of almond blossom. It is hard to know who is a god and who is a mortal. The warriors who gallop or saunter to battle on magenta chargers are the stuff of Persian epic. But the bangled beauty who plucks at her harp might be a human or a celestial. For the city, it seems, was home to many gods and heresies, infused by Buddhism and a host of Iranian deities and resurrection cults.

The long, crestfallen faces of the Sogdians' frescoes survive in their Tajik descendants. But as the Sogdians fled east, pushing into gorges now choked with their wrecked castles, their language

303

and their blood became mixed with others'. The Sogdian tongue seems to have lain close to the Persian of the great Achaemenian kings, and to the sacred language of Zoroastrian scripture. But it was already dying out among the Zerafshan oasis peasantry a thousand years ago, and the ancient idiom of Persia – the language of Cyrus the Great, Darius the Great, Xerxes – had vanished long before.

But high in the Zerafshan watershed, I had heard, where Oman and I pursued our way in silence, a few villages of the secluded Yagnob valley still spoke a remote dialect of Sogdian. Their isolation had fossilised them. Squeezed between precipitous mountains, and cut off half the year by snows, they had lived in enforced wretchedness and purity. Somewhere, I hoped, just beneath the avalanche-blocked pass of Anzob, we would find the valley entrance. But Oman only sighed at this foolishness. Such a people no longer existed, he said.

Around us bloomed orchards of pomegranates and the ances-tral Sogdian apricot, until the Zerafshan dropped into a long abyss, and the villages found only precarious perches on mats of green beside it. We clanked over a bridge and up a jagged gorge, following the Fandariya tributary. The villages grew guttural Sogdian names. I imagined a half-lost elegance about their bird-like women, whose hair occasionally flamed from their dark heads in a shock of auburn. The farmers seated in the tea-houses seemed to mimic their frescoed ancestors; but their bowls brimmed with noodle soup instead of wine, and in their laps the gilded swords had perished to knobbled sticks.

Sometimes the river stilled to a flood below sheer cliffs, and our road weaved alongside between precipices which refracted each other's light and sound, and tossed down threads of water-fall for hundreds of feet. We were close beneath the pass now, and had entered a stark gallery of ravines, roughed up by winds which blasted through them inexplicably.

Soon afterwards our road crept under hanging snowfields through the shepherds' villages of Takfon and Anzob. The peo-ple seemed to grow ever more inbred. We came upon fragile academics crowned by high brows, women with bewitching green eyes and old men sporting Roman noses and Dundreary whiskers. Occasionally I would glimpse a disconcertingly European face, as if some friend from England were scrutinising me from under a skull-cap.

A little farther on, where the Yagnob valley opened, we found two men heaving goats into the back of a truck. They wore old jackets and split boots. Shyly, feeling suddenly intrusive, I asked them their origins.

Yes, they said, they were Yagnobski. They all spoke Sogdian in the home, young and old, and had inherited the language from their parents, by ear. They sat before me by the river: an old man with a face of grizzled peace, and a pale-eyed youth. They shared the same lean features and retracted brow and chin. For months a cassette-recorder had lain neglected in my ruck-sack, but now I pulled it out and asked the old man to talk for me.

He settled nervously before it. The only sound was the rush of the river. Then he began to speak as if in a reverie: an elusive language filled with gutturals and soft plosives, and a sad, rhythmic energy. He concentrated on it as if remembering a song, his eyes overhung by tufted black brows and his knees locked in big, liver-spotted hands. He kept his stare on the recorder's winking lights. The youth joined him in a pattering tenor, and fell into the same melancholy cadences, until all their sentences seemed to wilt away in disillusion.

I listened almost in disbelief. This, I told myself, was the last, distorted echo of the battle-cries shouted 2500 years ago by the armies of the Great Kings at Marathon and Thermopylae, all that remained from the chant of Zoroastrian priests or the pleas of Persian satraps to Alexander the Great. Yet it was spoken by impoverished goatherds in the Pamirs. Once or twice some fragment floated up to me with the eerie resonance of a common Indo-European tongue – 'road' sounded identical in English, 'nose' was 'nez' – but the rest was incomprehensible.

I thought they must be declaiming poetry or saga, but no,

305

they said in faltering Russian, they were simply talking about the hardness of their lives. They bought goats in these mountains and sold them 200 miles down into the plains. As for the past, the old man knew that his people had been driven here by invaders, and that they had carried with them records inscribed on horse-skin vellum. But he was vague about all dates.

The young man too looked blank. The Yagnob villages were dying, he said. Life there was too isolated, too cold. In the early sixties people had begun to leave for Dushanbe and for lowland towns to the north. He himself had been born on a state farm in the plains. 'That's where our people are now. On the collectives. We hear Sogdian only in the home. I had three years in school, and nobody taught it.' He looked content with this. 'It belongs to the past.'

*

Oman and I returned down the bitter valley of the Fandariya, then up over the last range of the north-west Pamir, meeting the snowline at 11,000 feet, where he dashed icy water recklessly over the boiling radiator and engine. Then we descended to grasslands and at last into the farmed and industrial plains which flow north towards Tashkent. He stopped only to buy two giant carp at a fish-market, then sped on grimly into the night. We were both exhausted as the city outskirts limped past us. But as we neared the house we became aware of a blaze of lights and merriment, and a horde of children ran out to kiss him.

He looked bewildered. 'We've got guests.'

Then Sochibar and his daughter-in-law ran out too, and embraced him. It was his eldest son's birthday, and he had clean forgotten it.

The party was on its last, drunk legs, and half the forty guests had gone. The remainder were all relatives, together with Oman's mysterious middle son and a clutch of in-laws. Two long tables had segregated the sexes, and still groaned with uneaten salads, fruit and sweets.

A hard core of celebrants greeted us, and in no time we were sunk in shouting revelry. They were gross, simple men who bawled jokes in Uzbek, which scarcely bore translation, and plied me with mutton and vodka. Everyone was drunk. I sat between a post-office official and a chef on the railway, who jabbed me in the ribs or shoulder whenever he wanted to speak. I felt numbly detached. Meanwhile the women murmured together at their own table, not drinking, or fluttered about their husbands, hoping to leave. But the men went on bellowing and quipping and roaring in crescendoes of boorish glee.

Sochibar's father – a tiny, gnarled teacher, long retired – sprawled across the table to kiss and embrace me. 'I know all about English history,' he babbled. 'You have a dynasty, the Stuarts, and your queen is Elizabeth III now ....' His eyes peered half-seeing into mine. 'Oliver Cromwell, he was a man of the people ....'

Slowly, I realised, the men's table was dividing. At first Oman had sat wanly toying with his food, and once we had caught each other's eye and smiled complicitously from the bond of our journey. But now he was drunk again, and was accusing his sons of fecklessness. The eldest boy, in whose honour the party was being given, stared doggedly back from the head of the table, waiting for his relatives to go, while Oman's words reeled about him. Sometimes his pretty wife darted up behind, whispered things and took his arm. But Oman railed on, now turning on his second son, who sat down resignedly beside me. He was a handsome twenty-year-old, with an undirected urge to work in pop music, and a look of helpless charm. Once he tried to defend himself, but three or four men of Oman's age at once assailed him, shouting and wagging their drunken fingers.

During a lull the youth turned to me and said: 'My father just talks. He only ever talks. My mother's wonderful. I owe everything to her ....' Oman, I knew, had deserted her long ago, and perhaps some buried guilt prompted his raging. 'I don't need his help,' his son went on. 'I don't need anybody helping me. *Nobody.*' And this too must have been Oman's trouble, that his authority was not embraced.

307

An hour later, as a new squall broke out, the men's voices jacked themselves up to a battering climax. A few Russian phrases laced the Uzbek clamour, so that from time to time a shred of meaning floated across to me. At first rival gangs of supporters had restrained Oman and one of his brothers-in-law from hitting one another. But now they all rose in fury and soon a battle was raging under the verandahs. At its root lay the dispute over Oman's sons, but other vendettas were rankling to the surface, and fighting had broken out among their supporters too, huge with grappling and fisticuffs, into which several wives threw themselves in a useless plea for peace, while the neighbourhood dogs set up a long, delirious baying.

The eldest son, whose birthday had slipped away at midnight, continued to look bored at the head of the empty table. I sat there too, an inviolable guest, surprised at my own peace. Once I thought of intruding; but I imagined their shame afterwards, and kept my seat. Meanwhile the fantasy of the extended family toppled in dust about me: its happiness, its pliant union. The figures dimly battling round the porch were raw with their own truth: parents who stop loving their children, ageing people who have no place.

Yet these families, I thought, more surely than Western ones, outlive their individual members, and cushion every loss. For better or worse, they superseded every loyalty outside, and often rendered public life shallow and nearly meaningless. And now Sochibar and others were breaking up the fights one by one, pushing and complaining at the men, while gradually the flung punches cooled to bravado and the pugilists disappeared through the gates still shouting their imprecations, and some grudging reconciliations and handshakes began.

As the last guest departed, the remaining women cleared away the china then folded the table-cloths over the debris of glass and cherry-stones and drained bottles. Meanwhile Oman was smoking, staring over the verandah into darkness. 'I'm sorry, Colin. I don't know why they behave like that. They were defending my sons against me....' He was black with misery.

308

For a long time he went on lighting cigarette after cigarette. How these sons had wounded him, why fecklessness so infuriated him, I never really knew: whether his own hardship had turned him intolerant, or whether he feared to see in them some continuance of his self.

We were deprived of any long farewell. It was scarcely dawn, and our heads were reeling. On the station platform we clasped each other numbly.

More than any facial expression, more than the dejected warmth with which he said goodbye, or the pudgy arms embracing mine, I remember Oman's back as it dwindled towards the exit. Steeped in a dogged gallantry, it seemed to voice in its small span all his resistance to the unjust world. I felt at once relieved and bereft as it receded without turning into the crowds, and my train began slowly to heave itself northwards into the steppes of Kazakhstan.

11

Steppelands

I was entering the fringes of a formidable solitude. For almost a thousand miles Kazakhstan stretched northward in rolling grass-lands and dust-coloured desert. For hours, on all sides, the land was the same: a treeless wilderness under a dead sky. It lay like a caesura in Asia's heart, as if this were the earth's natural state of rest. Here I was out of the tilled oases and into the nomadic hinterland, from where centuries of warrior-herdsmen had descended on the valleys of the south. Pink and yellow wild flowers still seamed the soil, but thistles were dying over the shallow slopes, and the passengers around me looked out on the sameness with a numb, unfocused gaze. Only occasionally the grassland became pimpled with volcanic-looking hills, where Hunnish, barrel-chested horses grazed, and nobody was in sight.

For more than a million square miles this opaque nation sprawled between China and the Caspian. It was the size of Western Europe. Its people had coalesced as late as the fifteenth century from Turkic tribes which had swept in from the north-east nearly 1000 years before, and from Mongol invaders, and the Russians found them sprinkled over their vast plains in three confederate hordes. As the czarist settlers inched towards the trading centres of the Uzbek valleys, and of Persia and China beyond, the Kazakhs fell first into alliance with Russia, then into servitude, until by the mid-nineteenth century they had all been overrun. But they had still been a nomad people, who circled with their herds over huge migratory paths, and Islam sat light on them. Even now, when most of them were grounded in state farms or cities, Moslem doctrine was buffered by ancestral custom, and a little unfamiliar. And the Russians' presence soon created deep changes. They settled as grain farmers, disrupting the pasturelands, and swelled to a majority in the region.

In time Kazakhstan became the waste-bin of Moscow's empire. A rash of labour-camps covered it, and Stalin transported whole unwanted peoples here during the Second World War. Then the Soviets chose it as their prime atomic and nuclear testing site. Entire regions were envenomed by radioactive dust, while the titanic factories of an antiquated heavy industry still suffocate others in a toxic fog.

This was the most Russified of Central Asian states. Its government, like most others, was composed of old Communists under a new name, barely irked by a mosquito-cloud of opposition parties. Yet now it had sponsored a drive towards privatisation which was biting deep in commerce and agriculture. Quietly, with independence, the climate was changing. The high native birth-rate had already lifted the Kazakh population just above the Russian, and the economic ties with Moscow were straining. The mineral and energy resources of Kazakhstan – the biggest deposits of iron, copper, lead and zinc in the old USSR – were alerting international business, and Western companies cautiously investing in its gas and oil fields.

Islam was only a gentle influence here, and the Russians and Kazakhs were interleaved by moderating layers of ethnic subgroups, some 20 per cent of the populace: a million Volga Germans, with exiled Crimean Tartars, Ukrainians, Poles and Meskhetian Turks. There were leftover Chechens and Ingush from the Caucasus, Uighurs who had fled China, Uzbeks, Kirghiz, Armenians, Georgians, Azerbaijanis, Kurds, Karakalpaks, Greeks and a cloud of others. I shared my carriage with three Korean women, whose families had been deported from Russia's far east in the thirties. They were bound for Moscow, they announced, then whispered that they were continuing to Warsaw but were afraid of the mafia, since travellers to Poland were known to carry dollars or merchandise. 'There's nothing but gangsterism now,' they said.

Beside me sat a genial Kazakh schoolmistress supervising an outing of fourteen-year-old Dungan girls – lissom, Mongoloid creatures, whose Chinese Moslem ancestors had migrated across the border a century before. They squeezed into the carriage to view me. They wore pink digital watches and cheap rings, and their nails were varnished. They all wanted to travel, then to become seamstresses. Under their fluent, high-pitched Russian, some scraps of Mandarin survived.

'They had to learn Russian before,' said the teacher, 'but now it's all changed and everyone wants to speak Kazakh. In business, in government.' She was a big, raw-boned woman with the inflamed cheeks of a cruel land. She looked as if she could bear anything. 'My husband speaks beautiful Russian, and is valued in his institute, but he talks Kazakh only poorly. I know it's strange, but there are Kazakhs like that. And now the world's turned over. On feast-days and at weddings all the old customs are coming back – the horse-contests, bridal games and costumes, and the drinking of mare's milk.'

Yet it sounded artificial as she said it, as if her people had become sightseers. 'What do younger people think?'

'Oh, the young are all right!' she said. 'It's the old who find it hard. My parents, for instance, don't like what's happened. My father remembers the war. Those were terrible times, and they bound us to the Russians. He fought at Stalingrad, and lost an arm.' Her jolly face cracked open on flashing teeth. 'And in the famine of the thirties, during the repression, my parents almost died of hunger.'

'Were they victimised?'

'No, no, they were just ordinary people on a state farm. Everybody suffered ... anybody who owned a few horses or camels might be liquidated. My mother remembers that time well, how people were eating anything – dogs, cats, their own shoes. One day she gave a little boy a handful of grain and he ate it too quickly and died in front of her. I think she remembers this often ....'

313

Yet the old people went on feeling nostalgia for the past. Their bitterness, where it existed, fell far short of their sufferings. In 1920–23, towards the end of the Civil War, almost a million Kazakhs died of famine, and later the forced collectivisation was crueller here than anywhere in the Soviet Union. Between 1930–33 a ferocious and chaotic campaign to settle the nomads and reduce the richer farmers led to Kazakhs burning their grain and slaughtering their cattle rather than let them fall into alien hands. Almost half the livestock of the steppes vanished. Some people fled towards China, but only a quarter survived the trek; others were killed by the Bolsheviks. Out of a Kazakh population of only four million, over one million died of famine or disease. By the end of the decade the Great Terror had decimated officials, teachers and a whole generation of early Kazakh Communists. Yet even now, with independence, people scarcely spoke of it. The tragedy had descended on them impersonally, perhaps, on native and Russian alike, and was scarcely scrutable.

The woman went on: 'My father still thinks things were better then. He says people were kinder to one another, that they had more heart. But now it's each for himself. Everyone's just bent on business. But I don't think we're really a business people, not like the Uzbeks.' She let out a crackling laugh. 'We're just used to rearing sheep!'

As I looked into her cheery Mongol face, it was simple to imagine her back in the grasslands where her people had roamed a generation ago. Yet she lived in a flat-block in Chimkent. 'Those places are wrong for us. I'd like a garden, or a dacha, but we haven't the money.' Then she perked up, as if all pessimism offended her. 'But we have our freedom now! We can speak the truth at last. That's the first, the most important thing: to speak the truth.' The common sense of this, which had eluded generations of her rulers, fell from her with the sturdiness of old platitude. She rummaged in her bag and pulled out a cold chicken leg. 'We will make progress now.'

Outside the window the grass had thinned over a plain dusted with saxaul. Only occasionally the land lifted to a far slope where sheep-flocks stuck like larvae, or a herdsmen's village fringed the railway with winter cattlesheds built in whatever lay to hand: fragments from dismembered trucks, old tyres, rusted bedposts. The solitary faces watching us pass seemed to replicate the featureless plain: a heartless waste flowing northward to Siberia.

I got out at the first town we reached. Turkestan was a poor, sleepy place, spreadeagled among dusty trees under a blistering sun. Tramping its streets and empty shops, I felt suddenly jaded and lonely. I wondered what Oman was doing. Some of the people around me were Uzbeks still – Turkestan was an early site of pilgrimage – but the stocky childlike Kazakhs were all about. They looked guileless and enduring. Their faces, economical with low brows and close-set ears, seemed shaped for battling head-winds. Epicanthic folds squeezed their eyes to humorous cracks, which sparkled out from a plane of thick-fleshed bones.

I found a hotel which charged me fifty pence for two nights, and shared my room with a Kazakh metal-worker from the north, who had arrived in a lorry to buy steel joists. Maruya was perhaps forty, but showed the boyish agelessness of his people. He blundered about the room as if he wasn't used to one. Out of his frayed haversack he pulled little bags of cheeseballs and bread, eight cans of pig fat, a toothbrush and a bundle of garlic for his wife. It was too cold to grow garlic where he came from, he said – a village near Dzhezkazgan, in his country's bitter heart. A foot of snow had fallen even in May.

We tramped into the town to a bare restaurant, which served up only *lagman*. Maruya stared about with a curious, blank confusion. 'I don't know this town,' he said. 'I can't understand what the Uzbeks say.' I warmed to him, in faint surprise. It is the traveller's illusion that everyone is assimilated except himself. But Maruya, trudging about with his gauche smile and his bag of garlic, was as much a stranger here as I was. My own alienness plunged him into mystified silences. His knees jittered under the table. 'Where I come from,' he said, 'there's a factory which the

315

British built years ago, for cloth-weaving.' He gazed at me with a renewed wonder. 'Then the British left in the Revolution.'

'And afterwards?'

'Afterwards the famine came. The old people still speak of it, but there are hardly any old people left. Almost my whole village died of hunger then.'

'How do you forgive that?'

'It was very big. Three million of us died, you know.' He gave a dulled, compensatory smile. He did not try to explain anything. This blackest estimate of three million was becoming truth all over the nation. 'But that's all over now. We're not haters. Our people get on all right with the Russians, I've plenty of Russian friends.' His voice lowered in old habit. 'But they've ruined our young people. They drink and drink. We never did that before. And many are out of work.'

'Do you intermarry?'

'Our men take Russian wives. But not the other way about. I've never heard of that. Our people won't do it.'

I asked again: 'How do you forgive it?'

But he only said: 'Everything's hard with us, and cold.'

*

Next day all the old Soviet Union arranged its business around the witching hour when a televised Mexican soap opera called *Rich Men Also Weep* sabotaged any other life. It happened once a week and was wending through 150 episodes. At four o'clock, all over Central Asia, workers and machinery glided to a hypnotised standstill. Turcoman farmers and Uzbek shopkeepers were alike caught up in the incandescent question: would Pedro marry Rosalia? Villages fell silent. City transport dwindled, and televisions in hotel lobbies attracted such crowds that I would imagine there'd been an accident. The characters in this melodrama inhabited a world of unreachable glamour, yet were household familiars and the objects of heated speculation. The very title *Rich Men Also Weep* suggested a subtle amendment to decades of other sympathies.

316

It was at this quiet hour that I approached the sanctuary which broke in incongruous glory beyond the shabby suburbs of Turkestan. The shrine of Sheikh Ahmad Yassawi, founder of a once-powerful Sufi order, had been inaugurated by Tamerlane in 1397, but never quite completed. Circled by battlements which had flopped into ruin, it broke through the wasteland in a tawny mountain of walls and gateways. It was the Kazakhs' holiest shrine. Pilgrimage here ranked second only to Mecca. In the Kruschev years it had been closed down and ringed with barbed wire, but now stood lavishly restored.

I approached a forbidding entrance. Its arch was flanked by rounded, Babylonish towers over a hundred feet high. Close behind, its cupola surged up in a glow of turquoise, and beyond it the ribbed dome over the tomb-chamber – more private and exquisite – rested on a stalk of lapis blue.

I might have been entering a fortress. It lay, after all, on the fringe of the steppe. Sufism here seemed to remember itself less as a mystical path than as a militant brotherhood which had carried the sword against the Mongols and czarist Russia. I stepped ant-like under the porch. Originally this whole façade must have been awaiting the glazed bricks that decorated the other walls. Then Tamerlane died. A later restoration faltered. Looking up, I saw the half-petrified beams of old scaffolding bristling high under the archway, and the towers still pocked with holes where the workmen had laid down their tools half a millennium before.

I crossed from dazzling sunlight into dimness. I bought a ticket to the central prayer-hall. I was amazed. I had entered a museum. Beneath the dome, whitewashed to a deconsecrated spectre, the walls were lined by display cabinets showing old photographs and a few charts. In other rooms hung prayer-rugs and armour, and here and there the engraved tombstones of Kazakh khans and sultans were duly labelled, and displaced from their dead. In one recess a dusty pyramid of Marco Polo rams' skulls – each weighing up to thirty-five pounds – lay heaped in a tumult of upcurled horns.

I sat here until past the hour when *Rich Men Also Weep* would end, and watched people straggling past the cabinets: urban Kazakhs in jeans and summer frocks, a woman in a denim dress labelled 'US Army'. But among them were others – farmers and some black-faced gypsies – who ignored the exhibits but touched their brows to the walls between, praying, and caressed the obliterating whitewash. I had the sensation of standing at a watershed, where sanctity was slipping into history; or perhaps history, instead, was resurrecting, and the cabinets would soon be gone and the muezzin calling. I could not be sure.

Beneath the apex of the dome stood the prime exhibit: a two-tonne water stoop hammered out of bronze, gold and zinc by Persian craftsmen, the gift of Tamerlane. The Russians had carried it off to the Hermitage in 1935 (dark legends accumulated about the premature deaths of the perpetrators: it was God's will) and it had returned triumphantly in 1989, hauled through the main doors by tractor. Now a rumpus of old women tucked their admission tickets into their stockings and mounted the steps to embrace it, while a line of urbanites photographed one another below.

I peered into the tomb chamber. It was surrounded by a ceramic frieze in opaline green, but was otherwise bare. A few pigeons perched like stuffed exhibits round the nephrite ceno-taph. After a while a party of old Uzbeks arrived like a gust from the fields, swathed in azure turbans. They were listening to a female guide with ferocious attention, and sometimes mewed in astonishment. It was curious. These village elders were being taught by a dressy young woman in high heels. Only one man – a loud-voiced ancient with a stick – occasionally interrupted her, but she would cut him off with a confident '*Zhok!*' – No! – and they all fell silent.

Later, after the men had gone, I drifted into talk with her. I had thought her Russian – a plait of fair hair coiled down one shoulder – but no, she said proudly, she was pure Kazakh. 'I come from a tribe of the Middle Horde, the Arghan. Lots of us are fair, and our eyes pale and rounder even than the Uzbeks'!'

But her own eyes were black and sharp in an ivory face, where blushes came and went. Only her blonde hair and her long red dress, belted at the waist, had deluded me. She had the bud-like steppeland mouth, and her cheeks were high and broad. She said defensively: 'We've been too much Russified. In Almaty many Kazakhs can't even speak our language any more, just bad Russian.' She hissed in contempt. 'But it'll all come back, our traditions.'

'And the veil?'

'No. Among us, women were always free.' She looked so too, open and natural. Her smile exposed a pair of buck teeth, which were perversely attractive. 'We Kazakhs never wore the veil, and never will. Our women were bards and warriors and even wrestled with our men.' We were walking among the labelled tombstones now. 'See how long-lived we were! We have good air and good soil. And our mares' milk has every vitamin! I drink it all the time!'

Among the tombstones of Kazakh khans and law-makers, she stopped at a block of grey-veined marble. It was eloquent with a shallow-carved inscription. Once, she said, it had covered the body of one of her ancestors, a sixteenth-century chief who had travelled as an envoy to St Petersburg. She touched the stone, as she would a charm. She was about to study Arabic and Turkish herself, she said, because she too planned to become a diplomat. Her tribe was the tribe of ambassadors, she boasted, they had always been intelligent. She already had an uncle in the fledgling foreign service at Almaty, and it was this man who had become her model and beacon, together with the one in the tomb.

We circled into a prayer-hall where the Sufis had once chanted. It was filled by a crouching host of white-clad women. In the dome's honeycombed acoustic, their prayers whined like gnats. Some wore plumed clasps like those of Moghul princes, which sprouted enigmatically from their scarved heads. One held a carrier-bag labelled 'Christian Dior'.

Had the girl ever seen Sufis here, I wondered?

'They're very few. But yes, I did once see a ceremony. About thirty of them came and prayed and chanted in the darkness. I never saw it again.' She went on almost fiercely: 'We can act without darkness now!' She looked bright with determination. 'It's *our* future. The Russians and Tartars and the rest won't count here in the end.'

I looked at her keen face and firm figure. 'No,' I answered, I gave them little chance.

*

For a day and a night my train curled north-east through grass-lands towards Almaty, the Kazakh capital. Now and again the land moistened to meadows where egrets paced, or smoothed into giant fields. An enervating heat descended. The passengers fanned themselves uselessly and fell into torpor. One by one the card games and conversations died, and the picnics of yoghourt and cherries were abandoned. A noon hush set in. Opposite me two policemen sat in silence together. But the moment either left our cubicle the other would agitate: 'How much do police earn in England? What's their life like? Do they carry guns? How much ...?' until silenced by his companion's return.

Slowly, as we laboured east, the land heaved itself out of its sleep, tossing shallow ridges at the horizon. Sun and wind had stripped all life from it. We went through old Silk Road towns, levelled by Mongol invasion. They had revived into a polluted industrial life: the bungaloid cotton centre of Chimkent, the grimy chemical plants of Dzhamboul. Then evening came down with its gentleness over enormous wheat-fields, more like feats of nature than of men, and the westernmost ranges of the Tienshan reared from the skyline in cloudy snows and down-land green with woods.

Rambling along the carriages to keep awake before night, I came upon Malik propped in the corridor and gazing on to the steppes. He was still young, but his thinning hair swept back from delicate, melancholy features. He was a visitor here like me, he said, and this displacement may have eased him into talk. His father had been Kazakh but his mother Russian, and there was no knowing which had bequeathed him the lemony skin which lent his face its epicene polish, or the sad brown eyes behind their spectacles.

'Those mixed marriages can be hard,' he said. 'Our nations are too different. My Kazakh grandfather, for instance, became engaged to my grandmother by throwing her on to his horse and galloping off with her. That was the way then. And it's not always so different now. My sister was kidnapped by her husband and driven away in a truck from Almaty to Bishkek. Then he telephoned to tell my father.'

These customs died harder around marriage, I knew. Communist propaganda had fulminated against the traditional price paid to the bride's family: it often far outstripped the dowry. Fifteen thousand roubles, I'd heard, was normal for an urban bride. 'Was your father angry?'

'Yes, furious. He even telephoned me, but I was a law student in Moscow at the time, and what could I do? Anyway, he couldn't get his daughter back – she'd already "put on the scarf", as we say. She'd become engaged. So they settled down to negotiate the bride-price.' He was smiling a little cynically. I did not ask how his sister had been valued. 'I think my father had forgotten his own youth. His mother slammed the door in his face when he arrived with a Russian fiancée, even though the Koran permits marriage to Christians. She couldn't bear him marrying outside her people. She only opened the door to them a year later, when I was born. A grandson solves everything!'

But he gazed out at the desert plain as if he had solved nothing. There was something fastidiously self-protective about him. The sun had impaled itself on the mountains, and gone.

'So you're a lawyer?'

'I live in Moscow. I prefer it.'

'I've heard it's hell.'

'It's better than here.'

'Why?'

But he avoided direct questions. 'I'm still interested in my people. I became quite passionate about Islam when I was at school, about Iran and Afghanistan, everything .... I wanted to study it as a career, perhaps to teach.'

Sometimes his expression did not look natural to him. I kept wondering what he had been like before, as a youth. I said: 'But you gave it up.'

'I did service in Afghanistan, between 1984 and 1986.' He looked suddenly abject. 'I was an interpreter, liaising between the Soviet and Afghan airforces near Kabul. I'd have been jailed if I'd refused to go.' His voice whispered above the train-wheels. 'I dressed in Afghan army uniform, with no stripes. In some areas where I worked the *mujahedin* and the Afghan army occupied different parts of the same town, and simply agreed not to fight. So in that uniform I wasn't fired on. I came and went among them, like a traitor ....'

'You killed a man?'

'I was responsible for men being killed.' He looked away from me, through the smeared window, at his darkening homeland. 'You could say I betrayed my own people, fellow-Moslems.'

I said: 'You're half Russian.'

But he only went on: 'So I lost my love of that part of the world. It wasn't to do with Afghanistan itself, but with my role there. It was like being soiled.' He lifted his glasses fussily to wipe them, disclosing tiny, homesick eyes. 'That is only why I say Moscow is better.'

*

It is strange. You arrive in a city by night, and staring down from a hotel balcony on its light-glazed streets, looking more secret and seductive than they will by day, you wonder how you will ever decipher it. But within a morning the puzzle unravels with desanctifying speed. A few hours' walk locates the main avenues, elicits a conversation or two, uncovers a mood, and you return to a hotel no longer swimming among mapless lights and possibilities, but anchored, grey and unlovely, on the corner

322

of Gogol and Krasin streets.

Yet from my balcony in Almaty there was no sign that I was in a city at all. I looked across parklands where the spires of a cathedral hoisted gold crosses against the mountains. Its people numbered over a million – more than half of them Russian – but its grid of streets, mounting southward to the Tienshan foothills, ran half-empty through hosts of oaks and poplars. Sometimes, so dense were these trees, I imagined I was walking along tarmac tracks through a forest. Behind them the chunky Russian offices and flat-blocks spread anonymous for mile after mile. The air blew up sharp and pure from the mountains. It was like a suburb to a heart that was missing.

It was the Russians, of course, who had raised and nourished it. All its institutes and monuments were theirs, from the fountained boulevard of Gorky Street (now renamed Silk Road Street) to the soulless hotels and war memorials. But now the city belonged to nobody. Communism, Marx and Lenin streets might be renamed after spectral khans who had ruled the steppes a century or two ago, and ministry façades be veneered with pseudo-Turkic motifs; but the Kazakh culture had no true urban expression. Less than three generations ago virtually the whole nation was split into a haze of migratory villages. Its early rulers were lost, most of them, even to saga; and its modern heroes had been selected by Soviet propaganda – secular poets and thinkers, whose statues adorned the boulevards unloved. For decades the Kazakhs had been a minority in their own country. And now this alien city had floated into their hands. They were curiously unencumbered, even by Islam: a *tabula rasa* for the future to write upon.

I made my way south-eastward through the city, and reached the gardens where parliament buildings loomed up in Stalin's perverted classicism. It was very quiet. The scent of syringa sickened the still air. A few hoardings still read 'Glory to the Soviet People!', and nobody had chipped away the Red stars splashing the pseudo-Ionic capitals, nor the Lenin in the rose garden. These, after all, were the symbols by which the present leadership had

323

climbed into place. It did not do to disturb them. In front of the presidential palace, which stood enormous against the mountains under its blue banner, a block of stone commemorated those who had stood against what was warily inscribed 'the dictatorship of the centre'. The stone was scattered with withered bouquets. Here, in December 1986, a demonstration had protested at Gorbachev's replacement of the long-standing Kazakh First Secretary Kunaev by a native Russian. The uncontrolled riots and violent deaths that followed sent tremors all through Central Asia.

Now Kazakhs and Russians moved together in the streets. The Mongoloid faces looked softened and pale. Their women walked in modest dresses. Their hair tumbled at their shoulders or was tied at the nape in gaudy clasps. Among them the Russians lumbered in a seedy ebb-tide of colonialism: tired civil servants, mini-skirted secretaries, pensioners with drink-dulled eyes. They inhabited streets which a newly liberated economy was hanging with advertisements.

In Shaggie's fast food restaurant (which a Korean entrepreneur had modelled on McDonald's) the sons and daughters of the élite – Kazakh and Russian together – were busy being Western, lounging in T-shirts blazoned with US baseball team logos, their ears clamped in headphones, munching cheeseburgers. Beyond, a broken funicular had once scaled the hill where restaurants and a guesthouse had been a haunt of the privileged in Brezhnev's time. Now stairways lurched up only to garish ruins, filled with splintered mosaics and refuse, and covered by graffiti.

Towards evening I strayed into the opera house, where a shrunken audience was watching a dance drama based on *Madam Butterfly*. Selection or training had endowed the Kazakh ballerinas with the long, flexible backs and legs of their Russian companions, so that they pirouetted and bourréed through the turgid choreography in a seamless corps. In the auditorium's dark, awash with confected Puccini music, I was seated beside a woman with the ballet-dancer's heart-shaped face and look of

324

extended youth. She had suffered a knee injury dancing, she said in the interval, and had become a teacher.

It did not seem strange, for some reason, that the Western artifice of ballet should have engulfed a Kazakh girl two generations from nomadism. And her battle to go on stage was typical of any star-struck schoolgirl in the West.

'My father was a war veteran, very strict. He hated the idea of my dancing even when I was little.' She smacked down the air in a gesture of suppression. 'He thought the dance flippant, and hoped I'd be a doctor. But by the age of six I was already secretly determined. And in the end he gave way.' She smiled to herself with the memory of the child's passion. 'My husband didn't understand the dance either. He thought it ridiculous, like my father did.'

'He died?'

'We parted. I didn't receive children' – she used the sad Russian expression, as if children came through the post – 'and he could not bear that. I should have married a Russian.'

Wasn't it unusual, I asked, for Kazakh women to marry Russians?

'Not here in Almaty. I know plenty. My sister is married to a Ukrainian, and happy. This is a town where we're close. I'm glad of independence, I suppose, but I feel myself Soviet. Here in Almaty there are plenty of people like that – and we can't turn back. Russia opened our eyes, you see. Russian music, Russian dance. We Kazakhs have nothing like that. Russia gave us so much, ah' – sometimes she ended sentences with a little suffix of emotion. 'Of course I'm Kazakh too. But when I hear Tchaikovsky, I become Russian in my heart' – and like a Russian, she talked much about the heart. 'How couldn't I? I danced *Sleeping Beauty* and *Swan Lake*. I was the star. It's in my veins now.'

As the curtain went up on the second act, I realised how many of her dancers were Kazakh – more than half, she said – and suddenly they seemed astonishing to me, glissading and fish-diving out of their gypsy ancestry, in an art whose origins

325

lay in the courts of Catherine de' Medici and Louis XIV.

'But our audiences have fallen,' she said, as we emerged from the theatre into twilight. 'Our lives are so hard now, everything expensive.'

I said doubtfully: 'My ticket cost five roubles.' That was three pence.

'But still there are those who can't afford it, and many out of work. And in winter, when it's dark, people are afraid because of thugs. That's new with us, but it's here now, at night.'

People were growing frightened of violent crime, I knew. As we walked through dusk down the long central avenue of Furmanov, scarcely a car passed. At sunset, the city went dead. I said: 'But you're used to cities.'

'Yes, I was brought up in Moscow and Kiev.' Her feet made an urban clopping beside mine, planted with the ballerina's open instep. 'But my father was born in a village, in the country near Dzhamboul, and I sometimes go back there. He's buried out in the steppes, where the air is pure, and he loved it. When I go back, people play the *dombra* in our old house, and ask me in for tea, and talk. Yes, I feel the steppe in my heart too, but not like Tchaikovsky, ah .... It was different for my father. He even knew Arabic, was taught as a child by mullahs in the village. But my place is here.'

She fell into melancholy silence. I feared for her a little. She seemed to have forfeited all her past to this engulfing Russia, and now it was ebbing away. As her career declined, she said, she was falling into impossible longings – to star again, to study modern dance, to travel to the West. 'I want to go to Mexico especially. We have a wonderful serial on our television now, *Rich Men Also Weep* ....'

*

In the city's parklands, where the hum of traffic becomes lost in pine and acacia groves, stands a monument to twenty-eight soldiers of the Panfilov division, raised in Almaty, who repelled an armoured assault during the Battle for Moscow in 1941. At

326

the end of the memorial avenue, where Kazakh urchins were kicking a football, I approached a sculptural triptych raging with outsize warriors wielding grenades and bayonets. It was one of those soulful hymns to glory and sorrow which scatter the battlefields of western Russia with a proud melancholy. I stared at it with disquiet. Far from the pain and chaos of real war, these inflated heroes – impossibly grim and muscled – breasted their plinths in a Socialist Realism which stopped reality dead and turned their action unimaginable.

I lingered here while wedding parties came and went for their photographs. A Kazakh groom in a stick-up collar and scarlet bow-tie showed off his dark bride gleaming with amulets and a pleated silver dress. An embroidered gilet and velvet waistcoat covered her breast with crimson – the ancestral colour of fertility – while a steeple headdress reared from her temples like that of a medieval chatelaine.

Alongside, a Russian wedding party posed: the bride fair in white, her sergeant groom stiff in green dress uniform. For a moment, as the camera flashed, they and their whole party, replete with medals and lariats, froze into a tableau of wooden prestige while the Kazakhs grinned and chattered. But the brides laid their bouquets of lilies and pink carnations at the same spot near the eternal flame. Then they went away in cars fluttering with the same ribbons, sporting identical dolls on the bonnet.

The Kazakhs seemed doomed to mimic their conquerors. For days you might hunt here in vain for native artefacts. Even the city's origins were Russian, founded in 1853 as the wood-built garrison-town of Verny. Squashed among stucco and concrete, a few timber survivors, carved with gables and filigreed eaves, evoked a homely, unceremonious place, like a frontier village. Even the gingerbread cathedral, tossing up spires and domes scaled like fantastical fish, inhabited its parkland with a florid innocence, as if a child were celebrating God. I imagined it built of brick or stone. But when I tapped its walls and pilasters, they gave out a thump of stuccoed wood.

Nearby, under a towered belfry, stood Verny's old officers'

club. But now it housed the heart of the culture its officers had
conquered: a choice display of Kazakh musical instruments.
These rough, wild attendants of wedding and funeral had come
to rest in glass cabinets, handsomely displayed. They hung there
like caged birds: the fish-shaped *dombra* lutes and three-
stringed violas, many quite plain, played by long-dead masters.
Many a *kobiz* viola had been scooped crudely out of logs, and
cabinets trimmed with a barbarian cacophany of wooden horns,
zithers, goatskin bagpipes and horse-hoof cymbals.

Beneath some instruments you could touch a switch and start
their recorded music. Under the wooden harps, shaped like
antelope horns, trembled a noise like dripping rain, silvery and
inconsolable. Then came the scratchy energy of the *dombras*,
the throaty flutes and the meanderings of the *kobiz* whose mel-
low phrases made unexpected starts and ends. As I turned more
switches, the noises seemed to intertwine sadder and sadder,
until the little hall had filled up with a twanging and fluting at
once uncannily clear – I could catch each husky uncertainty of
the woodwind – yet emotionally remote, as if emanating from a
steppeland which had vanished.

Bards were the keepers of Kazakh culture. They sang heroic
sagas yet gave voice to common feelings. Their music pervaded
all events – the leaving and return to war or pasture – and conveyed an ancient morality. But their mantle had fallen on
nobody. Music and literature paled under Soviet censorship, and
I wondered – now that independence had dawned – what had
become of the Kazakh drama, once the purveyor of Socialist
Realism?

But Mukhtar Auezov, patron saint of the Communist Kazakh
theatre, still sat in bronze outside the playhouse entrance where
one of his best-known works was showing that evening. The
auditorium was packed and vibrant with the scuttling lisps and
gutturals of Kazakh, and everyone seemed young. Only on stage
an aged hero relived in dream sequence his rite of passage
through the twentieth century. One by one, in a stilted drama of
ideas, this protagonist fell foul of Islam (portrayed in flagrant

contempt), czarist Russia and Stalinism, then strode into a flag-waving paen to the Marxist future. At one point the actors vaulted into athletic still-life, holding aloft a spotlit hammer and sickle, and the audience broke into spontaneous applause, not for Communism, the woman beside me said – 'it's another sort of people who do that' – but for the theatrical beauty of the thing.

But this evening the play ended differently. A contemporary writer had devised a final scene. As the last act reached its climax, the red banners of the old finale suddenly drooped and the Marxist hymns died away. Demonstrations broke out – recognisable to the audience as those of 1986 – in which the hero's daughter was killed. Here he broke from his reverie (at the age, I reckoned, of 110), laughing at the tragic foolishness of history, and trailed away with a fallen banner, a little tired. But the banner read 'The Kazakh earth for the Kazakh people' and brought the audience to a storm of rhythmic clapping. They were cheering their own nation, I knew, as much as the actors or play – but without aggression or bitterness – then jumped to their feet and overlapped the stage with flowers.

But as we tumbled out of the theatre, everyone beaming and chattering, I felt a curmudgeonly qualm. Auezov's play had been corrected as remorselessly as all previous thought had been corrected. It was still a hostage. Only when it was allowed to return to its own thin truth, I supposed, would these people really be free.

'But you're seeing a renaissance!' cried a law student as we jostled together at the exit. He was a southern Kazakh, vivid and earnest. His friend and fellow-student came from the north and was silent. 'Before, this place was nearly empty! It just showed Soviet propaganda, not life at all.' He gestured at the announcement of future programmes. 'But now we're finding ourselves again. There's a play coming by Makataeb – you haven't heard of him? He was virtually a dissident, died twelve years ago. His plays have only just begun to be shown...and there's a play about a Kazakh hero who fought against the czars. It was banned before ....'

'Boring stuff,' said the northerner.

'I know we can't go back,' the southerner rushed on, 'but we have to rebuild ourselves. What about our city? Do you like it? Is it eastern?'

It was an odd, naïve question. He wanted it to be eastern. He was hot with rejection of European Russia. I said unkindly: 'It's playing with eastern motifs here and there. It's modern.'

But he was undeterred, filled by the passion to repossess his origins, as if they would tell him who he was. We were outside the theatre now, looking back at its façade, and could see the circus building opposite, like a deflated Buddhist dagoba, and a tatty wedding palace.

'They were built by the same architect, as an ensemble!' He talked as if it were the Centre Pompidou or the Lincoln Center. 'This is our national architecture! I think it's Kazakh. In the south we've kept the knowledge of Kazakh things. In the north, where he comes from' – he pointed at his friend, who looked darker and coarser than he – 'in the north, they've lost it. Even the language he speaks is poorer than mine.' The friend grinned and said nothing. 'In the north they're swamped by Russians. But in the south we're in the majority, and we've kept our epics and history alive. I know them, but he doesn't.' The friend continued grinning, like a comedian's stooge. 'He went to Russian school, but I went to Kazakh school.'

'You get on all right with the Russians,' I began – an old mystery had resurfaced – 'but I've read about what happened in the thirties. Three million dead, people say ....'

'But we've passed through that. The people who remember and suffered that are few now. You see how young people are!' They were flowing down the steps all around us: girls confident in their modern prettiness, and groomed youths escorting them.

The northerner suddenly said: 'But we've been surrounded by Russian culture always. We've received a lot from it. The Baltic states reject it wholesale, and Uzbekistan falls back on its past, but we haven't got a past like that. Almost everything we have

330

comes from Russia.'

'But we've been blinded by it!' said the southerner – they were being tugged away by the crowd. 'We were told we were part of this great movement forward, and all the time our own past was being buried.'

'But our past isn't enough ....' began the northerner, then they were swept away in a slipstream of friends, and I was left standing by the statue of Auezov, avuncular and balding in his armchair.

Back in my hotel – a tomb for tourists, where nothing worked – a group of languid prostitutes, mostly Russian, had bribed their way in off the streets. The concierge on my floor ushered one down the lift in resignation, almost with pity. 'That's the only way we can live now,' she said. 'Nobody on a salary can survive any more.'

She looked as if she too had fallen on hard times. She was fifty, perhaps, but the lines dribbled down from her eyes and over her cheeks in a map of long distress. A floor-lady's wages were pitiful. I asked: 'How do you manage?'

'I trade things from over the border with China. I buy sports shoes and jackets, and sell them here.' I could not imagine this, she looked too delicate and enclosed. But the cross-frontier commerce was booming, I knew. Already a railway linked Almaty to Beijing, joining the China Sea to Istanbul – and soon to the Persian Gulf – and one day might unravel the whole of Central Asia. 'That trade is all I've left to live on. My husband's gone. One trip to the market and my weekly salary's gone too. Another trip, and my son's has gone. Another, and my daughter's. We can't buy clothes any more.' She dashed a hand down her thin black dress. 'All our clothes are old.' She followed me to my room and stood uncertainly in the doorway. 'My children are both married now, and happy. But we still all live together in a three-room flat. We're like that here, collective, and poor....'

At first I had thought her Russian but she laughed for the first time when I mentioned it. It was a sad sound. 'I'm a western

Kazakh, from the Sachs tribe. We're paler there, with quite European faces and big eyes. We're the original Kazakhs.'

I looked doubtfully back at her. Perhaps this tribal claiming of fair skin and big eyes was a legacy of Russian colonialism. She said: 'My friends are many of them Russian. But whether we'll start to feel differently about one another now, I don't know. It's peculiar.'

Yet she was a little too old deeply to care, I thought. She looked somehow spent. 'Things will only change slowly,' I said, not knowing.

'When I saw you,' she went on, 'I thought you were one of our Soviet people, you seemed so open.' Then she said artlessly: 'I'm looking for a man now. I'd like a companion. Not for a family, but for the heart.' She plucked at her breast. She must once have been rather beautiful, I thought. Her mouth and cheeks had slackened round fine bones, and an old pride stayed in her manner. 'Would it be possible for us to meet, do you think, if you're here longer? Or for me to come to England?' Her voice had dropped to a sentimental contralto. 'Sometimes when I see people, I think, I could be happy with him, he's open and decent. I thought that when I saw you.'

In the face of this vaulting trust I felt complex, not open or decent at all. Her warmth and directness, even the cloud of her hennaed hair, reminded me of Russian women. She knew nothing at all of England, or of me. She simply swam in the tide of her instincts; and when I told her of a woman in England, she accepted this with a smile as if a chance accident had blocked an open road.

*

A few years ago the circus, like the ballet, was a showcase for Soviet culture. No city of the empire was complete without its circular theatre spinning with a galaxy of acrobats, trapeze artists, fire-eaters, conjurors, ventriloquists, bear-tamers, clowns and contortionists.

That summer a Moscow troupe was visiting Almaty, and the

332

spectators were undiminished. More than a thousand banked up to the theatre's gallery, where a twelve-piece band sent up a boisterous overture. Children and adults gazed with the same wonder into a spangled, hyperactive world whose vivid physiques and matinée-idol grins exuded an aura of other-worldliness. They gasped at the sleek-haired conjuror whose fingers sprouted spoons, respectfully applauded the performing yak, set up rhythmic clapping at the dancers meshed in twenty-foot pythons, and maintained a pindrop silence while a man with a cowhide whip at twenty feet flicked a rose from a girl's lips.

High in the apex of the dome, where a cyclorama of stars circled through darkness, a team of trapeze artists in phospho-rescent leotards dispersed and reunited. The music stilled to an unearthly trembling. Weight lost its meaning. They swam above us in a night ballet whose noiseless ease turned it to an exchange of ghosts, and grasped and released one another so effortlessly that had they failed, I imagined, the discarnate bodies would scarcely fall to earth.

Yet already a feel of archaism intruded. Musical references to *Swan Lake* abounded, and the clowns' jokes about *perestroika* seemed coined in another era. Towards the end a shambling brown bear was led into the ring's centre to play the accordion. It looked drugged and old. It reeled on its podium. The accordion was strapped to its paws like handcuffs, so that a few melancholy notes rose involuntarily as it swayed. It was at once ridiculous and heart-rending. The audience cheered. They were simply seeing a collusive beast, I suppose, pretending to be human. The animal, I think, saw almost nothing. Its eyes were inscrutable beads. Maybe only I, fancifully, was seeing in its tot-tering bulk the Russian Bear on its last legs.

*

In a park near the city's centre, under an avenue of ash trees, I met a girl named Dilia who dreamed of becoming a conductor. Every other evening she sat with an orchestra following the score in rapt, near-hopeless ambition, and returned at day to her job of accompanying singers on the piano. In her still-young face the classic Kazakh features looked simplified and intense. Her eyes slanted fine and dark under sleek brows, and beneath them the delicate mouth and cheekbones might have been limned on to her face by a miniaturist seeking perfection. But a pair of thick spectacles seemed to repel intrusion, and the score of Brahms' *A German Requiem* lay open across her knees on the bench.

'The conductors here tell me it's hopeless my wanting to conduct. They say "Give up! It's no good!" But I don't listen.' Her laugh was tinkling steel. 'They think I should concentrate on my piano playing. That's a woman's role. It's good work, but some of our singers have God-given voices which they scarcely cultivate, and then I'm angry. I'm hard on them, and they resent it. They don't think it's my place!' She sliced a hand across her throat, as if she were committing suicide, then her voice darkened into mockery which was not yet cynical, but might become so. *'No, no, you are just a woman, Dilia, you should do as you're told* …. But I've never done that. The Russians say "If you're afraid of wolves, don't go into the forest", but I've gone in and I'm not coming out now.'

She looked so young, I found myself saying: 'What do your parents feel?'

'My parents are dead. I live alone. My father was a railway engineer and she a teacher, but ill all her life. She was glad I loved music, but they wanted me married. They wanted grandchildren.' She took off her spectacles and lifted her face in profile, consciously stilling herself. Without her glasses, she appeared harder. 'Nobody understands my not marrying. But I never liked the men my parents produced. I've always liked older men.' She looked momentarily shy, as if this were a vice. 'When young men courted me, I pushed them away. It was sensitivity I wanted, and intelligence.'

'And children?'

'Children aren't important to me. It's only important that the man should love me.' She turned from my gaze again, but her hands wrenched at one another above *A German Requiem*, and her voice assumed its mocking lilt. '*Oh no, you must have children and live among saucepans, Dilia. Don't you want that? What's wrong with you?*' She laughed again, buoyantly. I could not foresee when this laughter would grow bitter.

'You may still marry,' I said. She was, in her hard way, beautiful.

But she dashed this aside with her hand. 'With us, women often marry at seventeen. Twenty-three is old – and I'm thirty-one!'

'But still ....'

'Marriage here can be terrible. When women get what they want, all they do is whine for more money. Men drink and beat their wives, and the women are silent and cover their bruises.' She closed the score on her lap. '*But you want a career more than a family, Dilia? Oh no, that's terrible.*'

She would have been unusual in any country, I thought, but here in the man's world of Kazakhstan she was extraordinary and moving. We sat for a while, silenced by her impasse, until an old man tottered towards us, his chest ribboned with war-medals. His was a near-ancestral face of Russian suffering, its lines deep-etched in hopelessness, its eyes bleared. As he stooped down to us, he breathed out beer fumes. 'I need to eat, young people ... I need to eat.' He waved at a tea-house through the trees. His slack mouth rambled between obsequiousness and a ghost of dignity. 'Is it possible for you to give?' Dilia raised her clinical profile to him, said something distantly, and we both gave. 'Thank you, thank you.' He scrutinised the money in his palm, then bowed to us frailly and stumbled away.

She said: 'I feel sorry for these old Communists who fought in the war, and believed. They've got nothing left now. Everything they valued has collapsed, everything they lived for. That must be hard.'

I liked her then. I had expected the old man to awaken her intolerance: his mind and body ransacked by himself and the world, his past so far from her imagined future. He would not have guessed her sympathy.

She went on as if no one had interrupted: 'Everybody apart from me seems to accept things. Perhaps I should not have been a woman.' She smoothed her hands over her face, as if eradicating lines, which were not there. It was an ageless face, without discernible expression; and her figure androgynously slim. 'But there was a man ....'

He had been a visitor to the concert hall, a Lithuanian Jew who had encouraged and perhaps loved her. He had invited her to Vilnius, but her parents had been horrified.

'Because he was Jewish?'

'No, no! Because he was not Kazakh. Men can do what they like, but a Kazakh girl must take a Kazakh husband!' Her hands wrenched in her lap again. 'But I deceived them, and went, and we were happy. We walked in the park, and talked. He was forty-five.' She looked suddenly naïve, forlorn. 'Now he's in America, and thinks I should go out there too. But what would I do? I could bear to work as a waitress for a year or two, but after that, if I didn't become a musician, I'd starve inside.' She touched her heart in the Russian way. 'I don't know what I'll do. Here I have my music. But over there I think I might have nothing.'

'Perhaps this friend would help you.' But I did not know what was happening inside either of them.

'Perhaps. When he telephones from there, he sounds happy. It's my voice that sounds sad to me .... I feel sad after he's gone.' She replaced an imaginary receiver. 'Lonely.'

So she remained between her lesser world and the cruel challenge of America, and did not know what to do. Only the small, determined mouth and tightened profile said that she was not to be pitied.

*

Next morning I flew to Karaganda, the second city of Kazakhstan. This was no more than a feint into the heart of a

336

steppeland spreading thinly peopled towards Siberia, for you could travel it for weeks and encounter no one. Far down, under the wings of our groaning Tupolev, drifted an unchanging, dun-coloured earth, where cloud-shadows moved in grey lakes and there was no glint of life. It was hard to look on it without misgiving. In these secretive deserts and the grasslands lapping them to the north, the Russians had for decades concealed an archipelago of labour camps, nuclear testing sites, ballistic missiles and archaic heavy industry. It was the dumping-ground of unwanted nations. Around the handful of those exiles it hammered into stature – Dostoevsky soldiered here in disgrace, Solzhenitsyn festered – millions more succumbed into death or obscurity. Trotsky spent two years banished in Almaty, before the murderer's ice-pick found him in Mexico.

From time to time the land had floated visions. In the late 1950s Russians and Ukrainians flooded into the northern steppes to plant a hundred million acres of wheat and barley on Kruschev's 'Virgin Lands' (lands not virgin at all, but Kazakh pastures) and for a few years the scheme flowered spectacularly, before soil erosion called it to heel. From the Leninsk space centre near the Aral Sea the first Sputnik shot into orbit, the first dog ascended, then the first astronauts.

But the testing sites near Semipalatinsk have left half a million people ill with radioactive sickness, some of them – in Stalin's time – exposed intentionally as guinea-pigs. Over a region now riddled with unfissioned plutonium, some 500 bombs, exploded over forty years, have undermined a bewildered populace with cancers, leukaemia, heart disease, birth defects and blindness, so that the first act of an independent Kazakhstan in 1990 was to ban all tests on its territory. All across this blighted country, lead smelters and copper foundries, cement and phosphates works still plunge the skies and waters in poisonous effluent, and some two million Kazakhs and Russians are rumoured chronically sick from the pollution.

But as we floated above it, the steppe looked untouchably vast. Here and there a green valley scored it, the excrement of a

337

mine appeared, or a lonely quadrangle of wheat; and as we descended towards Karaganda a speckling of dark cattle and pale sheep, invisible before, emerged against the void. Beyond the airstrip the road travelled across an empty plain. The sky thundered. After a long time villages of dachas and allotments started up, many half built and all deserted. Then came steel-works bannered in smoke; and suddenly the suburbs of Karaganda shot up in twenty-storey flat-blocks like a futuristic Hell. They clustered in concrete islands, separated by wasteland, so that the whole city was ringed by these desolate micro-regions too far from one another.

We jolted down splintered streets. It was a young town, founded in 1926, and it seemed ownerless. In western Russia it was the butt of black jokes: a synonym for nowhere. Its only purpose was the coalfields on which it sprawled. Of its 700,000 inhabitants, most of them Russians, one quarter laboured under the ground. Above ground, it looked half abandoned. To these choking warrens the Second World War had added an arsenal of iron works. All through the Stalin years the place was filled with ex-convicts still half in exile. From its railway station, still grim with floodlights, the packed Stolypin carriages had shunted their prisoners to a nest of surrounding labour-camps, and lorryloads of others vanished to nearby Samarka and Kengir, whose inmates in 1954 at last revolted – men and women together – until tanks overran them leaving 700 dead.

My hotel stood in the centre. Its concrete was cracking, and it owned a gaunt restaurant selling black market drink. When my room's telephone rang a woman began to enquire after her son, whom she had lost. She had dialled the wrong number. Her voice echoed from another time.

I went out into the streets. They were enormous and near-empty, their buildings the colour of dust, undecorated. Hammer-and-sickle banners still dangled across the roads, and a few people lingered at bus-stops or beer-wagons, as if in refuge from something. On the façade of the Miner's Palace, a screen of gross columns, sprouting figures of workers and soldiers, concealed some cringing Arabic arches; while opposite, in an ensemble of brutish, soot-coloured brotherhood, a Russian and a Kazakh miner upheld a chunk of coal. In its terrible isolation, I thought, the city might have been going mad. Its coal was poor, and produced a corrosive ash. Its river was strangled by radioactive waste, its air tainted with carbon. In winter, they said, snow turned black before it touched the ground.

When the labour-camps were broken up in 1956, Karaganda was flooded by ex-convicts, some of them educated liberals, who could not go home. They settled here beside their ex-jailers, and for a generation the city took on a gentler tinge. But it remained a wilderness of exiles, forced or voluntary. Now, at the end of Peace Prospect, the wooden concert hall, long closed, was falling to bits. Even the KGB headquarters – a Doric palace stuccoed grey and white – looked unoccupied (but was not). Outside a cake shop I passed 200 people queuing: doughy women in plain scarves and skirts who might have belonged in the forties, but for a dash of lipstick.

The German was queuing too: a man with glittering blue eyes and an uprush of grey hair. It was a face with more delicacy than life had allowed its owner. 'Nobody belongs in this town,' he said. 'It's vile. My home was in the Ukraine before the war, but my father was shot in the repressions four months before I was born' – he marked the months off with his blistered fingers – '... March ... April ... After that the bits of my family moved to East Germany, then to Siberia, and now here.' He said 'here' with a sour shudder. 'I've worked here twenty-four years as a builder, and it's become hopeless. I haven't been paid for three months. There's no law, nothing. Even the Russians don't have a country, nobody has a country. I want my son to go to West Germany, and I too. I'd rather be buried there.' His smile dispersed over a mouthful of gaps and stains. I remembered my gap-tooth and grinned back at him. 'I'm not afraid of work. And I'll pick up the language.' He hoisted a few German words into his Russian, but they came thick and distorted. 'Anywhere's better than here.'

Roaming the outskirts next day, I believed him. The coal-mines ringed the city in waste-heaps where the shaft-wheels turned in their scaffolds as if this were the thirties. So steeped was the place in secrecy that visiting delegates from Europe, suggesting aid, were offered no geological maps. The safety regulations (an official confided) were routinely flouted. There was no money left. Inside grim offices, where I was refused permission to go underground, illuminated cabinets glowered with the penants and medals of Soviet labour awards.

Yet the surface lethargy deceived. In 1989 these fearful tunnels spat out their miners in a strike which was echoed across the Union. Its men were young, angry and organised. They demanded, and won, an independent trade union. After sixty years of servitude, the workers were on the march. But their model, they said, was the United States of America.

12

The Mountains of Heaven

It was almost July. For over a hundred miles the Alatau mountains, the western ranges of the Tienshan, shadowed my bus
south along the Kirghiz border, while the road ran dead-straight
in their lee, seeking out a pass. Beyond a velvety massif of
foothills, the snow-peaks frothed in backlit clouds, as if swept
by pale fire.

Beside me sat a shy Kazakh girl who was studying electrical
engineering, and was going home. Sometimes she turned a
child's face to mine and questioned me about Europe. She
spoke in a whisper, through goldfish lips. Whenever I asked
anything about her, she whispered 'Who? Me?' as if no one had
ever enquired about her before. She got out in the middle of
pastureland, clutching a watercolour of roses, and walked away
towards a herdsmen's village in the hills.

After two hours the bus crested a pass and entered tablelands
of grey rock sheened in grass and flowers. We had crossed
unsignalled into the mountain state of Kirghizstan, the easternmost reach of Central Asia before it drops into the deserts of
Xinjiang. Of all these troubled nations, this was the most remote:
an Alpine sanctuary of less than four and a half million people.
When independence came, power slipped from the grip of the
old Communists, and the liberal president – alone in Central
Asia – ruled by political concensus, and was trying to free the
economy.

Around me in the bus sat the nation in miniature: some
Russians, Uzbeks and a scattering of fugitive minorities. But in

the ascendant, a jovial, rustic people – perhaps related to the Kazakhs – bellowed and slumbered and guzzled gross picnics. Seven hundred years before, the Kirghiz ancestors, harried by the armies of Kublai Khan, had migrated from the Yenisei river in Siberia, and centuries later percolated the Tienshan, mingling with the valley tribes. Their Islam was thin. They were nomad warriors, whose currency was the sheep and the horse. Divided by steep valleys, they had thought of themselves less by nation than by tribe, until Stalin rooted them in villages, and decided who they were. Then their language was codified with Russian loan-words to split them from the Kazakhs, and their boundaries fixed.

Towards sunset our bus climbed to a rain-swept plateau which rolled its polished rocks to the skyline. In the distance, shoulders and haunches of mountain came lurching out of clouds. Then farms and small factories appeared, and the long suburbs of the capital, Bishkek: Slavic cottages with carved eaves and fences frail in a tangle of vines and vegetables. Blonde women were basking on the verges in the last sunlight, grazing a goat or a few chickens. Everything seemed smaller than elsewhere: the flat-blocks, the streets, even the statues of Lenin diminutive in their workshop courts.

Night had fallen before I reached a hotel – an ornate Stalinist survivor, rowdy with Kirghiz farmers in from the mountains. But I was sick of the leathery mutton and *solyanka* soup in the hotel restaurants, with their sodden rice and sweet fruit juices, and I wandered out, warm with expectation, into the town's dusk.

It was filled with the scent of chestnut trees, and a sliver of moon was rising. I felt I was not in a city at all. It seemed only obscurely inhabited. Every path and avenue was wrapped in a thronging bank of trees, where the streetlights hung in lonely orbs, like outsize fairy-lights. It was as if its builders had tunnelled the place out of forest, gouging dark glades and country lanes, which sometimes opened on woodland clearings inexplicably ablaze with buildings.

From end to end of the city's heart, the boulevard once

named from Dzerzhinsky, but now Peace, pushed through indecipherable foliage where a few lovers sat, not kissing or
fondling, but curled together in a kind of speechless longing.
Once a gaunt equestrian statue loomed above me. Its arm
stretched black against the black sky, but I could not discern its
face, nor read its inscription. I stopped on a railway bridge of
rotting wood. A Russian couple was embracing in silence, her
back arched over the parapet as they kissed. From here the city
lights glimmered against a starlit glacis of mountains, and I suddenly dreaded the daylight, which might return the place to
Soviet drabness.

Yet at first, dawn revealed nothing. It seemed a city built for
farmers. Rustic cottages crammed its alleys, slithering with canals
where gardens of cherry and apricot flowered. A rural invasion
of Kirghiz was infiltrating the suburbs and crowding the shops.
They looked like last-generation herdsmen, coarser and burlier
than their Kazakh cousins. I watched them in fascination. They
lumbered along the streets as if breasting mountains, and would
drop unthinking to their haunches on the pavements. Their mas-
tiff necks rolled into barrel chests. Their hair was cropped into a
utilitarian black bush, beneath which the jowled, brachycephalic
heads belonged in Mongolia. In fact a physiognomic map (if it
omitted Tajikistan) would find Turkic features inexorably flatten-
ing eastward from the Caspian, until it arrived at these shambling, short-legged mountaineers with their full lips and ruddy,
fierce-boned cheeks. Many looked like pantomime peasants.
Their rolling-pin arms swung out from muscle-bound shoulders,
and their felt hats lent them a doltish gaiety. But within a generation they could refine to a tenuous urbanity, and these other
Kirghiz too were all about, running small businesses in the liber-
alised economy, percolating the civil service.

As I neared the city's centre, the streets still burrowed through
oak and acacia, and parks blossomed with syringa and handker-
chief trees; but the forest was teeming with traffic now, and at
the end of streets I glimpsed factory chimneys.

Suddenly, without warning, the greenery opened on stone-paved desolation. On one side stood the marble parliament, with the marble state museum behind. There was a pale hotel complex and a blank war memorial. A bullying Lenin, huge on his pedestal, commandeered the main square. All at once the city had lost touch with its people, who clattered round it in old Zhiguli and Moskvich cars, or walked numbly in the void.

Yet in a city still full of Russians, this Soviet order, I supposed, evoked nostalgia for a time when prices were stable and people knew where they were. Now everything had changed. The future belonged to the backwoods Kirghiz.

'They're flooding in everywhere,' said a Russian lorry-driver. 'When my people came down from Siberia in 1945, this town was all Russian and Ukrainian, with a few others. You didn't see these black people about. You have blacks in England? What's their position?'

'It's different.'

'Well, we have these blacks in the city now, as many as forty per cent. They come in from the state farms because they don't want to work. I don't remember them here when I was a boy. We used to go out into the countryside and view them there, like monkeys. And now they're here, not working at all, just buying and selling and apeing about.' A pair of Kirghiz girls sauntered by, trim in black skirts. 'They can dress all right,' he went on, 'because they're in commerce. They even get foreign money.' His eyes drifted over me, then unfocused. 'But they haven't got anything else. No industry, no brains.'

'But they're getting jobs.'

'There aren't any jobs. My sons have to work as teachers, on hopeless salaries. But where can we go? My parents are buried here, and my young sister ....' A spasm of misery twitched him. 'I can't go back to Siberia, so I'll stay. But many have gone, many, many ... anyone who could.' He planted his legs apart, and spat. 'Now these blacks think they're the bosses.'

I crossed the bleak spaces to Lenin Square, and walked along the tended rose-beds of the presidential office. Out of the quiet came the long ringing of an unanswered telephone. I mounted

344

the podium under Lenin's statue, and stared down on the avenue for those vanished May Day parades of orchestrated happiness. All round the square the loudspeakers tilted disused on their posts, and in the podium centre, where a microphone had once relayed leaden exhortations, the wires drooped in a tangle of dead worms.

I descended a flight of derelict steps to the rooms locked beneath. The marble passageway was discoloured and its balustrades falling. I trod gingerly, as if backstage. A broken water-pipe was dripping into the stair-well, and there was a stench of urine. The steel doors were barred, but already rusting away, and I peered through them into a sanctum of fetid emptiness.

*

Trespassing off First of May Street along the stairs and passage-ways of the Writers' Union – once a bureaucratic hub of mediocrity and obstruction – I met a writer named Kadyr. His urbanity and circumspection, even the cadaverous sensitivity of his face, seemed to set him generations away from his compatriots in the hills. Yet he had been born in a mountain village, he said, on the borders of China.

We sat in someone else's office by a deserted boardroom, on whose door the name of Chingiz Aitmatov, the expatriate Kirghiz novelist, was inscribed reverentially as if he were still inside. I asked what people did here now.

'They don't do anything,' said Kadyr. 'We've hundreds of writers, but no money...and our publishers can't get paper. It used to come to us from Russia, but now everything's atrophied. So at last we have our freedom to write – but no paper!' His lank hair and glasses lent him a juvenile charm which drifted on and off. An ingrained wariness pervaded him. Questions turned him vague. 'There was always too much that we couldn't say. We couldn't draw on our traditions or write our own history. Now our spiritual situation is richer, far richer, but our material one is hopeless.'

345

'What did you used to write about?'

'My novels were about nature,' he said quickly, as if exculpating himself from something, 'how the mountains sit in people's spirits, and how people relate to them and to one another. There are inhabitants of Bishkek like that, and I suppose I'm one of them.' He studied his hands. They looked too big for his body, which tapered away. 'People call us "the mountain people", because we've never really left the wilds.'

To write of the mountains, I supposed, was a covert way of expressing patriotism.

'It wasn't dangerous,' he said. 'Nature is nature, whoever is in power.' He picked a paperback from a shelf. 'This is by me ....'

It was a flimsy guidebook to Kirghizia. Opening it at random, I read: 'Just as the eagle flies up from his eyrie my people have risen to the heights of unprecedented creative achievement thanks to their Soviet homeland ....'

'Did you ask to write this book?'

'Yes, yes. I approached the publishers in Moscow – and they said Fine, fine.' His wariness had slipped away. He looked proud.

I fingered the passage miserably, then pushed it under his eyes. I heard myself say: 'Did you have to write that?'

He stared at it. 'It was a kind of ... well ... formula.' He did not look at me. We both laughed abruptly. For who was I to blame him? I had not lived in his grey nightmare. He began: 'There's nothing like that in my novels, of course. They're about how the mountains sit in people's spirits ....'

But his voice flaked away.

*

The Lenin Museum had been renamed the History Museum, but the history inside it was thin and distorted. Its lower halls were given over to a shadowy tide of Turkic peoples: Tartar warriors who had ridden these valleys in the eighth century with their battle-maces and round shields, sleepy stone menhirs that had stood above nomad graves, bronzes from lost Buddhist temples.

346

To these the nineteenth-century remnants of the Kirghiz lent only a more intimate variation. The rag dolls of their children were here; so were their lutes and square-shouldered fiddles which had wailed to the chanting of the *Manas* – the Kirghiz' *Iliad* which contains their whole history like a mighty palimpsest. With such instruments it was for centuries carried from yurt to yurt by the *manaschi*, travelling bards with prodigious memories, who only died out a generation ago. In the museum vitrines were goatskin bottles too, and leather funnels for the fomenting of mares' milk, while the mountain horses – tireless creatures with stone-hard hooves – had left behind fragments of harness and stirrup-irons.

Yet within the decade of the thirties this timeless cycle had dropped to earth. Even the most remote yak-herders were collectivised, and the first wheat-fields were creeping over the valleys. Bolshevism was celebrated in the museum's upper storeys by a collection which was already itself history. It was like wandering the church of a dead religion: life-size gilded maquettes of canonised historic episodes, and cabinets of facsimile letters and documents, all caressingly laid out as if they were originals. But in fact there was nothing here at all: just the memory of propaganda. The busts of its proletarian gods and saints seemed to gaze out from centuries ago. They were soon to be removed.

On the floor above, newly installed, were photographs of Stalin's purge victims and of the exhumation of a mass grave.

*

One morning, as I strayed round a collective warehouse near the western market, I heard distant chanting. At first I thought somebody had left a radio playing, then I emerged from passageways into a room hung with striplights. A woman in white chiffon was playing on an electric harmonium, while a projector threw on to a little screen some Baptist hymns in Russian. Among makeshift chairs some thirty people were singing in wavery unison. They looked like stocky Chinese: clear-eyed women and children in pressed frocks, three fresh-faced youths

347

and a line of elderly men. Nobody had dared remove the Communist standards dripping from the walls of their rented hall. The only other decoration was a vase of plastic carnations beside the harmonium.

> *Mortals built a house, and the rains came,*
> *And the floods rose, and the house fell ....*

Above them the head of Lenin bristled out of a poster charged 'Our beloved leader', and a red banner was slung along the back wall, blazoned 'The People and the Party are One'. Sometimes the crash of lorries intruded, rolling through the market beyond, and the distant shouts of bargaining.

> *This house is built by you, and the rains come*
> *And the floods rise, but the house stands,*
> *The house built by Jesus ....*

A pretty woman with a ravaged face conducted the congregation by hand, smiling with a pert, manic radiance, and the people copied her gestures as her hands fluttered and twirled in illustration of the hymns. 'Jesus loves me' – the palms alighted on the heart. 'Jesus loves you' – and the fingers shot out in front of them. 'Jesus ....'

It dawned on me that they were Koreans. They sat motionless, as a pastor addressed them. He came, I later learnt, from South Korea, and was speaking the native language which many of them had forgotten. He stood with his feet together and his hands laced in front of him. A puerile lock of hair fell over his face, which shone with a strenuous happiness. Towards the end of the service he called out the name of a girl new to the congregation, and summoned her to 'bear witness'. She stepped up in terror, dressed in an embroidered velvet jacket and matching hair-ribbon. 'I am very glad,' she began, 'I am so glad .... I am so happy ... happy ....' then faltered into blushing silence, while everybody clapped.

Then the pastor noticed me. 'We have a guest,' he said. He beckoned me up, and I heard my voice announcing my pleasure that I was amongst them, while the ranks of faces smiled back out of their excoriating goodness, and I grinned weakly. It was inspiring to see their little church growing out of oppression, I said – and as I uttered the words, they became true.

Yet their happiness, their conviction of divine sanctuary, was tremblingly frail in the banner-hung hall, and now the din of the bazaar – where Kirghiz and Russians mingled – almost drowned out their singing.

> *Jesus forever loving*
> *Beautiful Saviour ....*

At the end everyone embraced his neighbour on each side, murmuring the ritual 'I love you', and I found myself in the arms of an embarrassed taxi-driver. The community had only been worshipping here seven months, he said, and I must excuse the red banners. The hall was rented from a defunct Komsomol.

But how had Baptists evolved in Central Asia, I asked?

The taxi-driver knit his brows. 'After independence a rich Korean Christian came here from Los Angeles and asked us what we were. We said we thought we were Buddhists, but we didn't know. But the man said No, you're Christians. And so we became Christians.' The tale on his lips took on a biblical weight. His frank eyes examined me from a trusting face. Only a frail smile twisted his mouth, which seemed to acknowledge some strangeness in this. 'Now there are seven hundred of us Baptists, and we increase all the time.'

We walked into the blinding sun. I saw that his eyes were softened in smile-lines, and his springy hair touched with grey. His people had lost their history, he said. Even his name, Pasha, sounded synthetic. His ancestors had moved from Korea to Sakalin island. 'But in 1937 Stalin transported them in cattle trucks to Kazakhstan. I was born there, and my father died....'

'Why did your people leave Korea?'

349

'I don't know.'

'Were you Buddhists before?'

'I don't know.' He looked faintly distressed. 'But we became Communists in a way. I was a Young Pioneer and a member of Komsomol. But we didn't believe anything. We were nothing.'

We had turned our back on the market and were walking along a lane where a line of poverty-stricken youths and women squatted on wooden boxes. Each had laid out a few garments, cigarettes and tooth-paste on dirty newspaper in front of him, but two policemen were harassing them to go.

'They're selling things you can't get in the shops,' Pasha said. 'They buy them up cheap on the side. That's the only way they can live.'

They sat in resigned tiredness, while the police harangued them. Then, slowly, they upturned the boxes and packed their goods away. They couldn't afford the price of a market stall, Pasha said.

An old man craned angrily above them. He clutched a vodka bottle wrapped in a cloth. 'I work!' he bellowed. 'But what do these young people do? Sitting in the dirt!' Work: it was the Communist shibboleth, from the years of faith and full employment. 'Why don't they do something manly?' He shook his stick, but no one was listening. Behind his smeared, drunk eyes sat a whole era of failure.

'What can they do?' said Pasha. 'We're all just sitting about now. I spend my life waiting at the railway station. But there aren't any tourists, and only two trains a day from Moscow.'

The police had gone, and the black marketeers were setting out their wares again.

Pasha said: 'For seven years we've been told everything will get better, but I don't believe it. Nobody here believes it.'

*

The giant equestrian statue which had loomed above me in the night turned out by day to be a monument to Mikhail Frunze, the Bolshevik conqueror of Central Asia. In a standing insult to

350

those whom he had vanquished, the town was renamed Frunze in 1926, and only reverted to the homely Bishkek with independence. But his statue still rode its plinth undamaged, and the thatched cottage where he had been born remained enshrined in a portentous museum. Piously preserved artefacts filled its modest rooms: ink-wells and gloves, a hanging cradle and a miniature rocking-horse, the veterinary bag of his Moldavian father still lying in the hall. Respectable poverty shaped the ideal Soviet shrine.

But I was the only visitor, and someone had plastered the door with 'I love Kirghizstan' stickers. The Kirghiz attendant sat engrossed in a romantic novel. When I asked what people thought of Frunze now, her nose wrinkled. 'Old people may like him, but young people don't.' She flushed. She was very young. 'He killed too many.'

On a Sunday evening an old lady sits in the oak-filled park near Frunze's statue. Her blue eyes are filmed over, and their brows almost gone. Her hands interlace over the haft of an ebony walking-stick. But beneath her headscarf the face shows an intermittent brightness, as if some memory woke it. Then the sunk eyes seem to see again, and she smiles a pale-lipped smile, and looks almost beautiful. 'What is the time, young man?'

I always get the time wrong in Russian, and she laughs. She is not Russian, she says, she is Polish, born in Vilna.

'And what did you do there?' I ask.

I am used to Polish immigrants claiming titles and estates; but she says: 'We had a back garden, and some pigs, and we grew things.' Through the shifting oak-branches the street-lamps light up a face webbed in lines and hung with a fragile nose. 'But the Germans came and smashed the town, and burnt our cottage.' She strikes an imaginary match against her dress, 'And we fled.' I realise suddenly that she is not talking about the Second World War, but the First. 'Then I worked in a hospital.'

'As a doctor?'

'No, I'm not educated. Just as a helper.' She shudders, even in

351

the warm night. Her legs disappear into woollen socks and bed-room slippers. She looks institutionalised. 'Then I went to Vladivostok and was married to a surgeon – but he died long ago – and I came to Almaty and then here.' Her stick taps the ground. 'I'm ninety-six years old now, and my daughter is seventy-four, and some of my grandchildren are worrying about their pensions. So I'm old.' She laughs almost coquettishly at the thought, it still seems to surprise her. 'Look, wrinkles!' She lifts her face to me. It is pale and sunk, but her eyes have come alive in it. 'And my hands!' She spreads them before me. 'Look at them.' Their veins coil like ropes under the mottled skin. She gazes at them as if they were someone else's. 'But whether things are worse with other people, or the country, I don't know. I'm an old woman and I don't know anything. I never did know about politics.' Perhaps some inner safety-valve locks them out. She has not lived through the Stalin years for nothing. 'And what do you do? You're from England, ah yes, and you have your family there,' she decides, 'and things are peaceful.' She locks her fingers over the stick again, pleased. 'Yes.'

*

Across the footbridge over the railway trickled workers from the suburbs, with a drift of the unemployed bent on petty trade, or on nothing. To the north the city crouched in its forest, throwing up an occasional roof or a factory above the trees, while to the south the Alatau mountains shadowed the high-rise suburbs with a glitter of cloud-hung snow. Sometimes the whole bridge shook under me as a train packed with mountain marble rumbled west towards Russia, and hot diesel fumes blasted up from the track.

Marble was handsome building material, said the man beside me, but the Soviets had always bought it cheap. He was a builder himself: a haggard Kirghiz on sick-leave. He glared down on the cargo rattling below. 'My firm put up half the old buildings here,' he said. 'We even built the ministries. But now look! These new blocks are hopeless. Their concrete's made of sand and little pebbles, and stuck up with steel bought from

352

Russia. They don't last. The rooms are boiling in summer and freezing in winter.'

'And the work's made you ill?'

'It's an illness of my profession. I'm a plasterer, and I've got trouble with my arms. They ache all the time.' He looked older than his thirty-four years, all the youth worn out of him. 'That's the block we're working on, there!' He jerked his head at a concrete shell where a crane stooped idle. 'But the work's stopped because the steel hasn't come through. It's all like that now. I'm on half pay anyway, sixteen hundred roubles a month.'

That was less than fifteen pounds. 'You have a family?'

'My wife looks after the children at home. That's our Kirghiz way.' He turned his back on the suburbs. A momentary happiness entered his thoughts. 'I've got a little plot of land where I grow carrots and tomatoes, and one day I'm going to build a house somewhere, away from all this.'

'That's hard ....'

'The law allows it now, but often nothing happens. If you want to buy land, the local collective farm may just say No, and you'd have to bribe a chain of officials to get it. It's all mafia.' He was sounding like Oman now. 'One day, when I'm finished, I'll go back to the mountains. But it takes four days to reach my home village, first by plane, then on the hill tracks, it's that far. People work for almost nothing there, but that's where I'll go back.'

He was smoking fiercely, then throwing the half-finished stubs on to the track below. 'Look at this town. It never used to be like this. Even I can remember when it was grass and trees.' He gazed bitterly at the city as if it were a steelyard. Above it the mountains were shaking off their clouds across half the horizon. 'In those days a cool wind came in with the summer night,' he said, 'but skyscrapers shut it out now.' He looked down at the rail-track, gripping the parapet. In its flaking brown paint were lightly scratched graffiti. His wrists were like white stalks.

I could not suppress the feeling that his illness flowed from some mental hurt. He had drifted into the city as a labourer, learnt on the job and married at twenty-one. Then his life had set. For fifteen years he had built a town he increasingly hated. Concrete was so much coarser than the old brick, he said, and even brick was inferior to the native *saman*, which you never saw now. Perhaps the sickness in his arms was as much a toxin from his mind, so deep was his reaction against the suffocation of his mountains. He said again: 'In the end I'll go back there.'

The bridge was shuddering under our feet above another goods train. Someone had stuck a Soviet flag to its prow. He gave it a mock salute. An old instinct for labels, for the comfort of identifying, made me ask: 'You don't feel Soviet?'

'No.' It was a dislocated sound, as if he were answering some unfamiliar language. 'Or not very.' He was looking expressionlessly at the mountains again. The lines pinching his eyes were already scarring his cheeks too. 'Soviet? Soviet? They tried to make us feel that about Afghanistan, but nobody did.'

'You served there?'

'No, but many of my friends served, and some never returned. Only Moscow knows how many disappeared, deserted perhaps .... Others came back in coffins, to be buried here. None of them wanted to fight. My friends say that whenever they aimed their rifles they thought "Shall I fire or not?" But of course they were afraid.'

'There are Kirghiz in Afghanistan?'

His voice fell out of focus again. 'I don't know, I don't think so.' Even nationality clothed him only thinly.

'But fellow-Moslems ....'

'Yes.' He contemplated this. 'Although we Kirghiz are not strong Moslems.'

'No.' Their Islam was like the Kazakhs', I knew: drawn lightly over nomadic shamanism.

The builder seemed, for a moment, to elude all personality: a man on a railway bridge, in a grey suit and sandals. 'But look at Afghanistan now. How useless it all was!' He dropped his last cigarette butt on to the departing train. 'You know, if anybody started shooting from a village, the Russians just wiped that village out: old people, women, babies. It still makes my friends sick talking about it. And they participated.'

We went on looking down on the track. Soot-coloured crows were pecking among its sleepers. The man's knuckles clenched white on the parapet. Beneath them in the paintwork somebody had scratched 'Aleksis loves Anfisa'. I wondered vaguely who had carved it, Aleksis or Anfisa.

The man said: 'Those Afghan people are more like us than the Russians are.'

'Yes.' A lingering pedantry made me want further to place him. But if he looked grim, I knew, it was because he was wondering about his family, not his nation. It was I, not he, who was teased by the flux of his identity: by the light or half-repressed Islam of all these lands, their diminished loyalty to clan or tribe, their Soviet veneer, their shallow-rooted sense of nation. But he did not much care. He did not miss allegiances which his people had never felt. He had his wife and children in a brick-built flat to the north, and a patch of tomatoes. Only I was trying to redefine him. He, meanwhile, was stranded at a watershed timeless in this land: the divide between the urban and the pastoral.

He wanted to go back to the mountains.

*

Outside the railway station at dawn, I found Pasha, the Korean Baptist waiting for the first Moscow train of the day, dozing in his taxi. An hour later we were driving eastward down a silent valley to where the Tienshan cradle Lake Issyk-kul and carry the last thrust of Kirghizia into the Chinese deserts. To our south, out of sleepy hills, the Alatau massifs cut up a blue sky. To our north the Chu river idled through meadows. The air was thin and cool. The valley's fertility, ringed by its astral mountains, bathed it in an illusion of happiness.

But the Russian and Ukrainian cottages along the way marked the bloody incursions of nineteenth-century Cossacks, and in 1916 a Kirghiz uprising was savagely repressed. The herdsmen's flight over glacial passes eastward into Xinjiang was repeated in the 1930s, as over quarter of a million tribespeople fled collectivisation, driving their horses, yaks, camels and sheep deep into the Pamir.

Now the valley seemed at peace. Other dwellings interspersed those of the invaders, and soon their villages dwindled away altogether and we moved down avenues of willows and wheatfields. In this solitude, close by the river, all that remained of the city of Balasagun was sinking into fields of horse-high grass. It had been founded in the tenth century by a wave of Karakhanid invaders, and had petered away with their empire.

Pasha had no heart for it. He took out his Bible, wrapped in an old *Izvestiya*, and settled in the taxi's shade. I was left to wander the town alone. It lay inscrutably in ruin. A rectangle of crushed ramparts traced itself in the grass, and a farmer was grazing his donkey among the thistles over a buried palace. Nearby rose the minaret of a vanished mosque. Earthquake had broken it in two, but the eighty-foot stub, banded austerely in decorative brick, burgeoned from a huge octagonal plinth in a lonely manifestation of the city's power.

I roamed the site in ignorance. A millennium before, it had blossomed into scholarship and piety. The Silk Road, splintering through the valley, had deposited here a flotsam of trade and knowledge, and the bodies long crumbled in its mausoleums had left behind Chinese coins and bracelets of Indian cowrie shells. Iron swords, bronze lamps and amulets had been found too, and crosses carved in stone by Nestorian Christians: and a little museum had collected them all.

Straying round the levelled walls, I came upon a crowd of stone effigies, gathered here from distant nomad graves. Flat boulders, lightly incised, they were survivors from the vast western kaganate of Turkic tribes which had overswept the southern steppes and hill valleys between the sixth and tenth centuries. Now some eighty of these *balbali* stood in the long grass. Thin columnar noses bisected their faces, and dribbled slight moustaches. They were at once crude and unsettling. They looked like profane dolls. Beneath their pear-shaped chins they cradled goblets, and sometimes swords. Their close-set eyes held a sleepy simplicity. They seemed to be portraits: or slabs of stone which had grown expressions. Some believe them to be the images of slain enemies who become servants of the dead in the underworld.

A woman was scything the grass around them in careful strokes. She spoke of them affectionately, caressing the word *balbali* as if they were her babies. She understood the pagans' creating them, she said. Her own people, at Bairam, would banquet round their family graves and would imagine that the dead were feasting with them. That, she supposed, was the purpose of the *balbali*. She looked round them in tender authority. 'They are alive in a way, and they share with us.' She fondled a stone head. They stared away, all facing the dawn.

On the anniversary of a funeral, she said, her family would set aside food for the departed. But women never wept at the graves. They had to weep at home, or their tears would disturb the dead. She said this hotly, as if she wished it otherwise. Around us the variety of stone expressions, carved by intent or the wind, turned the *balbali* to a living audience. If mourners wept, she added, the waters would rise round the ghosts, and they would drown. 'All the same, we pray there,' she said, caught up in some private grief, 'and we imagine he is with us.'

Eastward the Chu river closed in and the grass peeled off the valley-sides from rocks of crumbled gold. As we neared Issyk-kul, we twisted through a defile and passed a spring hung with the rags of pilgrims. Then, suddenly, the cliffs cracked open and we looked down at mountains parted along a 120-mile corridor of sky-coloured water, dusted with tiny clouds.

A lacerating dryness had descended. The whole land looked burnt. A commotion of flayed foothills gnawed at the snowline, and around us the willows and poplars had gone prematurely russet, as if scorched by a sirocco. Westerly winds habitually blew the lake's evaporation eastward, where it fell on hills out of sight. But here the shore stretched unsoftened, like an

357

abstract painting.

Beyond the town of Balikchi we started along the northern coast in mesmerised silence. Across the water, and far ahead of us, the foothills were thinned away by haze, but strung above them, thronging the sky from end to end, the snow-peaks of the Tienshan hung in unearthly amputation. No wind touched the water. Close in to shore it shone aquamarine, but farther out it darkened to a deep, intense indigo, in which the reflected summits left a chain of icy lights.

Our road was deserted. It ran down a shelving passageway between mountains and sea. Sometimes the stain of a watermark 200 feet above lake-level, or a deep, pebble-strewn strand, signalled that for centuries the water had been evaporating. This was a mystery. Many streams flow into it, yet none ever flows out. Brackish, pure, oddly warm, it marinates in its own solitude. For 3000 square miles – five times the size of Lake Geneva – it smoothed before us in a glittering wilderness: the deepest mountain lake on earth.

Pasha drove at a stately 40 mph. He had been here as a boy, he said, on an expedition with the Young Pioneers, when his Communist zeal was still intact. 'And that was long ago!'

I did not know he had ever felt such zeal, I said.

'Yes, I did. Yes.' He smiled. The lake's calm soothed him. 'Even when I was in the Komsomol, I believed a little. It was like a religion, you see. But when I started my first job – then I gave up. When I saw how the local Party bosses cheated us of our wages, and how they secured perks, then I gave up believing.'

'You were seventeen?'

'Even younger.' He was talking with vague surprise, as of a distant relative. 'But my generation was the last to believe like that. My two sons never wanted to attend those political meetings. They just played truant. Everybody did, not only we Koreans. The Russians, too. They thought it all boring and laughed at it. And that was the end.' He had turned a little sombre. 'When I think how my parents trusted Stalin, even though

358

he repressed them! They thought he could not have known about their persecution – as if he was elevated above it! People died in the war with his name on their lips, you know ....'

His separation from his native Korea, I thought, had fitted him a little for Communism. It had offered a new sureness. He still hankered after Soviet rule, when everything, he said, had been at peace. 'I'm not sure exactly where my people came from. We were in Sakalin for two hundred years maybe, I don't know. It's wrong not to know your history. Educated people know their history. But here *nobody knows.*'

'Haven't you traditions left?'

He frowned. 'We have a special way of preparing noodles! And some of the older people sing songs which we younger ones don't know. But even our language has changed. When I talk with our pastor from South Korea we can hardly understand each other.'

We stopped near the lakeside to eat a picnic of dried bacon, kept cool in his Chinese thermos. The sunlight dazzled the thin air. I ambled across the shore, where boulders had been cast up by the withdrawing waters, to a miniature bay of mouse-coloured sand. The ground was starred by mauve and white convolvulus, and sea-lavender sent up a dry, crushed fragrance. The silence was absolute. Grey and salmon pebbles scattered the sands with a pastel delicacy. There was no sign that anyone had ever trodden here. The lake lisped in warm wavelets against my hands. Opposite, fifty miles across the water, the snow-peaks hung in nothing.

As I rested, a dinghy glided out of nowhere and cast anchor in the bay. Two fishermen, bearded piratically and almost tooth-less, clambered ashore with home-made rods to dig for bait. A century ago the lake had so brimmed with fish that the Cossacks of the Russian explorer Semyonov had harvested 400 pounds of carp by slashing at the surface with their sabres. But now, said the fishermen, a vicious pike-perch introduced from the Volga had upset the natural balance by gobbling herrings. Yet the bottom of their boat brimmed with blue-tinted scales, and soon

359

they rowed laughing away, calling after me: 'England! ... Football! ... Hooligans!' Their voices died over the silence. 'Better off ... here ... fishing ....'

Into the afternoon Pasha and I dawdled east. Half way along the shore, where the rains begin to colour the hills, a straggle of holiday camps and sanatoria appeared. Then came a presidential rest-house, built to simulate the cruiser *Aurora*, whose guns sparked the October Revolution. But beyond, the solitude intensified. A few villages, pretty with toy cottages, clustered among cherry and apricot orchards, and in the Kirghiz graveyards the castellated mausoleums looked grander than the houses of the living, crowned by Islamic crescents or the Communist star, or both.

But as the lake narrowed, and evening glassed it over, the Tienshan rose in jagged fangs to the south-east, angrier and even higher, streaming with clouds. They were reaching towards their savage climax, still invisible beyond, where the *syrt* plateaux hang in unchanging ice and stone, and glaciers laden with boulders and limned in bluish weeds slide imperceptibly down the chasm shoulders. In this tremendous labyrinth the Syr Daria rises, while other rivers spill over the watershed into Xinjiang; Khan Tengri, 'Lord of the Spirits', erupts in a trihedral pyramid of pink marble, and the 24,400-foot Mount Victory glimmers over China.

Yet where we went, skirting the lake's end, the river had left sodden meadows. The marijuana crop which had flourished here in the Brezhnev years had been put to the torch; but the Chu valley was still full of it, Pasha said – half the farmers smoked it – and from all over Central Asia, I'd heard, the white opium poppy was finding its way as heroin to Europe via the Baltic and Ukraine. Yet for the moment only acacia was in flower along the shore, and as we approached the whitewashed town of Karakol, the orchards became lush tangles of apple trees, where cockerels and ganders paraded.

In Karakol, for the first time, we felt the closeness of China. On a bluff high above the lake, where the explorer Przhevalsky was buried in 1888, a bronze eagle spread its talons over the unfurled map of his journeys: the Gobi, the Kun Lun, Tibet .... A cuckoo was cleaning its wings in the birch trees above.

The town was full of Uighurs, whose ancestors had migrated from Xinjiang a century before, and we came upon a mosque built in 1910 by Dungans who had fled the Taiping rebellion. It was surrounded by a Russian stockade, and its shutters and window-frames might have belonged to a Ukrainian cabin. But the dragon cornices and smiling roof were those of a Chinese temple; it was built in unfamiliar, grey-blue brick, and its minaret was a wooden pagoda.

Pasha stared round it blankly. 'They come from China, but they face Mecca! How did they grow to believe in this?'

I said: 'I don't know. How did you believe in Christianity?'

He turned a tranquil, humourless face to mine. 'I grew curious,' he said. 'I wanted to see this South Korean pastor who was sent to us. We all did. Because he came from the Capitalist world.' We had stopped where the stockade sprouted a Chinese gate with upswept eaves. 'But later we went on going to church because we felt a bit sorry for him. If we didn't go, he'd be alone. And he'd come all that way .... Then I found I was starting to believe. I don't know why. But at that service everything's happy. You've heard how we sing. I feel my heart lighten.' He lifted up his palms. 'Out in the streets everything's getting grimmer. There's no peace any more, and nobody knows what may happen. But in there .... I think we need God, don't you? If a man commits a crime, and there's no God, how can he be made to fear?'

These questions fell unanswered under the Chinese porticoes, with their synthetically painted beams. God gave meaning in a chaotic world, he said, He was a vital commodity. Sometimes I could not decide if Pasha were naïve or cynical.

I said: 'You can't create God because you need Him.'

But Pasha had read through the New Testament twice. While I had been admiring the pagan *balbali* in the grass at Balasagun, he had been finishing the Revelation of St John the Divine. 'I used to worry all the time about the future,' he said, 'especially

361

about my children. But now I've stopped. After all, if God gives something, that's good. If he doesn't give, that's His will also. So what have I left to worry about?'

It was easy to understand: the cloistered refuge of the little chapel, with its clean people singing of forgiveness, and the love of a Father less fallible in history than Lenin hectoring from his poster. 'I think many are there because they are unhappy,' Pasha said. 'Their husbands have died or left them. And nobody knows the future now that the Kirghiz and Russians are grating worse on one another.' He ground his knuckles together. 'But when we sing, we forget that.'

'You have Kirghiz converts too?'

'Yes, almost seventy, and it's harder for them. They're frightened the Moslems may kill them.' We peered into the prayer-hall spread with Chinese rugs under Chinese lanterns. Its strangeness seemed to deconsecrate it. 'Islam isn't really strong in Kirghizia, but nobody can read Arabic, so people don't know what the Koran says and if some mullah yells "Kill all the Christians" – they just may.'

These nightmares filled people's imaginations now. The misty promises of Communism and *perestroika* had peeled away from a horizon of black ignorance. For Pasha, the Marxist paradise-on-earth had been delayed too long, and all his people, he said, had long ago sickened into disbelief. 'But I suppose the Bible says that too, doesn't it?' he asked suddenly. 'That there's a future paradise.' He looked quaintly disconcerted.

I said: 'Yes. I think the Bible says "Wait."'

'Wait,' he repeated wanly. Something familiar and bitter was clouding him. 'Ah yes.'

The eastern end of Issyk-kul is haunted by tales of drowned cities. Early maps located a thirteenth-century Nestorian monastery here enshrining the corpse of St Matthew, and a century ago Russian expeditions glimpsed brick foundations under the surface, where the waves cast up shards and human bones. Dim memories circled a creek near the village of Koysary, and

Pasha drove there next morning in tired fatalism. While I had found a dormitory in a bleak hotel that night, he had slept in his car to prevent it being stolen. 'Fear of the law fades out here,' he said.

We crossed fields of young wheat. A heron clattered into the sky like a broken umbrella and descended ungainly at the lagoon's mouth. Then our track ended at a gateway between high turrets, and a secretive huddle of buildings in barbed wire. It was an armed naval base. It looked run-down and its watch-tower hung empty. But we had blundered almost to its gates, and I glimpsed a sentry's blond, nonplussed face, before Pasha swerved aside down a track along the inlet.

I joked: 'The Soviets are still here!'

'That's our army too,' Pasha said. 'The Commonwealth of Independent States ....' He seemed to be trying out the idea. 'There are our men in it.'

I had heard of a secret Soviet installation on the lake years before, built for the testing of torpedoes. Inhabitants of Bishkek had been mystified by naval uniforms appearing in the streets of a city fifteen hundred miles from any ocean. Now Pasha stopped the car among trees and I walked alone along the shore. There was no sign that the lake-level had ever receded. Instead its banks plunged to lapis-blue inlets glazed with water-insects, then eased into momentary rock-shelves and sank out of sight. I looked in vain for any drowned building. Only an abandoned flour-mill hovered above a cove among fir trees raucous with crows. Farther out, the lake was smeared with tracks like the wake of vanished ships.

I squeezed between the locked gates of the mill. On its jetty the wheels and hoists were rusting away, and the shadow of a barge lay ghostly and aslant beneath the water, under a sparkling rain of gnats. Nearby, a few blocks of granite shone on a spur, as if some citadel had been half absorbed into the earth.

I loitered here in faint bemusement. For a long time nothing moved or sounded except the wheeling crows. Then I heard something stir behind the gutted mill, and I remembered that I

363

was trespassing, perhaps in a military area. If I were a soldier from the naval base, I thought, and discovered an Englishman with an air navigation chart of his region and a journal full of indecipherable notes, I would demand an explanation more convincing than some tale of an underwater city. I padded to the mill's perimeter and squirmed under the wire. A sand-coloured hare skittered into the trees. Covered in dust, I prowled round the outer wall and found myself face to face with an old woman.

Her red fist was closed round a walking-stave, and her body heaved in its threadbare coat. We stopped a foot from one another. I looked into a primordial Slavic face, its nose a retroussé stub. But in it I saw a maternal and eccentric benevolence. She was beaming. I had encountered this face, I thought, a thousand times in the vanished Soviet Union. It looked old yet benignly half-formed: the gross, fleshy protoplast of Mother Russia.

I began chattering, trying to explain my presence. It was a beautiful shore, I said, but it looked so derelict now. I thought of the half-abandoned naval base. Everything seemed in retreat, I said. My gaze floundered over her frayed jacket and dress. Life had become so hard ....

But she cut me off. 'No! Everything's fine, it's wonderful!' Her jaw set. 'When people say how terrible everything is, I ask Why? What does everybody want?' She planted her trousered legs apart. They descended to woollen socks and split boots. She seemed instantly to have forgotten the oddness of meeting a gap-toothed foreigner coated in dust. 'Why can't people be content? I have a little garden over there' – she waved at the skyline – 'where I grow cherries and nuts, and there's a plot of land for pensioners where we plant potatoes. I've got everything I need. My teacher's pension is just nine hundred and five roubles a month but it's all right. The sun's good, the earth's good and the winters are mild here!'

I grinned back at her. Her comfortable face dispelled all anxiety. Where had she come from then?

'I arrived from Siberia thirty years ago. Everything was good up there too. Hard, but good. We had three cows, and that was enough. Milk, cheese, butter! Everything's fine, and it always was.' She rooted her stave between her feet. 'Our Gorbachev did the right thing.'

It was the first time I had heard anybody here praise him. 'Yes, in the West we admire him. I know he made mistakes ....'

'Who doesn't make mistakes? Nobody is walking on this earth who hasn't made mistakes. But it's a good thing the old Union has split up. It was finished anyway. And now these small countries will have to stand on their own feet. They'll have to grow up! They'll have to *work*!' She thumped the dust with her stave. 'Let every nation own its own earth, and every person own a little bit of it! Then they'll feel responsible.'

Only once her expression of gritty contentment buckled into displeasure. 'But I was ashamed,' she began, 'yes, ashamed, when Gorbachev said his pension was insufficient, and when Yeltsin asked the West for charity. Ask for credit, yes, but not for charity!' Her voice darkened with disgust. 'And our Gorbachev! When he complained about his pension, I wrote him a letter offering him two hundred roubles out of mine! I told him I could manage on seven hundred and five, even if he couldn't get by on four thousand.'

I stared at her in astonishment. She dashed back the white hair drifting from her scarf. Her quilted coat gushed wool stuffing out of every seam. I said: 'Did he reply?'

'No, of course not,' she answered. 'He was too busy lecturing in America, making money.'

Then she laughed stoically, and marched away.

*

Pasha and I left the lake behind us in a fading afternoon. For a while we followed the Tiup river through valleys awash with lucerne. The water ran golden between green banks below us. We were travelling along the last salient of Central Asia eastward before its mountains unravelled into China. In the villages the

365

Russians had vanished. Red stars disappeared from the cemeteries; Islamic crescents multiplied. Burly men clasping whips and booted on their horses followed their sheep-flocks across the hills, and women stood up in the meadows to watch us pass. Hunters of gazelle with the goshawk and the falcon, these tough herdspeople were nourishers of handsome cross-bred horses and astrakhan wool. With every few miles their villages became wilder and more Mongoloid. Their black eyes were slit almost to blindness; wispy moustaches and Mandarin beards trickled from their nostrils and chins.

Abruptly the valley narrowed. Pastures lacquered in creamy flowers swept against the road as we ascended, and fir trees gathered on the hills. Beyond them on either side, the unchanging snow-peaks kept pace with us, channelling us to China.

Once, from a roadside watch-post, three policemen flagged us down and ordered us out of the car. They had harsh, ignorant faces, and fingered revolvers. 'Are these maps secret?' They turned on Pasha. 'Is he a spy?'

'No,' said Pasha matter-of-factly. 'He's a historian.'

They scrutinised my passport and noticed old Chinese visas. The road to China was closed, they said. The only pass open lay through Torugart, far to the south. We were not travelling to China, I said, and they sent us away.

Our road turned to stone. Around it the hills crowded in velvet spurs, shutting out the mountains. The river spun below. In this sudden emptiness, at once verdant and sombre, only a few glossy and masterless herds of horses wandered. For miles the hills folded about us like lightly covered bones, then their rocks burst through the grass and littered the valley-sides. We passed another police-post, abandoned. For the first time Pasha became nervous. The sun set, but in the cleft of the pass ahead its afterglow illumined a surge of glacial mountains, the last barrier before Xinjiang.

Here, at the end of the world, on the rim of a bare valley, we came upon a monstrous *kurgan*, a grave-mound of rocks sprawled in a grim tumult fifty feet high: the sepulchre of some

Scythian or Turkic chief. I reached it over a grassland light with buttercups and harebells. But a cold wind sprang up down the valley, and the mountains were waning in the last light. Around the excavated crater of the grave, an arc of shrubs shivered with votive rags. But no one was there. They might as well have been tied by a pilgrimage of ghosts. I peered down into the pit of the tomb. It was two thousand years old or more, and violated long ago.

Beside it reared the hill of stones. Steel-grey, russet or pink, and silvered with lichen, they might have numbered fifty thousand: it was impossible to compute. They had been raised in awed memory of a single man; but a legend had accrued to them. It was said that Tamerlane, passing east with his army, ordered every soldier to gather up one rock and pile it in the pass. Years later, on his return, each man took away his stone to Samarkand, and those that remained became a cenotaph to the fallen.

As I climbed them in the silence, they rattled and clashed against one another. Each was the size that a man might carry. Under that twilit sky, circled by mountains, they became a nameless commotion of dead: a monument raised by the wasted to themselves. A few were blood-red or marmoreal white. They clattered like skulls under my feet and rolled down on one another.

Then I heard Pasha calling me to return. It was late and dark, he said, and this was not our country.

Index

369

373